Studies in African Literature

The Poetry of Commitment
in South Africa

▼▼▼▼▼▼▼▼▼▼▼▼▼▼▼▼▼▼▼▼▼▼▼▼▼▼▼▼▼▼▼▼▼▼

Studies in African Literature

A New Reader's Guide to
African Literature
Edited by HANS ZELL, CAROL BUNDY
and VIRGINIA COULON

Homecoming: Essays
NGUGI

Writers in Politics
NGUGI

Morning Yet on Creation Day
CHINUA ACHEBE

African Literature in the Twentieth
Century
O. R. DATHORNE

Protest and Conflict in African
Literature
Edited by COSMO PIETERSE and
DONALD MUNRO

An Introduction to the African
Novel
EUSTACE PALMER

The Growth of the African Novel
EUSTACE PALMER

The Novel and Contemporary
Experience in Africa
SHATTO ARTHUR GAKWANDI

The Literature and Thought of
Modern Africa
CLAUDE WAUTHIER

New West African Literature
Edited by KOLAWOLE OGUNGBESAN

The African Experience in
Literature and Ideology
ABIOLA IRELE

Perspectives on African Literature
Edited by CHRISTOPHER HEYWOOD

Aspects of South African Literature
Edited by CHRISTOPHER HEYWOOD

African Art and Literature: The
Invisible Present
DENNIS DUERDEN

The Critical Evaluation of African
Literature
Edited by EDGAR WRIGHT

Four Centuries of Swahili Verse
JAN KNAPPERT

African Writers Talking
Edited by DENNIS DUERDEN and
COSMO PIETERSE

The Writings of Chinua Achebe
G. D. KILLAM

The Writing of Wole Soyinka
ELDRED JONES

The Poetry of L. S. Senghor
S. O. MEZU

The Poetry of Okot p'Bitek
G. A. HERON

Understanding African Poetry
KEN GOODWIN

An Introduction to the Writings of
Ngugi
G. D. KILLAM

The Novels of Ayi Kwei Armah
ROBERT FRASER

The Writings of Camara Laye
ADELE KING

Stylistic Criticism and the African
Novel
EMMANUEL NGARA

Ngugi wa Thiong'o: An Exploration of
His Writings
Edited by DAVID COOK and
MICHAEL OKENIMKPE

The Writings of East & Central Africa
Edited by G. D. KILLAM

The Poetry of Commitment in South Africa
JACQUES ALVAREZ-PEREYRE

Art and Ideology in the African Novel
EMMANUEL NGARA

African Writers on African Writing
Edited by G. D. KILLAM

CRITICAL PERSPECTIVES

Critical Perspectives on Chinua
Achebe
Edited by C. L. INNES and BERNTH
LINDFORS

Critical Perspectives on Amos
Tutuola
Edited by BERNTH LINDFORS

Critical Perspectives on V. S.
Naipaul
Edited by ROBERT HAMNER

Critical Perspectives on
Nigerian Literatures
Edited by BERNTH LINDFORS

Critical Perspectives on Wole
Soyinka
Edited by JAMES GIBBS

The Poetry of Commitment in South Africa

▼▼▼▼▼▼▼▼▼▼▼▼▼▼▼▼▼▼▼▼▼▼▼▼▼▼▼▼▼▼▼▼▼

JACQUES ALVAREZ-PEREYRE
Professor of English Language and Literature
Grenoble University, France

Translated from the French by
Clive Wake
Professor of Modern French and African Literature
University of Kent at Canterbury

LONDON
HEINEMANN
IBADAN NAIROBI

Heinemann Educational Books Ltd
22 Bedford Square, London WC1B 3HH
PMB 5205, Ibadan · PO Box 45314, Nairobi

EDINBURGH   MELBOURNE   AUCKLAND
HONG KONG   SINGAPORE   KUALA LUMPUR
NEW DELHI   KINGSTON   PORT OF SPAIN

Heinemann Educational Books Inc.
70 Court Street, Portsmouth, New Hampshire 03801, USA

© Jacques Alvarez-Péreyre 1979
© In English translation Clive Wake 1984
First published as *Les Guetteurs de L'Aube:
Poésie et Apartheid*, Presses Universitaires de Grenoble, 1979
First published in English translation 1984

British Library Cataloguing in Publication Data

Alvarez-Pereyre, Jacques
   The poetry of commitment in South Africa.—
   (Studies in African literature)
   1. South African poetry (English)—20th
   century—History and criticism
   I. Title   II. Les guetteurs de l'aube. *English*
   III. Series
   821   PR9360.5
ISBN 0–435–91056–6

Set in 9/10 pt Plantin by
Wilmaset, Birkenhead, Merseyside
Printed in Great Britain by
Biddles Ltd, Guildford, Surrey

To the memory of
    my aunt, Pauline Blann (Auschwitz, 1944)
    Onkgopotse Tiro (Gaborone, 1974)

▼▼▼▼▼▼▼▼▼▼▼▼▼▼▼▼▼▼▼▼▼▼▼▼▼▼▼▼▼▼▼▼▼▼▼▼▼▼▼

The ivory tower is unknown to those who are assailed by history.

Charles Dobszinski

Contents

▼▼▼▼▼▼▼▼▼▼▼▼▼▼▼▼▼▼▼▼▼▼▼▼▼▼▼▼▼▼

Acknowledgments   ix

PART I   The South African Writer and the Problem of Commitment   1

Chapter 1   *When There Was Still Hope*   3
   The Importance of education   3
   Why the English language?   4
   A concrete example: Es'kia Mphahlele   6
   The spirit of the 1950s   8
   The repression – Sharpeville   10
   Notes   11

Chapter 2   *The Dark Years after Sharpeville*   14
   The English-speaking white writers   14
   The 1960s and the problem of commitment   17
   General survey of committed writing   21
   The writer, censorship and the public   23
   The committed Afrikaans poets   25
   Notes   30

Chapter 3   *South African Writing since 1968*   35
   The early 1970s   35
   The black writer today   38
   The political importance of the black theatre   41
   The South African writer and exile   43
   Notes   48

PART II   The Liberal Conscience and White Power   51

Chapter 4   *A Forerunner: Thomas Pringle*   53
   Notes   59

Chapter 5   *The Limits of Liberal Thought*   61
   Alan Paton   61
   Anthony Delius   67
   Notes   81

Chapter 6   *Total Commitment: Lewin and Evans*   84
   Biographical summary   85
   Presentation of the poems   86
   Notes   94

Chapter 7 *The New Prophets*	96
Peter Horn	96
Wopko Jensma	104
Notes	113

PART III The Black Poets and the Struggle for Power — 115

Chapter 8 *Vernacular poetry*	117
The Xhosa poets	117
The Zulu poets	122
Notes	128

Chapter 9 *The First Generation of Committed Black Poets*	130
Dennis Brutus	130
Cosmo Pieterse	145
Arthur Nortje	153
Notes	167

Chapter 10 *The Black Man Holds Up His Head*	170
O. M. Mtshali	170
Wally Serote	186
Don Mattera	196
Notes	204

Chapter 11 *The Black Man at the Crossroads*	207
James Matthews	207
Sipho Sepamla	215
Mafika Pascal Gwala	227
Notes	243

Conclusion and Evaluation	249
General characteristics	251
Common themes	254
A widening of the perspective	257
Reflections on language	261
What can poetry do against apartheid?	264
Notes	267

Appendix	269
Bibliography	270
Index	276

Acknowledgments

▼▼▼▼▼▼▼▼▼▼▼▼▼▼▼▼▼▼▼▼▼▼▼▼▼▼▼▼▼▼▼▼▼▼▼▼

The author wishes to thank his many friends and acquaintances in and outside South Africa for the help they have provided during his research.

He also wishes to express his gratitude to his wife for her support and for the additional insight she has enabled him to get, in the last stages of his work, into the situation prevailing in her native country.

FMACU — WFUCA
42, avenue Raymond-Poincaré
75116 PARIS - France

This book has been published with the help of the World Federation of Unesco Clubs and Associations

PART I
The South African Writer and the Problem of Commitment

To draw the portrait of the typical South African writer today is a difficult, if not impossible, task: the policy of apartheid has meant that the communities are separated and the living and working conditions of the individuals that make them up are both different and unequal. This division recurs in the literary sphere as well, and writers have no option but to take it into account, even though they deplore it. Thus the white poet Douglas Livingstone said a few years ago that he tried to imagine the life of a black poet in South Africa, but that he could only perceive certain aspects of it dimly.[1] For his part, the black writer Es'kia Mphahlele has said that he did not want to write about white people because he did not know them well enough: 'I don't know how they are born, I don't know how they grow up in their homes, I don't know how white people get married except what I see in the movies or what I read in books.'[2]

A similar dichotomy exists to a large extent on the level of the role that the writer wishes to play in his society. Uys Krige spoke for many, though not all, white poets when he said that the closer the poet moved to the politics of his own time, the more insignificant he became – and this after stating, rather paradoxically, that 'the poet's job is to express . . . what is common to all people'.[3]

On the other hand, the black poet Kgositsile asserts that oppression forces the writer to be didactic: he must choose, he says, between being a tool of that oppression and being an instrument of liberation.[4] As to the thematic level, one needs only to listen to Sipho Sepamla to find yet again this same division. Sepamla distinguishes between the poets who 'sing of love' and those who treat relevant issues, and he goes on to say: 'We don't write the same thing as most white poets write about. We write about the situation . . . And that is what is called relevant.'[5]

Whether one likes it or not, and in spite of the desire not to reproduce apartheid at the level of literary criticism, one is therefore forced to discuss South African writers on racial lines, stressing when one can those exceptions that really exist. Yet a parallel study of this kind would be inadequate if one did not take into account at the same time the order of events. The situation evolved very noticeably during the last three decades, and the political events, the racial separation and literary works are closely interconnected and, to a large degree, they illuminate each other.

Notes

1. 'I try to imagine the unseen aspects of a Black poet's life in this country, in this century: the early struggles. Education in what is essentially a foreign tongue – English. The dangers, poverty and exhilaration of township life. The inhumanities and indignities suffered in racially oppressive situations. Their determination to make over their lives. Mastering and expressing themselves in the subtleties and grandeurs of English poetry. All these I can share with them, sometimes with immediacy and impact, sometimes only dimly . . .' In 'the Poetry of Mtshali, Serote, Sepamla and Others in English: Notes Towards a Critical Evaluation', *The New Classic* (1976), no. 3.
2. 'There is a big barrier between us and the whites. We are looking at each other through a keyhole all the time. I don't want to write about white people because I don't know them that well . . . I don't know how they are born . . .' *Issue*: A Quarterly Journal of Africanist Opinion, vol. VI, no. 1, Spring 1976, ed. B. Lindfors, p. 15.
3. 'The poet's job is to express what is lasting and abiding, what is common to all people. The closer you move to the politics of your own time, the more insignificant you become.' *The Star*, International Weekly Edition, Saturday, 20 November, 1976, p. 16.
4. 'In a situation of oppression, there are no choices beyond didactic writing; either you are a tool of oppression or an instrument of liberation . . .' *Issue*, op. cit., p. 35.
5. Interview for the BBC.

Chapter 1
When There Was Still Hope

▼▼▼▼▼▼▼▼▼▼▼▼▼▼▼▼▼▼▼▼▼▼▼▼▼▼▼▼▼▼▼▼▼

The importance of education

From the beginning of European colonization, the African saw education as a way of improving his material condition and that of his community. Very quickly, however, and certainly by the last quarter of the nineteenth century, he realized that his traditional weapons would not defeat the more sophisticated arms of the whites; if he was to defend the land that remained to him and also obtain justice, he must give priority to political negotiation.

This was the change of approach, in which education would play a major role, that the Xhosa writer Citashe proposed to his contemporaries at the end of the 1880s, calling on them to lay down the gun for the pen.[1]

Already at that time, Xhosas and Zulus were being educated in the mission schools of the Cape Colony and Natal. Some of those who became teachers, pastors and journalists were subsequently to become the leaders of their people. At the time, the choice was obvious and hopes were very high: without education it was impossible to make oneself heard, impossible to show the white man that the African was not a savage, that he was as able as his conqueror, if only he were given the opportunity and the means to show it.

However, the means were limited and the schools few in number: while free and compulsory schooling was introduced for the whites in the early 1920s, the Africans had still to depend mainly on the mission schools for their secondary education.

The mission schools accepted African, Coloured and white pupils belonging to different social levels, without distinction. In allowing them to compete according to the sole criteria of work and example, they helped to give the young black students confidence in their potential. But on leaving school, these same students found themselves in a fundamentally unequal world in which their certificates were of little use against laws that protected even the most uneducated whites. Besides, the legislation reserving certain categories of work for whites, introduced by the Pact government in 1924 and expanded over the years that followed, was a serious obstacle to the vertical mobility of the African, who found himself doubly disadvantaged, first by his colour and secondly by his university diplomas: white employers were afraid of Africans with too much education.

This lack of mobility, which always goes hand in hand with inequalities in salary, even for people with the same qualifications, is one of the reasons why sociologists hesitate to use the term 'bourgeoisie' when talking about the most highly educated and the most prosperous Africans.[2] There were, however, among the latter – whether they be pastors, missionaries, small shopkeepers, lawyers, doctors or teachers – the elements of an emerging petty bourgeoisie: their income was higher than that of manual workers and servants, they lived better and were held in respect in their own community. But nothing, neither the fact that they were relatively well-off nor their education, could exempt them from having to carry a pass, from having to observe curfews, from police checks and humiliation. Even during the short period of the Smuts government (1939–48), the 'exempted Natives' had only limited privileges which disappeared as soon as the Nationalists came to power. And even if their income enabled them to live in the better and less dangerous townships, they were still not regarded as permanent residents.

Thus, because racial policy before 1948 and subsequently apartheid did not distinguish people on the basis of their education – or the fatness of their wallets – but according to the colour of their skin, the African intellectuals could not dissociate themselves from the masses, even if they wanted to. In any case, the great majority of them, primarily the teachers and social workers, were too much in contact with the injustices and inequalities perpetrated in the name of the 'system' to remain neutral or indifferent. Neither a true bourgeoisie nor a proletariat, but somewhere between the white bourgeoisie and the black proletariat, the category of educated Africans from which the first writers came was to express the deeper feelings of the vast majority of black people. It is not difficult to understand how the worsening of conditions due to the radicalization of apartheid from the early 1950s could only strengthen this tendency. As Lewis Nkosi wrote in 1965: 'In South Africa we were *saved* from the emergence of a Black Bourgeoisie by the levelling effect of Apartheid.'[3]

This representative character of the black intellectual and writer gave some of them, more than is the case in any other society, an official status as spokesmen, although it was a status not entirely without ambiguity inside their own community.[4] This is one of the reasons why they continued to insist that education should not be reserved for a small category of people who were better off or more fortunate. At the end of his collection of essays, *The African Image* (1962), completed in the years following his departure from South Africa, Es'kia Mphahlele argued, with a resentment that can be to some extent explained by the deterioration of the situation, that the African must be given the opportunity to 'wrench the tools of power from the white man's hand', and that literacy and a language common to all ethnic groups (at that stage, for Mphahlele, this meant English) was an essential weapon:

> Now because the Government is using institutions of a fragmented and almost unrecognizable Bantu culture as an instrument of oppression, we dare not look back. We have got to wrench the tools of power from the white man's hand: one of these is literacy and the sophistication that goes with it. We have got to speak the language that all can understand – English. But the important thing always is that we daren't look back, at any rate not yet.[5]

Why the English language?

'The language that all can understand'. This defines the prime value of a lingua franca which would not only enable the people of southern Africa to communicate with those of the rest of English-speaking Africa, but would also serve to cement the emerging nationalism of the Africans: a unifying force against the attempts to divide, a means of communication at world level against the attempts to impoverish through tribalism. For the 'return to the tribe' is a key phrase of the Afrikaner government alone, anxious to divide in order to rule, under cover of reproducing its own history for the 'good' of the other racial groups, of which it had assumed the guardianship.

However, the linguistic cohesion of the African tribes, chieftaincies and kingdoms had been prepared by the missions, mainly British and American, which evangelized through the medium of English from an early date, whereas the Afrikaners established their own missions only at the end of the nineteenth century, nearly three generations behind.

Apart from the fact that Afrikaans did not have any of the prestige enjoyed by English, after 1948 psychological factors came into play alongside those mentioned above. As soon as the Afrikaner became the real master of the country, the link was made between the oppressor and his language, and Afrikaans became associated with Nationalist policies – to such an extent that when Noni Jabavu, the daughter of the African leader, returned home after a long absence, she could talk of feeling the racial atmosphere building up around her and of the guttural sounds everywhere to be heard:

> I could feel the racial atmosphere congeal and freeze around me. The old South African hostility, cruelty, harshness, it was all there, somehow, harsher than ever because Afrikaans was now the language. You heard nothing but those glottal stops, staccato tones; saw only hard, alert, pale blue eyes set in craggy suntanned faces.[6]

English, then. But which English? And for whom?

Guy Butler, in his 1959 study of English-speaking poets, defined the English linguistic domain as being that of the million people who had learnt English 'on their mothers' knees'. This definition is, in fact, both a political and a literary one: Butler reserves the term 'compatriots' for the Afrikaners only, and he allows the South African poetic Muse the leisure to express itself only in one of the major languages – or in the 'argot of the townships'.[7] His criteria led him to include an English poet, a certain Margaret Buckton, who had written verse on South Africa but *had never set foot there*, whereas the only indigenous poet writing in English, H. L. Dhlomo (*The Valley of a Thousand Hills*, Knox, Durban, 1941), who could have provided an authentically South African voice for the anthology, is not even mentioned. Butler was to admit – but fifteen years later – that Dhlomo was a remarkable pioneer of African literature in English and that the black writers of the fifties were genuine men of letters with a complete command of the English language.[8]

These same writers were educated in the multiracial mission schools, before going on to university, and it was there that they discovered or perfected their knowledge of English. The lyrical way Lewis Nkosi tells of his double discovery of English and its literature is shared by nearly all the writers of his generation.

> I was reading an incredible amount, reading always badly without discipline; reading sometimes for the sheer beauty of the language ... I walked about the streets of the bustling noisy city with new English words clicking like

coins in the pockets of my mind; I tried them out on each passing scene, relishing their power to describe and apprehend experience.[9]

The same reaction is found in Brutus and Pieterse, and along with Mphahlele they also have the same taste for the most demanding English poets: Donne and Hopkins. While they were looking towards England, Peter Abrahams – born, like Mphahlele, in 1919 – found in the library of another multiracial institution, the Bantu Men's Social Centre in Johannesburg, the works of American blacks which were to influence his writing in the future.

It was therefore in English, and not Afrikaans or any of the vernacular languages, that the black man was to pursue the struggle to improve the lot of his people; it was in English that the black writer was to try and get through to the white man of his country and beyond him to the whole world, called upon to take note of the evils of South African racial policies. This fact is worth stressing: in the struggle against colonialism, the return to the vernacular languages has invariably been a political and cultural gesture. For English-speaking Africa, and particularly for South Africa, English was a gift from the colonizer.[10]

A concrete example: Es'kia Mphahlele

The example of Mphahlele provides an excellent illustration, in fact, of the life, education and working conditions of an English-speaking African writer during the 1940s and 1950s. Mphahlele's curriculum vitae is similar to that of many of his black compatriots.

Born in 1919 in the Transvaal, of very humble parents (his mother was a domestic servant and his father a messenger), Ezekiel was transplanted from the ıcity to the country when he was five years old and for a while he looked after the family's small herd of donkeys and goats. On the other side of the Leshoano river lived the 'heathens'; Es'kia, like the rest of his family, was a Christian and remained one until the birth of his first child.

He then went to live in a slum outside Pretoria: daily life there was like that of many other African families struggling against poverty and need on very low wages. Their tiny incomes had to maintain parents, children, grandparents and relatives. As the eldest, Es'kia had to do the housework: he got up at four in the morning, lit the makeshift brazier, made coffee for the family and tea for his grandmother, then set off for school. On his return, he had to prepare the evening meal.

Because of his household tasks, the child could not start his homework until ten in the evening, when everyone had gone to bed; there was little room – the only bed was occupied by his grandmother and young cousins, while the rest of the family slept on the floor.

Under these conditions, school did not attract him much at first. But he soon acquired a passion for reading, very quickly made up what he had lost and did so well that, thanks to his mother's financial sacrifices (his parents had separated in the meantime), he was able to go as a boarder to St Peter's, a school run by the Community of the Resurrection, where he had Peter Abrahams as a classmate.

After passing through Adams College, a teacher-training college run by American missionaries, on a bursary which enabled him to complete his studies, Mphahlele taught for several years at Ezenzeleni Blind Institute, described by Paton in *Cry, the Beloved Country*. He began writing: in 1947, he published a small collection of short stories, *Man Must Live*. The following year, the Nationalists came to power, and they immediately set up a commission to plan the changes in African education that were to be introduced by Parliament a few years later. These required an absolute separation of races at school level; the mission schools had either to cease admitting African pupils or scuttle themselves, which some in fact did.

Mphahlele, like many of his black colleagues, had no illusions about the implications of these changes now gradually being put into effect: to assist in the implementation of the new education policy was to connive at an inferior education in which everything – syllabuses, period of schooling, books – bore the marks of Christian National Education (CNE). CNE defines the role that religion must play in the individual's life: it declares that there must be no mixing of languages, culture or 'races'; it lays down that the subjects taught must conform to received Christian dogma and that therefore the theory of evolution must be condemned because it is contrary to the doctrine of predestination, that history and geography must teach that God gave each people its country and its customs and that South Africa is, therefore, God's 'gift' to the Afrikaners; and, finally, that no one who does not adhere to these principles may be employed as a teacher.[11] The new system denied the teacher the right to object, even as a simple individual: an official circular made it clear he could be dismissed if he did. This was the fate of Mphahlele and many others, although in some teachers allowed themselves to be officially 'converted' so as to be in a better position to continue the fight.[12]

Mphahlele had meanwhile continued studying by correspondence, obtaining his BA from the University of South Africa; he now came up against the laws reserving certain work for whites and temporarily found himself working as a messenger, as his father had done. He then taught in a school run by Father Huddleston's community, but in a private capacity, finally joining *Drum*, the popular African magazine founded in 1951, as a journalist and assistant editor.

The ignorance and contempt for the Africans to be found among a majority of whites emerge from the personal memories scattered throughout his book, *The African Image*, which existed at the time in embryonic form in his Master's thesis. This is how Mphahlele relates his interview with one of the editors of the big Johannesburg daily, *The Star*:

'Would you be interested?' the big man asked.
'Depends on the kind of thing you want.'
'Have you ever written regular features before – for any paper, I mean?'
One has learnt to take South African whites literally, so I replied:
'I'm on *Drum* and I write regularly for *Golden City Post* – er – that's our sister paper, by the way – a Sunday paper. It's published by *Drum*.'
'Is *Golden City Post* published in English?'
'Entirely,'
'Well, you see, what we want need not be terribly good English. We can always knock it into shape. I know the Bantu have a peculiar turn of phrase when they write in English. But you shouldn't let it worry you, see what I mean?'[13]

In spite of working for more than two years (1954–7) on *Drum*, Mphahlele did not feel satisfied; he wanted to return to his true loves, creative writing and teaching. But teaching had been closed to him as a profession since his dismissal and the accompanying ban on teaching, and this in spite of his having obtained his MA with distinction in 1956. In any case, how could he accept for his own children a system which he had himself criticized and refused to approve?

His journalism left him little time for writing and he was unhappy about it on other counts as well. He had to conform to the policy of the editorial board, which thought it knew what kind of reading the Africans of the cities 'wanted',[14] and he had to contend with the censorship of his editor when he wished to write of the options available as he saw them. In fact, he had either to go on playing an endless and wearisome game of evasion or make up his mind to go into exile. This last choice was to prevail: in 1957, Mphahlele left for Nigeria, to take up a teaching post there. Some years before him, Peter Abrahams had described, with all the precision of a medical diagnosis, the dilemma that was to face many South Africans: 'I had to go or be for ever lost. I needed, not friends, not gestures, but my manhood. And the need was desperate . . . Perhaps life had a meaning that transcended race and colour. If it had, I could not find it in South Africa.'[15]

The spirit of the 1950s

This was a period of intense political activity, both inside and outside Parliament.[16] Although the Afrikaner Nationalists had won a majority of seats in Parliament and therefore the power to legislate, they were far from having a majority of votes in the country, and there still seemed a chance to stem the tide of fanaticism and racism which now began to erupt 'officially'. Democratically minded people from all the communities sought ways of opposing the new tide of racist legislation.

Several mass demonstrations took place, the most important of them being the Defiance Campaign (June–October 1952), during which thousands of people were arrested. More protest activities were organized in 1955. Two of these were failures – the campaign against the destruction of Sophiatown and the evictions of black people carried out in the context of the Group Areas Act, and the attempt to boycott the 'ethnic' schools set up under the Bantu Education Act – but the Congress of the People was a huge success.

This great demonstration united the African National Congress (ANC – founded in 1912 but really active only after the war with the creation of the Youth League, in which Nelson Mandela soon made a name for himself), the South African Indian Congress (under the leadership of Gandhi, who lived in South Africa from 1893 until 1914, the Indians had started to use the passive resistance campaign as a weapon), the Congress of Democrats, which included Communists and non-Communists, the South African Coloured People's Organization, founded in 1953, and the recently formed South African Congress of Trade Unions (SACTU), with a membership of 30,000, mostly black. A Freedom Charter was adopted on 25 and 26 June 1955; it was ratified by the ANC, but encountered opposition from Robert Sobukwe's pan-Africanist wing.

These activities were the beginnings of the 'common society' every freedom-loving person was calling for, from the newly formed Liberal Party (1953) to the ANC. There was a sense of mutual respect; people valued each other's contribution, and were aware of the other man's qualities. Many of them wrote for progressive newspapers and reviews, especially *Fighting Talk*, the monthly *Drum*, *Post* (the Sunday paper associated with it), and *Africa South*.

Under the guidance of the young Anthony Sampson,[17] who was editor-in-chief until replaced by Sylvester Stein, *Drum* was to provide the emerging black talent with the experience and the platform they needed. Many well-known writers worked on it in their early days: apart from Mphahlele, there were Casey Motsisi,[18] Bloke Modisane,[19] Arthur Maimane,[20] Todd Matshikiza,[21] Can Themba,[22] Richard Rive,[23] Nat Nakasa,[24] Lewis Nkosi and Henry Nxumalo.[25] Can Themba, paying homage to Henry Nxumalo after his murder by tsotsis, tells how much he was the image of the true reporter, always taking personal risks and never hesitating to write about the abuses he uncovered. On one occasion, he had taken a job as a casual worker so as to reveal the ill-treatment of African workers by some white farmers.

Many of *Drum*'s articles, short stories, essays and news reports were autobiographical; the short story, in fact, seemed to be the form best suited to the hectic life led by these journalist–writers always on the move, often threatened, sometimes arrested by the police – like Can Themba, accused of trying to pray in a white church! They read a great deal, and from the best sources, they had a racy style, making considerable use of irony, and while they had the gift of putting their material across in a very personal way, they provided a true portrait of their community. For Lewis Nkosi, *Drum* was more than a magazine: it was the symbol of the 'new African' who had broken his ties with the tribal reserve and become the complete city-dweller, vital, brash and voluble.[26]

Just as Es'kia Mphahlele was about to leave South Africa, a new quarterly review made its appearance: this was *Africa South*, edited by Ronald Segal. The scope of this new publication was very wide, ranging from politics to literature, and its significance is even more striking when one considers the importance of the events taking place at the time: the Cato Manor riots were in fact to be a prelude to the Sharpeville massacre and were to inaugurate a decade which was to be even darker than that of the fifties.

In *Africa South*, one finds few professionals from the field of literature; the latter had too recently come into being, even among the whites. But one does find a large number of men and women from all political persuasions, apart from the Nationalists, and belonging to all the ethnic communities in South Africa. These include clergymen, notably the Rev. Ambrose Reeves, Joost de Blank, the Archbishop of Cape Town, and a Rabbi, André Ungar; liberals, like Paton and Patrick Duncan; some who were not politically involved, like Helen Joseph, Secretary of the Federation of South African Women; trade unionists, like Joe Matthews; and Communists, like Brian Bunting and Professor H. J. Simons. The whites, as one might expect, are in the majority.

The articles are very varied. There are reports on the major events of the day, the most important of which was the Treason Trial,[27] critical comment on recent racial legislation, and investigations,[28] but also articles of historical and/or literary interest: a study by the Xhosa writer, A. C. Jordan, on Xhosa literature, short stories – one, in fact, by Es'kia Mphahlele – a few poems, among them 'On the Gold Mines' by the Zulu writer Vilakazi, which Jordan translated into English, and extracts from the work of two white poets, Guy Butler and Anthony Delius.

Generally speaking, *Africa South* undertook to demystify apartheid, showing it up for what it was. Its analyses acquired considerable weight from the fact that they were the work of people highly placed in the hierarchy of the English-speaking South African churches, or of (white) MPs who still represented (but not for much longer) the black population.

But, although *Africa South* was often essentially concerned with journalism, the literary dimension was fully present in an attempt to convey a symbolic view of the situation: the 'Grim Fairy Tales' of E. V. Stone, *The Last Division* of Delius, under its original title of *The Great Divide* and subtitled *A Fantasy*, or an essay like 'The Village and the Castle' (Kafka in South Africa). On the one hand a demonstration of a variety of talent on either side of the colour bar, *Africa South* was also, in the late 1950s, the demonstration and the symbol of the open society that the majority of its authors wished to see.

The repression – Sharpeville

The titles of the articles in *Africa South* of a general political nature give a sense of the growing tenseness of the situation in the country; although the last issue of 1958 contains an article by the jurist Julius Lewin entitled 'No Revolution Round the Corner', all the 1959 issues return to this theme and end, on the eve of Sharpeville, with an editorial which announces: 'Revolution is now'. The events that followed showed that this was not in fact to be the case and that it was, on the contrary, the counter-revolution – as Leo Kuper, the historian and sociologist, put it – which was to triumph.

A new culture was, however, clearly in the process of being born: countering the criticism of the Nationalists, even before they came to power, that the mission schools were producing 'black Englishmen', Luthuli said that they were at the confluence of two cultures which were enriching without destroying each other.[29]

This last statement must be taken with caution, for one cannot really talk of the survival of an African pastoral civilization in the cities, or even in the tribal areas, where everything was changing as a result of new standards being imposed by the whites. There is, however, no doubt that the 1940s and 1950s were a cultural melting pot and that this could only be to the advantage of both communities. That it was occurring especially in cities like Johannesburg, Port Elizabeth and, to a lesser extent, in Cape Town, cannot be denied. Paton, who spent the whole of the forties at Diepkloof, speaking through John Kumalo (intended to represent one of the 'new Africans'), said that a new society was in the process of emerging in Johannesburg.[30]

The same point was made a few years later by Mphahlele, when, speaking of the fifties period, he stressed the vitality of this new culture that the Africans of the cities were creating:

> These South African writers are fashioning an urban literature on terms that are unacceptable to the white ruling class. They are detribalized or coloured (of mixed blood), not accepted as an integral part of the country's culture (a culture in a chaotic state). But, like every other non-white, they keep on, digging their feet into an urban culture of their own making. This is a fugitive culture: borrowing here, incorporating there, retaining this, rejecting that. But it is a virile culture. The clamour of it is going to keep beating on the walls surrounding the already fragmented culture of the whites until they crumble.[31]

The government met the new alliance brought into being by the adoption of the Freedom Charter with police raids on the offices of the different Congresses, banning orders of all kinds and the arrest of 156 political and trade union leaders, white as well as black, who were accused of nothing less than high treason.[32]

At the same time, the government provided itself with yet new means for dealing with opposition. In 1955, at the time of the Congress of the People, the Criminal Procedure and Evidence Act was passed, authorizing the police to search without a warrant. The following year, the Riotous Assemblies Act, which defined the word 'riotous' in very broad terms, allowed the police to arrest and prosecute anyone suspected of organizing 'stay-at-home' campaigns among the workers – these campaigns were included in the definition of the word 'riot'. Again in 1956, as a result of a further piece of legislation, the urban authorities were empowered to expel any African whose presence was deemed undesirable. In 1959, a law relating to the prisons defined as a crime the publication of 'false' evidence about prisoners or the administration of the prisons.

In March 1960, just as the ANC was finalizing preparations for its passive resistance campaign against the pass laws, Robert Sobukwe – who two years earlier had led his followers into a new organization, the Pan- Africanist Congress (PAC), hostile to any common action with the other non-black opposition groups – called for demonstrations against the pass laws throughout the country.

On 21 March 1960, the police opened fire on a crowd at Sharpeville, a small town in the Transvaal. The death toll was heavy: 72 people were killed, while more than 200 were wounded. Everywhere violent demonstrations followed; in the south of the country, the demonstrations were met with gunfire. A few days later, the government banned the PAC and the ANC, declared a state of emergency and arrested hundreds of whites and 'non-whites', holding them in prison without trial for several months.

Notes

1. For Citashe see below, Part III, Chapter 1.
2. Notably Leo Kuper (*An African Bourgeoise*, Yale University Press, New Haven and London, 1965) and Michael Banton (*Race Relations*, Tavistock, England, 1967).
3. In *Home and Exile* (Longman, London, 1965), p. 45. Reprinted as *Home and Exile and Other Selections*, Longman, London, 1983.
4. They arouse respect, envy – suspicion, too – as Leo Kuper's study shows (*An African Bourgeoisie, op. cit.*, Chapter 12).
5. *The African Image*, 1962 edition (Faber & Faber, London), p. 193.
6. Noni Jabavu, married to a white, had left to live abroad. See *Drawn in Colour* (John Murray, London, 1963), p. 3.
7. *A Book of South African Verse* (Oxford University Press, Cape Town, 1959), p. xvii.
8. During an address at York University in April 1975.
9. *Home and Exile, op. cit.*, pp. 9–10.
10. Cf. the following comment by Lewis Nkosi, made at a meeting of English- speaking African writers (Kampala, June 1963) and reported by Philip Segal: 'Whether delegates wanted it to be so or not, it seemed to me that what linked various African peoples on the continent was the nature and depth of colonial experience; and this was the final irony. Colonialism had not only delivered them unto themselves, but had delivered them unto each other, had provided them, so to speak, with a common language and an African consciousness; for out of rejection had come an affirmation.' *Contrast 6*, Autumn 1963, vol. 2, no. 2.

    More recently (March 1975), the Nigerian critic, Abiodun Jeyifous, stressed the need for a continental language which could surmount the linguistic barriers between African countries and went on to say: 'Without English, I am simply a stranger in certain parts of Nigeria. It's that fundamental,' *Issue*, Vol. VI, no. 1, Spring 1976, ed. B. Lindfors, p. 9.

11. Leo Marquard, a liberal historian respected for his impartiality, reads 'Christian National Education' as 'Calvinist Nationalist Education', so infused is it with Afrikaner Nationalism. For a detailed study of CNE, see Marquard, *The Peoples and Policies of South Africa* (Oxford University Press, London, 1969), p. 197; and more particularly 'Appendix Two: Christian National Education' in *Education beyond Apartheid* (Spro-Cas, Johannesburg, 1971), as well as 'The Role of Secondary Education in English-speaking White South Africa' by M. Ashley, in *Student Perspectives on South Africa* (David Philip, Cape Town, 1972).

12. Thus, a black teacher interviewed by the team of the sociologist Kuper confided that he interpreted the white civilizing mission in Africa to his pupils in such an ingenious way through the skilful use of antiphrasis that he taught them the exact opposite: 'I overcome the problem of being used as an instrument by telling them that the Jews suffered in Egypt for many years, but they had a hope for a deliverer who will come one day to free them from slavery. I always tell my children that God created four continents – Asia for the Asiatics, Europe for the Europeans [America for the Americans], and Africa for the Africans. He separated these people by seas, which is apartheid. Afterwards God decreed the boundaries and allowed these races to come to Africa to teach us Christian religion and civilization, and now those people have done their work, their mission is over. My feeling now is that freedom is at hand although we are still being dominated by these foreigners. In other words, the Messiah has come to lead us out of bondage, and that is why there is a scramble out of Africa.' Quoted in Kuper, *An African Bourgeoisie*, op. cit., p. 190.

That the teaching profession can, in spite of the system, be approached in a way advantageous to the black masses is proved by this recent statement by a young (19-year-old) African, a pupil of the most radical of the secondary schools in Soweto (the Morris Isaacson High School): 'My main aim is to educate the masses, particularly in politics. For this reason, I have chosen teaching as my profession when I leave school.' *The Star*, International Weekly Edition, 24 December, 1976, p. 10.

The whole chapter Kuper devotes to the black teachers, although written in the early sixties, is still relevant.

13. *The African Image*, op. cit., p. 97.
14. ibid., pp. 187, 194.
15. *Tell Freedom* (Faber, London, 1954), p. 311.
16. For a vivid account of the period, see Nkosi, *Home and Exile*, op. cit., and the article by Daniel Maximin, *'Drum ou la génération perdue'*, in *Afrique du Sud aujourd'hui*, Présence Africaine, 1978.
17. Sampson has since become known through several books, notably *The Anatomy of Britain*, later revised and republished under the title *The New Anatomy of Britain* (Hodder and Stoughton, London, 1962 and 1971).
18. Figures in several anthologies, notably in *Modern African Short Stories*, ed. Charles R. Larson (Fontana, Glasgow, 1971), Modern African Stories, eds. Komey and Mphahlele (Faber, London 1964), *South African Writing Today* eds. Gordimer and Abrahams, (Penguin, Harmondsworth, 1967), *Africa in Prose*, eds. Dathorne and Feuser (Penguin, Harmondsworth, 1969).
19. Author of an autobiography, *Blame Me on History* (Thames & Hudson, London, 1963), and co-author, with Lewis Nkosi, of the script for the film *Come Back Africa*.
20. Has written essays and also figures in *Ten One-Act Plays*, ed. Cosmo Pieterse (Heinemann, London, 1968).
21. Author of the libretto of the well-known musical comedy *King Kong* and an autobiography *Chocolates for my Wife: Slices of My Life* (Hodder & Stoughton, London, 1961).
22. Themba, born in the Transvaal in 1924, a bursary student at Fort Hare, obtained a first-class degree in English, took a teaching course, taught, then became a journalist. He went into exile in Swaziland in 1963 and died there in 1968; a selection of his writings has been collected under the title *The Will to Die* (Heinemann, London, 1972), with an introduction by Lewis Nkosi.

23. Rive was born in 1931 and brought up in Cape Town's notorious District Six where a large Coloured community lived until their eviction, when it was turned into a white residential area. He obtained his BA at the University of Cape Town and his Ph.D. at Oxford. He now teaches English and Latin at a school for Coloureds. He has written a novel, *Emergency* (Faber, London, 1964), and a large number of short stories. A selection of his writings was published by Ad. Donker, Johannesburg, in 1977. His autobiography *Writing Black: an author's notebook* was published in 1981 by David Philip, Cape Town. He is also a literary critic.
24. Nat Nakasa (born in 1937) will be mentioned frequently in this study; he was a brilliant journalist and editor-in-chief of *The Classic*.
25. Nxumalo (1918–57) was born in Port Shepstone and went to school at St Francis, Marianhill; he was obliged to give up his studies before his matriculation for family and financial reasons. He did a number of jobs before joining *Bantu World* as a sports journalist. He fought with the South African armed forces during the Second World War and became a sergeant; away from his country, he rubbed shoulders with many people on an equal footing and noticed how different conditions were from those in his own country; he returned very frustrated. He worked on *Drum* from 1951 until his death.
26. *Home and Exile*, op. cit., p. 10.
27. See below.
28. The carrying of passes by African women, the people who had been banned (whom Helen Joseph had been to see). See her book, *Tomorrow's Sun* (The John Day Company, N.Y., 1967).
29. See *Let My People Go* (Collins/Fontana, London, 1963), p. 29.
30. See *Cry, the Beloved Country* (Penguin, Harmondsworth, 1958), p. 34.
31. *The African Image*, op. cit., p. 192.
32. The Treason Trial was to last several years before ending in 1961 with the acquittal of all the accused.

Chapter 2
The Dark Years after Sharpeville

▼▼▼▼▼▼▼▼▼▼▼▼▼▼▼▼▼▼▼▼▼▼▼▼▼▼▼▼▼▼▼▼▼

The English-speaking white writers

An incursion into the world of the white writer is necessary at this juncture, partly so as to provide this half-literary, half-sociological outline with some perspective, and partly because the majority of black writers left South Africa immediately before or after Sharpeville. The white writer was therefore the only one, for a time at least, who was able to give an account of the realities of the South African situation – provided, of course, that he wanted to do so; here attitudes vary.

Two theoretical statements by two personalities belonging to the white literary world will illustrate this. On the one hand, there is the text of a lecture given by Paton in Johannesburg in 1956, 'The South African Novel in English'; on the other hand, Guy Butler's anthology, *A Book of South African Verse*, which includes a long introductory essay by the editor on South African poetry in English (1959).

While the author of *Cry, the Beloved Country* makes direct reference to the 'situation', one is struck by the minimal place it is accorded in Butler's essay. Paton seems to have written his lecture with his windows wide open to the sounds from the street and fully aware of the pressures exerted by apartheid even on literature. Butler, on the other hand, seems to have written his study sitting on Sirius or, at least, in a padded room far from the noise and fury of the world. And nothing could constrast more than the conclusions reached by the two authors. There can be little doubt that, beyond the differences of personality and temperament, we have here two very different sets of political attitudes.

Paton, in fact, takes the opposite view to a statement apparently made by Guy Butler during a broadcast on the BBC (in 1955?), which served as the basis of his essay. He argues that in contrast to the English-speaking *poet*, who looks towards England, the South African prose writer is deeply rooted in his own society. Paton lists as evidence the novels of Olive Schreiner, Sarah Gertrude Millin, William Plomer and others including Nadine Gordimer, who had just begun to publish. The proof is that among these writers one theme predominates and overshadows all the others because the very life of the countryside pushes it firmly into the forefront – the theme of the racial problem: 'Race is not a plot, or a structural pattern, or an obsession: it is the very stuff of our lives, and it is life that is the making of a story.'[1]

There is nothing new here: already in 1949, Paton had stressed the fact that the pressure of everyday realities upon the South African liberal writer was such that it gave the racial theme precedence over all others.[2] After him, Nadine Gordimer stated at Harvard in 1961, with as much emphasis, that the dominant factor shaping South African customs and social attitudes has always been, is and will continue to be, the colour question.[3]

Another difference of opinion between Paton and Butler concerns the English language. In contrast to the latter's exclusive vision, Paton makes no distinction between those writers for whom English is the mother tongue and the others. He goes on to mention Peter Abrahams, whose novels were beginning to be published abroad.

Finally, when he comes to pose specifically – since the conference organizers had asked him to do so – the problem of the novelist's social role, Paton, although very prudent in his approach, stresses the importance, in a country so divided by apartheid, of seeing the novelist interpreting and showing the country and its inhabitants to their contemporaries and the world at large: this vision of oneself through the eyes of others has an inestimable value, he says. Nothing could do more to give us a better understanding of ourselves, of others, and of ourselves in relation to others.[4]

Paton willingly admits that this revealing of one's country to oneself can be extremely painful but this baring of the truth, he insists, is indispensable.[5]

Butler's essay has a completely different resonance.

Guy Butler was born in 1918 into a well-off Cape family: several of his uncles ran prosperous farms there, while his father was editor-in-chief of the *Midland News and Karoo Farmer*. On his father's side, he was descended from an old South African family: a Quaker grandfather well disposed towards the Boers, and a grandmother descended from the 1820 Settlers. On his mother's side, however, Butler's links are with England, from where his mother came.

References to Europe are frequent in his work: he lived there on several occasions, in Oxford first, where he finished his university studies, then during the Second World War, when he was involved in various theatres of military action. His first volume of poems was called *Stranger to Europe* (1952).[6]

Between the publication of this collection and *A Book of South African Verse*, Butler published two plays: *The Dam* (1953) and *The Dove Returns* (1956).[7] As Professor of English Language and Literature at Rhodes University, Grahamstown, he was already by the end of the 1950s a member of the English-language establishment.

It is doubtless futile to look for the degree of 'Englishness' of a member of the Empire or British Commonwealth who is an emigrant or descended from emigrants. Doris Lessing, who was born in Rhodesia of parents who described themselves as 'English', has shown in an essay full of irony and dry humour how contradictory such a definition really is.[8] As far as concerns Butler and his assertions that the English-speaking South African poet is turned towards England, there is no doubt that, from the historical point of view and up to the time of the declaration of the Republic in 1961, very strong and complex links existed between English-speaking South Africans and their country of origin. One should, however, add that in his desire to show that South Africa is not isolated from the rest of the world from the cultural or literary point of view, Butler overestimates the links that still bind it to English civilization. In contrast, he presents the environment in which the white poet lives as still wild, therefore inappropriate for the poet to identify with. The way he describes the country and its inhabitants, especially, in no way provides a true picture of the South Africa of the forties and fifties:

Industry and commerce have brought towns and cities, and these, alas, are populated not by the protagonists of a vital culture, sure of its values, but by those of a decaying one, internally divided, offering to the tribesman, as he steps out of the sorcerer's ring of bones, a choice of beliefs ranging from Catholicism to Communism.[9]

The term 'tribesman' is significant: Butler constantly uses it to designate the African and he persists in talking of 'primitivism' to describe the latter's mode of life and civilization.[10]

Thereafter it is easy to follow the dialectic of Butler's introduction: if the white poet cannot find his identity in an Africa he says is still semi-barbaric, if he cannot, either, identify with England in spite of all his ties with it, where is he to find his roots? And to what must the 'traveller', for this is how Butler sees the white poet, cling? To the great truths? But for the most part these are trampled underfoot by the 'European' himself . . .

So, the first conclusion to which the poet comes is that he must turn back into himself, he must return to introspection: 'It is not therefore surprising that much recent South African poetry is inward. Our journeys bring us back to ourselves.'[11]

It follows that the poet's scepticism is going to lead to a detached attitude to society and the country but, paradoxically, also, says Butler, to 'a sharper or different sensual awareness of the world' and to a return to nature. It is, finally, the poet's ability to give an accurate account of this relationship between the world and the self and between the self and the world that enables him to 'rediscover' himself ('only in finding the right image, an image which is a clear reflection of ourselves in the world and the world in us, do we achieve, however briefly, a homecoming'.[12]

To conclude that the attitude thus described is rather Byzantine is perhaps going too far, but it does certainly lead to an 'ivory tower' outlook; it is exactly the opposite of the one preached by Paton and Nadine Gordimer. A reading of the poems included in the anthology confirms this view: very few refer to contemporary South African society. The only allusion to apartheid occurs in the selection of Delius's poems ('The Ethnic Anthem'), which is also the only critical glance in that direction.[13]

The image of South Africa that emerges from the majority of the poems is that of a primitive, tribal Africa, not at all the South Africa of the townships, bursting with vitality and source of the talent mentioned earlier; a conventional Africa, in short, which corresponds to the image the Nationalists have tried to create.

In fact, this stress on the primitive and tribal side of the African, imprisoning him within these two adjectives, this exaggeration of the gulf between the cultures in manifest contradiction of the attempts made by individuals belonging to all ethnic groups to bridge that gulf, and, finally, the argument that Africa – and therefore its black inhabitants – have a congenital resistance to change, was preparing the public for the policy of enforced tribalization and 'Africanization' propounded by Verwoerd and was justifying in advance the application of a different status, and therefore a different treatment, of the indigenous community.[14]

Is Butler indulging in politics, then? If so, certainly unconsciously, as he is not a racist but rather the victim of his own ignorance and his own marked exclusivism.[15] But there is no doubt, however, that through the anthology and his introduction to it, he is perpetuating or reinforcing the prejudices common to a majority of white South Africans.[16] The book was reprinted several times during the sixties without any change to the introductory essay or the choice of poems.

The 1960s and the problem of commitment

The nineteen-sixties and *Sestig* began with Langa–Sharpeville, deepened to the State of Emergency that before long was written in to the ordinary laws and permanent practices of the land, and that saw the outlawing and virtual destruction of most of the broad liberatory Movement and the imprisonment, banning, gagging, pegging, banishment and exile of members and supporters of this movement. The sixties was a period of brutal repression, of imprisonment without trial, of death in detention. It was a time of grim-lipped silence; but it was also a time of rumours, persistent rumours, dark rumours of torture, persecution and victimization. It was a time of political trials.[17]

This is how an Afrikaner, P. P. Louw, writes in an article in which he analyses the *Sestigers* movement (from *Sestig*, meaning 'sixty') – a group of Afrikaans writers who wanted to break with the conformism of the Afrikaner world. There could not be a briefer, more concise summary of the eventful decade of the sixties.

Organization of the resistance began immediately after Sharpeville. On 16 December 1961, the anniversary of the Voortrekkers' victory over Dingaan at Blood River in 1838, ten explosions rocked the cities of Port Elizabeth and Johannesburg: the first acts of sabotage had been carried out by armed units of the banned ANC, now calling itself *Umkonto We Sizwe* ('the spear of the nation'). The new organization had abandoned passive resistance in favour of sabotage aimed at opening the eyes of the white electorate and warning the Nationalists of the hardening of its position.

Also in 1961 a new underground movement was created, called the African Resistance Movement, or ARM (also known as the National Committee for Liberation, or NCL), consisting mainly of whites, young liberals for the most part. They, too, rejected violence against persons, attacking only installations of little importance.

At the end of 1962, another resistance organization emerged, called Poqo, from the Xhosa word for 'pure'; it was the armed wing of the PAC and its units did not hesitate to attack individuals.

Simultaneously, the government intensified its repressive measures. Also in 1962 it introduced the Sabotage Act (only one of whose twenty-two clauses is concerned with sabotage properly speaking). This new act made it possible to place a number of the regime's opponents under house arrest and to extend bannings of all kinds. The Congress of Democrats was banned in September 1962: its members, whatever their political affiliations, were all declared Communists in terms of the Suppression of Communism Act. The following year, the General Law Amendment Act allowed for the detention without trial, for a renewable period of ninety days, of any person the police wished to question. Suspended in 1965, it was replaced by an even more draconian piece of legislation, the Criminal Procedure Act.

An important trial took place in 1964: this was the so-called Rivonia Trial, in which the chief accused were the leaders of the armed resistance belonging to all the ethnic communities: Nelson Mandela, Walter Sisulu, Dennis Goldberg, Govan Mbeki, Ahmed Kathrada, Lionel Bernstein, Raymond Mhlaba, Elias Motscaledi and Andrew Mhlangeni. All except Bernstein were condemned to life imprisonment.

The same year, Bram Fischer, one of the leading barristers who had defended Mandela and his companions, the son and grandson of Afrikaners well known for their role in the affairs of the Orange Free State, in his turn joined the underground movement. Fischer had belonged to the South African Communist Party in the thirties and, as a barrister, had defended several opponents of the regime. He was 56 when he joined the underground. For more than a year he evaded capture by the police, before he was finally arrested and condemned to life imprisonment.

The last of the major trials of this period was that of John Harris. He joined the ARM in 1961 and was involved in several acts of sabotage with fellow members, including one in July 1964 which resulted in one person being killed and several injured. He was arrested, tried, condemned to death, and hanged in April 1965.

The culmination of this period was another law which permitted the government to hound an even greater number of its opponents: this was the Terrorism Act of 1967, which provided a definition of the term sufficiently vague to cover any act of opposition and to allow the authorities to strike wherever they wished. This law was made retrospective to 1962, enabling the government to prosecute and imprison opponents who had so far eluded its clutches.

Where, in fact, during this period of continuing crisis about the basic freedoms, were the white South African writers and intellectuals? Better equipped than most of their compatriots to respond to the events of the time, could they – should they – have remained indifferent? What English- or Afrikaans-speaking groups protested in 1963 or in 1966 against the silencing of the near totality of black writers? The Afrikaans poet, Breyten Breytenbach, wrote a few years later: 'Isn't it astounding that the blossoming-time of Sestig – that period during which we gathered in our nice, fat prizes, and when we wanted to fight to the death about who should get the Hertzog Prize – coincided with a period in which more and more writers were banned? Have you also got that nasty flavour of shame in your mouth?'[18]

The debate about the relations between literature and politics is, of course, never-ending: some writers – the majority – insist that the two must be kept separate, some arguing for the 'purity' of literature, others that literature can have no effect on events.

Immediately after Sharpeville, supporters and opponents of writers' commitment clashed in a new literary review launched in Cape Town, *Contrast*. In no. 3, an unsigned editorial entitled 'The Liberal Conscience' set out to assess the arguments.[19] According to the author – probably Philip Segal, editor-in-chief at the time – part of the English-speaking community was suffering from a sense of guilt towards the Afrikaner and towards the black man. The liberal writer who makes this guilt the subject of his books takes on the role of pamphleteer, with disastrous consequences on the artistic level, for the racial theme distorts the vision ('it must be questioned whether work recorded through the distorting lens of the "race theme" can attain to artistic truth and life at all'). The conclusion of the editorial then simply repeats Butler and Roy Campbell:

> The prayer of the South African writer to his or her Muse should be in the first place for a vision penetrating beyond the silhouettes to the man and woman of reality, a sensuous identity with this world and people. He may then beg for the time and inner stillness to perfect his craft, to weigh every word and

syllable and pause so that their effect strike like iron to the reader's heart; to strive for style which our work lacks, and hold not to the forms of truth only but to its mood and inward spirit.[20]

While noting the generosity of the beginning of this definition, we must not be misled: a vision in depth of the Other ('a vision penetrating beyond the silhouettes') is impossible in a society which denies the Other when he is black and abolishes all possibility of contact with him, be it direct or through the medium of the written work. This desire must remain therefore a pious hope for so long as this same society has not changed. To whom must this task be given, then? To the politician, of course! Thus it is that the writer excuses himself from the task of contributing to this change and can devote himself exclusively to his art ('to strive for style'), if he has the leisure and the intellectual freedom, two elements which do not belong to the life of the black man.

Taking the opposite view are the progressive writers of whatever nationality who, following Maïakovski, insist that the 'fable' of apolitical art should be laid to rest once and for all. Chinua Achebe, the non-Marxist Nigerian novelist, sums up their position when he says that the theory of art for art's sake is equivalent to saying that all is for the best in the best of worlds:

> A writer who says that art is for art's sake is clearly saying – 'The political situation is all right as it is. Don't upset it'. That is what you are saying. And those in power will say, of course: 'This is real writing. He knows his job, you see. He's not disturbing us'. And so it is a deeply political, a highly committed stance to take.[21]

This is certainly how Paton and the majority of the leading South African novelist and short-story writers have understood it. And this is perhaps a possible meeting point for black and white writers who do not want to close their eyes to the real situation in their country: people of all colours brought together, all communities made one, those who believe in Heaven and those who do not. George Orwell had already said as much when he wrote in 'Writers and Leviathan' that 'the experience of the German occupation taught the European peoples something that the colonial peoples knew already, namely, that class antagonisms are not all-important and that there is such a thing as national interest'.[22]

If 'race' is substituted for 'class', or if one bears in mind that in South Africa these words are synonymous, then Orwell's words can be applied to the situation of the sixties and seventies in South Africa. This is doubtless why the statements of South African writers are also so reminiscent of those made by the French writers of the Resistance, echoing one another through time and space:

> One may have dedicated one's life to poetry but first and foremost it is to the defence of man, to the defence of life that I am attached. (Pierre Seghers, France)[23]

> You are committed to certain values, you are committed to life, long before you sit at the typewriter. What comes out are the outer trimmings of your commitment, waiting for use. (K. Kgositsile, South African writer in exile)[24]

> Who then will give witness to our time? Who will tell of life, that incredible and threatened thing, that daily legend, that gaunt and hungry beast with its tongue

hanging from its mouth? What is wanted are poets of blood, poems signed with our suffering. (Luc Bérimont, France)[25]

We need now an artist who is the sort of human being who is moved to protest when his sense of humanity is outraged and who, being an artist, makes his protest articulate in terms of his art . . . Who is going to do for Sharpeville what Picasso did for Guernica? (Neville Dubow, South Africa)[26]

> How can I speak to you of flowers
> When there are only cries in everything I write?
>
> (Aragon, France)[27]

> It is said
> that poets write of beauty
> of form, of flowers and of love,
> but the words I write
> are of pain and of rage.
>
> (James Matthews, South Africa)[28]

One could go on listing parallels, so alike are the two situations in terms of oppression and the climate of conflict. We can leave it to the French poet Pierre Emmanuel to conclude this discussion; the length of the quotation is fully justified, for no one could better express the problem of the relationship between Morality and Art or better explain the true ambition of a literature which, in the face of Tyranny, has less the desire to last than to serve Man at a time when his Humanity is being so seriously threatened:

> For so long as each of us has not come to the realization that the present time is the ultimate absurdity of man, from whom all meaning has perhaps been stolen; for so long as we are incapable of recognizing, in its least everyday manifestation, the threat that is being forced upon us by that vast enterprise of human abasement whose methods and effects we are already beginning to experience; for so long as we fail to understand that through it it is himself that man is trying to destroy and that it is successfully counting on all the destructive forces hidden within us; and finally for so long as we do not, with all the violence of our despair, stand up to these monsters that we dare not acknowledge outside ourselves because they are so cleverly hidden within us, we shall remain insensitive to the true significance of the drama being played out. However imperfect it may be on the level of art, the most dynamic poetry of today seeks to create the conditions of lucidity needed for a total awareness, for an offensive on the part of liberty. It does not have the pretension of producing, right away, the definitive works of the period, but to prepare the right climate for them.[29]

Armed with this 'viaticum', we can return to Uys Krige's remark quoted above,[30] and ask what *all men* have in common if it is not the legitimate desire for liberty, dignity and equality of opportunity, and the meaning of the equation: 'The closer you move to the politics of your own time, the more insignificant you become', when absolutely everything in South Africa represents a political act, even entering a public lavatory or a sports stadium reserved for another racial group.[31]

General survey of committed writing

What then is the committed writer to do?

It would be more accurate to ask: what can the committed writer do? The reply depends a great deal, really, not only on the writer's own temperament but also on whether or not he is actually in South Africa.

Alan Paton and Nadine Gordimer have already replied on behalf of the prose writers. In their view, the essential thing is not to turn one's back on reality, however unpleasant, but to reveal it to the public – mostly blind or unconcerned – so as to oblige it to reflect and to stir its conscience, and perhaps even move it to react. This idea had already been expressed by Sartre[32] and was to be 'reactivated' in the sixties.

So, during an international conference of writers at Uppsala (Sweden) in 1967 on the theme of 'The Writer in Modern Africa', in which the South African writers Alex La Guma, Nkosi, Brutus and Mphahlele took part, Albert Memmi declared, on behalf, it seems, of a majority of them:

> The true commitment of the writer does not therefore consist in signing manifestos, deciding whether or not to vote, but in daring to depict reality as it really is. And this will necessarily lead to conflict with most other people because in general they cannot see this reality.[33]

We shall see how the leading South African prose writers give shape to the problems confronting their country and portray characters who take part in the Resistance, commit acts of sabotage and are sent to prison: their works will be relentlessly banned. This was the fate of C. J. Driver's *Elegy for a Revolutionary*, Jack Cope's *The Dawn Comes Twice* and Mary Benson's *At the Still Point*, while Nadine Gordimer's *The Late Bourgeois World* incurred the wrath of the censors for other reasons.[34]

The prison literature that 'flourished' during the same period suffered the same fate, as, for example, the book by the journalist Ruth First, *117 Days*, which gives an account of her imprisonment and interrogation against a background of contemporary events (among which the dramatic arrest of Dennis Brutus stands out), and Helen Joseph's *Tomorrow's Sun*, which describes the growing involvement of a woman who has remained outside politics.

As far as the black prose writers are concerned, the pressures of everyday life on them were so strong that they wrote only short works (short stories, essays, articles), as long as they stayed in South Africa. But during the sixties most of them went into exile, and they now wrote longer works: narratives and novels dominated by the autobiographical element, which far exceeds in intensity anything that fiction could depict: Alfred Hutchinson's *Road to Ghana*,[35] in 1960, followed by Alex La Guma's *A Walk in the Night* and *And a Threefold Cord*,[36] in 1962 and 1964, Bloke Modisane's *Blame Me on History* (1963),[37] *Drawn in Colour* and *The Ochre People*,[38] both by Noni Jabavu, in the same year, and *The Stone Country*, also by Alex La Guma, in 1967.[39] Among those who stayed, Richard Rive and James Matthews published short stories, some of which appeared in the collection *Quartet* (1963), while the following year Richard Rive published his novel *Emergency*, which unfolds against the background of the events of Sharpeville.[40]

With one or two exceptions, poetry gave way to prose in this task of conveying the surrounding reality. Yet a lot of poetry was written during this period: but even when it was of high quality, as that of Sydney Clouts, Ruth Miller and Perseus Adams,[41] it generally remained peripheral to the 'situation'. This was particularly true of the poetry published in the review *New Coin*, founded by Guy Butler in 1965.

While *Contrast* (1960) continued to maintain a certain neutrality, Lionel Abrahams's *The Purple Renoster* (1957) and *The Classic* (1963) (the latter intended mainly but not exclusively for African writers still in South Africa) published more committed writing. The same applied to *The New African*, founded in Cape Town by Randolph Vigne, who had belonged to the Young Liberals (Lewis Nkosi was for some time its editor-in-chief), and *Sechaba*, the political and cultural organ of the ANC in exile.

Thus, a continuous but limited trickle of poetry gave witness to the present. Sometimes, it was occasional poetry reflecting an immediate reaction to a specific, traumatic experience: the Sharpeville massacre, the fate of John Harris, the accidental death of Chief Luthuli. At others, on the other hand, the poem tried to show the hidden significance of an event, by presenting reality in the form of more or less clear symbols which were rather like training a projector secretly or insistently on to the hidden depths of the collective unconscious.[42]

The committed poetry of the period that stands out above the rest and reveals a certain continuity of thought is the work of four writers: a white, Delius, and three Coloureds, Brutus, Pieterse and Nortje.

In *Black South Easter*, analysed in a later chapter, Delius uses a 'vision' to convey his conception of an ideal South African society. His poetry had opened out considerably after the publication of *The Last Division*, but in this poem the beauty of the images and the rich rhythms are the vehicle for ideas that are not very convincing in spite of their liberal quality. Delius settled in London in 1966; he worked at the BBC, where he welcomed visiting South African poets, notably Brutus and Pieterse. The latter had just published in the United States *The Ballad of the Cells* (1965), and Brutus, whose first volume, *Sirens, Knuckles and Boots* (1963), had appeared while he was under house arrest, was preparing to leave for London. *Sirens* had won the Mbari Prize for poetry, founded by the Nigerian review, *Black Orpheus*, at the same time as the poems of a young disciple of Brutus's, K. A. Nortje. It was Nortje who, amid the silence of the general lack of communication, was to compose poems which most effectively expressed the deeper reality of the sixties and became their tragic symbol as a result of his death in 1970 during his brief period of exile in Canada and England.[43]

In 1967 and 1968 respectively, there appeared two anthologies: *South African Writing Today*, compiled by two Johannesburg writers, Nadine Gordimer and Lionel Abrahams, and *A Book of South African Verse* by two Cape Town writers, Jack Cope and Uys Krige.[44] The latter was an improvement on Guy Butler's anthology in that it included English translations of poets writing in Afrikaans and in the vernacular languages. However, English-speaking African writers are missing from this anthology too, and the Coloured poet Adam Small is included among the Afrikaans writers for a poem originally written in English![45]

The anthology of Nadine Gordimer and Lionel Abrahams is more 'ecumenical' and more representative of contemporary South Africa. Prose is well represented but would nevertheless be no more than a postscript to the period of the fifties if it did not include two important texts: Mary Benson's 'Twelve Years! It's Nothing! (A Letter to James Baldwin)' which gives frank and inspiring witness to the cruelty of the period, but also pays homage to the courage and heroism of those who

The Dark Years after Sharpeville

resisted; and Lewis Nkosi's 'Black Power or Souls of Black Writers', which belongs to the debate on commitment and in which the author distances himself from most of his black contemporaries.[46] In the section devoted to poetry, which is much shorter and less original, one poem, however, stands out above the others: 'The Taste of the Fruit'. Its author, William Plomer, writing from his English retreat which he now never leaves, has managed to find the right words to bring together in a single homage two highly talented people who both committed suicide within three days of each other in July 1965 – Ingrid Jonker and Nat Nakasa, whose sensibilities were unable to cope with the separation and division organized by the regime:

> Let those who will savour
> Ripeness and sweetness,
> Let them taste and remember
> Him, her and all others,
> Secreted in the juices.[47]

Finally, the anthology includes the last scene of *The Blood Knot*, a play by Athol Fugard which was first performed in 1961.

Fugard, born in 1932 of an Afrikaner mother and an English-speaking father, is really the whole of the South African theatre of the sixties. As the main dramatist writing during that period, Fugard would stand out for that fact alone, if his plays – he wrote several during the sixties – were not also intended to bear witness to their period.

In 1958, Fugard was working in a magistrate's court which dealt with infractions of the pass laws at the average rate of three a minute. This brief experience of the administadministration of apartheid was a revelation to him.

Fugard settled in Port Elizabeth after a long period of travels during which he was a seaman in the Far East and did his apprenticeship in Europe and America as a theatre and television director. He married an actress, Sheila Meiring,[48] and founded, at the request of Africans living in the township of New Brighton, an experimental theatre company known as the 'Serpent Players', which exists to this day.

The plays he writes, either alone or on the basis of improvisation by members of his group, all have their source in the life of poverty in the townships, in the problems posed by discrimination and the frustration that it causes. *The Blood Knot* is the story of two brothers, the one black, the other with a lighter skin, trapped within the prison of the prejudices that they reproduce, in spite of themselves, in their relationship. While *Hello and Good-bye* (1965) takes the audience into the twilight world of the 'poor Whites', *Boesman and Lena* (1969) returns to the ambiguity that the regime, associated as it is with the colour white, continues to foster.[49]

Until 1962–3, Fugard and the actors who worked with him encountered no problems other than material ones in rehearsing together and performing to mixed audiences. Then segregation became more strict and Fugard reluctantly had to agree to put on performances for separate audiences, or to give up the theatre.

The writer, censorship and the public

Fugard's position could not be a better illustration of the triangular relationship between the writer, the various forms of censorship and the public.

What is literature, in fact, if not a means of communication? Between writers, between the writer and his readers or his audience, between readers, between reader or audience and the writer . . . If we add the different South African communities, what a large number of variables there are!

The law has instituted two different regimes, one for the white 'tutor', the other for the black 'pupil'. In the sphere of theatre, this means that the majority of foreign plays are not shown to the blacks. Early in his career, Fugard asked overseas playwrights to forbid the performance of their plays in South Africa, in the hope that this pressure would lead to a change of policy. The 'boycott' was organized and gathered momentum. The South African government then passed the Piracy Bill, which deliberately violated international agreements by allowing theatre directors to ignore the wishes of foreign playwrights.

It was then (in 1968) that Fugard changed his approach:

> Anything that will get people to think and feel for themselves, that will stop them delegating these functions to the politicians, is important to our survival . . . There is nothing John Balthazar Vorster and his Cabinet would like more than to keep us isolated from the ideas and values current in the Free Western World. These ideas and values find an expression in the plays of contemporary writers. I think we South Africans should see these plays.[50]

This point of view has been much discussed.[51] Fugard has, nevertheless, produced plays for separate audiences which would not have been available to them otherwise, foreign plays 'banned' by their authors. The problem was different when the bannings were the work of the government itself, and these were to increase in number during the sixties.

In a society in which there are no legal channels by which the communication, or at least the expression, of millions of people can pass (Parliament, trade unions and political parties are all closed to the blacks), there are only the writers who can fulfil this essential role. And if they are in turn banned from speaking, unhappy the country that deprives itself of this permanent and ready 'wire-tapping kit'.

Nadine Gordimer and Lionel Abrahams both protested against the total censorship affecting forty-six South African writers then living in exile, among them the big names in black writing in English. Nadine Gordimer, after pointing out that only three of those affected by this measure had been engaged in politics, went on to say that South Africa was doing itself irreparable harm by suppressing the least trace of these writers, who, she argued, provided a first-hand insight into the lives of people living out of sight of the whites and into the unexpressed thoughts of black people. Lionel Abrahams posed the problem, on the basis of the Brutus case, of the responsibility of 'free' writers in the face of the censorship affecting their black colleagues.[52]

But it is this white public which the committed writer is trying to reach – for it is they who hold the power and abuse it, even if it is the government doing so in their name – willing to listen?

Sociologists who have studied the white community of the sixties conclude that, on the whole, one is dealing with a conservative majority, and this includes the English-speaking South Africans whose liberal tradition has been greatly exaggerated. Although there is no aggressive racialism among many of them, prejudices and stereotyped attitudes towards the black community as a whole, and not only towards the Africans, abound – we saw an example of this in the case of Guy Butler. Professor Colin Gardner, in a study of English-speaking whites,[53] points out that, if his compatriots are less than enthusiastic about apartheid as a doctrine, they nevertheless hide in the shadow of the Nationalists, either from opportunism or fear. The existence of a Westminster-type parliament, which has only a semblance of legality since it functions only for the whites, is all they want.

The cultural and psychological links that existed with England until the proclamation of the Republic and the break with the Commonwealth grew weaker during the sixties and English-speaking South Africans lost their standoffishness and arrogance towards the Afrikaners: a not insignificant proportion of them voted for the Nationalists.

As for the immigrants coming from Britain, far from introducing a breath of fresh air into the country, for the most part they quickly adopt the prevailing prejudices. David Stone, in his book *Colonist and Uitlander* (1973), shows the often unconscious connection between the latent racism to be found in Great Britain, especially since the fifties, and the rapid adherence of the immigrants to a regime based on racism.[54]

Colin Gardner is therefore right when he concludes that on the level of everyday life the theoreticians of apartheid have no cause to complain about their English-speaking compatriot: 'In practice, apartheid is for him the sum total of South Africa's racial situation.'[55]

As has been pointed out in connection with religion – and a study published in 1975 confirms it[56] – liberalism in South Africa is a marginal phenomenon and commitment or real involvement (as opposed to concern) is to be found only among a minority of the minority. It is therefore easy to understand why the South African committed writer has the impression that he is crying in a desert, and the radicalization of literature after the sixties was inevitably a direct result of the growing refusal of the white community to listen.

The committed Afrikaans poets

At the turn of the sixties, a group of Afrikaans writers endeavoured to get rid of certain taboos which had until then restricted the development of Afrikaans literature: they are known as the *Sestigers*.[57]

Afrikaans literature is young – it dates only from the beginning of this century. It has been closely associated with the development of Afrikaner nationalism, of which one of the binding forces was the Afrikaans language, to which its writers gave its letters patent of nobility. Many are the heroic or pastoral poems which have responded to the expectations of a simple, rough audience, sure of the justness of its cause against the oppressors of the day, the English. Until the sixties, Afrikaans literature, especially its poetry, has provided a particularly effective support for the strongly pro-government Afrikaans cultural organizations.

Signs of cracks in this solidarity began to appear at the end of the fifties and in the early sixties: the reasons were political or humanitarian, but also cultural.

In fact, culture, as the Nationalist leaders understand it and seek to impose it in the name of the survival of the white race and the Afrikaner 'nation' in South Africa, is turned in on itself; it is not outward-looking as culture should be. It places people into categories, says Adam Small, and instead of bringing them together, it does everything in its power to drive them apart ('It is not in the first place a possibility or complex of possibilities of communication between men; it is not in the first place oriented towards human understanding, but rather towards misunderstanding').[58]

To this we can add the observations of another *Sestiger*, Breyten Breytenbach:

> One wanted to believe in a miracle. One wanted to believe that in this country it might be possible to write as a person about people, for people. But the poison of racialism flows so deeply in our veins. Even in our language, our beautiful language, our miraculous vehicle. We speak of man and woman, boy and girls. And if they're not quite pale enough? *Kaffer, hotnot, koelie, houtkop, outa, aia, jong, meid, klong, skepsel* – yes, one of our leading Sestigers speaks of 'skepsels' in his most recent work, though to his eternal credit let it be said that he refrains from speaking of 'skepselwyfies' or 'skepselooie'. We have renounced some of these terms under the pressure of growing consciousness, but will we ever accept the entire, self-evident humanity of the 'others'? Now we have come to rest at a self-satisfied *Bantu* and *Coloured*. In besmirching others we foul ourselves. Then our language becomes filthy jargon. Is it so very difficult to address others in the terms they use to describe themselves?
>
> Do we want it to be said later on that in this land of sunshine there were two species of homo sapiens – man, and the white man?[59]

Small and Breytenbach, along with Ingrid Jonker, who has already been mentioned, are three major committed poets of which South African protest literature can be proud.

Ingrid Jonker (1933–65), the daughter of an important figure in the Nationalist Party, was brought up by her mother, who had separated from her husband, and had a difficult childhood, chiefly on account of their poverty. After their mother's death, she and her sister went to live with their father and his new family, but they did not become part of it. Her first volume of poetry was ready when she was only 16, and was published in 1956. In conflict with her father and then with the Afrikaner community because of the racial policies of her country, she travelled to Europe with the prize money she won for her second collection, *Rook en Oker* ('Smoke and Ochre'), published in 1963.

Rook en Oker contains, among others, a fine poem written to the memory of the children who were victims of the Sharpeville, Langa and Nyanga massacres, 'The Child who was Shot Dead by Soldiers at Nyanga', which her editor preferred to publish under the less compromising title of 'Die Kind' ('The Child'):

> The child is not dead
> the child lifts his fists against his mother
> who shouts Afrika! shouts the breath
> of freedom and the veld
> in the locations of the cordoned heart
> The child lifts his fists against his father
> in the march of the generations
> who shout Afrika! shout the breath
> of righteousness and blood
> in the streets of his embattled pride.
>
> . . .
>
> The child is present at all assemblies and law-giving
> the child peers through the windows of houses and into the hearts of mothers
> the child who just wanted to play in the sun at Nyanga is everywhere

the child grown to a man treks through all Africa
the child grown into a giant journeys through the whole world
Without a pass.[60]

The collection that appeared after her suicide in 1965, *Kantelson* ('Setting Sun'), contains poems of disillusion whose bitterness and discouragement derive from her vision of life as being based entirely on division.

Adam Small, three years younger than Ingrid Jonker – he was born in 1936, in the Cape Province – belongs to the Afrikaans-speaking Coloured community. After studies at the University of Cape Town, then at Oxford, he taught philosophy at the Coloured University of the Western Cape.[61] Small, who is also a playwright, has written a great many poems. His main collection, *Kitaar My Kruis* ('Guitar my Cross'), appeared in 1962; some of the poems are written in the Coloured patois of the Cape which is close to Afrikaans and which Small refers to as 'Black Afrikaans', while others are in English, a language Small handles well.

The three keys to a correct understanding of Small's poetry are his deeply religious nature, his love of satire, and the role played in his poetry by repetition and incantation.

Like George Orwell, he sees satire as having an extremely important role to play in the twentieth century. His own satire gains considerably from his very skilful use of religious references and quotations. However, it would be a mistake to think that it is merely a question of skill or technique. Small is deeply Christian, but not in the manner of most of his white compatriots. For him, as for Paton, the message contained in the First Epistle of St John is crucial: 'How can a man who does not love the brother that he can see love God, whom he has never seen?'[62]

This is how we should read his poem – frequently quoted but often misconstrued – 'There's somethin'', originally written in English and reproduced in the anthology edited by Cope and Krige:

> You can stop me
> drinking a coke
> at the Cafe
> in the Avenue
> or goin' to
> an Old Nic revue,
> you can stop me doin'
> some silly thing like that
> but o
> there's somethin' you can
> never never do . . .
> you can't
> ever
> ever
> ever stop me
> loving
> even you![63]

Although the word 'Christian' can be used to describe the readiness of the oppressed to forgive their oppressors, the former often invoke the support of the Old and New Testaments to denounce the false religion of the majority of the whites. It is this explicitness which makes it impossible to compare many of Small's poems to true Negro spirituals for, although full of allusions which are obvious to a coloured audience, they are far more biting than the works of American blacks. In addition, the biblical terminology and place names retain all their relevance here, for the Afrikaners have used the place names mentioned in the Bible for their own towns, villages and hamlets. In 'Groot Krismisgabet' ('Great Christmas Prayer') it is an easy transition from the biblical Bethlehem to the South African one, dragging in its wake the other places where Man is daily humiliated:

> Lord
> now we praise you again
> you who came for the salvation of the world
> you who were born so many Christmases ago
> in Bethlehem
>
> yes in Bethlehem Lord
> in the stall
> near the donkey
> near the cow
> in the crib
> on the ground
> on the dirt floor Lord
> in a place that stank
> in a place that made you sick from the stench
>
> we know places like that Lord
> yes we know them
> we have duplicates of them all over
> in Windermere
> in District Six
> in Blouvlei just behind Wynberg near Retreat
>
> and therefore we praise you again this Christmas Lord
> only you
> only you who have the greatest experience of all
> of this kind of place
> only you can help us
>
> only you can for us
> perhaps again this Christmas Lord
> let a new Moses be born here
> a new Moses
> a new Moses
> o Lord, our Moses –
> we'll hide him Lord, we have lots of hiding-places[64]

It is easy to understand how Small finds in the discrimination he encounters every day and in the physical and moral misery he can see all round him, the themes of many poems of which recrimination is always a part. 'De Lô' ('The Law'), for example, explicitly attacks the Immorality Act by telling the story of two young people, a white woman and a Coloured man, in love with one another but driven to suicide by the law, which opposes their love and has led to their being jailed. The law? asks Small in an insistent refrain, what law?

Diana was 'n wit nôi	Diana was a white girl
Martin was 'n bryn boy	Martin was a Coloured boy
dey fell in love	they fell in love
dey fell in love	they fell in love
dey fell in love	they fell in love
sê Diana se mense	said Diana's people
what abou' de lô	what about the law
sê Martin se mense	said Martin's people
what abou' de lô	what about the law
sê almal die mense	said all the people
what abou' de lô	what about the law
sê Martin sê Diana	said Martin said Diana
watte' lô	what law
God's lô	God's law
man's lô	man's law
devil's lô	devil's law
watte' lô	what law
sê die mense net	the people only said
de lô	the law
de lô	the law
de lô	the law
de lô	the law
what abou' de lô	what about the law
what abou' de lô	what about the law[65]

Small's attitude was to become more radical during the year that followed, under the influence of Black Consciousness and, after having considered himself for a period as an Afrikaner and a 'Bruin Sestiger' ('Brown Sestiger'), he went over to the new movement.

The third Afrikaans-speaking committed poet is Breyten Breytenbach, younger than Ingrid Jonker and Adam Small, for he was born in 1939. He was brought up in a very conservative family living in a small Boland village in the Cape, but he broke early with the Afrikaner tradition by going to the English-speaking and liberal Cape Town University instead of the University of Stellenbosch. Without waiting to graduate, Breyten left for Europe, for he was deeply interested in painting and also wanted to write. He finished by settling in Paris in 1961 and there he married a young Frenchwoman of Vietnamese origin.

In his correspondence at the time with his friend André Brink, another Sestiger, there is a letter in which he poses the problem of the Afrikaans writer's commitment:

> Why do we intellectuals not adopt a more positive, even a militant attitude? Are we looking for a change of heart (magnanimity!) in the Afrikaner, or do we want justice and a recognition of human dignity in SA, in spite of the prejudices of the sly White devils? I myself will only acquire respect for the Afrikaners (for

myself) when I learn that 'Jan Smit' has been placed under house arrest or has vomited all over himself with electrodes attached to his fingers . . . Where are the Afrikaners among the accused of the Rivonia trial?[66]

Breytenbach's first two books, a volume of poems, *Die Ysterkooi Moet Sweet* ('The Iron Cow Must Sweat'), and another of short stories, *Katastrofes* ('Catastrophes'), appeared in South Africa in 1964 and earned him a literary prize. But, as he set out to receive his prize, Breytenbach realized that his wife was an undesirable in the eyes of the law and that, in accordance with the Immorality Act, he was even liable to imprisonment; as a result, he felt even more strongly the need to act against apartheid.

In 1967, Breytenbach collaborated in a special number of the *UNESCO Courier* on apartheid: his name stands alongside those of Paton, Nkosi, Brutus and Ronald Segal. His article was entitled 'The Fettered Spirit' and in it he stressed the impoverishment apartheid caused in the sphere of relationships and at the cultural level, and concluded that the masters of the country were committing cultural suicide.[67]

It is this same idea, but presented in much stronger and much more bitter terms, that he developed in a collaborative work published in 1970, *Apartheid: A Collection of Writings on South African Racism by South Africans*. Breytenbach himself stressed the responsibility shared by all Afrikaners in perpetuating apartheid:

> The tendency is there sometimes to think that apartheid is an unpopular dogmatism devised by a few bureaucrats and some perverted theoreticians and imposed [also] on the majority of Afrikaners. One must point out that the Afrikaners are responsible for apartheid, collectively and individually. If the Whites as individuals, if all those who practise culture (the intellectuals, the academics, the artists, the authors, etc.) were to withdraw their direct or implied support of apartheid – not only of a particular government, but of the ethics of Albinohood itself – it could not last.[68]

Breytenbach's own position also became more radical: this change is perceptible in a letter he wrote in 1969 to André Brink: 'You seem to want to improve your society, making it more human; for me that can happen only if the present power structures are broken down by destroying the very foundations on which they rest.'[69]

Thus, as we progress through the sixties, we become aware of an increasing impatience among the intellectuals and the committed writers: already some of them – Dennis Brutus, but also Hugh Lewin and David Evans – had chosen the path of resistance. At the time when Breytenbach wrote this letter, the last two had begun to serve their prison sentences for sabotage.[70] The end of the sixties heralded a decade in which the outlook of the young blacks was not to be the only one to undergo a radical change.

Notes

1. 'The South African Novel in English', in *Knocking on the Door* (David Philip, Cape Town, Rex Collings, London, 1975), p. 140. Paton adds: 'It is the English novel of South Africa that is therefore nearest and truest to South African life.'

2. See below, p. 66.
3. 'The Novel and the Nation in South Africa' in *African Writers on African Writing*, ed. G. D. Killam (Heinemann, London, 1973).
4. *Knocking on the Door*, op. cit., p. 146.
5. ibid., p. 147. It is striking to see how Nadine Gordimer arrives at the same conclusions: 'We have a great deal to learn about ourselves, and the novelist, along with the poet, playwright, composer and painter, must teach us. We look to them to give us the background of self-knowledge that we may be able to take for granted.' ('The Novel and the Nation in South Africa', op. cit., p. 37.)
6. *Stranger to Europe* (Balkema, Cape Town, 1952).
7. *The Dam* (Balkema, Cape Town, 1953), *The Dove Returns* (The Fortune Press, London, 1956).
8. Doris Lessing writes in 'In Pursuit of the English': 'In the colonies or dominions, people are English when they are sorry they emigrated in the first place; when they are glad they emigrated but consider their roots are in England; when they are thoroughly assimilated into the local scene and would hate ever to set foot in England again; and even when they are born colonial, but have an English grandparent. This definition is sentimental and touching. When used by people not English, it is accusatory. My parents were English because they yearned for England, but knew they could never live in it again because of its conservatism, narrowness and tradition. They hated Rhodesia because of its newness, lack of tradition, lack of culture. They were English, also, because they were middle-class in a community mostly working-class.' In *Alienation*, ed. Timothy O'Keefe (MacGibbon & Kee, London, 1960).
9. *A Book of South African Verse* (Oxford University Press, Cape Town, 1959), p. xxviii.
10. Cf. 'Fighting for "Afric's race reviled"' [an allusion to Thomas Pringle, discussed further on] has proved a difficult task. This is not entirely the fault of white self-interest and un-Christian prejudice: it is quite as much owing to the intimidating distances between primitive tribal life and even the most unsophisticated European existence', ibid., p. xxxi).
11. The passage is worth quoting in full: 'Most of our poets have tried to belong to Africa, and finding her savage, shallow and unco-operative, have been forced to give their allegiance, not to any other country, but to certain basic conceptions . . . What rest and stability they find is not in any particular place, but on principles: the integrity of the individual; the duty to seek the truth and proclaim it; the command to love thy neighbour. All these concepts are alien to an Africa:

> Indifferent to love or hate
> Incomprehensible to placate
>
> (Peter: 'Christmas on Three Continents')

These "European" principles are difficult to transplant among tribesmen, particularly when Europeans themselves tend to lose them. We have to re-discover them and realize them afresh in their African context. Like Delius's Livingstone, we frequently find ourselves

> bent above the growing chart,
> of savage and amazing truth.
>
> (ibid., pp. xxxvi–xxxvii)

12. ibid., p. xli.
13. See below, p. 69.
14. The essentials of this argument can be found in a lecture Butler gave on the BBC (in 1955, according to him) 'The English Poet in South Africa', in *Fact Paper* no. 51, 31 January 1958 (A Supplement to the Digest of South African Affairs, Pretoria).
    Here are some extracts from this text:
    'The word "impersonally" is the clue to the new sensibility. One cannot commune with Africa as Wordsworth did with the Lake District. As Aldous Huxley has suggested,

lines like those written above Tintern Abbey are not produced when there are tigers about, nor in a country where devastating drought and tribal wars are frequent.'

'South Africa is still a frontier society: in the absence of a common view of our past or future, or of any basic mutual acceptance of each other, the mere presence of members of other races makes us feel like exiles in our own land.'

'Until recently, our poets looked at Africa geographically; they were excited by its topography, its flora and fauna. Although this excitement has not died, they are now trying to make sense of it, to put it into perspective of time, to fill, or abolish, or redeem the culturally empty centuries behind us.'

15. A lecture Butler gave in 1964 reveals his evolution on this subject as he calls for exchanges between the South African cultures: Butler argues that the country has everything to gain from the encounter on African soil between 'the white Apollo and the black Dionysos' ('The terrified White Apollo will be less scared once he discovers and acknowledges the Apollo in his Black opposite number; and the African Dionysos will be less inhibited if he can exchange rhythms with his brother inside the White man'). In 'The Republic and the Arts', Witwatersrand University Press, 1964.
16. See below, pp. 24–5.
17. 'The Sestigers: A Post-Mortem', in *Bolt*, no. 9, 1973, p. 23.
18. 'A View from Without', in *Bolt*, no. 12, 1974, p. 53.
19. It comes after an exchange of articles between Neville Dubow, a Cape Town art critic, in favour of commitment on the part of the writer (see also below), and the novelist Mary Renault.
20. 'The Liberal Conscience', in *Contrast*, vol. I, no. 3, Winter 1961, p. 9.
21. *Issue*, vol. VI, no. 1, Spring 1976, p. 37.
22. 'Writers and Leviathan', in *The Collected Essays, Journalism and Letters of George Orwell*, vol. IV (*In Front of Your Nose*, 1945–50) (Secker & Warburg, London, 1968), p. 410.
23. *La Résistance et ses Poètes* (Editions Seghers, Paris, 1974), p. 90.
24. *Issue*, op. cit., p. 34.
25. Quoted in *La Résistance et ses Poètes*, op. cit., p. 125.
26. *Contrast*, vol. I, no. 1, Summer 1960, pp. 80–1.
27. *Le Musée Grévin* (Editions de Minuit, Paris, 1946), p. 71.
28. *Cry Rage!* (Spro-Cas Publications, Johannesburg, 1972), p. 1.
29. Quoted in *La Résistance et ses Poètes*, op. cit., pp. 205–6.
30. See above, p. 2, note 3.
31. Cf. Breytenbach's views on this in *Bolt*, op. cit.
32. In *Qu'est-ce que la littérature?* (Gallimard, Paris, 1948), p. 104. See below, p. 112.
33. P. Wästberg (ed.), *The Writer in Modern Africa* (Scandinavian Institute of African Studies, Uppsala, 1968), p. 83.
34. *The Late Bourgeois World* (Jonathan Cape, London, 1966); reprinted in 1976. Nadine Gordimer has said that she did not set out to write a work of propaganda or to prove anything, but that the book displeased the censors because its conclusions did not fit in with the official view of the period on the acts of sabotage of 1963–4, which served as a backdrop.
35. Gollancz, London, 1960.
36. *A Walk in the Night*, published in Ibadan in 1962, was reissued by Heinemann, London, in 1967. *And a Threefold Cord* (Seven Seas Books, Berlin, 1964).
37. *Blame Me on History* (Thames & Hudson, London).
38. Both books were published in 1963 by John Murray, London.
39. *The Stone Country* (Seven Seas Books, Berlin, 1967).
40. *Quartet. New Voices from South Africa* (Heinemann, London, 1964). *Emergency* (Faber, London, 1964).
41. Sydney Clouts, *One Life* (Purnell, Cape Town, 1966). Ruth Miller, *Floating Island* (Human & Rousseau, Cape Town, 1965). Perseus Adams, *The Land at My Door* (Human & Rousseau, Cape Town, 1965).
42. For three typical texts, see 'Sharpeville Inquiry', by Ann Welsh, also author of *Set in Brightness* (New Coin, 1968), in *Contrast 8*, Autumn 1964; 'The Dead at Sharpeville' by

Makhudo Ramopo, in *The New African*, June 1966; 'Pursuer and Pursued' by Hilda Brooke, in *Contrast 3*, Winter 1961.
43. See below, study on Nortje.
44. Both published by Penguin, London.
45. Cope and Krige leave no doubt about their aims: 'African poets still speak largely in collective and impersonal terms and songs may be found of true poetic value which are in fact products composed by a wedding choir or a location musical band. The poem of total individualism or of alienation and despair is likely to come from the man who has strayed far from his people, perhaps into exile, and probably will be written in English, not in his home language.' (op. cit., p. 19.)
46. Nkosi's thesis is that there are too many writers who, under cover of literature, indulge in propaganda. While essentially in agreement with Orwell about commitment, he asks – as Orwell does too, in fact – that the artist should remain strictly independent of all ideologies. For him: 'Unless he is variously talented the best way a writer can contribute anything of worth towards the development of his society is simply by writing – and writing as well as he knows how' (*South African Writing Today*, op. cit., p. 198), and he adds further on: 'For me the function of literature is still to provide an atmosphere of life, by which I mean all those sentiments which bind us to one another in a great compassionate humanity. The function of literature is pre-eminently moral; it is to insist upon the value of aesthetic experience in the original sense of that word. Poetry will have failed if it ignores its main function which is to make us perceive better and experience more' (p. 202).
47. *South African Writing Today*, op. cit., p. 256.
48. Sheila Meiring also writes poems under the name of Sheila Fugard.
49. The three plays have been collected together in *Three Port Elizabeth Plays* (Oxford University Press, London, 1974).
50. ibid., p. xviii.
51. See *Index on Censorship*, vol. 4, nos 1, 3, 4, for the debate which was initiated, in South Africa and in the rest of the world, on the problem of the cultural boycott and Athol Fugard's change of attitude.
52. For Nadine Gordimer's article, see 'How not to know the African', in *Contrast 15*, vol. 4, no. 3, Autumn 1967, p. 47. For Lionel Abrahams, see *The Purple Renoster*, 6, Winter 1966.
53. 'The English-speaking Whites', in *South Africa's Minorities* (Spro-Cas, Johannesburg, 1971).
54. *Colonist or Uitlander: A Study of the British Immigrant in South Africa* (Clarendon Press, Oxford, 1973).
55. 'The English-speaking Whites', op. cit., p. 43.
56. Cf. Jeffrey Butler, 'Changes within the White Ruling Class' in *Change in Contemporary Africa*, ed. L. Thompson and J. Butler (University of California Press, 1975).
57. To the writers mentioned in these pages must be added Jan Rabie, a novelist and short-story writer, and Etienne Leroux, the author of a trilogy which caused an outcry in South Africa (English translation: *To a Dubious Salvation*, Penguin, London, 1972).
58. 'Towards Cultural Understanding' in *Student Perspective in South Africa* (David Philip, Cape Town, 1972), p. 203.
59. 'A View from Without', op. cit.
60. Ingrid Jonker, *Selected Poems* (Jonathan Cape, London, 1968), trans. Jack Cope and William Plomer.
61. He subsequently resigned and now works in a bookshop.
62. 'A Conversation with Adam Small', in *Bolt*, no. 6, November 1972.
63. *Kitaar My Kruis* (Hollandsch Afrikaansche Uitgevers Maatschappij, Cape Town, 1973), pp. 55–6.
64. ibid., p. 19.
65. ibid., p. 52.
66. Quoted in 'The Breytenbach File' by André Brink, *The New Review*, vol. 3, no. 25, p. 5.
67. *UNESCO Courier*, March 1967.

68. *Apartheid* . . . , ed. A. La Guma (Lawrence & Wishart, London, 1972), p. 140.
69. 'The Breytenbach File', op. cit., p. 6.
70. See below, studies on Lewin and Evans.

Chapter 3
South African Writing since 1968

The early 1970s

The year 1968: the United States and Europe are shaken by protest; the revolt against the older generation had begun, and not even South Africa was to be spared. In that country, radicalism had taken refuge in the universities, where the students belonging to NUSAS (National Union of South African Students) reacted vigorously against each new erosion of civil liberties, while SASO (South African Students' Organization) gained an active foothold in the 'ethnic' universities. From the early seventies, students and teachers were to be caught up in demonstrations against repression which were to transform the campuses into enclosed battlefields given over to strikes, expulsions, conditional reinstatements and prison sentences. When the protesting university teachers were silenced by the authorities the students took over from them . . .

And, in fact, it was the student members of SASO who gave Black Consciousness its initial impetus. Tired of being under the tutelage of NUSAS, from which they detached themselves in 1969, and influenced by the pan-Africanist ideas that had dominated the previous two decades, by the writings of Nyerere and the example of the struggle in which the American blacks were engaged,[1] they could see no other way out of oppression except by creating a unity that would enable them, eventually, to confront the whites from a position of strength.

Their immediate aim was to develop a community consciousness that would lead blacks to act as a community and give them pride in belonging to that community. The word 'black' was adopted in place of the term 'non-white', which they saw as an expression of the whites' Eurocentric outlook in relation to the various black communities. All the activities undertaken by the numerous associations that came into being in the wake of SASO gave a sense of reality to black solidarity and were aimed at developing self-awareness among the blacks. The aim was to free the black from his inferiority complex, to give him the courage to lift up his head with pride and to realize that it was up to him to achieve his liberation once and for all. Even the white liberal was regarded as a hindrance to the achievement of that liberation because he had always urged patience and preached a gradualism which had never got anywhere. When accused of being racists in reverse, the young activists of the Black Consciousness movement replied that their movement was not directed against the whites as individuals but against 'white values'.[2] Hence their determined rejection, too, of those blacks who tried to imitate the whites, even to the extent of lightening their skins, and of those who played the separate development game in the Bantustans.

In the religious sphere, the Cottlesloe consultation (December 1960), which took place in the wake of the Sharpeville massacre, led to a questioning, and criticism of, the Dutch Reformed Churchs tenets on apartheid even from within their ranks. A journal, *Pro Veritate*, was launched in 1962 by several leading ministers and theologians, and the Christian Institute was founded a year later, with Dr Beyers Naudé as its Director.[3] This, and other reappraisals of the general attitude of the Church towards apartheid, eventually led to the distribution of the *Message to the People of South Africa* (1968), which called on Christians and all men of good will to choose between obedience to the principles of brotherhood and justice on the one hand and blind adherence to apartheid on the other. From 1968 the approach was to combine criticism of the existing institutions with concrete proposals for the establishment of a new society.

Parallel with the Black Consciousness movement there developed a 'current' of White Consciousness which, without being as widespread as its counterpart, sought to reassess the traditional values of western civilization and test them against the social, economic and political realities of South Africa.

For instance, Richard Turner, who had obtained his doctorate in Paris in 1966 and taught political science at the University of Natal, published *The Eye of the Needle*, subtitled 'An Essay in Participatory Democracy' (1972), in which he tried to show that the establishment of a more just society could not be achieved without a change in personal attitudes. Another work in which Turner collaborated, *White Liberation* (1972), asserted that the whites themselves needed freeing. These two books, published by Spro-Cas (Study project on Christianity in apartheid society, later to become Ravan Press), called for a new kind of democracy in which the citizen would have a real choice. Both books were soon banned and Turner himself was banned from teaching or publishing. He was murdered in 1978.

New poetry journals came into being, some of them – such as *Wurm* and *Izwi* – enjoying only a brief life, while others – such as *Ophir* (in Johannesburg) and *Bolt* (in Durban) – survived several years, all of them indicative of a sharper awareness of contemporary realities. In *Ophir* (1967–76), for instance, social, racial and political themes became the subject of poetry and the work that was published, drawn from all parts of the world, broke down South Africa's narrow horizons. Young black writers like Serote, Mtshali and Pascal Gwala contributed poems, while whites like Peter Horn, Wopko Jensma and Walter Saunders expressed their revolt against authoritarianism in poems in which satire played a significant part. The anthology published by *Ophir* in 1974, entitled *It's Gettin' Late*, contained a warning to South Africa which others were to echo.

Indeed, during the same period, the effects of the country's racial legislation on employment, which seriously restricted its economic growth, began to make themselves felt, and economists and industrialists began to cast doubt on the *practicality* of apartheid. Colin Gardner stresses this chance 'alliance' between the intellectuals and high finance in his study of English-speaking South Africans.[4] Faced with a shortage of skilled labour and inadequate white immigration, the Chambers of Commerce began to press the government to allow all blacks to take on skilled jobs and to make discrimination less inflexible.

However, although some of the more visible signs of apartheid tended to disappear, it remained unchanged in its essentials: even after the upheavals that shook the whole of South Africa in 1976 and 1977, Vorster declared that nothing would change, blacks would not be allowed to live in the cities, they would not be granted rights, nor would there be any alteration in the Bantustan policy. The only reform was to provide the possibility of compulsory education for the blacks, but only at the primary level, which had not been affected by the riots. There was also the promise of new dispensations which would allow for representation of the Coloureds and Indians in a tri-cameral Parliament, although the basic laws regarding segregation would not be affected.[5]

Meanwhile, for the very first time, in 1973, a book in Afrikaans was banned: it was *Kennis van die Aand*, by André Brink, who translated it himself into English the following year and had it published in London in 1974.[6]

Since the late sixties, Brink had distanced himself from the other *Sestigers* by his more militant attitude, arguing that the Afrikaner writer should serve both his and the African communities by defying the most absurd and harmful expression of the South African state's authority: censorship. Brink had spent several years in France and he was in Paris with Breytenbach during the riots of May 1968. Although this can to some extent explain his views, Brink still really represents the moderate Afrikaner tendency, which rejects revolution and seeks to find a way of changing the Afrikaner community before violence breaks out.

To Breytenbach, this attitude was far too timid, for reform could not change South African society *fundamentally*. If the Afrikaner wants one day to be part of a liberated South Africa, he must show himself willing to oppose his own people.

Armed with a special visa, Breytenbach took part in the *Sestigers* Festival at Stellenbosch in February 1973 and made an outspoken speech to an audience that included several high-ranking members of the Nationalist Party. He stressed the importance of the present over the eternal, and declared that he could not find it in himself to remain unmoved by a situation in which the future of the Afrikaner, his culture and his language were threatened as they were. He wanted nothing more to do with what he called 'apartaans', that is, an Afrikaans which had become synonymous with oppression and white domination. He said that Afrikaans should have the same status as the other languages spoken in Africa, no more and no less. The only way for the Afrikaners and the whites as a whole to become a part of Africa, he said, was to destroy the walls the Afrikaner had erected around his 'purity', share South Africa with the rest of its peoples and abandon the *laager*, the closed world of the present, which could only lead to destruction.

Breytenbach was loudly applauded by his audience, proving that the poet–prophet is no more taken seriously than the clown is, for he is, like him, paid to produce laughter or a moment of fear, to play his role as a contradictor who has been given the right to protest just so that people can say they live in a democracy. A few months later in Cape Town, Mtshali was applauded by an audience consisting mainly of whites for poems which were all the more moving for being the product of the cruelty of the whites . . . which led Mtshali to reflect on the cynicism of his audience.

Proof of this is to be found in the fact that no one protested when, embittered by his continued exile and the absence of real change in his country, Breytenbach tried to make his commitment more real than it had been up to that point. He made contact with the resistance movement inside the country and allied himself with whites whose chief aim seems to have been only marginally the eventual overthrow of the present regime. Arrested in August 1975, he was solemnly tried in Pretoria. He stated during his trial that he had sought to follow the logic of his ideals and that in acting the way he had done he had wanted to come to terms with himself.[7] He was sentenced to nine years in prison.

André Brink, paying homage a few months earlier to Bram Fischer, who had died in prison after a long illness, said that, unlike other Afrikaners, he had tried to broaden the concept of Afrikanerdom itself.[8] This remark can be applied to Breytenbach as well, for he was guilty of placing the cause of Man above a partisan and fundamentally inhuman ideology.

The black writer today

The late sixties and early seventies saw a veritable flowering of poetry and drama in the black community. Apart from James Matthews, who abandoned the short story in favour of poetry, nearly all the new writers were unknown; many of them belonged to the Black Consciousness movement and adopted the verse form with remarkable ease.

This poetry revival can be explained in a number of ways. Experience had taught the blacks that prose was a dangerous instrument because too explicit. The government tolerated poetry more readily because it reached a smaller audience. But the poem is also a hiding place, and a marvellous short-cut to saying what is essential with great economy because it expresses the immediacy of emotion in a concentrated form.

Even more than the short story had done previously, poetry was able to reflect the troubled and hectic life of the majority of working blacks, with its constant insecurity and its lack of leisure, and of the students on the volatile university campuses. 'It's becoming a fugitive means of expression,' Mphahlele was to say.[9]

Poetry has the additional advantage that, unlike the short story, it can be shared immediately, either by being recited or by being circulated in cyclostyled form. Mtshali writes: 'Poetry, music and drama can be shared with many other people at the same time'[10] – a real advantage during the period of agitation that was to develop at the beginning of the seventies.

Alongside leading figures such as Mtshali, Matthews and Serote who opened the way for the people of their own and the older generation, there were a number of writers, amateur as well as professional, who expressed, in poetic terms, the ideas and the aspirations that had been suppressed for a decade or more and that were crying out to be put into words. Poetry seemed now to have acquired the double objective of continuing to speak to the whites while addressing a larger black audience.

It was this that led to the publication of the anthology edited by the white poet Robert Royston in 1973, entitled *To Whom It May Concern*,[11] which brings together Mtshali, Serote and other poets of all generations who had not yet established their reputation. They included two members of the older generation, Casey Motsisi and Stanley Motjuwadi, whose work had appeared in *The Classic*, and a few others who had not published in book form but whose talent is obvious from the poems chosen for this anthology, notably Njabulo S. Ndebele, Pascal Mafika Gwala and Sydney Sepamla, author of the poem which gives the collection its title.[12]

The small events of daily life in the townships or 'white' cities project a way of 'being-in-the-world' which is peculiar to the urbanized black during the seventies.

They can be related with a certain detachment and the general approach can be one of acid humour rather than complaint. It is nevertheless a fact that we have here a 'present' which is very different in spirit from that of the sixties. Since the suppression of organized resistance, the black has picked himself up again; there is a new energy in his approach to his situation which augurs well for the future.

During the years that followed, these poets published more and more of their work. In 1973, Nadine Gordimer paid tribute to the new black poets in the last chapter of *The Black Interpreters* (Spro-Cas/Ravan, Johannesburg, 1973), stressing the two striking characteristics of this poetry – its hidden aspect and its eloquence.

However, in the wake of Matthews, who was not included in Royston's anthology, probably because of the banning of *Cry Rage!*, a number of poets were no longer willing to content themselves with alluding to things. With them, poetry became a vehicle for slogans, angry protest and a political message. They were thus able to reach a wider audience more likely to understand them, and their poems sometimes appeared in publications that were less bothered about polished style than the more serious, conventional journals.

For instance, *Blac* (Black Literature and Arts Congress), printed in the Cape Province, varies from four to eight pages and publishes texts directly inspired by the political events of the day. A poem in the second number celebrates the entry of the FRELIMO troops into Lourenço Marques after its evacuation by the Portuguese. The third number appeared just after Soweto and took the form of a 'homage to the martyrs'. Matthews's anthology, *Black Voices Shout* (which was immediately banned), was conceived in the same way.[13] In this case however, it is more a question of Black Power than Black Consciousness.

There is the same preference for direct language in Don Mattera (born 1935), whose life has been a more agitated one than Mphahlele's. This is how he writes in 'No Time, Blackman':

> Stand Blackman
> and put that cap
> back on your beaten head
> Look him in the eye
> cold and blue
> like the devil's fire
> and tell him enough
> three centuries is more than you can take, enough.[14]

This is intended to show the white the reality of the life he has created in every particular for the member of the black community which he *does not know*; above all, it is intended to stir the black from his apathy, to rouse him from the sleepy state of the slave who has got used to his slavery and remind him of the courage of his forefathers. These are all aims which, given the subject matter, could get lost in abstraction or in the prosaic muddle of propaganda. However, nothing of the kind happened. In fact, as we shall see later when we come to study in detail the work of the major poets of this period, Mtshali, Serote, Mattera, Matthews, Sepamla and Gwala, this is a pre-eminently concrete, precise poetry, although often allusive, full of new images and sounds, and with plenty of humour, subtlety and irony, too. But it is also devoid of any desire to form or belong to schools, and it is remarkably free of ties with the 'Great Tradition'. It is as if the void of the preceding years had in the long run been to its advantage, as if it had gained from not having any clumsy models to imitate. Left to themselves and under the pressure of circumstances, these young poets led poetry out of the ghetto in which the purists and the traditionalist anthologies had imprisoned it, and they gave it a new life.[15]

Indeed, the black writer of the seventies was, with very few exceptions, the product of the apartheid period. He had grown up in separate institutions, he had not been able to benefit from the teaching or culture dispensed by the missionaries, he had not had the opportunity to learn to speak an educated English, he had had no contact with the whites except in the context of his oppression and he had had to stand by and watch as the straitjacket of the law had closed in upon him. With a clarity unknown to his elders, he was forced to ask himself the question: what future do I have in this kind of society? He had realized that he was on his own and that his salvation depended entirely on his own initiative.

Although he was older and better-off on the social level, Sepamla expressed a number of the preoccupations and points of view of the majority of the new black poets when he said, during a lecture he gave in 1975, that Shakespeare, Dickens, Lawrence, Keats and many others had given him a great deal, but that he would *also* have liked to nourish his spirit on the banned black writers, those of the United States as well as those of South Africa, for they and he had been born of the same mother.[16]

Sepamla is not ashamed to admit that his education has many gaps in it and that this handicap prevents him from doing as much as he would like, and that in any case the 'situation' effectively determines the choice and variety of the themes he can treat. He stresses, however, that anything is preferable to silence and isolation: the black writer must go on writing and publishing, without deluding himself that he can change his readers, but with the reasonable certainty that he can influence them and give them food for thought. Sepamla believes that he must continue doing this in English, not only in order to reach the white community, which is still so shortsighted, but even so as to be able to talk to other blacks.

Sepamla emphasizes, in fact, the prestige of English, not only among the industrialists and the majority of white employers but also among certain layers of the black population and in the Homelands, where Afrikaans has been rejected as the official language and as the medium of education. Even 'broken, murdered English' is to be preferred to no English at all, argues Sepamla, who adds that the writer who wants to reach the widest possible audience must not be put off by the (white) critics.

It must, however, be pointed out that this tendency is not shared by all the followers of Black Consciousness, which calls for a return to the vernacular languages as an essential feature of the affirmation of black identity. Thus, while Adam Small, who until then had written mainly in Afrikaans, chose English to show his current hostility towards 'Apartaans –Afrikaans' and published a collection with the very explicit title *Black Bronze Beautiful*,[17] a writer like Mtshali said that he had returned to writing in Zulu 'to establish his identity', while continuing to describe in English what the reality – or rather the unreality – of his life was.[18] These two tendencies are not, however, mutually exclusive; they are both very much in evidence in the multiracial review *Staffrider*, launched in 1978. There one finds, side by side, poems in English and in the vernacular languages, as well as the resurgence of the short story with writers like Ahmed Essop, Mtutuzeli Matshoba, Mothobi Mutloatse and Mbulelo Mzamane.[19]

It is easy to understand how poets like Butler could admit to having experienced a sense of shock when they read the work of the new black poets about whom the white critics are divided. Some refuse to consider what they write to be poems, in the name of the 'Great Tradition' and formal considerations and because of the pervasive intrusion of social and political elements. On the other hand there are those who acknowledge the vigour and the vitality of this poetry and who argue that the black South African poet cannot cut himself off from the conditions to which he is subjected and which have inevitably influenced his formation and the way he writes.[20]

The same split is evident in the way white critics respond to the English of the new black poets. While Butler has come to accept that several kinds of English are spoken in South Africa, he nevertheless questions the real motives of the blacks and says they make the language their *servant* rather than *serving* it. There are other less clear-cut positions, but even well-intentioned critics are critical of deviations from standard English, which they often attribute to printing errors!

Taking the opposite view, Christopher Hope speaks for other white poets and critics in accepting that the survival of the English language in South Africa needs this enriching variety of forms.[21] And an eminent linguist at Witwatersrand University, Professor L. W. Lanham, even suggests that this new writing should be included in school and university syllabuses.[22]

It would, however, be to provide an incomplete picture if one were to limit an examination of black writing of the seventies to poetry.

The political importance of the black theatre

Theatre plays a critical role in the work of stimulating a collective awareness through creative writing, statements and speeches – what the partisans of Black Consciousness call 'conscientization': because communication is immediate for what is sometimes a large number of spectators; because the theatrical text does not have to pass through the hands of the printer or the publisher, who is still inevitably white; because it lends itself to the subtle play of allusion, to the wink and the gesture, while the inclusion of vernacular words can be shared by the author, his actors and those who listen.

Moreover, the dividing line between theatre and poetry is rather vague: the theatrical production is often a mixture, a collage of short texts – in prose or verse – of song, dance and slides or extracts from films. The production entitled 'Black Images' was like this – it was put together in 1973 by the Theatre Council of Natal (TECON) and ended, after homage was paid to the distant and more recent 'historical' heroes (Chaka, Dingaan, Mandela and Sobukwe), with an appeal which was eloquent in its very simplicity:

> Everyone says Yes to FREEDOM
> Everyone says Yes to BLACKNESS
> But how many are prepared to die?[23]

Nothing could better stress the functional character of this literature conceived as a psychological, but also a political, weapon of liberation. The impact of Matthews's poems, examined in a later chapter, or of the many theatrical productions, can be gauged in the light of the events of Soweto, Langa and Guguletu: while they both give warning of the revolt to come, the spirit of revolt itself is fortified by these unpretentious songs that show that it is stirring once again.

Many recent plays contain eloquent examples of this subversive writing. For example, in *Sizwe Bansi is Dead*, written by Athol Fugard, John Kani and Winston Ntshona, the hero, Styles, enacts by himself a scene in which the 'boss', *Baas* Bradley, tells the workers of the Ford factory he manages that the 'big boss' is coming on a visit:

'Tell the boys in your language, that this is a very big day in their lives.'
'Gentlemen this old fool says this is a hell of a big day in our lives.'
The men laughed.
'They are happy to hear that, sir.'
'Tell the boys that Mr Henry Ford the Second, the owner of this place, is going to visit us. Tell them Mr Ford is the big Baas. He owns the plant and everything in it.'
'Gentlemen, old Bradley says this Ford is a big bastard. He owns everything in this building, which means you as well.'
A voice came out of the crowd:
'Is he a bigger fool than Bradley?'
'They're asking, sir, is he bigger than you?'
'Certainly . . . [blustering] . . . certainly.'[24]

The whole scene illustrates the same biting humour, and the subversion, similar to that of life itself, lies in part in the white man's ignorance of the language spoken by his workers.

A little further on, a reference to the Homelands makes it possible to improvise and adapt the play to the place where it is being performed. In October 1976, as a result of just such an adaptation of the text, Kani and Ntshona were arrested and detained for a few days in the Transkei because their criticism of 'independence' had displeased Matanzima.

The play *Confused Mhlaba* (1974) by Khayalethu Mqayisa (born in Port Elizabeth in 1952 and educated in fact in the Transkei) was in due course banned as soon as its subversive nature had been deciphered by the censors. Several scenes in the play are intended to make the black spectators reflect on their lot. Through his characters (James Menzi, an ex-teacher who has sought escape in drink, Joyce, a nurse whose religion is her great support, and Hlubi, who has just left prison where he has served a long sentence for his involvement with the ANC), Mqayisa, whose ninth play this is, tries to provide a concrete representation of the different options available to the blacks. In Scene V, James and Joyce are arguing, because Joyce refuses to hide Hlubi – she is afraid of getting into trouble:

'I don't want to be followed, James. I don't want them to search my house, I don't want to be woken up at ungodly hours. I don't want to lose my job, James.'
'There is no need for all this.'
'There is! I want to sleep without disturbance, keep my job. I want to retain my freedom.'
'Freedom! What are you speaking about?'
'I'm not as learned as you are, *boet** James. But you know what I mean. I still want to make up and do all the things I'm allowed to do.'

---

* *boet*: brother.

'Yes Baas, no Baas, I'm sorry Baas and laugh even if you don't want to. That's what you are trying to retain.'[25]

Further on (Scene VII), Hlubi enters, with flowers in his arm, and addresses the audience:

'Brothers and sisters, I've made it. Father Mbopha introduced me to Bishop Russell of St Mary's Cathedral. Bishop Russell was so delighted to see an ex-politician active in church circles. We had tea, together, and discussed petty apartheid. Yes, we agreed that through prayers a change will come in this country.
After this meeting Father Mbopha made me to be a Sunday School teacher. I'm teaching my young brothers and sisters to be faithful to the laws of this country and to their inevitable emancipation. I'm teaching them about the oppression of the Israelites at the cruel hand of Pharaoh. After these lessons, I give them sweets and they sing.'[26]

We have here a good example of antiphrasis and indirect criticism reinforced by the acting and the gestures. As we shall see with Sepamla, some sentences – such as 'we agreed that through prayers a change will come in this country' – produce an immediate reaction of laughter before the deeper, serious, meaning dawns.

The government has, however, found a way to parry this subtle interplay of author, actors and spectators: a recent law requires acting companies to submit a copy of the play they want to put on to the censor and sometimes they are asked to give a sample performance. One can see, therefore, how difficult it can be to reach the public with any theme. The various companies have also been badly hit by arrests, restrictions to residence and other kinds of banning orders. We should not have any illusions about the fact that Breytenbach was *also* in prison; as in the sixties, it is the *black* intellectual, writer and protester who are the favourite targets of the authorities and a new diaspora has taken place in recent years in the direction of several independent African states, as well as the United States and Great Britain. South African literature is therefore a literature of exile and we must end on this theme.

The South African writer and exile

In considering the options open to the South African writer faced with the burning issues of his country, we have seen the relative importance of the retreat into the 'ivory tower', of 'sensual' identification with the land and its people, of literary and armed commitment. There is a further possibility when all the others fail – exile, by choice for some and forced upon others.[27]

In the 1920s, Plomer, Campbell and van der Post sought to get away from the narrowness of the South African scene and the South African mentality which, for a period, they had tried in vain to shake from its self-satisfied lethargy. Several other whites have, since then, followed them: Sydney Clouts, Anthony Delius, Dan Jacobson, Jillian Becker.[28] Among the blacks and the Coloureds, virtually all the writers of the fifties and sixties sought refuge abroad, and a few recent writers, Mtshali, Serote and Langa, later joined them.[29] Here, too, however, there is a distinction to be made, since the white writer can, for the most part, return to

South Africa from time to time to renew his contact with the environment, whereas the black writer, the true exile, must wait and live on hope.

And yet, whichever group they belong to, they all continue to speak about their country, to write about it, if not for it: the black writer knows that without subterfuge that is difficult to put into practice on a large scale his books cannot be read by his contemporaries,[30] except for a tiny minority able to buy them while travelling abroad.

The black writer finds himself, therefore, in the same position as the Soviet writer who has been expelled from his country but whose works are banned there and can only be circulated, often with difficulty, by the *samizdat*. How does the writer react to this situation? How does exile change the themes he decides to write about, the tone he adopts?

The reply, as one might expect, varies according to his temperament but also according to circumstances and the place where the writer has taken refuge and tried to start his life again. A writer like Plomer, born in 1903 – the same year as Paton, but famous earlier than he for his novel *Turbott Wolfe* (1924) – eventually settled in England where, from 1950, he became Benjamin Britten's collaborator in all his major operas. From time to time Plomer has continued to write, if not about South Africa – *The Taste of Fruit* is an exception – at least with and for South Africans: in 1949 he wrote a preface for a collection of short stories written by Pauline Smith, another exile, about the Afrikaner peasant community (*The Little Karoo*).[31] In 1966, he contributed a short introduction to Guy Butler's *South of Zambesi*, and, with Jack Cope, published a translation of Ingrid Jonker's poems. But Plomer has written a number of other books which have no connection with South Africa:[32] so, is he an English or a South African writer?

On the other hand, Dan Jacobson, Clouts and Delius, although they live in England, only ever speak or write about their country of origin; they are not banned from living there and can, like Plomer before them, return for brief visits. They do not speak about exile, and even though Jacobson sees himself an outsider wherever he goes, this is not necessarily because he is a Jew – so, too, is Sydney Clouts.

It is a totally different story for Breytenbach who, although he is white, is a political exile. His success as an artist and a writer is of little consolation to him away from his roots. Hence his poems express a very deeply, intimately felt sense of exile:

> you ask me how it is living in exile, friend –
> what can I say?
> that I'm too young for bitter protest
> and too old for wisdom or acceptance
> of my Destiny?
> that I'm only one of many,
> the maladjusted,
> the hosts of expatriates, deserters,
> citizens of the guts of darkness
> one of the 'Frenchmen with a speech defect'
> or even that here I feel at home?
>
> yes, but that I now also know the rooms of loneliness,
> the desecration of dreams, the remains of memories,
> a violin's thin wailing

> where eyes look far and always further,
> ears listen quietly inward
> – that I too like a beggar
> pray for the alms of 'news from home',
> for the mercy of 'do you remember',
> for the compassion of 'one of these days'.[33]

We have seen what his resentment at having to live away from home has done to him – his frustration at living so far away and being so useless, at not being able to live in his own country *at peace with his conscience*. There only remains then the enduring agony that precedes the suicidal gesture that contradicts these lines written ten years previously:

> I've been thinking
> if I ever come home
> it will be without warning towards daybreak
> with years of hoarded treasure
> on the backs of iron cows.[34]

However, exile broadened his outlook: from the late sixties onward, the exile preoccupied with his own suffering, the lyric poet singing his love of his wife, the elegiac poet singing of exile, speaks in a way that shows his deep concern for all the oppressed people of his country. In his collection *Skryt*[35] he identifies with the resisters who plan their return to the 'promised land' from their exile, evokes the black children dying of malnutrition in the resettlement camps, attacks the 'butcher' Vorster, whom he also calls the 'rotten tail' (from a play on words on the Afrikaans *vrotstert*). Lyricism has become a weapon of war:

> *and you, butcher*
> you burdened with the security of the state
> what are your thoughts when night begins to bare her bones
> when the first babbling scream is forced
> from the prisoner
> like the sound of birth
> and the fluids of parturition? . . .
> *tell me, butcher*
> so that the obstetrics you're forced to perform
> in the name of my survival
> may be revealed to me
> *in my own tongue*[36]

Another case of exile: that of Mphahlele; in him, too, we find the same acute awareness of exile, with the ability to express it in verse and in an eminently poetic prose.

Having barely arrived in Nigeria, his thoughts turned back to the country he had just left and he wrote his autobiography, *Down Second Avenue*,[37] the shanty-town street where he had lived for several years. The last lines of the book foreshadow the poem he was to write in Nigeria, 'Exile in Nigeria'; it is a long poem dedicated to the north wind just as Shelley had dedicated his to the west wind. In it, Mphahlele describes his feeling of emptiness: accustomed to violence and to reactions of defence or counter-attack, he found it difficult to get used to the peace of Nigeria which had yet to experience its own fratricidal struggle. Accustomed to being always on the go, he could not understand the meaning of this cessation of movement and whether it was a sign of resignation or numbness. But he was determined to avoid these and to continue the struggle – it was out of the question to give up now:

> My claws have poison:
> only let me lie down a while,
> bide my time,
> rub my neck and whiskers,
> file my claws and remember.
> Then my mind can draw the line between
> the hounds and hunted of the lot
> in the blazing painful south of the south,
> use their tools and brains –
> thanks for once to ways of white folk.
> And in yonder land of peace and calm,
> you think I'll change my spots?
> No matter,
> no regrets:
> the God of Africa
> my Mother
> will know her friends and persecutors, civilize the world
> and teach them the riddle of living and dying.
> Meantime,
> let them leave my heart alone![38]

He had to do more than just live; he had to create, a task made all the easier by his choosing to conduct his fight in the cultural arena. In the years that followed, Mphahlele continued teaching and writing: a collection of essays, *Voices in the Whirlwind*, the updating of *The African Image*, a novel with the significant title *The Wanderers*,[39] and a long prose poem which, coming more than ten years after 'Exile in Nigeria', showed very clearly that he had not lost sight of his native country. On the contrary,

> I live in a glasshouse, the one I ran into 17 years ago. It's roomy but borrowed ...
> I could if I choose renew my lease indefinitely in this glasshouse, quite forget write off my past take my chances on new territory. I shall not. Because I'm a helpless captive of place and to come to terms with the tyranny of place is to have something to live for to save me from stagnation, anonymity. It's not fame you want it's having your shadow noticed it's the comfort that you can show control over your life that you can function.[40]

For Kgositsile, exile is a luxury one can only afford to toy with because there are other, more important things on his mind:

> Against these two
> pillars and the evening
> sun stands the baobab

> as I stand
> between memory and desire.
> Afrika! the memory
> that lingers across the hovering
> womb of my desire at dawn.
> Afrika, the stench of absence
> Afrika, the fragrance of rebirth.[41]

Not that he did not undergo periods of intense self-interrogation, looking in on himself, during pauses in his activities. Then he asked himself:

> Who are we? Who
> were we? Things cannot go on much as
> before. All night long we shall laugh
> behind Time's new masks. When the moment
> hatches in Time's womb we shall not complain.[42]

But this man who was born in Johannesburg in 1938 and who arrived in New York in 1961 knew very well where he was going. He was a true revolutionary who identified with the struggle of the Afro-Americans because he found himself in America when it occurred. What interests him is the lot of the black man, whether he be African, South African or Afro-American, and for him, wherever it occurs, the struggle has the same appearance, the same enemies: capitalism and the false values of the white man by which the black has all too often allowed himself to be deceived:

> You who swallowed your balls for a piece
> Of gold beautiful from afar but far from
> Beautiful because it is coloured with
> The pus from your brother's callouses
> You who creep lower than a snake's belly
> Because you swallowed your conscience
> And sold your sister to soulless vipers.[43]

Kgositsile sided with Black Power without needing the experience of Black Consciousness. This is why he was from the outset more radical than they were, more violent, having had less difficulty exorcizing the demons of submission, resignation and broken promises:

> This wind you hear is the birth of memory,
> When the moment hatches in time's womb
> There will be no art talk. The only poem
> You will hear will be the spearpoint pivoted
> In the punctured marrow of the villain; the
> Timeless native son dancing like crazy to
> The retrieved rhythms of desire fading in –
> To memory.[44]

Kgositsile who, for Mphahlele, stands astride two continents, is a true citizen of the Black World, more American than South African in his style and his themes.

But his second book invokes H. L. Dhlomo; it links Sharpeville and Watts in its symbolism and celebrates at random—because they belong to the same fight – David Diop from Senegal, Rap Brown and Malcolm X the Americans, Lumumba from the Congo, Mandela the South African, and Césaire the West Indian. In this way he is able to call his second collection *My name Is Afrika* – exile has given it its true dimension:

> But the day is not here yet to sing:
> No more blues. No more stale tears
> To claw some nigger's way to crumbs,
> Slime dripping down the long-broken spine.
>
> The day is not yet here to sing:
> No more snow-crust blues when
> The warrior leaps to act, eyes
> Spitting fact of this moment
> When our children and us turn
> Adult, knowing,
> The roots of the uprooted knowing
> No more hesitation.[45]

Notes

1. On this point, see especially John Kane-Berman, *Soweto – Black Revolt, White Reaction* (Ravan Press, Johannesburg, 1978); Gail M. Gerhart, *Black Power in South Africa: The Evolution of an Ideology* (University of California Press, Berkeley, 1978); J. Alvarez-Péreyre, *Les Guetteurs de l'aube: poésie et Áparthéid* (Grenoble University Press, Grenoble, 1979); Baruch Hirson, *Year of Fire, Year of Ash – The Soweto Revolt: Roots of a Revolution* (Zed Press, London, 1979).
2. See the definition of Black Consciousness in *SASO Newsletter*, vol. 5, no. 3, November–December 1975:

   BLACK CONSCIOUSNESS IS:

   1. an attitude of mind, a way of life:
   2. its basic tenet is that the Black man must reject all value systems that seek to make him a foreigner in the country of his birth and reduce his basic human dignity:
   3. it implies awareness by the Black people of the power they wield as a group, both economically and politically and hence group cohesion and solidarity are important facets of Black Consciousness:
   4. The Black man must build up his own value systems, see himself as self-defined and not defined by others:
   5. Black Consciousness will always be enhanced by the totality of involvement of the oppressed people, hence the message of Black Consciousness ˙.as to spread to reach all sections of the Black Community:
   6. Liberation of the Blackman begins first with liberation from psychological oppression of himself through an inferiority complex and secondly from the physical one accruing out of living in a white racist society:
   7. Black people are those who are by law or tradition, politically, socially and economically discriminated against as a group in the South African society of their aspirations.

3. On these questions, see Peter Walshe, *Church versus State in South Africa* (C. Hurst & Company, London, 1983). Dr Naudé was tried in 1973 for refusing to give certain evidence regarding the Christian Institute, and banned, together with several other people, in October 1977.
4. 'The English-speaking Whites', in *South Africa's Minorities* (Spro-Cas, Johannesburg, 1971), p. 45.

South African Writing since 1968

5. A new Constitution was eventually voted in (November 1983) after a referendum concerning white voters only. By then, P. W. Botha, Vorster's former Defence Minister, had become Prime Minister.
6. *Looking on Darkness* (W. H. Allen & Co., London, 1974).
7. 'The Breytenbach File', by André Brink, *The New Review*, vol. 3, no. 25, p. 7. Breytenbach was freed in December 1982. For a recent interview of Breytenbach see *Index on Censorship*, London, vol. 12, no. 3, June 1983.
8. In *South African Outlook*, vol. 105, no. 1248, p. 68.
9. *Issue*, vol. VI, no. 1, Spring 1976, ed. B. Lindfors, p. 21.
10. ibid., p. 28.
11. *To Whom It May Concern* (Ad. Donker, Johannesburg, 1973). *Black Poets in South Africa* (Heinemann, London 1974).
12. See below, section on Sepamla.
13. *Black Voices Shout* was first published in 1974 (BLAC Publishing House, Athlone, Cape). It was subsequently reprinted by Troubadour Press, Austin. The collection contains poems by Austin Cloete, Christine Douts, Mike Dues, Pascal Gwala, Ilva Mackay, James Matthews, Wally Serote, Steven Smith and Benjamin Takavarasha.
14. *Azanian Love Song* (Skotaville Pub., Johannesburg, 1983), p. 46.
15. See 'Conclusion and Evaluation' in the present work.
16. 'The Black Writer in South Africa Today: Problems and Dilemmas', in *The New Classic*, no. 3, 1976, p. 19. 'I was brought up on Shakespeare, Dickens, Lawrence, Keats and other English greats. True enough they opened my eyes, they gave me inspiration. In short I received a rich sustenance from these men. But for my body to have remained healthy, for my eyes to have kept me on the right course I would have liked to have been fed on Mphahlele, La Guma, Themba, Nkosi. I would have liked to have laid my hands on the "unrewarding rage" of Richard Wright, James Baldwin, Le Roi Jones (Iman Baraka) and other Afro-American writers. These men I would have liked tenfold because they have all sucked from the tits of my mother. But alas! For me this has been denied.'
17. *Black Bronze Beautiful, Quatrains*, by Adam Small (Ad. Donker, Johannesburg, 1975). Here are quatrains 11 and 34:

    > I am warm: gather my myrrh with my spice
    > and earthy: eat my honeycomb with my honey
    > I wasn't born from that White Womb, so cold
    > of glaciers and eons of chill ice.

    > Their vineyard's keeper thought they I would be,
    > harvesting their grapes: their wood to hew
    > But the Sun, intoxicating, would not let me be
    > Would not let me break my dark beauty.

18. *Issue*, op. cit., p. 27. 'I write English for my present state of reality or unreality, and I write in Zulu to establish my identity which will be translated by posterity. Only then will my past heritage be accorded its right and respectful position.'
19. See Ahmed Essop's *The Hajji and Other Stories* (Ravan Press, Johannesburg, 1978), Matshoba's *Call Me Not A Man* (Ravan Press, Johannesburg, 1979), Mutloatse's *Mama Ndiyalila* (Ravan Press, Johannesburg, 1982), Mzamane's *Mzala* (Raven Press, Johannesburg, 1980). Essop and Mzamane have each also written a novel, *The Visitation* (Ravan Press, Johannesburg, 1980) and *The Children of Soweto*, (Longman, London, 1982), Matshoba, a play, *Seeds of War* (Ravan Press, Johannesburg, 1981), while Mutloatse has edited *Forced Landing* (Ravan Press, Johannesburg, 1980), and *Reconstruction* (Ravan Press, Johannesburg, 1981).
20. Generally speaking, the first tendency would be represented by Guy Butler, Jack Cope and Douglas Livingstone, the second by Nadine Gordimer, Sheila Roberts, Christopher Hope, Walter Saunders and Mike Kirkwood. For echoes of the controversy which opposed some of the above-mentioned critics at the Poetry Conference held in Cape

Town in 1974, see *Poetry South Africa*, eds., Wilhelm and Polley (Ad. Donker, Johannesburg, 1976).
21. Cf. Christopher Hope, 'The Elephants are Taking Driving Lessons', in *Bolt*, no. 10, May 1974. See below, p. 264.
22. Professor L. W. Lanham, 'English as a Second Language in Southern Africa since 1820', in *English-speaking South Africa Today*, ed. A. de Villiers (Oxford University Press, Cape Town, 1976).
23. Quoted in 'Black Theatre in South Africa', *Fact Paper no. 2*, June 1976, International Defence and Aid Fund, London. This is, in fact, one of the poems produced by the prosecution during the trial of the leaders of SASO and the BPC in 1975. For an excellent introduction to black South African theatre, see Robert Mshengu Kavanagh's essay in Kente et al, *South African People's Plays* (Heinemann, London, 1981).
24. *Statements* (Three Plays) (Oxford University Press, London, 1974), p. 7.
25. *Confused Mhlaba* (Ravan Press, Johannesburg, 1974), p. 22. Ravan have published a number of plays in their Ravan Playscript series.
26. ibid., p. 32.
27. There is no intention of dealing fully here with an extremely important theme which recurs in nearly all South African writing.
28. Dan Jacobson (*The Evidence of Love*, 1959; *The Trap* and *A Dance in the Sun*, 1955; *The Price of Diamonds*, 1957; *The Beginners*, 1966) and Jillian Becker (*The Keep*, 1967) are, with Nadine Gordimer, the best known. The works cited are all published by Penguin, London.
29. Mtshali has since returned to South Africa.
30. Dennis Brutus managed to get himself read in South Africa in the seventies under the pseudonym of John Bruin (John Brown, the Coloured). See *Thoughts Abroad* (Troubadour Press, Austin, Texas, 1970).
31. A book originally published in 1925 with a preface by Arnold Bennett. In 1950 Plomer wrote a preface for a new edition published by Jonathan Cape, London.
32. For a full biography of Plomer, see John Robert Doyle Jr, *William Plomer* (Twayne Publishers, New York, 1969).
33. Breytenbach, *And Death White as Words*, a bilingual text with English translations, selected, edited and introduced by A. J. Coetzee (Rex Collings, London, in association with David Philip, Cape Town, 1978), p. 51.
34. Breytenbach, *In Africa Even the Flies Are Happy, Selected Poems 1964–1977*, trans. Denis Hirson (John Calder, London, 1978), p. 30.
35. Published in Holland in 1972 with drawings by Breytenbach himself.
36. *And Death White as Words*, op. cit., p. 87.
37. Seven Seas Books, Berlin, 1962.
38. 'Exile in Nigeria' in *Poems from Africa*, ed. Langston Hughes (Indiana University Press), p. 122.
39. *Voices in the Whirlwind: Poetry and Conflict in the Black World* (Hill & Wang, New York, 1967). *The Wanderers* (Macmillan, London, 1972; Fontana, London, 1973).
40. *Issue*, op. cit., p. 16. It is as a result of this anxiety, but also because of the fear that there would develop in exile a literature cut off from its natural environment, in which the artist might be tempted to 'act out' his role as an exile without being able to share in the life of his country, and in spite of the risks involved in doing so, that we must see the reason for Mphahlele's decision finally to return to South Africa, as Oswald Mtshali had done.
41. 'Flirtation', in *My Name is Afrika* (Doubleday & Co., New York, 1971), p. 50.
42. ibid., p. 64.
43. ibid., p. 64.
44. ibid., pp. 65–6.
45. 'No Celebration', ibid., p. 57.

PART II
The Liberal Conscience and White Power

The committed poets dealt with in the following chapters belong to a minority of the white population who have opened their eyes to the position of the colonized people of South Africa and who have continued working to bring injustice to an end and to achieve the conversion of the whites.

A whole range of attitudes will be found here, as a result of the worsening of the political situation, but also because of the individual temperament of each of the writers. It goes from verbal protest (Paton) to total commitment (Lewin and Evans), via other forms of attack: satire (Delius), and philippic and prophecy (Horn and Jensma). The work of these white committed writers represents well, therefore, the different viewpoints dictated by the liberal conscience. But it is also a seismograph constantly measuring the shifts of the South African state of mind and the upheavals that shake the country, often deeply.

While the commitment of the white poet is, above all, the product of a personal choice which allows him to reconcile moral or political principles with the way he conducts his life, it is also evidence of the white poet's desire to influence men and events. We shall therefore see in the following pages that the question of the role they wish to play vis-à-vis the authority of the State and vis-à-vis their contemporaries is posed more or less explicitly by each of them. It is this spectrum of attitudes and their motivation, in so far as they can all be seen in the life and work of these writers, that will be dealt with in the chapters of this section. It makes sense, however, to begin with the forerunner of white committed poetry, Thomas Pringle, the Scottish poet who settled in southern Africa at the beginning of the nineteenth century.

Chapter 4
A Forerunner: Thomas Pringle

▼▼▼▼▼▼▼▼▼▼▼▼▼▼▼▼▼▼▼▼▼▼▼▼▼▼▼▼▼▼▼

The white poets who are preoccupied with the racial problem to the extent of making it the most important, if not the sole, subject of their work have a forerunner in Thomas Pringle.

Pringle, who was born in Scotland in the year of the outbreak of the French Revolution and died in London in 1834 immediately after the abolition of slavery in the British colonies, lived in South Africa for only six years (1820–6). He is nevertheless regarded not only as a South African but also as the father of South African poetry in English.

Pringle was very attached to his native Scotland, and remained so all his life, but the situation of his family, like that of many of the less well-off in the wake of the Napoleonic wars, was so bad that they decided to exile themselves to South Africa, with the intention of settling there permanently. Pringle belonged therefore to the first wave of British settlers who were sent out to the eastern 'frontier' of the Cape Colony in 1820. He took very seriously his responsibilities as leader of the little expedition that was gathered under his wing: the emigrants were expected to set out in small groups, and it was practically the entire Pringle family, along with a few friends and their servants, who emigrated.[1]

Pringle was 30 at the time; in Scotland he had been employed as a clerk, a not very onerous job which had given him the leisure to write. In addition to the publication of a small volume of poems in 1819,[2] his activities had included the editorship of two literary reviews, *Blackwood's Magazine* and *Edinburgh Magazine*. His natural inclination to daydream had undoubtedly been reinforced by a physical infirmity which left him with a lifelong limp and even obliged him to use crutches; this handicap did not, however, prevent him from undertaking long excursions on foot or on horseback into the Scottish highlands, and later into the region granted to the colonists in South Africa, for the contemplation of nature always gave him considerable pleasure.

The young poet enjoyed the protection of Sir Walter Scott[3] and hoped this would eventually help him to obtain employment in Cape Town more in keeping with his literary tastes and his physical abilities. In the meantime, he took his full share of the work during the first two years he lived on the frontier. For there was everything to be done at Glen Lynden; to start with, a road had to be made for the horses and the heavy ox-wagons. Pringle and his party cleared the land and the forest and laid out the first roads; and, adopting methods borrowed from the Africans, Pringle built himself a thatched house and one for his brother, whose arrival had been delayed. He also made rudimentary furniture, constructed the tiny colony's bread oven, planted and sowed . . . Finally, he took on the role of doctor in order to treat simple illnesses and acted as preacher for his companions and their servants. There is frequent reference in his writings to Robinson Crusoe, with whom he often compared himself – except that he was not alone, since he had married before leaving Scotland and his wife's sister still lived with them.

This highly intelligent and insatiably curious man literally immersed himself in the distant and recent past of the country he was making his own, studying its inhabitants, both white and black, and their languages. He consulted the accounts those who had preceded him had left of their travels, but he also made a point of getting to know the officers, ministers, missionaries and older settlers who lived in the same region as he did, and was always ready to travel several hours, sometimes even days, on horseback in order to meet them.

He was interested in the Boers, whose land the new immigrants had inherited after its confiscation by the English government following the events of Slagter's Nek;[4] but he was even more interested in their slaves and black servants. Their lot, at a time when the new laws aimed at undoing some of the injustices under which they had suffered in the past had as yet had little effect, could not fail to shock and upset him: shock him as a Christian and upset him as a man. But Pringle was not merely an admirer of the 'noble savage', in common with many of his European contemporaries, he was truly and genuinely opposed to tyranny and oppression in any form.

The journal which he kept fairly regularly, and which he used to write the first classic of South African colonial literature, *Narrative of a Residence in South Africa*,[5] shows that he also took a close interest in the flora and fauna of his new country. Some pages of his journal are as interesting as those written not many years later at Concord in the United States by another pioneer and committed writer of his day, Henry Thoreau.

The Cape was governed in the 1820s by a man whom some have portrayed as a petty tyrant and despot, others as a benefactor. While Sir Charles Somerset deserved the gratitude of his fellow citizens for a number of useful innovations, he is chiefly remembered by posterity for the dislike he showed the new arrivals, and especially for his opposition to the establishment of a free press in Cape Town.[6] It was particularly in this last connection that Pringle came into conflict with him and earned his enmity.

Having established the tiny family settlement to everyone's satisfaction, after two years on the 'frontier' Pringle set off for Cape Town, where the patronage of Sir Walter Scott had secured him a position in the government library. Since his salary was very small, Pringle started a private school under the direction of his friend Fairbairn, whom he had persuaded to join him in South Africa. The launching and publication of the first numbers of a journal edited by the two friends attracted the suspicion and then the open hostility of Sir Charles Somerset. If Pringle was generous by nature, he was also a poor diplomat and an obstinate man. He met Somerset head-on and lost his post in the library. The parents of the pupils attending his private school withdrew their children one by one from the establishment of the man who now passed as a 'radical'. Deprived of his income, Pringle first went back to Glen Lynden. He stayed there for a further two years or so, devoting most of his time to studying the condition of the slaves and the Hottentots; the result was the publication in 1827 of an article on slavery[7] which was to change the course of his life. Feeling himself to be the butt of Somerset's persistent animosity and anxious to obtain redress, Pringle decided to return to

England to put his case. Soon after his arrival there, he was appointed secretary of the Anti-Slavery Society, founded in 1823 by Wilberforce, whose attention he had attracted by the publication of his article. Pringle had the satisfaction of witnessing the abolition of slavery, brought about largely by the combined efforts of Wilberforce, Zachary Macauley and other active members of the Anti-Slavery Society. He died shortly after, in 1834, from a lung infection, just as he was planning to return to South Africa.

Busy as he was, first at Glen Lynden then in Cape Town, Pringle had continued to write. Judging by a letter to Fairbairn, his literary activities to an extent troubled his conscience.[8] Yet an examination of his poetry shows that it was profoundly marked by the situation he found around him: more than half the poems he wrote deal with the plight of the black people, and only rarely do they come from the pen of a traveller stirred by the exotic.

In fact, Pringle's avowed intention was to reorientate his Muse, already active in Scotland, so as to record his response to the reality that confronted him now:

> I tune no more the string for Scottish tale;
> For to my aching heart, in accents wild,
> Appeals the bitter cry of Afric's race reviled.[9]

With this aim in mind, Pringle proceeds in various ways: he attacks oppression, tyranny and slavery generally, but in a number of poems of varying lengths he also concentrates on precise issues and evokes the human tragedies that result from the scourges he denounces.

The poems that illustrate the first kind of approach might sound, not surprisingly, pompous to the modern ear; their rhetoric is a little cold and their imagery is closer to that of the eighteenth than to the nineteenth century. For all that, Pringle has a very clear perception of the evils of slavery as an institution, and he is the first to point out that the oppressor is inseparably bound to his victim:

> Oh, Slavery! thou art a bitter draught!
> And twice accursed is thy poisoned bowl,
> Which taints with leprosy the White Man's soul,
> No less than his by whom its dregs are quaffed.
> The slave sinks down, o'ercome by cruel craft,
> Like beast of burthen on the earth to roll.
> The Master, though in luxury's lap he loll,
> Feels the foul venom, like a rankling shaft,
> Strike through his veins. As if a demon laughed,
> He, laughing, treads his victim in the dust –
> The victim of avarice, rage, or lust.
> But the poor Captive's moan the whirlwinds waft
> To Heaven – not unavenged: the Oppressor quakes
> With secret dread, and shares the hell he makes.[10]

Much simpler and more concrete in their conception are the poems in which Pringle portrays people whose lot has moved him. Thus, in 'The Forester of the Neutral Ground',[11] subtitled, in a very Scottish way, 'A South African Border Ballad', he tells the story of a young Boer who wants to marry a young Coloured woman employed as a servant on his father's farm and who, faced with the open hostility of his family, ends up by taking refuge with his companion – sold by his family and repurchased by himself – in another part of the Colony, where they intend to wait for better days:

> Then tell me, dear Stranger, from England the free,
> What good tidings bring'st thou for Arend Plessie?
> Shall the Edict of Mercy be sent forth at last,
> To break the harsh fetters of Colour and Caste?[12]

Elsewhere, in 'The Bechuana Boy', Pringle starts from an actual event, his meeting with a young Bechuana who had sought his protection and whom he was later to take to England with him, to show the absolute power over the slave that slavery gives to the master. The poem, which is rather long, contains scenes of the kind Harriet Beecher-Stowe's book was to popularize some forty years later – for example, the slave auctions and the enforced breaking-up of African families.

In what amounts to a veritable portrait gallery, Pringle presents some of the people who were linked with the history of the Colony in its early days – the missionary, Dr Philip, and the French Huguenots – as well as the indigenous inhabitants of southern Africa at the time. These sketches are rather reminiscent of those eighteenth-century full-length portraits in which the subject is painted in his most characteristic clothes and stance, while in the background, standing out against the countryside or against the sky, appears the incident to which they owe their fame or their disgrace: 'The Hottentot' and 'The Caffer' are treated in this way.

Not infrequently in his poems, Pringle allows the oppressed to speak for themselves, giving himself the opportunity in this way to relate the main events in the history of black South Africa. In each case, a large body of notes provides additional historical, religious and anthropological information. Thus Pringle is the first to write about, and portray in a favourable light, the black hero Makana.

In all these very varied poems,[13] either directly or through the characters he evokes, Pringle constantly emphasizes the responsibility of Europe and Christianity towards Africa; for he took very seriously the influence he could exert in revealing to the English in England, who at the time held the reins of power, what was being done in their name in the southern hemisphere. Thus, in 'The Emigrant's Cabin', a long poem which is in effect a one-act play, Pringle uses his own family and his friend Fairbairn, supposedly visiting them at Glen Lynden, as a pretext for describing not only their daily life but also their objectives:

> And thus, you see, even in my desert-den,
> I still hold intercourse with thinking men;
> And find fit subjects to engage me too –
> For in this wilderness there's work to do;
> Some purpose to accomplish for the band
> Who left with me their much-loved Father-Land;
> Something for the sad Natives of the soil,
> By stern oppression doomed to scorn and toil:
> Something for Africa to do or say –
> If but one mite of Europe's debt to pay –
> If but one bitter tear to wipe away.[14]

A Forerunner: Thomas Pringle

Pringle is often much more violent in his criticism than this, and there can be no doubting his calling into question of the so-called civilizing mission of the Europeans who preached principles they rarely practised when they could be to their own disadvantage. In this, as in all his efforts to show the true facts, Pringle is a worthy forerunner of Paton and the 'new prophets'. Their tone is different from his; yet one finds in both cases the same criticism of their contemporaries. And we also find in his work an expression of the firm conviction that it is the writer's duty to denounce injustice at all times. These themes recur constantly in his work, for the poet has an obligation to relate

> A tale of foul oppression, fraud and wrong,
> By Afric's sons endured from Christian Europe long,

and to accomplish this great task

> By flashing Truth's full blaze on deeds long hid in night.[15]

It seems then that Pringle should be linked with a tradition which existed already in Europe and which was on the verge of spreading to the United States – the tradition of the militant missionaries, philanthropists and writers who were determined to combat tyranny, even if it meant the sacrifice of their own lives in the process.

But Pringle inaugurates, for southern Africa at least, yet another tradition: that of the white liberal who is unable to resolve the contradiction between his role as the denouncer of tyranny on the one hand and the accomplice of colonization on the other.

Pringle's 'relationship' with the Bushmen illustrates this phenomenon: the poet spoke often and at length of the earliest inhabitant of southern Africa, both to sympathize with him and to defend him, and there can be no doubt that it is with the greatest sincerity that he makes him say:

> Thus I am Lord of the Desert Land,
> And I will not leave my bounds,
> To crouch beneath the Christian's hand,
> And kennel with his hounds.[16]

This does not prevent Pringle the colonist, as distinct from Pringle the poet, when he is victim of the attacks of marauding Bushmen trying to survive after the destruction of their hunting grounds, from requesting the intervention of those very commandos whose appalling excesses he has previously denounced.[17] Replying to his friend Fairbairn, who pointed this out to him, Pringle wrote: 'You see, we back-settlers grow all savage and bloody by coming into continual collision with savages.'[18] Two months later, Pringle returned to this subject, disclaiming any wish *on his part*, to take up arms against the Bushmen.[19]

On a par with this kind of embarrassing contradiction, one encounters in Pringle an attitude which seems, if not to run exactly counter to his liberalism, at least to suggest its limitations: 'Afar in the Desert' provides proof of this. This is a poem which, in the setting of the South African Karoo, expresses the Romantic idea that civilization is bad and that Nature provides the man who flees it with a refuge. This poem, which Coleridge praised to the skies when he read it,[20] and which is certainly not without poetic quality, consists of six stanzas of unequal length incorporating the refrain which gives it its title:

> Afar in the desert I love to ride
> With the silent Bush-boy alone by my side.

An odd stress on company – albeit silent – which is contradicted in other parts of the poem:

> I fly to the Desert afar from Man . . .

and

> Oh! then there is freedom, and joy, and pride,
> Afar in the desert alone to ride . . .

up to and including the last stanza, which is nevertheless not lacking a certain grandeur:

> And here, while the night-winds round me sigh,
> And the stars burn bright in the midnight sky,
> As I sit apart by the desert stone,
> Like Elijah at Horeb's cave alone,
> 'A still small voice' comes through the wild
> (Like a Father consoling his fretful Child),
> Which banishes bitterness, wrath, and fear –
> Saying – *Man is distant, but God is near!*[21]

The reader may well wonder how much humanity is in fact accorded this 'present–absent' Bush-boy who, by his presence, could only have facilitated communication between the white man and the tribes they encountered. It is true, of course, that he is in a Desert! This is clearly a poem in the extreme Romantic manner which is only partially autobiographical,[22] but this does not alter the fact that there is a contradiction in its very terms, and that the black man is here invisible, or only partially visible – and this will continue to be the case until decolonization is properly achieved.[23] This lapse is all the more surprising in the light of Pringle's life and of the assertion contained in the same poem that 'My soul is sick with the bondman's sigh'. Pringle's writing seems, therefore, to show that, even in the case of a liberal like himself, it is difficult to reconcile one's principles with everyday practice and that the white man still has a long way to go before he will be able to identify with others so different from himself.

Was Pringle himself conscious of these contradictions and of his own limits? He may have seen in his enforced return to England a way to dispel these ambiguities. No longer a colonist, that is to say, no longer directly tied to the exploitation of the country and its black inhabitants, but associated instead with the exalting task of the Anti-Slavery Society, of which he had high hopes, Pringle must have felt at peace with his conscience. Unintentionally, his quarrel with Sir Charles Somerset had provided him with a perfectly honourable escape from his dilemma: he was leading the way for other liberals to choose exile rather than condone colonization by their presence. It was also possible, at the time Pringle was writing, to believe that the abolition of slavery would fundamentally alter the lot of the blacks and the Hottentots in southern Africa. It was, however, to be another hundred years or more before other English-speaking white poets were to return to the problem of racial oppression in South Africa.

In 1883, on the other hand, Olive Schreiner, South Africa's first woman novelist, set her *Story of an African Farm* against this tormented background. And in 1908, in an essay which is too long to quote here in full, she was to write these words, which showed the feminist she was to be concerned in a wider sense with the plight of people dominated by others:

> If blinded by the gain of the moment, we see nothing in the dark man but a vast engine of labour, if he is to us not a man but a tool, if we force him permanently, in his millions, into the locations and compounds and slums of our cities . . . If, unbound to us in gratitude and sympathy, and alien to us in blood and colour, we reduce this vast mass to the condition of a great, seething, ignorant proletariat – then I would rather draw a veil over the future of this land.
>
> As long as nine-tenths of our community have no permanent stake in our land, and no right and share in our government, can we ever feel safe? Can we ever know peace?[24]

With William Plomer, fifteen years later, the racial question came to the fore as a theme in the plot of *Turbott Wolfe* (1923).

It was, however, with Paton that it was to appear again and to constitute the core of the work of an English-speaking South African writer.

Notes

1. Pringle was the best educated in the group and it was he who took charge of all the formalities in Scotland and the negotiations concerning the small settlement in South Africa.
2. *The Autumnal Excursion*, or *Sketches in Teviotdale: with Other Poems* (Edinburgh, Constable, 1819).
3. Sir Walter Scott had read and liked Pringle's first poem, 'The Autumnal Excursion', which Pringle had sent him in 1816, when it appeared in *Poetic Mirror* (edited by James Hogg).
4. Place of the rebellion by the Boer farmer Bezuidenhout, in the very region that was to be allocated to Pringle and his family (Baviaan's River).
5. First published as the second part of *African Sketches* (London, Moxon, 1834). The notes refer to this edition.
6. Cf. Jane Meiring, *Thomas Pringle: His Life and Times* (Balkema, Cape Town and Amsterdam, 1968), p. 112.
   Somerset was recalled to England, where his conduct had often been debated in Parliament. He resigned in 1827.
7. 'Slavery or "The State of Slavery at the Cape"', in *New Monthly Magazine*, XVII (1826).
8. Meiring, op. cit., p. 123.
9. In 'The Emigrants', *African Sketches*, op. cit., p. 99.
10. ibid., p. 66 (the poem dates from 1823).
11. 'Neutral Ground' here refers to the no-man's-land which the government was hoping to establish between the advance guard of European colonization and the first Xhosa villages.

12. *African Sketches*, op. cit., p. 57.
13. This variety is to be found not only in the forms used but also in the tone; 'The Emigrant's Cabin' and especially 'The Lion Hunt' are narratives full of humour.
14. *African Sketches*, op. cit., p. 30.
15. 'The Emigrants', op. cit., p. 99.
16. 'Song of the Wild Bushman', *African Sketches* op. cit., p. 12.
17. In several places in this *Narrative* and in 'The Caffer Commando', *African Sketches*, op. cit., p. 38.
18. Meiring, op. cit., p. 115.
19. ibid., p. 115.
20. Quoted in *Thomas Pringle*, by John Robert Doyle, Jr (Twayne Publishers, New York, 1972), p. 161.
    'Afar in the Desert' is Pringle's most frequently anthologized poem.
21. *African Sketches*, op. cit., pp. 9, 11.
22. Pringle did journey across the Karoo, but in the company of his wife and some friends.
23. A theme taken up again later by Mtshali and Sepamla (see below).
24. Quoted in Uys Krige, *Olive Schreiner, A Selection* (Oxford University Press, Cape Town, 1968), p. 189.

Chapter 5
The Limits of Liberal Thought

▼▼▼▼▼▼▼▼▼▼▼▼▼▼▼▼▼▼▼▼▼▼▼▼▼▼▼▼▼▼▼

The ironic tragedy of the liberal's position in a colonial situation is that, whatever he does, he is doubly suspect: many in the colonized community reproach him for his purely verbal commitment which is the product of his position of privilege, and the State, which he attacks by drawing general attention to its abuses, accuses him of subversion and 'opening the gates to communism'.

Paton and Delius are good examples of the South African liberal, the former more than the latter because he speaks throughout his work from within the country, which he has never left. Delius, who has lived outside South Africa since 1966, without being an exile, can use his situation as a resident abroad to justify adopting a middle-of-the-road position which seems to take account of the different points of view. It is easy to understand, therefore, that to speak in this context of the 'limits' of liberalism is likely to be confusing, unless one adds that this term takes into account the point of view of the colonized population and that, in the way it sees the black man, it betrays the influence of the society in which it exists. As one might expect, those concerned defend themselves against this charge, and Paton has done just this, not without humour, in a piece entitled Case History of a Pinky. *The aim of this chapter is to 'test' what the liberal has to say, as we did in the case of Pringle, without wishing in the least to underestimate his genuine contribution to the struggle against apartheid.*

Alan Paton

The whole of Alan Paton's work is a long indictment of apartheid. From 1948, when his first book, *Cry, the Beloved Country*,[1] appeared, until 1973, which saw the publication of *Apartheid and the Archbishop: The Life of Geoffrey Clayton*,[2] he unswervingly pursued the same objectives: to expose the injustices of the system set up by the Afrikaner Nationalists, to show the humiliation it causes, to constantly stress the immense responsibility for this that falls on all the country's whites, and to insist on the need for radical changes, before it is too late and love turns to hate. After Pringle, and before Nadine Gordimer and Dan Jacobson, Paton feels and expresses this fundamental truth which was or will be theirs: 'where life and race are inextricably intertwined, it follows . . . that if one is writing about life, one is writing about race also'.[3]

But writing does not mean refraining oneself from acting to change this totally unacceptable everyday reality; on the contrary. Paton's work is never intended to remain theoretical: whether writing precedes or follows action, or whether they occur together, it is impossible to detect in him any divorce between public life, private life and 'literature'. Even if we did not have his semi-autobiographical narrative, *Kontakion*,⁴ written after the death of his first wife, we would know that after devoting fifteen years of his life to running Diepkloof Reformatory, an institution for black juvenile delinquents, he devoted as many again to the Liberal Party, of which he was the joint founder and the president. *Cry, the Beloved Country, Debbie Go Home, Sponono*, and the articles he published in *Contact* are all the products of this experience.⁵

Besides, if it is at all possible for a man to represent an idea or a philosophy of life, Paton would be the one who could best personify the liberal, both with his qualities and his limitations. It is not for nothing that in the two biographies he has written Paton has drawn the portraits of his friend Hofmeyr, a 'proto-liberal', who served for a long time as his political model, and of Archbishop Clayton, who typifies for him the committed churchman.

Between 1948, the date when he began writing the first of these biographies, and 1964, the date when he finished it, came Hofmeyr's death, the dark days of the victory of Malan's Nationalists, the formation of the Liberal Party and the tightening of the grip of apartheid. There was also the separation of South Africa from Great Britain, Sharpeville and its innocent dead, and then John Harris.

John Harris is in a way an example of Paton's failure on the political level: by dint of preaching the respect for justice and the obligation to suit one's actions to one's words, Paton became the inspiration of a group of young liberals who took what he said very seriously. For them with Sharpeville the day had come when to speak and not to act was proof of impotence and self-betrayal, when to act in complete solidarity with the oppressed seemed henceforth inescapable.

But for Paton, between the word and armed struggle lay the rejection of violence, even in response to the growing violence of the regime. Paton never gave up 'knocking on the door', but he always did so respectfully – he always respected the country's institutions, even though they had been established and maintained in the most arbitrary manner.

Finally, the unwavering principle of a life at first devoted to education, and then to the defence of the oppressed, has always been the Christian ideal. His religious writings occur at regular intervals in his work: *Christian Unity: A South African View* (1957), *Meditation for a Young Boy Confirmed* (1959), *Instrument of Thy Peace* (1969).⁶ It is not by chance, either, that the heroes of his two main works, Arthur Jarvis, Kumalo and Pieter van Vlaanderen, are all dedicated Christians.⁷

Paton's influence does not stop at the fact that he planted the seed of liberalism in many consciences; in his varied work, where one finds side by side pamphlets, poems, novels, short stories, musical plays, one book stands out – *Cry, the Beloved Country*. In advance of its time, this very popular work on the racial question in South Africa incorporates the main themes which will be taken up by white poets, and to a lesser extent by black poets, during the next twenty-five years.

Through the overlapping destinies of the families of the Reverend Kumalo, a Zulu, and James Jarvis, an English-speaking white, Paton develops several themes: the theme of the false image South Africa has sought to present of itself, and its corollary, the need to discredit the official version of the situation; the theme of the fear and the absence of love, of the blindness of the whites; the theme of the impoverishment of the cultural and spiritual life as a result of the way South African society has been divided and partitioned. In fact, the whole book could be seen as a metaphor of the first universal epistle of St John the Evangelist. Indeed,

The Limits of Liberal Thought

Jarvis, the father, is saved only when he realizes after the death of his son, Arthur, that he has been content to love God without loving his neighbour, without loving Kumalo, who lived and performed his ministry right beside him at Ndotsheni. This 'revelation', which, on the eve of the 1948 elections, Paton could feel was not too late, underlies the quest for one's fellow man, for the outsider who should never have become one. This is indeed the real subject of the book, along with the idea that once this discovery has been made no sacrifice is too great to achieve the change of heart upon which the fate of the country hangs. Arthur relives, in a sense, in his son, who begins to learn Zulu from Kumalo, so as to be better equipped to understand the black man.

Cry, the Beloved Country is not simply a fictionalized treatment of the themes that the expanding grip of apartheid was to make even more evident during the fifties, sixties and seventies. It is also a poem, a symphony of voices and a dramatic oratorio. Though it is the poetic feeling that dominates, the prose that serves as the medium for the story is itself transformed at times into real poetry.

Paton's lyricism strikes one first of all in the nature scenes, which are like love songs dedicated to the African land: here already, the form Paton adopts is inseparable from the theme. The opening of the novel delimits two kinds of terrain and two separate destinies; it establishes, in the names evoked and invoked, which link Afrikaans with English, Zulu and Xhosa, the unity that lies behind the differences; and it stresses that the land thus named belongs to all the communities:

> There is a lovely road that runs from Ixopo into the hills. These hills are grass-covered and rolling, and they are lovely beyond any singing of it. The road climbs seven miles into them, to Carisbrooke; and from there, if there is no mist, you look down on one of the fairest valleys of Africa. About you there is grass and bracken and you may hear the forlorn crying of the titihoya, one of the birds of the veld. Below you is the valley of the Umzinkulu, on its journey from the Drakensberg to the sea; and beyond and behind the river, great hill after great hill; and beyond and behind them, the mountains of Ingeli and East Griqualand.[8]

Elsewhere, we find the barely disguised songs that facilitated the adaptation of the novel for the American stage by Maxwell Anderson and Kurt Weill (who composed the music for the *Threepenny Opera*).[9] It is in this context that we can justifiably talk of a 'symphony of voices' – the black voices in Chapter 9, the white voices in Chapter 11: laments, lullabies for the child who is about to die, or breathless sentences that convey fear[10] and open up into full-blown prayers or prayers that are incorporated into the overall 'sermon'[11] of the book. The sentences, here, have a strong rhythm which coincides with the rhythm of human breathing and is frequently reminiscent of the poetic prose of the Psalms:

> Who indeed knows the secret of the earthly pilgrimage? Who indeed knows why there can be comfort in a world of desolation? Now God be thanked that there is a beloved one who can lift up the heart in suffering, that one can play with a child in the face of such misery. Now God be thanked that the name of a hill is such music, that the name of a river can heal. Aye, even the name of a river that runs no more.[12]

This style is characteristic of Paton; it recurs often in his work, whether the typography is explicitly that of poetry or not, and justifies his considerable reputation as a poet.[13] It is not, however, this style that one will find later in Horn or

Jensma but rather, along with the themes listed above, the language of prophecy, the lyrical insistence on the desire for a 'togetherness' which will transcend racial and religious barriers, and, finally, the fear engendered by ignorance and separation.

On the other hand, Paton's successors will also resort to the symbolism he used twice in his first novel, a symbolism which is all the more effective for being expressed with simplicity:

> All roads led to Johannesburg. Through the long nights the trains pass to Johannesburg. The lights of the swaying coach fall on the cutting-sides, on the grass and the stones of a country that sleeps. Happy the eyes that can close.[14]

> In the deserted harbour there is yet water that laps against the quays. In the dark and silent forest there is a leaf that falls. Behind the polished panelling the white ant eats the wood. Nothing is ever quiet, except for fools.[15]

Such is the importance of *Cry, the Beloved Country* that it unjustifiably eclipses the rest of Paton's work, including his poetry. It needed the publication of a mixed selection of prose and verse in *Knocking on the Door* (1975) to obtain a global picture of his poetic work, comprising no more than thirty or so poems. Must we, therefore, regard it as insignificant? I think not. There is one point that must be made: Paton's poems are not so much arms for the fight – he leaves this function to his pamphlets, articles and editorials – as the reflection of the self-questioning of a man who feels intensely his personal responsibility in a society which claims to be Christian but which is nevertheless unjust. Paton provides an admirable picture of the anguish of conscience of a man torn between indifference towards the world and the call of this same world, of a writer caught between the desire to act concretely and the desire to devote himself entirely to literature but fearing that, in satisfying this wish, he will altogether fail in his duty.

If the first of these conflicts was evident in him from the thirties onwards, the second emerged with the publication of *Cry, the Beloved Country*. In fact, surprised and delighted by the success of his book among the general public who, through it, were being informed about the South African situation, Paton withdrew from public life in order to write. Very soon, he realized that withdrawal was impossible; the political events of the day demanded the involvement of all men of good will, and Paton was now convinced of the need to found the Liberal Party, which he and a few others believed would rally those South Africans who were determined to oppose Nationalist policies. Paton's withdrawal was short-lived, but the inner debate between literary and political action went on. Poetry was not, however, for him, as too for Dennis Brutus later, the vehicle for political ideas, for he had plenty of other platforms from which to express these. That is why one only occasionally finds poems concerned with the criticism of apartheid, while those expressing his reflections on the theme of commitment are more frequent.

Among the former, one must mention, because it is so untypical, 'My Great Discovery', the light-hearted tale of an imaginary machine capable of changing people's pigmentation; its white inventor prefers to destroy it rather than be the first to be transformed into a black! The poem is a spirited satire of pseudo liberalism and the racial theories of the day (it was written in 1953):

> I sat astounded
> Completely dumbfounded
> By the epoch-making

> Breath-taking
> Discovery . . .
> I seized the telephone
> And in a voice unlike my own . . .
> Government, I said
> The girl said, what division?
> I said, no divisions any more.
> She said, I mean what section?
> I said, no sections any more.
> She said, I'll report you,
> (Or, deport you,
> I can't say
> I'm not au fait
> With recent legislation).[16]

The poems belonging to the same group illustrate another of his favourite techniques, the use of indirect criticism he terms 'accusing by implication', although it has limitations which he readily admits.

The best example of this is provided by 'We Mean Nothing Evil Towards You', which is a criticism of the scheme to send Africans back to the Reserves fostered by Verwoerd and which Delius was to satirize – in a different way, it is true – in *The Last Division*. Only the end of the poem, however, avoids the pitfalls of an over subtle presentation inaccessible to the very people to whom it is addressed:

> Can you for whom we have made this reparation
> Not give us something also, not petition
> The gods of all the tribes we create
> To call you back in one migration
> North to the beating heart of Africa?
> Can you not make a magic that will silence conscience,
> Put peace behind the frowning vigilant eyes,
> That will regardless of Space and Time
> Wipe you from the face of the earth?
> But without pain . . .
> For we mean nothing evil towards you.[17]

The poems that deal with the theme of commitment are of a quite different order, without at all departing from Paton's normal non-sectarian attitude. 'The Hermit', which dates from 1931, treats this theme antiphrastically and is the direct forerunner of 'Poems at Bargain Prices' by Peter Horn. Paton, whose outlook had been considerably broadened after a visit to England in 1924, realized that he could no longer live with the same innocence as before in what he had once believed to be a Paradise on earth: he wants to avoid becoming like his hermit, who has shut himself away from the world so as not to have to listen any more to the cries of those who suffer:

> I have barred the doors
> Of the place where I bide,
> I am old and afraid
> Of the world outside.

> How the poor souls cry
> In the cold and the rain
> I have blocked my ears,
> They shall call me in vain . . .
>
> *Do they think, do they dream*
> *I will open the door?*
> *Let the world in*
> *And know peace no more?*[18]

The fact that the temptation exists, however, is shown in the short piece entitled 'Trilemma', which reveals the complexities of the human soul and the tensions that act upon every individual. The author–narrator dreams he sees three students 'nobly degreed and capped and gowned', passing by a field where a humble labourer is tilling the ground. While two show indifference or disdain, the third joins him in his work. What puzzles the author, though, is that each face is his own:

> But most absurd of all was me,
> The real me, not the other three,
> Going from hood to hood to see
> Which of the three was really me![19]

'Could You not Write Otherwise' (1949) best shows the pressure of everyday reality on the themes of the committed writer. This poem was the conclusion of a lecture which Paton gave in the United States that year, entitled *Why I Write*, in which he illustrated his points with recent poems. He used the poem to reply to criticism by a woman reader of the interrogation in the title:

> Simple I was, I wished to write but words,
> And melodies that had no meanings but their music
> And songs that had no meaning but their song.
> But the deep notes and the undertones
> Kept sounding themselves, kept insistently
> Intruding themselves, like a prisoned tide
> That under the shining and the sunlit sea
> In caverns and in corridors goes underground thundering.[20]

The whole of Paton is here, and nearly all white committed poetry. The whole of Paton because it expresses his overriding preoccupation with the responsibility of the white man whose eyes have been opened to call upon his contemporaries for a change of heart. Changing people through literature, through the power of words and situations, is a lofty, some would say an unattainable ambition. The fact that Paton realized that something more was needed is evident from his entry into the political arena some years later; but he was to continue 'knocking on the door', in the real sense as well as metaphorically.

This call for a change of heart was prompted by another belief to which he has always remained faithful, even in the face of the continuing blindness of the whites: the need to uncover the reality, hidden beneath the reassuring official image of a prosperous South Africa bathed in sun ('under the shining and the sunlit sea'), of a so far contained, but still a threatening force ('a prisoned tide', 'goes underground thundering'). So, once again, poetic themes that were to become those of the next generation.

But another characteristic just as peculiar to him: those songs which he can only describe as 'sorrowful' are the songs of the oppressed: further on in the poem, he talks of 'artless songs become the groans and cries of men'. In fact, whether it be the black characters of *Cry, the Beloved Country* or those who appear in the few poems in which Paton speaks through them, we only find the suffering, pleading side of the black man, and not the militancy of which he is capable, nor his vitality, humour, irony or the spontaneous gaiety with which he can defend himself. It is in this respect that he differs from Peter Horn and especially Jensma.

It is also through his poetry that Paton clearly shows, therefore, that he has gone to the heart of the problem of commitment: here, as in the case of the themes that have become those of the 'new prophets', Paton shows that he is more than a forerunner. In fact, this man who was born when the English colonies of the Cape and Natal on the one hand, and the Afrikaner republics on the other, were emerging from the Boer War, has closely identified himself with his generation. His life and his work reveal just how closely he has observed South African society and just how well he has perceived, long before many of his contemporaries, the potential tragedy and the means to avoid it. If relatively few have followed in his footsteps, it is because the majority of his white compatriots have not had his faith in man, guided as he has been by the Christian ideal.

But the weight of colonization lies heavily on him as well, and, albeit reluctantly, he is one of its representatives. He illustrates the uncomfortable and increasingly indefensible position of the liberal, who draws the criticism of both the Afrikaner Nationalists and the supporters of Black Consciousness. The former blame him for breaking the united front of the group and spreading doubts about the 'civilizing mission of the white man'; the latter accuse him of continuing to preach moderation and patience in the last quarter of the twentieth century, in the face of all the evidence of the last thirty years. Even some of his former colleagues and disciples accuse him of having moved to the right. And it is true that Paton now defends the Bantustan policy and has made himself, with a few others, the spokesman of a federalism in which the whites would be able to retain their majority in some provinces.

In order to reach the 'new prophets' and those who have tried to fully apply Paton's own principles and to believe in the redemptive role of a revolution, we must cross the dark years that separate the legal establishment of apartheid from the events of Sharpeville. It was Anthony Delius, a parliamentary journalist engaged in the daily sounding of white society, who was to predict the conflagrations that were slowly festering in the ranks of those he called the South African moujiks.

Anthony Delius

Anthony Delius figures in the African *Who's Who* as a journalist, but it is more likely that his name will go down in posterity for his contribution to the literature of his country, and chiefly for his poetry.

Delius was born in Simonstown, in the Cape Province, in 1916. On his mother's side, his family has been in South Africa for three or four generations, while his father, who was of English origin, was related to Delius the musician. After spending most of his childhood on a farm in the Transvaal, Delius studied at Rhodes University; he had just finished when war broke out. During the war, he served in the South African Intelligence Corps. After the war, he went into journalism and founded the Port Elizabeth *Post*, on which many of the younger generation gained their experience; he then became a parliamentary journalist in Cape Town and, in this capacity, followed the debates of the South African Parliament during the eventful fifties. It was from his experience with the *Cape Times* that came the poem *The Last Division*. Extracts first appeared in the review *Standpunte*, of which he was at the time editor-in-chief, and in *Africa South*, edited by Ronald Segal; it was published in its final form in 1959.

In the meantime, Delius published a collection of poems, *An Unknown Border* (1954), and two travel diaries. In 1960 appeared a play inspired by the personality of Cecil Rhodes, *The Fall*, then, in 1962, more poems, *A Corner of the World*, and a political novel, *The Day Natal Took Off*. Delius left South Africa in 1966 for London, where he worked for ten years on the African Service of the BBC. He retains his deep attachment to South Africa and belongs to the editorial board of the review *New Coin*, edited by Guy Butler, in which his long poem, *Black South Easter*, was published in 1965.[21]

While one finds in Delius most of the themes present in the work of the South African poets of his generation, particularly that of the identity of the white poet in Africa, his originality, and also his merit, lie in having dealt directly with the most important problem of his time: the problem of a society dominated by the policy of apartheid. *The Last Division* is to this day the monument, and certainly the *chef d'oeuvre*, of English-speaking satire directed against apartheid: here Delius links up with Paton in his condemnation of a system erected by the Afrikaner Nationalists, and he later expressed, but much less felicitously, in *Black South Easter*, his attitude towards interracial relations in South Africa.

The Last Division is a long poem of about 2,500 lines, divided into three cantos composed of stanzas of unequal length; each stanza resembles the movements, or tableaux, of a play which derives its dramatic elements and its comic effects from tragi-comedy, but which, given the lesson it seeks to draw from its symbolism and the events it evokes, also owes something to the mystery play.

We learn in Canto I that the Abbot of a Tibetan monastery has, in response to the appeals of an English monk who has had a series of frightening premonitions, summoned two sages (whom the author refers to sometimes as 'wise men', sometimes as 'seers') to help him interpret them: a Russian who has survived a Stalinist prison camp, and a Bushman who, with a handful of others, has survived the genocide to which their race has been subjected over the centuries. The choice of these characters seems to suggest that Delius has as little sympathy of left-wing totalitarianism as he has for white colonialism in southern Africa. In fact, while, as the rest of the first canto indicates, Delius's criticism is fairly general, he feels a certain indulgence towards his fellow South Africans. The conversation between the three men serves as a pretext for strong criticism of the United Nations' powerlessness to restore peace to countries torn by war, as well as for condemnation of the conflict between the great powers, which places the entire planet at risk. In between, he draws the disillusioned portrait of a standardized, antiseptic, materialistic humanity which places excessive faith in Science, avoids introspection and relies on received ideas, be they those of Darwin, Marx or Freud. All this is not an unnecessary digression: the Abbot and his companions conclude that, in order to cure this insane humanity, they must show it a portrait of

The Limits of Liberal Thought 69

itself in miniature, in the form of a country embodying all its iniquity and condemned in consequence to extinction. But where are they to find a suitable country, whose inhabitants would be likely to acknowledge their folly?

It does exist, Delius tells us through the Bushman who even, with a generosity which is a little surprising coming from a person who has seen so many of his own kind decimated by the colonists, goes on to appeal to the Abbot to show mercy. The Abbot promises to spare the South Africans and to frighten rather than harm them. By way of introduction, before switching the action to Cape Town, where the Parliament buildings will become its focus, Delius outlines the current South African ideology. It is presented with devastating satire as a heterogeneous jumble of ideas and prejudices dating from a past age:

> Ha, all the world's old clothes turn up at last
> In Africa, to find their second youth,
> And intellectual discards of the past
> Can spend an Indian Summer in the South.
> Ah, what a rig is there, a cast-off world,
> Divine rights, Hindu caste, imperialism,
> Tricked out with new democracy and twirled
> With dialectical materialism!
> Civilization's Sitting Bull or satrap,
> At half-remove from the good naked state
> With liberal clichés down to Nazi claptrap
> To clothe in second-hand the second-rate.[22]

In Canto I, Delius concentrates his attack mainly on the world of the fifties; in Canto II, he expresses his criticism of his own country, while at the same time advancing the action. As the parliamentary debate on Nationalist policies towards the black people unfolds, the inhumanity of the arguments vies with their absurdity, and concludes with the balance of the action being quite literally tipped in an unexpected direction.

Delius cleverly uses the international situation of the day, with its focus on Cyprus,[23] to create a terminology which, while deriving from a specific set of events, can be applied very appropriately to the Nationalists. Thus he terms 'ethnosis' the Afrikaner strategy aimed at securing complete independence from Great Britain on essentially racial lines. Verwoerd, as Minister of Native Affairs and future Prime Minister, is given the title 'Ethnarch', while the Nats (the Nationalists) become the Neths, to fit in with the rest. The national anthem – the Ethnic Anthem – lists the main segregation laws of the racist State, Ethnasia, providing Delius with a fine opportunity to satirize its stupidity:

> Ethnasia will last a thousand years
> Our land is studded with its glories
> Its monuments are separate bars
> And separate lavatories.
>
> God has through us ordained it so
> Post Offices are split in two
> And separate pillar-boxes fix
> That correspondence does not mix,

> No one has ever managed better
> To guard the spirit – and the letter . . .
>
> We've split all difference so fine
> No wider than a hair or skin,
> To foil the trick of traits and needs
> So shockingly the same in breeds –
> For such success in our researches
> We thank Thee Lord in separate churches.
>
> How wondrous is our work, our way,
> And Thine as well, Great Separator,
> Who separating night from day
> Left us to sort out the rest later.[24]

Delius uses imaginary names, which are nevertheless quite transparent to his contemporaries, to attack the politicians most in the public eye. Chief among them, the one who holds the centre of the stage for the whole of the second and third cantos, is Verwoerd, who was at the time responsible for the planning and application of apartheid and the policy of 'separate development'. Giving him the name Beleerd,[25] Delius paints an historically accurate portrait of Verwoerd, who had set himself up as the guardian of the white race in South Africa and was regarded as epitomizing Afrikaner virtues, honour and glory, in spite of having been born in the Netherlands. First as minister, then as head of the government, he was to relentlessly pursue the implementation of his plan to achieve the strict separation of the 'races' and to ensure white domination for a very long time:

> Statistics, numbers, races fill his vision,
> Ransacked from Europe, Africa, Asia
> And patched together with a schooled precision
> To form a bold methodical fantasia,
> His Hundred Year Design, His Master Plan
> To keep the Neths the masters – and their clan.[26]

This relentless policy had led Verwoerd to attack the rights of the Coloureds, which had always been regarded as inalienable. Delius thus denounces the Nationalists' manipulation of the Constitution and satirizes the parody of democracy they had set up. Still in Canto II, he attacks the inhumanity of the Population Registration Act and the Group Areas Act, but his main target is the brand new policy of 'separate development'; the poet–journalist reveals it for the political and cultural swindle it is, several years before it was put into effect. His criticism remains just as pertinent today:

> Study now this Great White Figure,
> Or kindly Governor of the black man's gaol,
> Locations and reserves, those somewhat bigger
> Lock-ups, to put the blacks beyond the pale.
> Head-keeper of the Bantu, he discusses
> Bold plans to modernize the penitentiary,
> Even give ruptured tribes some legal trusses
> To set them free inside a previous century.

The Limits of Liberal Thought

> Each race, or group, or tribe in like confinement,
> Fruitful by androgynous gestation,
> Develops its own lines of quaint refinement –
> Culture begins with tribal decoration.[27]

While the venom of his satire shows up the fanaticism, the authoritarianism and, in spite of their long-term plans, the narrowness and pettiness of Nationalist thinking, Delius does not deal kindly either with the Opposition United Party. He accuses the latter of lacking political vision and of being totally incapable of putting forward genuine solutions. Its racial policy differs little, he says, from that of the party in power.

> They no more wish the black among his own
> A man, than have him as their next-door neighbour,
> But want him in some neutral zone
> To buy their goods and be cheap factory labour.[28]

But an unexpected event brings the MPs' discussion temporarily to a halt: while Beleerd is expounding on the merits of the natives' returning to their ancestral customs, the Parliament building and the surrounding lawns suddenly sink into the earth and descend into the nether regions. Delius hastens to tell us that it is not really Hell, and not, therefore, final damnation, in accordance with the Abbot's promise to the Bushman. The opening of Canto III introduces us briefly to the symbolic Tree of Life, resembling an old baobab with its immense trunk, and it is still possible for the MPs to redeem themselves by climbing from its gnarled roots to its gigantic head of hair.

At this point, a new character takes the stage: his name is Harriman, the chief psychiatrist and director of the 'Rehabilitation Centre' which he invites all the MPs to enter:

> But as the change from your condition is abrupt
> I should advise a stay in Gateway Home,
> My Centre, to restore your psychic norm.
> It's simply a question of adjustment . . . but
> You'll like the place. The atmosphere is pleasant.
> It's round the corner of the Tree. The Gate
> Is there, goes up ten miles, and has a crescent,
> An arch made of rainbow, meant to counter
> Adverse propaganda with an image.[29]

Beneath the fable, it is easy to discern the serious point being made by Delius: the image of the rainbow signifies the simultaneous existence of complementary values, and one of the aims of the Centre is to restore the sense of relativity which is so lacking in the new arrivals who have as yet not learnt anything from their mishap.

The MPs refuse Harriman's offer: rather than try to integrate themselves with the outside world – they detest the word 'integration ' – they prefer to remain aloof and hope that the rest of the world will turn to them when it has realized that the so-called integration can only have disastrous consequences. They inaugurate their campaign with a polemical pamphlet, entitled 'Has Heaven got a future?'

But the old habits take a long time to die: the founders of Ethnasia will not be entirely safe until they have colonized the desert spaces to which they have been relegated and erected a protective wall around themselves. It is the Opposition, now reduced to a purely symbolic function but at last able to assume a constructive role, who are given this task. In order to economize on materials, in short supply in this region, they will use the bumf that the State, in its mania for legislation, endlessly accumulates. Endless, too, the construction of the wall, and the days spent waiting for 'the rest' to arrive. Only one, a drunken Coloured, wanders into this place; he immediately takes flight, accompanied by the black servant who brought the MPs their refreshments: the latter are now condemned to the void, to nothingness.

The Last Division is not boring to read, because above all the author shows himself capable of considerable wit. The enterprise was, however, a risky one, for the book is largely a battle of words. The plot itself was nevertheless an original one, even though it offered little potential for development: men have always enjoyed finding their own or their neighbours' misfortunes beneath the cloak of fable. Although real people are portrayed under fictitious names, the poem avoids becoming dated, as is almost inevitable with this genre, because, unfortunately, the spirit and the methods of the Nationalists and the supporters of White Power in South Africa have not changed at all in the last twenty years. For this reason, Delius's well-placed arrows always find their mark; for the poet is adept at finding the telling phrase and the concise expression. When he criticizes the anachronistic policies of the Nationalists, the accuracy of the point being made coincides with the forcefulness of the words chosen to express it:

> A Xenophobe Salvation Army they
> Make Bibles of the latest revelation –
> The mixture that mankind has reached today
> Must go no further, it's the consummation!
> Thus marching backwards to the future's danger
> Eyes fixed on dreams from which the past has woken,
> They see a truth from which all truth is stranger
> And keep a trust by which all trust is broken.[30]

Delius also managed to avoid the obstacle inherent in the lengthiness of his argument, either by alternating considerations of a general nature with specific criticisms of South Africa, as in Canto I, or by varying the stylistic devices. Thus, not only is each canto divided into stanzas whose length is calculated to maintain interest but the rhythms, too, are constantly varied. The Ethnic Anthem is a good example of a passage where the verve of the satire is sustained, strengthened even, by a change to a livelier rhythm. Elsewhere, Delius introduces 'sung' interludes in a different style: he does this for the passage concerning the liberals, where he abandons alternate rhymes in favour of the rhyming couplet, thus introducing a pause in the general structure.

> Ten little liberals waiting to resign,
> One went and did so, and then they were nine.
>
> Nine little liberals entered a debate,
> But one spoke his heart out, and then they were eight.

The Limits of Liberal Thought

> Eight little liberals saw the road to heaven,
> One even followed it, and then they were seven.

And so on, until only one is left, and even he . . .

> One little liberal found nothing could be done,
> So he took the boat for England, and then there were none.[31]

Finally, the element of farce created by the choice of situations, as well as by the contrast between the MPs' role and the frequent inanity of the debates, shows up the absurdity inherent in the day-to-day realities of the South African situation. Does Delius, though, make this absurdity too bearable? It is certain that it would not be possible to rewrite *The Last Division* now without being accused of insensitivity, after all the suffering that apartheid has caused and continues to cause. Films that look back at the past are only possible when the initial situation no longer exists, and this is not yet the case with South Africa.

Even though he wanted to censure the behaviour of his compatriots through laughter, Delius's intentions were entirely serious. To be convinced of this, one has only to read the warnings contained in the fable in order to give it greater force and to communicate a sense of urgency to his contemporaries about the need for a change of policy:

> Two parties of mistrust, one shrinks from right,
> The other fears their folk may shrink from wrong.
> (Alas my country in your fateful years
> That these two eyes of our one people's vision
> Should be, as the last chance of choosing nears,
> Squint of bigotry and blur of indecision!)
> Down deep in their subconscious thickets none
> Suspects his time, his destiny is reckoned,
> Nor sees pale hands press downwards from the sun
> And shadow rising round him by the second.[32]

The poem's virtue was to confront the white government and white public opinion with a magnifying mirror, held up not by a stranger to the country, or a critic determined to find fault wherever he could, but by a South African familiar with the political situation, someone who had closely observed individual and national weaknesses, and was not inclined to be excessively indulgent in his criticisms or to make concessions to personal pride. Afrikaners were divided on how to take this attack. 'It is an unpleasant little poem', wrote *Die Burger*, while the literary critic of *Die Transvaler* commented: 'If we could get more of this sort of work from every political standpoint it could have a clarifying effect on the murkiness of partisanship, and the tense grimace of politics could relax into the healthier smile at one's own expense.' You have, in fact, to go back to the period of Plomer and Campbell to find a similarly direct attack on South African society. But, whereas Campbell had mainly attacked the parochialism and the narrowness of outlook of the inhabitants of Natal, his native province, Delius, like Plomer (but in verse), was warning of the dangers inherent in a racial policy applied with such cold determination and so destructive in human terms. Delius, however, was also writing with a professional knowledge of the South African political scene which his predecessors had lacked, but this is an additional reason for having certain reserves about *The Last Division*.

Apportioning the blame to both sides, as Delius did, was not without risk: it could give comfort to the Nationalists in their policies. 'After all, the rest are no better!' they could think. It was also a dangerous approach with regard to the rest of the world, to which Delius seemed to be saying: 'Those people are obtuse, but in microcosm they are like you; pointless, therefore, to put pressure on them!'

Moreover, Delius's insistence on focusing his attack on Parliament alone seemed to suggest that the poet–journalist believed everything followed that route and no other. This is partly true, in that both legislative and executive control of the country resides solely with the whites. But this emphasis tended to give excessive weight to the political aspect in relation to economic and social factors, of which there is no mention at all in *The Last Division*. This is an oversight, because in 1955 South Africans were fighting, *outside Parliament*, against Nationalist policies, demanding the establishment of a true democracy and a fairer distribution of power. Even if one accepts that in *The Last Division* Delius is helping to strip Parliament, which in fact represents only a minority, of its false image, he still sins by omission: by alluding only to the time bomb of the racial situation and to the Bantustans he gives an incomplete picture of the South African situation in the fifties. In spite of these reservations, it is still a fact, however, that this poem is Delius's most important contribution to an understanding of this period and to the condemnation of apartheid at a time when this policy was being established with all the rigour we know. Compared to Paton, who was writing on the same themes at about the same time, Delius seems to be less idealistic, more pessimistic even, but, as the rest of his work shows, proposing equally vague solutions to the racial 'conflict', treating it all on the level of interpersonal relations and not in terms of power. If Delius pays more attention to the political situation as such, Paton, in *Cry, the Beloved Country*, provides a far more complete picture of the situation. The former appeals more to the reason and intelligence of his readers, the latter to their heart and their feelings.[33]

Black South Easter, which was written some ten years later, led Delius to abandon the field of politics proper for that of interracial relations on a personal level. The poet, who can here give free rein to his lyricism, turns out to be much less at ease with it than he was with polemic; it must be stressed, though, that the work, while much shorter, is also more ambitious. Whereas in *The Last Division* Delius had tried, through a poem of political fiction, to draw his fellow citizens' attention to the folly of their racial policies and to the dangers they were storing up for the future, in *Black South Easter* he returned to the past in search of evidence of a better future. But in incorporating his meditations, in the form of a 'vision', into his personal dilemma as a man and as a poet, in developing themes already dealt with in his preceding collections, all of them linked with the Ocean, Delius simply increased the number of obstacles and produced a confused work which was, nevertheless, an illustration of the difficulties confronting a white South African trying to think through the problems of a multiracial society. *Black South Easter*, intended as the 'constructive' side of the critique presented by *The Last Division*, came close, in fact, to undermining this very intention.

This corner of the world which is South Africa was already a turning point in the voyages of discovery of the first navigators, the place of storms they had to encounter before they could 'round the Cape'. The Cape/cape was the testing ground that separated the known from the unknown: some had the courage to cross to the other side, some died in the attempt, others returned, scarcely believing their good fortune, only to be wrecked on the way back, while others turned back, frightened by their experience and deciding they had gone far enough. Then, one day, the Cape of Storms became the Cape of Good Hope, which is not merely a matter of semantics, says Delius, in a collection aptly entitled *A Corner of the World*. Once the Cape/cape has been rounded, the traveller is on the threshold of a new world: 'man turns the tumultuous corner/to meet himself . . .' To the geographical and personal significance is now added a symbolic dimension:

> Still we learn, battered between hope and storm
> the beauty of becoming, and the need
> to die.[34]

The history of South Africa and personal history are mingled here – not only the history of the discoverers of the past, but Delius's also, thanks to his emigrant father, who chose to settle in this corner of the globe.[35] Cape Town, where the Atlantic and Indian Oceans meet and mingle, is also the meeting place of East and West, of the white and oriental people, on Africa's soil. Already in *The Last Division* Delius had noted the irony of the fact that the Nationalists were more intent on discrimination than the Ocean that had brought them to this place. For the theme of *Black South Easter* exists in embryo already in this earlier work:

> The ocean, with a calm sardonic titter,
> Eyes what five centuries of trade have swirled
> In tidal marks of civilizing litter
> About 'the fairest Cape in all the world' . . .
> And white bones rock in deep green hammocks under
> Where Indian and Atlantic mix their waters,
> Careless that whites ashore are torn asunder
> To choose what race shall wed their great-granddaughters,
> And pour out laws that lovers from the seas
> Must match the ladies on their knees.[36]

It is not a descent into hell this time, rather a dive beneath the seas: limbo and the empty spaces give way to the depths of the Ocean. The descent is simply an image of human introspection and the quest for the past; from the depths of history emerges the awareness of a common humanity.

Delius relates how, one stormy night in Cape Town, he leaves the newspaper offices to go home and is driven to the sea-front by the black South Easter, a wind that brings rain and change of weather to the extreme south of the Cape Province. In this place which has seen countless shipwrecks, his imagination conjures up a vision of shipwrecked people from all countries and of all colours, gathered beneath the waves and dancing to the music of a ghostly orchestra, while close by several people talk. The latter belong to the distant and recent history of South Africa and correspond to some of the present-day South African communities. Among them are Diaz, who represents the first western discoverers of the tip of the African continent and who was drowned off Cape Town; Woltemade, the Afrikaner farmer of German descent famous for his rescue on horseback of a dozen shipwrecked sailors whom he pulled from the raging seas, making several journeys before being dragged away himself; Makana, the Xhosa chief who made a reputation for himself during the border wars against the white invaders and who was drowned, during an escape attempt, off Robben Island, where he had been imprisoned; Barney Barnato, the English-speaking South African Jew who had built his fortune on the diamond and gold fields of southern Africa and leapt into the sea from the ship on which he was making the crossing from Southampton to Cape Town; finally, the only truly fictional character of the story, a young actress supposed also to have drowned.

History itself is reduced to its simplest expression: no events are recorded after the writer's fantasy or imagination has evoked his characters. We listen to their imaginary conversation, then the author-narrator – in effect the sixth character of the poem – departs, with his questions still unanswered.

The word 'conversation' does not really convey what is going on among the characters: it is more like a series of monologues which follow one another fairly naturally, an exchange of confidences without the proper dialectic of a discussion. Each of them is essentially telling the story of his own relationship with the world, through his sea adventure. The sea here plays a crucial role, as much on the symbolic level as on the level of events: it is at one and the same time the mother who offers protection and the cruel stepmother who despises human pride, forgetting man during her monstrous coupling with the wind, but also providing him with the opportunity to give of his best; she is the great unifier. The wind has scarcely less importance: Delius uses it as the symbol of tradition on the spiritual level and the instrument of change on the material level.

Black South Easter could be a poem about failure: two of the protagonists commit suicide and the author himself does not, in the final analysis, find the meaning of life. However, even though the poem effectively poses the question of success and failure in a modern world which, for Delius, has lost much of the courage, faith, imagination and love which the preceding centuries seem to have possessed, he presents as something to be envied that underwater interracial gathering – a chance gathering, it must be noted, called up by the author himself. These two themes are mingled, framed by Delius's own questionings about what he is and what he is doing in the world.

The first theme is evoked by contrasting the Woltemade–Makana pair, considered as positive, and its opposite, the pair formed by the millionaire and the actress, with Diaz occupying the intermediate, symbolic role of the eternal explorer dormant in all men. Woltemade personifies to the highest degree the sense of responsibility and commitment towards the human species. Delius makes him say of his reaction to the spectacle of the shipwreck:

> Was I to sit there and watch them [the breakers]
> Make a meal of my fellow men?
> The tattered-masted, shivering ship,
> And the pathetic littleness of hands
> And voices, stung, struck at my manhood.
> For each it swallowed, so much
> The sea diminished me.[37]

And further on, as if to stress his humanitarianism even more:

> But a man cannot always be calm
> Before the smug inevitabilities
> Of sea, or earth, or even heaven.[38]

Makana had allowed himself to be captured to save his followers; he personifies the spirit of sacrifice and respect for the ancestral traditions.

Opposing these two protagonists, the millionaire and the actress seem to stand for the modern world with its individualism, its fear of commitment (symbolized, in the case of the actress, by the rejection of maternity), the superficial character of its human relations, its lack of charity and, finally, its intolerable pride. All these weaknesses are presented as existing in the wider South African society. Delius takes the opportunity to attack the hypocrisy of the country's rulers ('furtive Calvinists cheating the Bible'), their pretentiousness in believing they possess the earth, their insensitivity and their small-mindedness in what is really a country of immense grandeur.[39]

The second theme is already contained in the choice of positive characters, Woltemade, a Boer, and Makana, an African. The reconciliation of the races is first of all Delius's with the Afrikaners, whom he had treated so harshly in *The Last Division*, while Makana, merely mentioned in a few earlier poems, is here elevated to the role of protagonist. There was certainly reason for the South African reader to be surprised by this exchange of courtesies between individuals traditionally separated (by custom and law) and here meeting on an equal footing. And, although Makana is not addressed as 'Mr', his interlocutor asks to be forgiven for unthinkingly(?) calling him a 'Kaffir'! Delius, in fact, makes things quite clear: after describing with obvious pleasure this underwater world where the continents have forgotten their differences in order to mix and blend, he adds:

> I doted on their multimillion
> Wealth of meeting, their endless tumult
> Of delight in one another, lost
> Forever to the bleak fanaticism of the wind
> That hollows heart and self.[40]

Once again, evoked in a paragraph which enumerates the variety of the professions, grades, colours and traditions, we find the symbol of the rainbow which Delius had offered to the South African MPs, through the medium of Harriman, as the ideal of a full and complete integration that must be sought. The underwater scene strikes one, in fact, as being a parallel to the church scene in *Cry, the Beloved Country*.[41] But it adds nothing to it; on the contrary. For Paton's scene had existed in reality, and he had made it the ideal to be sought, first of all socially, then politically; but does Delius's scene go much beyond the stage of an impossible dream? Is it not, in its very elements (a meeting of drowned, not living, people, in an 'extra-territorial' place, a succession of monologues and not a true dialogue), the proof of the difficulty, indeed the impossibility, of its realization in this world? Nothing is said, either, about the means by which this human harmony is to be achieved: equality, which is specifically referred to, implies a will to negotiate in the real world. But it is not the black who has opposed constructive dialogue for decades, but the white. And it is not difficult to imagine the latter's repugnance, supposing he can overcome his prejudices, for negotiations which would abolish his privileges. The underwater gathering is a confraternity that transcends the racial barriers, but remains on the level of a dream for 'the happy few'. And history itself is seen in the context of a tolerance which is singularly absent from the history textbooks placed before the South African schoolchildren who will, perhaps, be the rulers of tomorrow.

While on the subject of figures, we might ask ourselves if Delius himself respects in *Black South Easter* the equation he had put forward in *The Last Division* to sum up the numerical relationships in South Africa ('four blacks to every white, there's your equation')? Out of five characters, only one is black; the author respects not the spread of racial groups, but the national origins of the European colonizers – one Portuguese, one Boer, one English-speaking colonist, plus the (white) actress, included for good measure. Where are the characters representing the other communities which have contributed to the creation of modern South Africa? In the absence of a fair representation of blacks, where are the Coloureds and the Indians, especially in view of the fact that the latter have been as important for the development of Natal as the Tswana, Sotho and Zulu have been for the Rand? A petty criticism? Surely not! If, as Guy Butler asserts in his short introduction,[42] the work aimed at being representative on the historical level then it should have been genuinely so. There is no avoiding the conclusion that the poet's vision is a partial one: it is history seen by a white South African and written for white South Africans.[43]

Finally, what are we to make of a moral view that consists in drawing lessons from a past presented as being more human, more noble, than the present? Certainly, Diaz was a very courageous man, and Woltemade was a real hero. But the heroism of the colonists has mostly been one-sided: it coexisted with the relentless fight waged against the 'savages', who were themselves merely defending what belonged to them. The gulf between cultures was immense in the seventeenth and eighteenth centuries; if it has been rationalized since then, this was in order to serve the economic interests of the whites and to perpetuate their political domination. Yet it is in our own time that ethnocentricity could have the best chance of losing its virulence, if only official propaganda, in South Africa at least, did not work against the course of history.

However, the 'vision' Delius offers us sometimes reflects the prevailing prejudices, and the idea of reconciliation is undermined by the language. A study of the vocabulary associated with colour reveals a Manicheism which follows well-defined racial lines. Thus, the colour white is regularly linked with positive images, while the colour black most frequently indicates the threat of evil:

> The street was a long black tongue
> reaching out of a widened gullet.
>
> like black leaves in an evil wind
> they fell, from another winter of the heart.
>
> the winds
> changed, favourable or black.[44]

Is Delius, then, the unconscious vehicle for the racism which, according to the black American, Ossie Davis,[45] is contained in the English language, and do South African prejudices weigh more heavily upon him than he realizes? If the reply is in the affirmative, it must be recognized that the numerical ratio between the races is not unconnected with the fear that the white feels for the black and the colour black, and that this fear is itself part of a whole range of prejudices and inhibitions borne by the collective unconscious and which extends beyond the purely South African context.

In the light of all these reservations, it is difficult to consider *Black South Easter* as constituting a constructive complement to *The Last Division*: the criticism contained in the latter work was much more challenging than this 'vision', which takes little account of reality and remains, in its very language, ambiguous. These reservations evaporate when one considers Delius's latest poem.

'Meditation on Main Street',[46] in fact, wins one's accord immediately: it is a short work – some 150 lines – in which the author seems once again to have found the 'objective correlative' which enables him to express at one and the same time his fears and his love for his country, which he had left ten years previously, but has often revisited and which is always present to him, even in London. However, although Delius evokes South Africa with sober, but powerful, lyricism –

> where else such noon or morning;
> such delicate and violet depth to drown
> the day in fathoms of intensity

– his attachment comes through more strongly than it would if it were expressed simply through the celebration of the nature he loves: the people of his country, especially those who are oppressed, are strangely present in the poem. There is no plot, only a meditation, as the title indicates, occurring between two questions put to the powerful mining magnate of Anglo-American, Harry Oppenheimer, a passing back and forth between past and present, and the problem that has preoccupied Delius since 'Time in Africa': how to bring forth from the depths of the past a viable future *for everyone*.[47]

It is not by chance that the setting is Johannesburg: this city that mushroomed into existence barely eighty years ago – hence the phrase 'shallow past' used to evoke its history – is the symbol of the great industrial metropolis where live side by side, but purely ephemerally, financiers, managing directors and face workers. Delius has long seen Johannesburg in terms of this three-level cross-section: the skyscrapers, the domain of the executives; ground level, teeming with the multicoloured crowds; and the underground, where the miners work.

For Delius, however, the symbol of Johannesburg is also that of a country which should belong to all its inhabitants. A State, here invisible but omnipresent, has decided otherwise, and the evening trains carry away the black workers, who are forbidden to be in the city, except during the day. It is in this rejection, in this daily repeated expulsion, that the fault which contains the seeds of future disaster lies. According to Delius, in fact, the rejecter will one day be the rejected. And he evokes Solomon's judgement, here mercilessly pushed to its conclusion by the 'bad mother':

> Darkness comes three times –
>   for the regular thunder,
> also at the day's end,
>   then – some sudden news of war,
> calamity? – the trains
>   fill with black fugitives,
> not in the home-going of other cities,
> this is the law, decreed time of madness,
> state-appointed hour of rejection,
> the judgement when the child is cut in half:
> third clang of darkness is an angelus
> bringing sleep but no rest, and no amen.

The religious references are not unintentional; they emphasize the idea that sin has been committed. The warning that thunder is on its way is also justified: this thunder may be described as 'regular', but there is another fast approaching, it seems – the thunder of the conflagrations frequently prophesied.

Delius's argument is presented entirely, in fact, in terms of Time, which works inexorably against those who refuse to share. The land belongs to everyone, Delius says; bones mingle there as finally and as indissolubly as the drowned of all nations, races and colours mingled beneath the sea in *Black South Easter*. The same idea is taken up again here, but much more convincingly:

> Dumps of sand lie heavy
>   on Paul Kruger's bones,
> the shade of Sekukuni*
>   whistles in abandoned shafts.
> Old freedom-fighters still
>   your warriors and horsemen
> search for abiding homelands in our past.

Then, spontaneously, Delius uses an image which the black poet Sepamla also used, as we shall see later, at about the same time:

> The here and now of future history
> plays blues for both in a late afternoon
> shebeen. Whatever loyalties the trumpet
> pleads with, the wooden horse is time.

Hence his anguished plea:

> Listen, Johannesburg,
>   listen my childhood,
> heart needs horizon
>   as horizon heart,
> invert us as you will
>   the rough world rights itself.
> Who is rejected in turn rejects
> though victory is always a disaster.

A fine poem, in which generosity and clear-sightedness go hand in hand with the accuracy of the images and the symbols. With quiet lyricism, Delius expresses the ideas that preoccupy him; a prophet in his way, nearer in age, style and philosophy to Paton than to Horn or Jensma, but a prophet all the same, and a long-standing one. Hence the appeal to reason which the poet as Tiresias makes, knowing full well that no one will listen. And if he addresses it essentially to Oppenheimer and, through him, to the country's leading businessmen, it is because he believes that it is they who are the true supporters of the regime, and that it is they who are the real pressure groups:

---

* Sekukuni: chief of the Bapedi, a tribe from the Northern Transvaal.

The Limits of Liberal Thought

And here's my question—
      can it be forgiven
this profligate tearing
      out of heart and rock?
It's the cloud's shadow now,
      and the ground trembles
as we tremble at foreknowing buried
deep inside ourselves. Grey flanks of buildings
stand about us, a high sad trumpeting
darkens the air. Oh Mr Oppenheimer
mahout of these concrete elephants which way
now to escape the lightning? It will surely
strike somewhere out of these loving skies.

Clearly, Delius has not said his last word. When he retired from the BBC in 1976, he published a long historical epistolary novel, entitled *Border*, dealing with the 1820 settlers from Britain, as well as a poem, 'The Island', which evokes the prison island where the black detainees are held in captivity.[48] Delius has been awarded the Thomas Pringle Prize for his work as a whole; rarely has a literary reward been so completely in accord with the man whose ideas and talent it confirms.

Notes

1. Paton was 45 when *Cry, the Beloved Country* appeared, published in England by Jonathan Cape and in the United States by Scribner & Sons. The edition used here is the one published by Penguin, London, 1958.
2. David Philip, Cape Town, 1973. Paton continues writing articles in *Reality*, a journal which reflects liberal opinions.
3. *Knocking on the Door* (David Philip, Cape Town, 1975), p. 142.
4. The full title is: *Kontakion for You Departed* (Jonathan Cape, London, 1969).
5. *Debbie Go Home*, collection of short stories (Jonathan Cape, London, 1961), published in the United States under the title *Tales from a Troubled Land*. *Sponono* is a play in three acts (written in collaboration with Krishna Shah) based on three of the short stories from this collection.

   Contact was the newspaper published by the Liberal Party and was closely associated with the life of the party from 1958 to 1966.
6. *Christian Unity* and *Meditation* were republished in *Knocking on the Door*, op. cit. *Instrument of Thy Peace*, Fontana, London.
7. Pieter van Vlaanderen is the central character in *Too Late the Phalarope* (Jonathan Cape, London, 1953), the second of Paton's novels with an Afrikaner setting.
8. Carisbrooke is English; Umzimkulu, Ingeli, titihoya are African; veld and Drakensberg are Afrikaans. Note, too, that 'East Griqualand' brings in the Coloured community. The only absentee from this 'ecumenical' list is the Indian community, missing, too, from the 'author's note' at the beginning of the book; this omission is all the more incomprehensible in view of Paton's friendship for the Indians, about whom he has written very sympathetically elsewhere in his work (see *Knocking on the Door*, op. cit.).
9. In 1949, under the title *Lost in the Stars*. Another adaptation, in verse, and again for the theatre, was performed in London in February 1954; it was the joint work of Felicia Komai and J. Douglas.
10. See *Cry, the Beloved Country*, op. cit., pp. 71, 89.

11. This term is used by several black writers, sometimes pejoratively, to describe Paton's novel. See, especially: Es'kia Mphahlele, *The African Image* (Faber, London, 1962 and 1974); Lewis Nkosi, *Home and Exile* (Longman, London, 1965); David Rubadiri, 'Why African Literature', in *African Writers on African Writing* (Heinemann, London, 1972).
12. *Cry, the Beloved Country*, op. cit., pp. 56–7.
13. Whereas Cosmo Pieterse accuses Paton of watering down the message contained in *Cry, the Beloved Country* through excessive lyricism, Malcolm Muggeridge argues that it is not possible to describe Paton's imaginative writing as 'fiction' for, he says, 'although Paton invents characters and situations, he is essentially a poet rather than a novelist; more a saint than either, maybe. An earthly saint, as poets are; in his case, rooted in the South African country-side he describes so enchantingly'. (Foreword to *Instrument of Thy Peace*, op. cit.).
14. *Cry, the Beloved Country*, op. cit., p. 12.
15. ibid., p. 164.
16. *Knocking on the Door*, op. cit., pp. 118–21.
17. ibid., p. 115.
18. ibid., pp. 8–9.
19. ibid., p. 12.
20. ibid., pp. 82–3.
21. *The Last Division* (Human & Rousseau, Cape Town, 1959). Referred to as *TLD* in these notes.
    An Unknown Border (Balkema, Cape Town and Amsterdam, 1954).
    A Corner of the World (Human & Rousseau, Cape Town, 1962).
    Black South Easter (*New Coin*, Rhodes University, n.d.). Referred to as *BSE* in these notes.
    The first two collections are currently out of print.
22. *TLD*, p. 22.
23. The events in Cyprus occupied the whole of the fifties.
24. *TLD*, pp. 30–1.
25. An Afrikaans portmanteau word, which Delius himself translates as 'forcely learned'.
26. *TLD*, p. 32.
27. ibid., p. 34.
28. ibid., p. 43.
29. ibid., p. 54.
30. ibid., p. 23.
31. ibid., pp. 47–8.
32. ibid., pp. 47–8.
33. Although it would be a mistake to oversimplify, for by the introduction of Arthur Jarvis's journal Paton introduces a reflective element which is directed at his readers' intelligence.
34. *A Corner of the World*, op. cit., p. 68.
35. See *An Unknown Border*, op. cit., p. 7.
36. *TLD*, p. 26.
37. *BSE*, p. 6.
38. ibid., p. 7.
39. ibid., p. 9. Delius developed this theme in a long poem, 'The Possessor' (in *A Corner of the World*, op. cit., pp. 46–56).
40. *BSE*, p. 4.
41. On the occasion of Arthur Jarvis's funeral, his father mingles with blacks for the first time, and shakes hands with them. In fact, all colours and communities are represented: this scene is of great importance to Paton, and is essentially a barely fictionalized account of a similar event which occurred on the death of a white South African woman who was greatly loved by the black people, with whom she had frequent contact. (See especially 'A Deep Experience', reprinted in *The Long View*, ed. E. Callan, Praeger, London, 1968.)
42. 'The moment when the poetic imagination transforms *history* into myth is an exciting one in the growth of a literature' (Editorial). A slanted view of history, then.

43. Evidenced by the first reference to Makana in *BSE*, p. 2: 'I thought of *black* Makana on his rock'. Black South Africans know who Makana is and the rest should know as well, if he is part of South African history – but he does not belong to *their* history!
44. *BSE*, pp. 2, 3, 5. Delius does, however, reverse the equation white=good, black=bad, when he has Makana speak (*BSE*, p. 7).
45. An article by the American actor, Ossie Davis, which reproduces a lecture he had given to American teachers, is entitled: 'The English language is my enemy' (in *The American Teacher*, April 1967). The author quotes, in supporting his argument, Roget's *Thesaurus of the English Language*, where 'blackness' has 120 synonyms, 60 of which are obviously pejorative and none positive.
46. *Contrast 37*, Spring 1975, pp. 6–10.
47. In *An Unknown Border*, op. cit.
48. *Border, A Novel* (David Philip, Cape Town, 1976). 'The Island', in 'Poetry against Apartheid', *The Transatlantic Review*, February 1976.

Chapter 6
Total Commitment: Lewin and Evans

▼▼▼▼▼▼▼▼▼▼▼▼▼▼▼▼▼▼▼▼▼▼▼▼▼▼▼▼▼

Hugh Lewin and David Evans are the heirs of the liberal ideal as it was incarnated for the first time in literature in the hero of Cry, the Beloved Country, Arthur Jarvis. But they have been luckier than he: they were not 'killed' by their creator before they had the chance to commit themselves totally to what seemed to them to be a just cause.

The hero to whom Paton has given life but whose shadow is all that flits through the book enjoys, as a white man, all the privileges of his society. But he quickly discovers that the South African reality that his parents enabled him to discover is only part of the picture and that he knows nothing, or next to nothing, about the other members of the South African society: the Afrikaners and the men and women of the black communities.

He delves therefore into the history of his country and seeks to find out more about its inhabitants. Realizing the appalling destruction of tribal society as a result of industrialization and forced labour, he tries to relieve the blacks of some of the evils that beset them through his activities in the social and health spheres. But he is murdered, entirely fortuitously, by a group of tsotsis, before he gets the chance to carry the struggle into the political arena, where he senses the real battle must be waged.

The writings his father finds after his death – fragments of a personal diary, articles, social projects – move the old man deeply, and he realizes that the Christian education he has given his son was very limited, more pious than real. James Jarvis, converted by his son's example, devotes his wealth and the rest of his life to activities that bring great benefit to the Africans who have lived in poverty in the valley alongside his home without his ever knowing them.

The essential message Paton, via Arthur Jarvis, bequeathed, as it were, to the people of his country, before partially conforming to it himself during the course of his political life, is contained in the lines that follow. There can be no doubt that it was these words that prompted the actions of David Evans and Hugh Lewin and which continue to act as an inspiration for others like them:

> Therefore I shall devote myself, my time, my energy, my talents, to the service of South Africa. I shall no longer ask myself if this or that is expedient but only if it is right. I shall do this, not because I am noble and unselfish, but because life slips away, and because I need for the rest of my journey a star that will not play false to me, a compass that will not lie. I shall do this not because I am a Negrophile and a hater of my own, but because I cannot find it in me to do anything else.[1]

Biographical summary

DAVID EVANS was born in 1935 into a family belonging to the English-speaking community in the Cape Province. His father, a clerk, had served during the First World War and traditionally voted for General Smuts's party.

Having completed his secondary schooling, Evans began his career as a journalist. His professional activities led him to cover a meeting of the ANC at which Chief Luthuli spoke, displaying considerable ability and authority. This was the first time Evans had met blacks of his own intellectual level: this 'shock encounter' led him to try and make contact with them and to get to know them better. Still in his capacity as a journalist, he visited Southern and Northern Rhodesia; he realized the failure of the so-called policy of partnership between these two countries with radically different racial policies.

At the time of the Treason Trial, Evans went to work in Durban and soon joined the Liberal Party.

His association with black nationalists and whites belonging to groups politically opposed to apartheid, especially the Communists, caused difficulties with his paper, which he left to go and work with the more liberal *Evening Post* in Port Elizabeth. Here he became friendly with Dennis Brutus. It was the time of the emergency: Evans realized he could not continue as a journalist since it prevented him from telling the whole truth. He then went to work with Alan Paton, who was preparing his biography of Hofmeyr, and acted for a while as his secretary.

For long a supporter of non-violence, he eventually joined a clandestine group which committed acts of sabotage. First his freedom of speech and movement was restricted when he was accused of political agitation, and he was finally arrested after John Harris's bombing; he was sentenced to five years in prison at the end of the trial. During his detention, Evans studied for a university degree by correspondence, completing it at Oxford after his release in 1969.

Evans has settled in England; he has taught there and at present holds a full-time teaching post in one of the working-class areas of Liverpool. In 1973 he denied that he was a Communist, describing himself as a left-wing humanist, but said he was convinced, however, that young South African liberals ought to have allied themselves with the Communists. He criticized Christians like Paton for their passivity, their inability to reconcile the world of ideas with the world of action, which is what he had tried to do. He has followed the poems written in prison with other writings: love poems, 'not *poésie engagée* at all, unless love is a commitment, too', a novel and plays, all still unpublished, except for some of his poems.

HUGH LEWIN's 'itinerary' closely resembles that followed by David Evans: both born at almost the same time into white families whose only contacts with black people were those of the master–servant relationship, they both came, but by different routes, to an *in depth* understanding of the nature of the racial problem.

Lewin was born in 1939 in the Transvaal. His father, an Anglican priest, intended him for the priesthood and sent him to a private school (white, naturally) in Johannesburg. It was here that, a few years later, the young man met Father Trevor Huddleston, the Father Beresford of *Cry, the Beloved Country*. Thanks to him, he gained access to a mini-society in which the term brotherly love really meant something. The religious community directed and run by Huddleston was doing a great deal to relieve the misery of Sophiatown, and it opposed, albeit unsuccessfully, the eviction of the blacks from this township. Lewin observed these struggles at close hand and Huddleston, whom he saw frequently, acted as his confessor.

In 1958, Lewin entered Rhodes University, Grahamstown, where he obtained his BA three years later. Very soon, the young man became involved in NUSAS and took an active part in the demonstrations organized by the students to protest against the closing of Fort Hare.

Lewin joined the Liberal Party at this time and met Evans, who had become regional vice-chairman of the Party. He later declared:

> After university I continued to do what I could to focus attention on the laws which I felt prevented Africans from living a full and proper life. But my efforts seemed puny and hopeless. It seemed that nothing would awaken the Whites. At about this time I was approached by a friend who asked me to become a member of the 'National Committee for Liberation', a secret sabotage group. My lord, I was terrified. Instinctively I was opposed to any form of violence and I knew that I was not suitable to the active role I was being asked to play. In spite of this I decided to join.[2]

His membership of the NCL, which had meanwhile become the ARM (African Resistance Movement), lasted eighteen months, during which he took part in three sabotage operations, all against installations. It was he who was given the job of recruiting John Harris, whose indiscipline led to the bombing which caused the only victims of their activities. He was arrested in July 1964, only a few days after the bombing and when the ARM had decided to suspend activities which had proved ineffective. The Special Branch accused him of organizing the bombing and he was beaten by his interrogators. At the end of the trial, he was sentenced to seven and a half years in prison, where he met up again with his friend Evans.

Released in 1972, he left for London, where he resumed his career as a journalist, first with the *Observer*, then with *Drum*, after a period with the International Defence and Aid Fund. He now lives and works in Zimbabwe.

He published a few poems in journals, but in 1974 he published his main work, *Bandiet*, subtitled 'Seven Years in a South African Jail', which is an account of his detention at the central prison in Pretoria. Lewin had there found himself in the company of twenty-six other white political detainees (the blacks arrested because of their opposition or overt resistance are detained on Robben Island). Among his fellow prisoners were sixteen members of the Communist Party; there were twelve Jews. None of the prisoners was from the working class. His sober, but moving, account covers all aspects of prison life; the figures of his fellow detainees appear frequently, especially those of Dennis Goldberg, Evans and Bram Fischer. Warders, informers and interrogators complete the picture. Some of the most striking scenes recur in some of the poems discussed below. *Bandiet* is the work of a white South African who, through his opposition to them, has born genuine witness against his country's racial policies. It is this characteristic, and the generosity of his attitudes, that justify placing this book alongside Brutus's prose account of his own imprisonment on Robben Island.

Presentation of the poems

Each of Lewin's poems tells a story, whether it concerns him directly or not. He relates it soberly, advancing his narrative by the repetition of words or phrases, which builds up to what is usually a fairly abrupt conclusion. This repetition also has a poetic function already noted in the prose and verse of Paton; it serves to achieve a gradual release from tension or violence, which Paton and Lewin both abhor.

Thus 'The Wedding' is a very simple account of a completely unnewsworthy event which reveals, nevertheless, all the harshness and inhumanity of the South African laws. An Indian, Solly Nathee, who has been forbidden by an injunction from the Minister of the Interior from participating in any gathering of more than three persons, is able to attend his daughter's wedding only by watching it from the top of a hill near his home. Two police officers have been sent to ensure that he respects the law. It is only one at a time, as we learn at the end of the poem, that the guests can come and shake hands with the bride's father.[3]

In 'Japhta' (unpublished), Lewin is more prolix because he has more to say, although Japhta's life is summed up in two pages. Japhta Majola, a shepherd in his home tribe, has bettered himself by sheer determination: he has learnt to read and write, gone from school to Fort Hare University to fulfil his ambition to become a teacher. However, one year after the implementation of the Nationalist legislation on higher education, and when he has finally achieved his goal, Japhta commits suicide. The poem tells why.

Japhta, explains Lewin, who had clearly met him while at Rhodes University, which is Fort Hare's neighbour, was well known for his moderation and his sense of fairness, and had been elected by his fellow students as President of the Students' Representative Council. Japhta also had a sense of dignity: when the police invaded Fort Hare in order to expel the students protesting against the new legislation, Japhta the moderate, 'Majola the Just', said 'No!' This 'no' was enough, in the eyes of South African law, to make him an agitator:

> Japhta Majola, herd-boy, student, teacher – one year
>   after becoming a teacher – committed suicide.
> Why? Ask why? Ask. You must ask – why?
> And, in asking, imagine what it is to be a herd-boy on
>   the hills, who dreams of becoming a student – to become
>   a student, who dreams of becoming a teacher – to become
>   a teacher, and to be banned
>   from teaching.
> Banned. Restricted. Prohibited from teaching,
>   anything,
>   anywhere.
> Japhta Majola, teacher who would teach, should have
>   lived and taught.
> He died, aged 26.
> Ask why.

Poems depicting the evils of apartheid, such as 'The Wedding' and 'Japhta', are the most polished and come off best. 'A New Pieta', which is an attempt to look at the sculptural potential of black woman through the eyes of Michelangelo, fails because of its rhetoric and lack of originality. One is inclined to prefer a poem like 'Carpenter', in which Lewin, the Anglican, modernizes the theme of the Crucifixion with great conciseness, as Paton had done before him and as Horn and Jensma were to do after him.[4]

A second group of poems deals with his prison experience as such. They have the impact of the fists that struck his face. The sentences are short, almost prosaic: this is not 'literature'. The poems present the experience in its raw state and are an account of a life typified by peremptory orders and insensitivity, by the simple solidarity of the prisoners among themselves.

'Another Day' is dedicated to Bram Fischer, and the poem begins with this summary of a prison day:

> It was like any other day
> from unlock
> breakfast/wash-up/scrub/clean
> garden/lunch
> lock-up
> wash-up/scrub/clean
> shower/4 p.m. supper
> lock-up
> till un-lock next morning
> any day every day
> 14-hour lock-up
> every night.[5]

These documentary details are not gratuitous, for 'Another Day' is an account of the day when Bram Fischer was told, in the prison visiting-room, that his son, who had been seriously ill since childhood and had been kept alive by his parents' devoted care until he went to university, had died suddenly. And he had to go back to his cell, where he remained for fourteen hours (the '14-hour lock-up/every night') on his own. Nothing else: a day, in fact, like every other day; the law allows no exceptions.

Apart from 'Condemneds', which evokes the atmosphere of the prison's death row, through which Lewin had to pass every day (there were on average six executions a week), the other poems are linked to Lewin's personal experience. Three poems stand out: 'On Friday, 24 July 1964', 'Touch' and 'Three Friends'. The first describes the extremely violent interrogation to which he was subjected on that day (the same day as Harris's bomb attempt), for the police were determined to make him 'talk'. The poem evokes this interrogation, as if recorded on tape; it telescopes the interrogators' abuse, snatches of personal thoughts, the hammering of the blows, the synaesthetic impressions of the prisoner as he takes his 'punishment' and on whose mind, opposed as he is to violence, the scene has remained engraved. The narrative ends on an anticlimax: in the room above the one in which Lewin is being questioned, and from which has come the sound of blows and screams, John Harris has finally confessed.[6]

'Touch' is closely linked to 'On Friday . . .': Lewin lays himself bare to an extent that very seldom exists in prison literature; the emotion the poem evokes is, for that reason, perhaps, so much the greater. For he, the untouchable, but not the untouched, asks to be allowed to rediscover real human contact:

> When I get out
> I'm going to ask someone
> to touch me
> very gently please

>   and slowly,
>   touch me
>   I want
>   to learn again
>   how life feels.⁷

Finally, 'Three Friends' is a long poem in which Lewin reminisces aloud about his trial and interrogation, which remained vividly impressed on his mind for a long time: why are the three friends who have come in turn to give evidence *against* him in the witness box and not in the dock with him? Slowly the answer dawns on him; there is room for only one person in the dock.

This last idea which, in the context of the resistance to white policies, shows what solidarity really is, recurs in 'Song of the Shrine' (unpublished), which reveals another side of Lewin's poetry. It is, in fact, an account of one of the acts of sabotage in which he took part, written in prison and smuggled out. Few such actions have been related with such lyricism, but also with such simplicity; the event is presented just as it was lived; the unpretentious style of the narrative evokes the euphoria of the act itself, inviting the reader to share in it after the event, and conveys a certain grandeur already suggested by the title:

>   You can't stop now
>   so go in
>   bowed, silent
>   beneath the arching beams.
>   And the throbbing is in the ground
>   and in the sky all around
>
>   and the pylon legs so firm, so strong,
>   solid and immoveable
>   waiting impassively watching
>   indifferent.
>   Your packets so small:
>   mean gifts for a king.
>   . . .
>
>   Unburdened
>   you look up
>   before the last connecting
>   up
>   of King Pylon.
>   Tall,
>   indifferent.
>   (Big bastard isn't it?)
>
>   Set?
>   If we're wrong anywhere
>   it'll go now – and all of us
>   Set. Now
>   plug
>   carefully
>   in.

> And above the throbbing hum
> you can feel a quiet ticking –
> and the grass seeds begin to itch.
>
> We're not wrong.
> Right.
> Let's go.
>
> Tomorrow morning, you're going to fall big boy.

Thus, these few works, of which only the prose of *Bandiet* is available to the general public, contain the expression of a very personal temperament. Lewin's inspiration does not pass through a cultural prism, it is not the slave of a tradition, nor does it create one. What counts for him is the need to say what happened in the fewest possible words and in the truest possible way: 'to say it as it is' could well be the motto of a man whose essential quality, rare among adults these days, is his purity.

Evans has the same purity, but his approach is different; an older man, his literary maturity is also greater. He who, before his imprisonment, had, on his own admission, never composed anything more than doggerel verse for his friends, found that poetry was the medium that suited him best in his own situation. He wrote 'Love Poem 66' for his wife and smuggled it out of prison; the poem then found its way to London, where it was published under the initials D. E. in Canon Collins's *Christian Action Newsletter* (Autumn 1967).

The first stanza of 'Love Poem 66' provides the keynote for all of Evans's poems: it is less the event itself that interests him than its hidden meaning:

> It takes the dark to make me see.
> The daytime eye (being blind to all but fact)
> Sees just the gate, the bars, the walls,
> and not beyond.
> But night reveals
> Fugitive truths that hide by day,
> The lighted stage that once loomed like a world.

His poems are therefore essentially poems of revelation. They are without mysticism, however; they function rather through the discovery of symbols that illuminate the action, give it its real meaning and incorporate it in a 'history' which transcends the poet's personal adventure.

The myth of Prometheus is applied to the solitary prisoner tormented by his interrogators who come, one by one, to force him to give up his secrets, their patience equalled only by their imperturbable cruelty. For he, too, has defied the Gods, those who hold the Power; he has stolen from them fire, arms and explosives, and this fire transmitted to others is the spirit of resistance. Thus in almost exactly the same terms, 'Prometheus 70' once again takes up the theme announced at the end of 'Love Poem 66': '. . . I am not here to meet the entered debts/Prometheus paid them high upon the crag . . .'

Here, the narrative thread is barely visible; it is almost entirely dissolved in an atmosphere of nightmare, in which the night of the cell seeks to dominate the spirit, and the hectoring of the investigators mingles with the muddled thoughts

Total Commitment: Lewin and Evans

caused by the loneliness, while like a litany recurs the demand: 'Recant', which would release him from his misery:

> Girls
> come in their mini-skirts
> their smooth thighs moist for love;
> he feels paps soft upon his chest
> the sweet sap swell his horn
> hears the whispers in his ear . . .
> Recant . . .
>
> Hermes
> comes
> the messenger
> soft-footed in his brown-suede shoes
> exit permit in his hand:
> We drank together at the club
> you've only got to say the word
> sign here on the dotted line.
> Recant.
>
> Prometheus
> writhes against the rock
> teeth-torn lips spit out a groan
> I can't.

Nothing could be further from the spectacular, the sensational or the purely circumstantial: a lay 'passion' like Looksmart's.[8] There is no question of betrayal, because Evans is not alone:

> Herakles
> is far away
> beyond the reach of telegram
> while silent on the folded plains
> the unseen people
> seem to sleep.
>
> But
> smouldering in a sullen town
> a hut-fire gleams
> flares
> disappears.
> Prometheus
> endures.

This renunciation contains an act of love, and this is the second key to Evans's poetry, so much so that all his poems could be called love poems. 'Love Poem 66' is essentially a letter in verse in which Evans asks his wife's forgiveness for exposing her to having to face adversity alone. Significantly, Evans does not for a moment lament his own fate, but his wife's. For, paradoxically, it is the prisoner who is safe, and in order to explain this, Evans turns to a semi-religious vocabulary:

> Did I say safe? Yes, safe
> From sudden swoop of either right or wrong,
> Reluctant monks within our cloistered walls.
> You must be free to sin.

Then follows a fine love song, very classical in its conception. After comparing the caged bird he is to the free bird who 'with futile wings/frail flesh and bone and feather/flay[s] the mesh that traps the fluttered mate/ and fall[s]', Evans cries out:

> And you, my darling, cruelly locked outside
> What words are there to still the flapping heart?
> What hand to stroke tired feathers tinged with grey?
> What lips to soothe the itching of the skin?
> Not mine; not yet.

The poem ends with a plea to his wife:

> And as the soft dark hardens into day
> I can absolve – if you absolve in turn.

Another love poem inspired by his prison experience is 'Prison Visit' (unpublished). Here Evans uses the extended metaphor of the aquarium to represent in concrete terms the distance that separates him from his wife who has come to see him. The plexiglass partition barely allows the voice to pass through it and distorts faces and human shapes, hence the image of two fish which remain in two separate worlds, while the sharks swim about in the background.

The men Evans writes about in another series of poems are those who have managed to cope with the separation from their loved ones or who, on the contrary, have 'cracked'.

Among the first: Bram Fischer, again, and Dennis Goldberg, another of those convicted at the Rivonia trial, militants and therefore brothers in a common cause. It is from the great spirit of solidarity these two have patiently helped to build up all round them until it is real to them all that the detainees draw the moral resources they need to keep going for years on end – in some cases for the rest of their lives.

On the other hand, the political commitment which would have been their salvation was clearly missing from the lives of Nakasa and Nortje, to whom other poems are dedicated. This is the conclusion Evans reaches, but this does not prevent him from stressing the terrible solitude of the political exiles, uprooted in this way:

> And then,
> Nat,
> you learned,
> – if you had need to learn –
> exile was not escape.
> But only the sundering apartheid
> of self from self.
> The denying signs were there
> in private faces.

The political exile, in fact, is doubly in need of love, and he dies, too, from the indifference and selfishness of others. This explains why, at the end of a section in which he has invoked each of the American civil rights leaders in turn, Evans cries:

> The richest city of them all was not rich enough
> to keep one young man alive.[9]

In the poem dedicated to Nortje, the first version of which was read at the poet's funeral by Evans himself,[10] a greater distancing has been achieved, and Evans's meditation, while intensely lyrical, is also more serene. It leads him to reflect on the death of poets, as his 'If Poets must have Flags' was to be a meditation on their lives and art. While the poets who have died will be missed because they helped others to understand the world in its essence and as it reveals itself, those who only sing about what is beautiful and forget the ugliness and cruelty of the world will not fit into the global and non-reassuring vision of Art which Evans favours.

Finally, this man of high ideals, who, with the modesty of all true heroes, was little inclined to play at being a martyr for the cause, who had such a high conception of commitment that afterwards he refused to seek honour or profit from it, this man brings us back to the tensions that lie beneath the surface of all liberalism. Evans's present work seems to indicate that he is tending, not towards reconciliation as preached by the liberals even at the time of Soweto, a reconciliation between the sheep and the wolf which could only prepare the sheep for being eaten *with greater dignity*, but towards a true restructuring of society which would effectively vindicate the sacrifice of those who lost their lives. 'Revolution' and 'revelation' are ultimately synonymous for Evans, and in this the faithful successor of Arthur Jarvis prepares the way for Jensma and Matthews:

> They
> ask the poet to be
> a songbird in a cage
> a eunuch in a choir
> a slave of art
> manacling his anguish
> in tinkling silver chains
>
> We refuse.
>
> We'll go ugly and free
> exhuming the corpses
> releasing the rot
> revealing the holes
> ripped by the shot.
> We'll wrap around our banners
> the guts of the dead
>
> – if we must have flags
> let them always be red.[11]

Neither Lewin nor Evans regrets what he has done: they are not fanatics or hotheads, and the judgement expressed by Trevor Huddleston, then Bishop of Stepney, in his preface to *Bandiet* ('No one reading this book could miss the shining quality of the author's character'), is as valid for Evans as it is for Lewin.

In fact, these two men have done no more than apply, to the letter, the teachings of Paton himself, first in *Cry, the Beloved Country*, then after the creation of the Liberal Party and from 1958 at political meetings and in *Contact*, where he declared on one occasion:

> Where will we [the Liberals] be found? Counselling moderation in all things? God forbid. There can be no moderation in justice, mercy, and truth. They are what they are.
>
> One of our clear and insistent duties, and one which we have already accepted in the past, is to uphold the values of decent and civilized life, and the dignity of persons. These, being values of life, must be upheld in living, not only in speeches and sermons.[12]

Cut off from the rest of the world during their years in prison, Evans and Lewin are the turning point of the sixties and seventies, and it is far from certain that they did the immeasurable harm to the liberal cause of which Paton accused them at the time: by 1968, the days of traditional liberalism were numbered. Certainly, Paton and others from all the communities continued to be active, particularly at the South African Institute of Race Relations (SAIRR). But the most militant blacks were then on the verge of rejecting their gradualism and, finally, their braking role on black nationalist aspirations. Perhaps the polarization intended by apartheid was responsible for the inevitable failure of this tendency: a group aiming simply at exerting moral pressure could never become the third force it wanted to be. Evans, Lewin and a handful of whites, among them the eminent figure of Bram Fischer, were in fact preparing for a South Africa in which political action would not be based on the gulf between whites and blacks, but would occur at the level of battle between democrats, once apartheid had been abolished and all 'colours' and communities had been blended.

The writings of Evans and Lewin are by no means the only ones young liberals have contributed to their country; nor are theirs the most important. It is, however, the only writing[13] which has gone hand in hand with a total commitment, the only writing among the whites which has grown out of a direct experience of resistance to apartheid and the South African gaols. It is the only writing, finally, which has taken the form of poetry, and for this reason it constitutes a kind of postscript to the momentous early sixties for which we had only so far had the witness of the Coloured poet, Dennis Brutus.

Notes

1. *Cry, the Beloved Country* (Penguin, London, 1958), p. 151.
2. Statement made to the court during his trial in November 1964 and reproduced in *Bandiet* (Heinemann, London, 1984), p. 12.
3. Reproduced in *Poets to the People: South African Freedom Poems* (Heinemann, London, 1980), p. 81.
4. Paton, in *Knocking on the Door* p. 81; Horn, *Walking through our Sleep* (Ravan Press, Johannesburg, 1974), p. 41; Jensma, *Sing for our Execution* (Ravan Press, Johannesburg, 1973), p. 96.
5. *Poets to the People*, op. cit., p. 82–4.

6.   He was standing
      in front of me
      shouting – Jew bastard –
      You Jew bastard –
      which, as he well knew by then,
      was incorrect on both counts.
      Still he stood in front of me
      screaming
      – Jew bastard you Jew bastard
      I'll kill you –
      and a lot of additional filth
      about my mother, my grandmother
      all of it irrelevant
      The generations talked that night
      the generations screamed
      from the depth of the hulk
      in front of me
      screaming
      – Jew bastard Jew I'll kill you I'll kill you . . .

      (Unpublished.)

7. *Poets to the People*, op. cit., pp. 84–5.
8. See the study on Pieterse, below.
9. 'Threnody for a young man who committed suicide in New York' (unpublished).
10. See 'Conclusion and Evaluations', below.
11. *Poets to the People*, op. cit., pp. 20–1.
12. Statement made in 1958 and republished in *The Long View* (ed. E. Callan, Praeger, London, 1968), p. 72.
13. With that of C. J. Driver, who has written poetry (in Pieterse, *Seven South African Poets*, Heinemann, London, 1974), two novels (*Elegy for a Revolutionary*, Penguin, London, 1969; *Send War in our Time, O Lord*, Faber, London, 1971), and critical articles.

Chapter 7
The New Prophets

▼▼▼▼▼▼▼▼▼▼▼▼▼▼▼▼▼▼▼▼▼▼▼▼▼▼▼▼▼▼▼▼▼▼

The writings of Wopko Jensma and Peter Horn attest to the continuation of the white liberal voice. Their poetry, like that which was published in Ophir, *has become more violent in its denunciation of abuses, more vehement in its criticism of South African society, more direct in the expression of its likes and dislikes. Sign of the times: the language has changed, and the poetic style, too. Delius's classicism has been succeeded by a freeing of rhyme and structure, language has become more that of the man-in-the-street, even in the poetry of Peter Horn, an academic like Guy Butler. Can we attribute this new freedom to the fact that Horn and Jensma are of more recent South African stock and, as a result, perhaps more open, more daring, less slaves of a tradition whose constraints they have not experienced? This explanation is not enough: we must see in this new tendency the influence of currents of thought external to South Africa, but even more, certainly, the result of the growing impact of the political on the cultural.*

A change of tone, then, and a widening of horizons: social and political elements take precedence over description and attempts to identify with the South African countryside, while the more introspective poems reflect the preoccupations of people living in a society granted only to a small privileged group. There is also the increasingly apocalyptic vision of a violent future felt to be fast approaching, the expression of a society suffering from schizophrenia. There are other indications besides these two which lead one to refer to these poets as new 'prophets'.

Prophets are born in times when the world is perverted, when some turn away from the way laid down by God or simple morality. Addressing the leaders and policy-makers who have made themselves immensely powerful, and especially the citizens who have handed over to them their authority, the new prophets, as Paton had done twenty-five years previously, proclaim the urgent need for change and the poverty of a life based on constraint and fear.

Peter Horn

Totalitarian regimes have the citizens and poets they deserve, those who accept the bayonets upon which order is based and who, by their silence or useless chatter, make themselves the accomplices of those who rule. Peter Horn[1] is not one of these: he has chosen to be on the side of the oppressed, on the side of the future, of the dream of a multiracial society; in short, on the side of freedom. Making the most of his double privilege as a white and a poet in a country in which the whites are the masters and poetry the last remaining freedom, he challenges his fellow citizens, upbraids them relentlessly and prophesies the bad times ahead. Or else, slipping into their midst, he speaks on their behalf and says the things they do not dare to say out loud.

But there is also something of the strolling player about him, a mixture of the knock-about clown and the astrologer: of the first, he has the gift of the gab, of the turn of phrase that hits its mark, but there is seriousness beneath the wit. Like the astrologer, he invites his fellow citizens to read the signs of destiny written, not in the stars, but in their own actions, he draws on the symbols and myths that have the power to make apparent the latent tragedy of a situation on the verge of disaster and, using old fables and tales of other countries, he presents a theatre of shadows in which reality takes on fantastic and terrifying shapes.

Peter Horn is, in fact, anxious to change the society in which he lives and to show it to the outside world; if he has made himself its censor, it is because he wants to share in reshaping it.

At the same time, he constantly questions the value and effect of what he is doing. For, if he can say anything, or almost, who can listen to him and, especially, who is willing to listen to him? Is he perhaps allowed to speak out precisely in order to blunt the effect of his message? Does his freedom of expression put him in the category of people useful to the authorities, court jesters whose madness permits them to say anything because they are, in any case, irrational? This is how the problem of the power of poetry under a totalitarian regime could be expressed in concrete terms.[2]

Poems? You want poems? We got poems!

Thus begins 'Poems at Bargain Prices', with this line flung at the reader-listener. The poet–hustler, who seems to have set up his stall in the market place, has more than one poem in his bag: poems to help you to dream, poems to send you to sleep, poems that prevent the Sunday afternoon peace from being disturbed. Yet these are not the poems he likes best:

> Ah, you sleep?
> May you wake in peace!
> Because we got other poems.
> Poems which will disturb you
> With announcements of bloodshed,
> War, atrocities, atomic bombs and jails.
> Jails visible from the window
> Of your peaceful bedroom,
> Whenever you open the blinds.

There is no better way of defining oneself or of expressing more evocatively the elevated role one attributes to a poetry conceived, not as a soporific, but as a stimulator of sleeping consciences. This is certainly Peter Horn's aim in *Walking through our Sleep*, a collection of a little more than fifty poems which is addressed essentially to the white community. Twenty-five years after Paton, Horn returns to the theme of general blindness and imminent disaster; for, in spite of the prosperity, in spite of the silence of the slaves, the state of the country has deteriorated, South Africa has become a vast fortified camp in which the occupants live according to the law of the gun in a state of intellectual and moral poverty to which they are totally oblivious. In order to alert his fellow citizens, and also to inform the outside world, Horn has set himself the task of revealing above all a South Africa of which one is not generally aware.

To carry out his work of demystification, to start with, Horn substitutes an in-depth picture for the superficial reality of the publicity posters and the tourist brochures. 'Morning in Durban' is a development of the theme of the 'appearance and reality of the South African landscape'. The poem begins with a lively and happy description of the natural features which give the city its charm and which are much admired by the tourists. The sun, the bright light, never fail, and the sea, too, Horn tells us, 'rises with festive surf to greet the towering hotels/and cranes on the shore'.

The second stanza takes up the theme of natural beauty once more and sets it against the human activity. For Nature is only a décor and we know from Greek tragedy that a blue sky is by no means synonymous with peace and happiness:

> Beautiful, like rivers in flood, the widening streets
> carry the victims in cars and buses, a torrent of workers
> to ware-house and factory.
> Laughing policemen open and close the sluices.

These lines – a graphic description of alienation – emphasize the coexistence of beauty and suffering, while at the same time stressing that it is an organized and compartmentalized kind of society ('open and close the sluices'). The contrast between the fundamental inhumanity of this life and the laughing policemen whose job it is to ensure the maintenance of order accentuates the impression of an existence relentlessly geared to production and death.

The third and last stanza returns to the theme of Nature, which is now demystified, although Horn feels obliged to stress the 'lyrical illusion ' – the sky bends to 'caress' the sea and the trees – and to include an additional figure, a drunkard, who is the only one who does not share in the general process of mystification:

> Beautiful the blue sky under which the managers rise
> to their task . . .
> beautiful the blue sky under which hundreds will die of hunger.

Horn's second manner is to start from this apprehension and define a symbolic space and climate which create a new reality, at once unusual and disturbing, but whose elements are drawn from the daily life and which we only need the courage to look at in the face. 'Mobile' is reminiscent of the canvas of the Belgian Surrealist Paul Delvaux, in which the fantastic comes from the juxtaposition of the familiar and tangible with the unusual. It is the latter that creates a gap between the reality one is used to and the reality one suddenly perceives, a gap that provokes a feeling of unease, even anxiety:

> The confidence with which
> A man walks through the streets of this town
> Astonishes me: as if his feet
> Were treading on solid ground.

The use of slow motion intensifies the sensation of unreality. And yet, essentially,

Horn is once again treating the theme of blindness. For, in spite of appearances (once more), the ground is not firm: the rest of the poem, through the repetition of the question 'doesn't he see?' again stresses the blindness of the inhabitants of the town who fail to understand the 'signs' all around them:

> Rooted in the middle of the square
> I dare not move: I fear
> I might upset
> The delicate balance.

The overall burden of Horn's argument is that it is not the physical features of a country that reveal its soul, but the soul which transforms the landscape until the latter resembles it. Horn's picture of South Africa is one that has been adjusted so as to take the oppressed into account. Hence the cold, grey world, the twilight atmosphere that the poems depict, an absence of sun and warmth which is the very opposite of the usual picture of South Africa. Horn explains, in fact, that South Africa is only shown like this because this is the way people have wanted it, and he specifically names the guilty parties:

> You will ask me:
> what about the beautiful evening,
> calm and free? And is the fair and open face
> of heaven clouded by ideologies?
> Where are the blazing leaves of autumn trees
> and where the birds? The gorgeous bush shrike
> and the burning phoenix?
>
> Go look for them
> in the republic day address
> and in the balance sheet of Anglo-American,
> there you will find, advertising themselves,
> the mighty: Oppenheimer and Verwoerd.[3]

Thereafter, *Walking through our Sleep* develops like two ellipses which constantly cross one another: the one defining this new South African landscape, the other accusing those responsible for the disastrous transformation of a whole society. It is a highly symbolic landscape, with the symbolism acting as a stimulus for the imagination, but also developing into myth because it so vividly reflects the predominant characteristics of a society and its ideology.

To begin with, a space surrounded by barbed wire and divided into sections separated from one another by walls, fences and closed doors – a network of ghettos. This society is partitioned vertically as well as horizontally: at the top of the pyramid, are the invisible men from whom orders *that may not be questioned* emanate and who have at their disposition, to enforce them, a horde of policemen, informers and spies, in addition to the now indispensable executioners who must carry out the ever-increasing numbers of executions; right at the bottom, a people of troglodytes who only leave their caves or their shacks to do the work required of them; between these two, small groups of individuals who, in order to retain their privileges, are content to close their eyes, happy that someone else is willing to carry out the business of repression for them. A hypocritical society that betrays the religion to which it claims adherence. A society without a culture, or which is afraid of culture. A world without love.

It is not surprising, therefore, that the poet sees, in the tears shed around him and in the ashes scattered on the ground, the signs of a bloody future as the inevitable consequence of this heartless present:

> No heart this my heart is burnt out: see this
>   stagnating pool
> of black tears covered by ashes
> in the path of the future
> under the boots of the coming
> trampled to death
>   by friend and foe alike with
> no heart.[4]

It is a portrait etched in black, with very distinct lines. Horn can only be criticized for his Manichaean portrait of South African society if one forgets that this same society is so rigidly hierarchized that distinctions of colour totally outweigh those of class, wealth and education. Here the 'Them' and 'Us' dichotomy is that of white/black, rich/poor, oppressor/oppressed. If Horn adds to these poet/philistine, it is not only for good measure, but also because in this society poetry is worth no more than a can of beer.

Yet the depiction of this cold, grey world which has penetrated the very insides of the houses and colours even the most personal poems[5] gives the reader a feeling of unreality, as of something almost abstract. It seems as if Horn overdoes it and that, in his desire to counter the rosy myth of South Africa as the country of beautiful scenery and prosperity, he creates in his turn another myth, the myth of a totally 'black' South Africa, as oversimplified and misleading as the first. This is far from the complex world of Nortje, in which the sun and tyranny exist side by side, creating an inevitable malaise, as we shall see.

Of the three approaches adopted by Horn, only the first two thus restore a certain perspective and take account of the situation as a whole.

There is, however, another way to bring the citizens of a country around to reflecting on their universe: by calling them to account. In poetry, as in politics, this approach consists in asking questions, more questions, and still more questions. This is what Horn does.

For, if present-day South Africa is characterized by the disappearance of certain men and certain principles, and if the daily activities which elsewhere give life its substance are here lacking, then relentlessly asking questions of one's fellow citizens and of oneself is perhaps the only way to protest against the arbitrary despotism that dominates one's world and to try and involve others in one's protest. But this world, this society, is paternalistic and authoritarian; all the answers have been prepared in advance, ready to be trotted out as needed, no one even asks himself questions any more:

> They sit above, whom our song does not reach.
> For them there are no problems any more:
> there are only answers.
> Answers.
> Answers.
> Answers.

The New Prophets

'World opinion is organized against us'.
'Our country will fulfil its destiny'.
'White Christian people unite!'
'The *** leaders have been trained in communism'.

So many answers. Why do you still ask
questions? Why are you so stubborn?[6]

But in ending 'Letter to a Friend Overseas' with the cry,

But what is night? And what is dawn? And what is
pain? . . . What dream is this? And when shall I awake?

Horn is not in any way playing a new 1970s version of *Hamlet*; he is simply bringing out, by stressing its tragic aspect, the impasse to which the present policy of repression and suppression of liberties by the South African government has brought the country. The conclusion of 'For Autumn Poems use Mist and Rain' is even more pointed:

Tell us, tell us about Utopia, tell us
about China and Cuba, tell us about Marx, and –
tell us.
Where do we go in autumn
where do we go in the cold nights?
Unless there is a miracle?

The opposite world, which Horn longs for, appears in 'Voices from the Gallows Tree', and it is the child of redemptive violence. This hymn to change, this cry of hope sent up from the depths of the South African 'prison', is placed at the centre of his collection like a pearl in its matrix:

This is the language of the hurricane. The violence
of life reborn. We haul the flags down
for today and forever. We will awaken
the double-headed drums of the evening
and remember the parched lips of the
sand drinking the blood of the innocent.
For there: burning like grief
and brighter than morning a cry.
The cry of a people
smashing their cells and their
ghettos.

Here Horn clearly goes further than the simple adhesion in principle to the lot of the Spartacuses of his country; he acknowledges that their violence is alone capable of overthrowing the violence which has reigned for seventy years.

The rest of the poem is just as lyrical. The people liberated by the hurricane will try to regain the possibility they have lost during the years of oppression to reconstruct their relationships with others. This 'vision' ends symbolically with a word which has been banned for a long time, the word 'Together':

> I greet
> the audible the visible
> a new
> word: Together.

To see Horn purely in terms of the lyrical quality of his poetry, however varied it may be, would be to fail to do justice to the satirical poet who emerges from a reading of *Walking through our Sleep*. Besides invective, which Horn does not hesitate to use when he wants to make a direct attack without sidestepping any issues, his favourite weapon is irony. It is irony that enables him to achieve with the greatest subtlety his intention of lambasting the present regime and the whole of the white community. Rather like a Trojan horse brought into the fortress, the poet is in a position to spare nothing and nobody because he has had plenty of time to observe his fellows and has concluded that the chief evil from which South Africans suffer is hypocrisy and conservatism. Whether he is showing up, in the manner of the French poet Jacques Prévert, the bankruptcy of the gold and diamond magnates,[7] or suggesting, by explicit reference to Swift, a means of purging humanity of its harmful elements,[8] or whether he is addressing the congregations of dishonest faithful who, in spite of their pious words, crucify their Lord every day of the week,[9] it is always with the same objective in mind, it is always the same evils he is castigating. This is why the poem that best sums up his philosophy and his style is 'Why do we pray?' It is not without significance, therefore, that Horn indicates in a subtitle that the poem is a (fictional) reply to Dorothee Sölle, the German theologian who, following in the footsteps of Dietrich Bonhoeffer[10] and the German confessional churches, does not see religion as something set apart, cut off from the so-called secular world and its injustices, piously concentrating on the love of God. Dorothee Sölle, like Bonhoeffer (and it is also Peter Horn's position), believes that the best defence of the Christian civilization of the West (of which South Africans claim to be the authentic representatives and defenders in southern Africa) is to expunge all the evils men have allowed into it.[11] It is the political conservatives and the religious hypocrites who are in fact the real enemies of this civilization they claim to be defending. The criticism directed at them takes the form of a virulent attack on a materialistic world which condemns itself by its pursuit of gain at any cost.

Thus, in the poem, the perversion of the Gospel message is shown very effectively by the distortion of the Lord's Prayer, which Horn has recited by cynical old men and which is only superficially a 'fiction', for it is embedded deep in their hearts:

> Because we have betrayed
> the dreams of a young man
> who died two thousand years ago
> we old men sometimes say
> our father
> thou art in heaven
> for on earth
> you are too uncomfortable . . .
>
> Because we are citizens
> of a well-ordered state

> with laws for our benefit
> we say your kingdom come
> but not now

In this new *Waste Land*, which Horn has signposted throughout *Walking through our Sleep*, the paradox is not so much that, in spite of the difficulty he has in writing, his revolt and feeling of confusion are transformed into poetry,[12] but rather that he is determined to continue with his criticism when he knows full well that there is nothing he can really do to prevent the perpetuation of the *status quo*. Is it proof of an unwavering faith in the power of the word or the reflex of a man for whom poetry is as natural as the instinct of survival? There is matter for reflection here on the relationship between the Writer and Authority. For, if the former's aim is essentially a moral one, if his fables and his barely disguised symbols seek to convey a lesson, it is because he believes he can change things by 'speaking'. It is not by chance that the poem which immediately follows 'Voices from the Gallows Tree', the hymn to change, highlights both the paradox of this 'speech' which Authority allows him and the limitations to it that he encounters, limitations that include the feebleness of his influence on those in command, and therefore to effect change. It is as if in describing a totalitarian society the poet is denying from the outset that his poem can have any use whatsoever, except to the individual, for whom it serves as a remedy against despair or madness!

This acute awareness of the role to which the poet is confined – the role of the accredited clown (the expression is Horn's), who is at the same time *discredited* by what he says among the majority of whites – is very real to Horn, and his poetry gives concrete witness to it. For, sensing his impotence, the poet is ultimately driven to raising his voice and in the face of his contemporaries' deafness to calling for a fundamental change of regime, which will have to be achieved by violence, since the constitutional route is closed to the oppressed and the 'dialogue' offered by those in power is nothing but a pretence intended to postpone the event or to divide. This is where the poet falls into the trap set for him by the regime: since he can only preach the destruction of this society, which 'allows' him to express himself, he must surely be mad.

This is how we should read 'The Poet as a Clever Invention', whose subtitle could be: The Fool addresses the Society which maintains him. It is, in fact, as a clown that the liberal white poet depicts himself; the image is rendered more tragic than comic by the way it highlights his impotence:

> in purple shirt and orange tie
> I the accredited clown
> to this ailing society
> am allowed to tell you a few truths
> and similar nonsense
>
> so listen you christened dung-heaps!
>   I will lie for you
> everything: I can invent: everything . . .
>
>   looking at you I realize: 1 bottle of beer
> is better than 1 volume of poetry
> of any FORM & CONTENT poet

> looking at you I realize: the only
> adequate criticism
> of this society
> would be
> *to bash in your heads.*

Between the paroxysm of the poet's outburst against those who persist in not listening to him and his taking refuge in total silence, there is only one step . . . which the regime sometimes helps him to take. For the alternative to the freedom of expression granted the writer when his verbal outbursts are useful to the regime is the silence to which he is reduced when what he has to say becomes an embarrassment. He abandons the complex of the clown who screams to be heard through his audience's deafness, to assume the role of the modern Galileo, who proclaims loudly and ceaselessly what will be tomorrow's truth.

The comparison with Galileo is not fortuitous. Horn himself invites us to make it with his poem 'B.O.C.C.',[13] in which he evokes the fate of Galileo, silenced because he defied the ideas of his time by proclaiming his own discoveries and contradicting the official teaching of the Catholic Church on the nature of the world. Peter Horn's ideal, it seems, is that the poet should contribute to a Copernican revolution in people's minds.

But he knows the limits of his power; censorship has taken over from double meaning, the scissors and the gag have replaced the play performed in the town square, not to amuse the populace, but to set it thinking. It is not difficult to understand why the last words of *Walking through our Sleep* (coming at the end of a new series of poems, 'Profit and Loss', intended to draw a parallel between the failure of Ulysses who returns empty-handed to Ithaca and that which awaits, in the last analysis and inevitably, the European's quest to colonize Africa) should assert the power of writing to outlive the regime which has thought to suppress it for ever:

> The riches of love
> are stored
> for the future
> in dusty books
> banned by the state.

Wopko Jensma

There are not many South African authors who write both in English and Afrikaans; there are fewer still who publish in both these languages.[14] As for Jensma, he offers the peculiarity of including many African words as well in his poems.

This extension of his linguistic territory must not be taken as a desire to go one better or to surprise his readers, or even to confuse them. Clearly, the fact that he has lived in Swaziland, Botswana and Mozambique enables him to use the languages spoken in these countries that lie on South Africa's borders. It would perhaps be more accurate to regard his plurilingualism as a sign of what some might see as a wish to be 'ecumenical' or others as evidence of a political intention: to bring together and reunite in one place – the book being written – the languages of all those who live in southern Africa, and the people who speak them without really speaking to one another. The whole of Jensma's work invites this interpretation.

Jensma has published three collections of poetry, which also have the distinction of having been illustrated and type-set and/or page-set by the author himself. *Sing for our Execution* (1973) contains a series of remarkable woodcuts depicting strange, almost monster-like creatures, while *Where White is the Colour, Where Black is the Number* (1975) and *I Must Show You my Clippings* (1977) include collages and montages based on photographs by white and black artists.[15]

One influence is immediately obvious in Jensma's work, and it accords with his plurilingualism: the influence of jazz. It appears in the titles and form of several poems,[16] as well as in the dedications to various black singers and musicians. We must certainly see this as a homage to the black population which, in South Africa as in America, is the chief depository of this form of expression, but at the same time as a wish on his part to tell of his joy in sharing with communities from which he is separated by the law.

There is more: jazz requires people to participate fully in life, it makes them completely human because it enables them to infuse living with the rhythm and freedom which tends to be suppressed in everyday life; it is here that another essential characteristic of Jensma's poetry can be seen.

Much of what Jensma has written seems to have been the product of a spontaneous response, hence the exclamation, the cries and the harsh tone of his statements. For he listens to the world in which he lives, and it is a world that does not live on music, a world that is divided, a world that suffers, often without knowing it: Jensma feels all this with greater sensitivity than many others. The thematic texture of his poems provides not so much a picture of the unjust distribution of wealth and the misery that results from it as the representation, in a naturalistic and often symbolic form, of the suffering inflicted on others, which he regards as a crime. What Jensma says, without equivocation and without oversimplification in spite of appearances, is that a part of South African society, the whites, has made itself the gaoler of the rest. But in doing so, it causes itself the most appalling torments; and it is by no means accidental that the vocabulary and imagery of Jensma's poetry constantly refers to violence inflicted upon the living body, to bloodshed, explosions, self-mutilation, brutal killings and executions, all symbols of the price that has to be paid for the pervading lack of sensitivity.

'Misto 3' is a good illustration of the almost telegraphic style Jensma uses to convey his most urgent messages. The words seem to come out in the jerky fashion of a computer which has been programmed by a society bent on suicide and which in this way rediscovers its most secret obsessions and its enduring anxieties:

> Lets
> spit
> lets
> spill our names on blank walls
> lets
> spell it out: We have no future[17]

This staccato, halting, almost breathless style, like something that has been pummelled and beaten, also comes, and takes its form, from the intensity of the poet's perception of the impending danger, from his realization of the countless wounds from which the great body of South African society as a whole is going to die. These poems plunge the reader into the heart of a silent storm, less spectacular than the cataclysmic unleashing of the elements prophesied for the Last Judgement, but just as devastating and, in the final analysis, much more painful.

Jensma renders this feeling of the sinister dissolution of a whole society particularly well through the evocation of the unexpected and bizarre. This is the more reflective side of his poetry: everyday life is filtered through the poet's acute sensibility, which is able to express the result very aptly. Thus, it would be a mistake to see *only* surrealistic images in the scene described here:

> by the law of our country
> a plant was found guilty
>
> the sentence was carried out
> before the assembled people
>
> it was first stripped of fear
> and then hung by its conscience
>
> the children sang a sweet song
> and pressed leaves in text-books.[18]

This vision is only superficially strange; and there is a clear design beneath the apparent simplicity. The plant which is found 'guilty' is a good illustration of the degree of absurdity that the obsessive 'witch-hunt' against an illusory omnipresent enemy can attain. The execution scene with which the children are associated, perhaps only metaphorically, emphasizes the everyday character of the repression (or oppression) while at the same time introducing the theme of 'the ritual of the taming of the shocking' which the last line brings out particularly clearly. It is in fact typical of totalitarian regimes to allow the coexistence of the angelic and the demonic.

It is this 'monstrous' world – and one realizes the relevance of the visual representation which Jensma provides of it by his illustrations – which effectively predominates here, either through its psychological force or the power of the picture he paints of it.

But in order to convey it, Jensma does not have to resort to the extraordinary, to the fire and brimstone of Hell. The monstrous belongs to the everyday world, it is totally ordinary, it lies within each one of us.[19] Germany provided it with a fertile soil during the Nazi period, apartheid enables it to develop in southern Africa, but the way it is evoked by Jensma suggests that tomorrow the monstrous could be somewhere else.

His method – if it is a method – is simple, for it follows closely the lines of reality itself. Cain has killed Abel. Cain keeps his brother's still bleeding body. Cain talks to it, talks aloud *to himself*, and his waking dreams are heavy with this blood which he cannot wash away: a forerunner of Lady Macbeth, but worse than her, since it is his own brother Cain has killed. In fact, in order to show a South Africa sickened by apartheid, Jensma has chosen to speak in the first person, as both the hero–victim and the hero–murderer. But it is always the same 'I': it is the same person who suffers, the man who has been stricken by what he has himself conceived or done in a moment of aberration or madness. An inner universe takes shape, like the cross-section of a sick mind: it reveals the terrible schizophrenia of living all the time by two codes of conduct, one for one's family and (white) neighbour, the other for the sub-human black man cast in the role of servant. Thus the hero–victim dies a thousand times over, bleeding from a thousand wounds, while the hero–murderer constantly proclaims a brotherhood which is contradicted by the multitude of crimes committed against the flesh and the spirit of these 'unlike likes'.

'Lopsided Cycle', one of many like it, is an illustration of this kind of poem:

> i got a gash in my head
> blood spurts from it
> i must cut my head off
> i must hide myself
> no one must see me do it
> cause the blood is my guilt[20]

Through the theme of cheated brotherhood, Jensma returns to a theme common to all those who have written about South African society over the last thirty years: the theme of the guilt of a world that unjustifiably claims to be Christian. Jensma handles it in a thoroughly personal way, which is often reminiscent of a preacher exhorting a congregation of sinners. It is no accident that the quotation used as an epigraph for *Where White is the Colour* is taken from St Augustine: 'They love truth when it reveals itself, they hate it when it reveals themselves.'

It is a short step from preachers to prophets, and it is an easy one to take in Jensma's case for we clearly have here what one might call a new prophetism, a doomsday literature. The warning that the world is about to end is justified by the existence of the most glaring evils: the perversion of the Gospel message, the hard-heartedness of the Christian towards his fellow man and the systematic impoverishment of a whole people. The world that is depicted by Jensma is *infernal* for a host of reasons.

Hell as Jensma sees it around him consists in having only negative 'values' to share with others: bad conscience, lack of feeling ('Christ meant for a society turned stone'),[21] fear ('a communal fear unites us').[22] It is also the dark tunnel of identical days which are never lit except by the celebration of war, that is to say, more blood, and by protestations of peace that are contradicted by the sad reality:

> today is tuesday
> yesterday was monday
> tomorrow will be wednesday
> after that another day
>
> time after time the sea
> collapses to certain death
> on its burning beaches
>
> time after time our prime
> minister proclaims lasting peace
> and nails sharpeville on
> another burning cross
>
> today is dingaan's day
> yesterday was republic day
> tomorrow will be an ordinary day
> after that a similar day[23]

The form of this poem, which is rather like a counting rhyme, stresses the mechanical character of this daily life and its absurdity, while the time ellipse – Dingaan's Day falls on 16 December, Republic Day on 31 May – accentuates even more the sameness of the days that have gone by between these two anniversaries of Afrikaner revenge against the Zulus and the British.[24]

Hell, too, is the vast loneliness of the man separated from others, above all from his neighbour, that is, the neighbour who inhabits the same country but who belongs to *another* community, who lives in *another* ghetto. Here we again encounter the symbolism of the closed door and the closed house, of obstinate waiting, of the desire for communication and real contact. The following poems show the two sides of an identical reality, the man who is outside and the man who is inside expressing the same need *without meeting one another*:

> my lord
> i know my presence irritates you
> i want to enter your house
> and page through your thesis
> and have a drink with you
> and have a chat
> and have a laugh
> and smoke a pipe with you
> and tap you on the shoulder
> i am waiting at your door
> i'll wait i'll keep on waiting
> my lord[25]

> i open the door and see no one
> i always open the door
> i think i will wait
> someone may come some day
> someone who wants to see me
> someone who will listen to me
> one must have patience
> one must trust
> one must have faith
> i want someone to see me
> i want someone to hear me talk
> i want someone to knock on the door[26]

Over against this world, the desired world is present only as a hollow shape, in opposition, by omission, so to speak, because it does not yet exist or is barely perceptible. Yet it is already clear that it will come about through sacrifice, hence the many images of crucifixion, while the prohibitions inevitably evoke the idea of freedom, the continual repression the idea of liberation, and the absence of love, which is constantly referred to, proclaims the love that men long for.

Although there is an obvious moral intention, embedded in the lesson as a 'revelation' of the Evil all around, it does not lead to insipid sentimentality as could have been the case. Jensma's most personal and original contribution to this 'doomsday' literature is to be found more in his manner and his tone than in his themes themselves. Therefore, rather than quote poems that show a community of

The New Prophets

purpose with other writers who have stressed the 'Cain syndrome', it would be better to highlight those which characterize Jensma's own approach.

Once again it is the preacher or the prophet one thinks of when reading those poems in which Jensma expresses himself with passionate forthrightness in cries, exclamations, interjections and peremptory questions, as in 'Misto 3' and other poems from *Sing for our Execution*. Here, the poet's preoccupation with eschatology is made even more evident by the violence and the virtual explosion of the language. It is as if, in the intensity of his 'vision' and the urgency of his sense of the need for change as a matter of life and death, syntax were an obstacle to spontaneity, traditional structure a threat to writing that has become the immediate apprehension of thought; as if, too, spelling is a nonsense unless phonetic, unless an exact reflection of the spoken language.

But Jensma's most usual manner is to use stories, fables and parables aimed at catching the attention of the reader–listener and forcing him to think as he contemplates analogies that speak to the mind. Thus the parable that follows unfolds along the lines of a riddle, serving as an ideal introduction to a sermon on the evil which lies hidden in people's consciences:

> i am a dirty little room
> with spiders in the corner of my skull
> my mouth a dark pit
> into which human droppings disappear
> the speck of rust in my heart worries me
>
> many people breathe in and out of me
> i am at ease with the world
> only the speck of rust worries me[27]

Even clearer is 'Sometime next time', where the striking shorthand of the parable draws on religious symbolism to show the size and the difficulty of the task that has to be accomplished in South African society:

> i plant my corn on the rocks
>   it does not grow
> i plant my corn on fertile land
>   it does not grow
>   next time i plant
> i'll start beyond
> i'll start beyond the bread[28]

As for the doomsday scenes themselves, these appear in the form of visions and dreams that are deliberately left vague but which nevertheless convey their violence. In the last poem of *Where White is the Colour*, the narrator wakes from his nightmare in the corrugated iron shack which he seemed to have left only a moment previously in search of bread for his children. Yet there is no one there and the empty plates are covered with dust. At this point, the poet interjects: 'What did i live for? what am i going to die for?'[29]

These questions are in a way the key to Jensma's work. While he obviously condemns a kind of life that he considers wrong from a purely ethical, as distinct from a social, point of view, Jensma never sets himself *apart*, but always *inside* and *among*. The very fact that he speaks in the murderer's name as well as the victim's shows the extent of his attachment to his country. He must be capable of great love for him to be able to identify with all the South African communities, to conceive of them all as victims and to bring them all together. Tenderness is, in fact, a dominant feature of the second collection, just as a very black humour was characteristic of the first.

This tenderness appears in powerfully lyrical poems in which Jensma celebrates the dead and the martyrs of a cause he has made his own, the cause of freedom and reunion. While in 'We Children',[30] with sombre irony, he has the dead children of Sharpeville sing a hymn which ends with the expectation of more massacres, in 'In Memoriam Ben Zwane' Jensma is able to transcend the immediate factors surrounding the death of a friend in suspicious circumstances by generalizing the fate of the individual so that it encompasses the whole country and adopting the tone and feeling of the Negro spirituals:

> ma people, come an get ready
> train's a comin
> ain't no room fo sinners
> we're goin all da way
>
> i heard a word, ben
> but i fear t'say 't here
> tell azania
> i only say 't soft, not loud
>
> did you tumble down steps?
> did you slip on a piece 'f soap?
> what da hell did you do?
> tell me you died 'f tb
>
> ma people, god go ya covered
> let's rail away, all stoned
> 'f winin'n dinin all day
> gonna be great in south africa[31]

Similarly, 'Cry me a River' – a poem inspired by the fate of Bram Fischer, who was to die in prison from cancer at the beginning of 1975 – can be read without its specific political allusions as praising the example of a man who has devoted his whole life to a cause:

> who's that rowing a black boat
> through this black night?
> who's that not sparing his arms
> and rowing without end?
>
> who's that rowing a boat
> on the river without an end?
> who's that not giving up hope
> on a journey without end?
>
> who's that rowing a black boat
> black in the black night?
> who's that hearing the slave bell
> and beating the thud of his gut?[32]

The New Prophets

To which community does Wopko Jensma belong? The question is not as trivial as it may seem: so many voices mingle in his voice that one finds oneself thinking that he could represent the whole of South Africa. Before seeing his photograph, one could picture him as a Cape Malay, or a Tswana from a township where everyone speaks Afro-American slang, or an Afrikaner who has broken with Afrikanerdom, or an English-speaking South African who has spent his childhood among black people. Yet he is white![33] Still only in his forties, Jensma seems to have lived several existences in several communities, and this is something of immense significance in a country so compartmentalized and divided as South Africa. But the fact that he is South African cannot be denied, as the opening of *I must show you my Clippings* testifies:

> i was born 26 july 1939 in ventersdorp
> i found myself in a situation
>
> i was born 26 july 1939 in sophiatown
> i found myself in a situation
>
> i was born 26 july 1939 in district six
> i found myself in a situation
>
> i was born 26 july 1939 in welkom
> i found myself in a situation[34]

He depicts the white mentality too well *from the inside*, of course, to be considered an outsider, and his tone, here and there,[35] is too detached for it to be that of a black man. The word 'empathy', with all it suggests of generosity and ability to identify with others, does not adequately describe him. Jensma is certainly the one poet living in South Africa today who comes closest to being what one could, for the first time, call the voice of the South African nation – if such a nation really existed.

Is it possible to discern a distinct line of development in South African writing from Paton to Jensma? Protest and a sense of what is lacking in a society sick from apartheid lead to the vehemence of prophecy via total commitment to the cause of the oppressed and this movement corresponds to the three main stages in the evolution of the political situation in South Africa over the last thirty years: in the first stage everything still seemed possible in spite of existing legislation; then came Sharpeville and the short-lived resistance movement, and finally the 1976–7 riots, which saw the worsening of tension between the young black generation and a white authority rigidly set in its negative attitudes. With war and decolonization now on the country's borders, no poet at all sensitive to the society in which he lives could fail to realize the significance of the quite perceptible movement that is beginning to shake his world.

But it is normal, after all, that the white poet should be more sensitive than others to the signs of catastrophe: if it is to occur, in the near or distant future, it will be his community that will be the worst hit. One thinks of the lines Pierre-Jean Jouve wrote between the defeat of 1940 and the emergence of the French Resistance:

> The power of prophecy, by which poetry acknowledges catastrophe, elevates the art of the poet in moments of darkness: for none is more sensitive than the poet to the breaks and the cracks in the shaking edifice of civilization.[36]

Yet these same poets who have emerged from the white liberal milieu have done everything in their power to avoid the advent of the great day of reckoning and its inevitably violent outcome. The place taken up in their work by remonstration and pleas to share or surrender some, if not all, power before it is too late, the overt and indirect preaching, the parables and the fables, and, finally, the satire, all clearly show their will to *convert* their fellow citizens, to appeal to them on the level of morality to mend their ways and change their policies and institutions. This literature written *by* whites *for* whites is reminiscent of the situation described by Sartre in *What is Literature?*:

> If society looks at itself and especially if it sees itself being *looked at*, there is, as a consequence of this alone, a questioning of the established values and the state: the writer shows society its image and calls upon it to acknowledge it or to change. And it changes in any case; it loses the equilibrium formerly given it by ignorance, it vacillates between shame and cynicism, it engages in bad faith; thus the writer gives society *an unhappy conscience*, and as a result he is in perpetual conflict with the conservative forces which maintain the equilibrium he tends to break.[37]

'An unhappy conscience': this is what the committed poets studied in this section have tried to give their white compatriots.

During Pringle's time, the diatribes against slavery and the verse accounts of the abuses committed against peoples who were not yet completely subjugated, fell upon sympathetic ears. Wilberforce's influence in England was great, it covered a large section of society and united families of thought which were often far apart. But the majority in a colonial country, as it has been evident since Paton, can very easily live with an 'unhappy conscience', ready to prick up their ears when their interests are threatened and it becomes expedient to have, if not principles, at least the appearance of being 'generous'. The committed white writer is, ultimately, a moralist. Lewin and Evans, who hoped to convert their contemporaries by their deeds, and not by their poems, are not exceptions to this: the terrorist act (selective, as we have seen) is presented as a sermon. But broadcast throughout the country by press and radio, this was not how it was interpreted; it was seen rather as a sign of the disorder that could not fail to occur if power changed hands.

There remains the possibility of creating fear, of prophesying evil times ahead; of converting, not by a vision of Paradise regained or of the rainbow of 'races' and colours, but by the vision of a Hell in which everything one most wants to keep will be lost. In other words, a return to prophecy.

This is the line of development that links Paton to Jensma. The whole tragedy of the liberal conscience in a colonized country is its powerlessness to change the moral outlook of those in power, who resemble him like a brother. In the face of this 'resistance' to conversion, and often to the personal example that is set, the only option left is resistance to tyranny.

At this point, the scales are tipped on to the side of the oppressed. Some are tempted by the role of Spartacus: they realize that, all things considered, change can only come through their own action. To this end, the oppressed masses must first be freed from their mentality of consenting victims accustomed to their state to the extent of having forgotten the old virtues. They must be educated in a country where education for the slave is carefully restricted. They must be won over. They must be converted. It remains to be seen how language can be used to stir the oppressed into becoming the real force for change.

Notes

1. Horn was born in 1934 in Sudetenland. A South African since 1955, he teaches at the University of Cape Town. He founded the review *Ophir*, which he has edited with another South African poet, Walter Saunders.
   The poems quoted in this chapter are taken from *Walking through our Sleep* (Ravan Press, Johannesburg, 1974).
2. Horn has since published in *samizdat* a further volume of poems, *Silence in Jail* (Scribe Press, Claremont, Cape Town, 1979).
3. ibid., p. 5. The first four lines are clearly reminiscent of Wordsworth and Keats.
4. ibid., p. 25.
5. See ibid., pp. 2, 38.
6. ibid., p. 30.
7. 'Litigation: Being an exact transcription of the moving speech addressed to the mining magnates at their annual dinner' (*Walking through our Sleep*, op. cit., p. 35).
8. 'A Modest Proposal for the Universal Benefit of Mankind' (*Walking through our Sleep*, op. cit., p. 36).
9. 'An Easter Yodel for Unbelievers' (*Walking through our Sleep*, op. cit., p. 41).
10. Which was exemplified, during the Second World War, by his opposition to Nazism, an opposition which sometimes assumed a direct political form. Bonhoffer was in fact executed by the Nazis after the abortive plot against Hitler.
11. Horn takes this idea up again in one of his epigrams: 'The best defence/of Western civilization/is an attack/against it' (*Walking through our Sleep*, op. cit., p. 45).
12.
>   Sing how shall I sing
>   for God's sake how shall I sing
>   in a well organized prison
>   with this grinning mug above me
>   never mind Plato and Aristotle
>   just tell me
>   how do I sing
>   with a boot on my throat.

    In 'A Useless Plea to the boots of a Nameless Spy' (*Walking through our Sleep*, op. cit., p. 37).
13. 'BOCC', one of Horn's finest poems, but too long to quote here, plays on the word BOSS (Bureau of State Security), whose job is to track down the regime's opponents, and which has been responsible for a great deal of torture and extortion. The poem employs the terms used in connection with house arrest. (*Walking through our Sleep*, op. cit., p. 58.)
14. One can mention Dennis Brutus, Cosmo Pieterse, Adam Small, André Brink, Uys Krige.
15. Ravan Press, Johannesburg.
16. Several poems, whether specifically designated as such or not, are 'blues' or spirituals. Others are divided into 'riffs' (a jazz term referring to a fast, sustained melodic phrase), while yet others evoke South African (*marabenta, kwela*) or American (stomp) dances.
17. An analysis of this poem by Walter Saunders can be found in *Poetry South Africa*, ed. Wilhelm and Polley (Ad. Donker, Johannesburg, 1976), pp. 80–1.
18. *Sing for our Execution*, op. cit., p. 71.
19. Hannah Arendt noted this after following the trial of Eichmann in Jerusalem from start to finish.

20. *Sing for our Execution*, op. cit., p. 14.
21. ibid., p. 29.
22. ibid., p. 30.
23. ibid., p. 42.
24. The first is the anniversary of the battle of Blood River which saw the defeat of the Zulu armies of Dingaan (who had earlier massacred a group of Voortrekkers). Republic Day falls on the same day as the signing of the Treaty of Vereeniging, which brought the Boer War to an end.
25. *Sing for our Execution*, op. cit., p. 47.
26. ibid., p. 50.
27. ibid., p. 22.
28. ibid., p. 91.
29. *Where White is the Colour*, op. cit., p. 94.
30. *Sing for our Execution*, op. cit., p. 76.
31. *Where White is the Colour*, op. cit., p. 33. Azania is the name some want to give to South Africa once it is freed from Afrikaner domination.
32. ibid., p. 19.
33. Cf. Mary Morrison Webster in *Sunday Times* (Johannesburg, 1974): 'The reader's initial and, indeed, lasting impression is that Jensma is an African – possibly of Sophiatown.'
34. The names of places (towns or suburbs) *evoke* the various communities they are associated with.
35. *Sing for our Execution*, op. cit.; see 'Our Village'.
36. Preface to Pierre Emmanuel, *La Colombe* (LUF, Fribourg, 1943), p. 15.
37. *Qu'est-ce que la littérature?* (Gallimard, Paris, 1948).

PART III
The Black Poets and the Struggle for Power

▼▼▼▼▼▼▼▼▼▼▼▼▼▼▼▼▼▼▼▼▼▼▼▼▼▼▼▼▼▼▼▼▼

In literature, there is no such thing as spontaneous generation: literary forms take shape slowly, evolving under the impetus of various factors, some of which are specific to the period, dying, or surviving but taking on another name or another appearance. This is what happened in Europe, especially in the theatre and the novel, where the route leading to their modern forms passed via the mystery plays, the medieval narrative poem and the epic in a process that lasted several centuries. In South Africa, indigenous literature developed more rapidly from a core of oral expression that covered too wide a field to be adequately described by the word 'literature'. There was, certainly, a body of religious, philosophical and other notions, but these were contained in a way of life which was expressed through a multitude of customs and rites.

What we can designate by the restrictive term 'poetry' generally consisted, for the tribes and kingdoms of southern Africa, in praise poems, satirical narrative and tales in which were inextricably mixed music, passages that were spoken or sung, and dance and physical expression in the widest sense of the term. The transformation of tribal society undermined or distorted this art form; Christian education, particularly, by introducing the use of writing, gave it new possibilities while reducing the 'languages' that could be employed to the one which could be adopted to the printing process, and it oriented literary production, in the beginning at least, to those areas that seemed desirable in accordance with Christianity's own concerns. It was only with the passing of time, the progress of the struggle for emancipation and the extension of white hegemony that literate blacks, in order to make their protest at the lot reserved for them, turned to literary forms that were new to them, in which the old virtues could be given expression. Journalism was naturally foremost among these as it made it possible to conduct and sustain the political campaign; yet the black writer of the start of the century did not reject literary creation properly so called, as is illustrated by the Chaka of Thomas Mofolo (1876–1948), written in 1910 but only published in 1925, and the Mhudi of Sol T. Plaatje (1878–1932), published five years later. The first of these works was written in Sotho, the language spoken by Mofolo, who came from Basutoland (Lesotho), but Mhudi was written in English, as was a book written at the same time by the Zulu writer, R. R. R. Dhlomo (born 1901), entitled An African Tragedy (1928). In the years that followed works appeared both in the vernacular languages and, between 1928 and 1941, in English. Also in one or other of the indigenous languages and/or in English, there was a steady stream of protest poetry: right up to the arrival of the Nationalists in power in 1948, these poems provided evidence of the will to resist among the black population. Black committed poetry does not therefore begin in the present. Without attempting an exhaustive study which would be out of place here, it seems fitting, however, to draw attention to the forerunners.

This reminder will be all the more necessary in order to show the evolution of protest among the black peoples of South Africa. It is clear that it has followed the evolution of oppression and that protest has imperceptibly changed into revolt. It is the continuation and the worsening of this oppression that has led the colonized population to resort to the spoken word as one resorts to arms or to the loudspeakers, so as to make oneself heard by a much larger audience. There is a continuous link joining the forerunners to the poets of Black Consciousness, via the poets of the sixties.

Chapter 8
Vernacular Poetry

▼▼▼▼▼▼▼▼▼▼▼▼▼▼▼▼▼▼▼▼▼▼▼▼▼▼▼▼▼▼▼▼▼▼▼

Among the vanquished of history, national catastrophes cause reactions of defeatism or anger which the collective memory stores up and which, sooner or later, find their expression in literature. This was how, after the last Xhosa war, which had even further reduced the national territory, the first example of committed poetry by a black South African came to be written by I. W. W. Citashe, proclaiming his faith in the power of the written word:[1]

> Your cattle are gone, my countrymen!
> Go rescue them! Go rescue them!
> Leave the breechloader alone
> And return to the pen.
> Take paper and ink,
> For that is your shield.
> Your rights are going!
> So pick up your pen.
> Load it, load it with ink.
> Sit on a chair.
> Repair not to Hoho*,
> But fire with your pen.[2]

This poem was the signal that launched the tradition of black protest poetry in South Africa which was first to express itself in the vernacular languages and then, without exhausting itself in this form, in English also. It was, however, only with the growth of racial discrimination through legislation and the erosion of fundamental rights that what was only a continuous, but limited trickle was to become a growing torrent, and the black poets were to devote themselves entirely to their people's struggle.

The Xhosa poets

As part of their aim to restore their compatriots' faith in themselves and to show them how to learn from the lessons of the past, the exponents of Black Consciousness naturally conceived the idea of republishing works which were

---

*Hoho: mountain fortress.

mostly no longer in print but which bore powerful witness to the enduring spiritual resistance of the blacks.

Thus it was that in August 1971 appeared *The Making of a Servant*,[3] a slim volume containing eight poems originally written in Xhosa by seven different poets and translated into English for this edition by Robert Kavanagh and Z. S. Qangule; their composition and publication covered the period 1925–62. One of the fundamental characteristics of these poems is that they transcend tribal boundaries and old antagonisms. They reflect rather the trend towards unity which manifested itself in the political battles of the period from 1930 to 1960 and were therefore an opportune reminder to the younger generations that the struggle was above all a common one.

The compilers of *The Making of a Servant* could not but pay homage to the father and at the same time the giant of Xhosa literature at the beginning of the twentieth century, S. E. Q. Mqhayi (1875–1945). The author of several novels, Mqhayi was above all a poet whose influence and talent were recognized during his lifetime to the extent of earning him the title of 'poet among poets'. The form in which he excelled was the *isibongo*, or praise poem, a traditional form which had been very popular over the past centuries and of which chiefs and kings were not the only beneficiaries. The poem by Mqhayi in *The Making of a Servant* is taken, in fact, from a praise poem written in 1925 on the occasion of the visit to southern Africa of the Prince of Wales, heir to the British throne; often regarded as a parody and frequently reproduced in anthologies, the poem is famous for the question – surely not rhetorical! – which the African puts to Great Britain through the intermediary of his illustrious guest:

> Hayi, the mighty Great Britain!
> Here she comes with bible and bottle,
> Here she comes, a missionary escorted by a soldier,
> With gunpowder and guns,
> With cannons and breechloader.
> Forgive me, O Father, but which of these must we accept?

While Mqhayi's poem is interesting for its bitter irony, which was to become a favourite device among his successors, more important for an understanding of the forerunners of Black Consciousness are four other poems in the collection.

The first, entitled 'The Contraction and Enclosure of the Land' (1958), is the work of St. J. Page Yako: as its title suggests, it deals with the most serious problem facing the black man in southern Africa, the shrinking of his land:

> Thus spake the heirs of the land
> Although it is no longer ours.
> This land will be folded like a blanket
> Till it is like the palm of a hand.
> The racing ox will become entangled in the wire
> Too weak to dance free, it will be worn
> Out by the dance of the yoke and the plough.
> They will crowd us like tadpoles
> In a calabash ladle.

The poem is completely explicit, yet its tone, with its restraining lyricism, is perfectly controlled. There are no abstract words; instead, the imagery evokes very concretely the expropriation and gradual shrinking of the land that really belongs to the African ('Thus spake the heirs of the land'). The second part of the poem describes the resulting change in customs: less land, therefore fewer cattle, hence the corruption of the practice of *lobola*.* At the end the poem returns to the picture of a people reduced to living at a subsistence level; here, too, the imagery is both apt and eloquent:

> Yes, we fold up our knees,
> It's impossible to stretch out,
> Because the land has been hedged in.

'The Land of the People Once Living', by Sob. W. Nkuhlu, dates from the same period as the last poem; the author evokes the ancestral land that once fed all its sons. A deeply lyrical poem which, like most poems in the vernacular languages, draws on the animals and plants of South Africa, it blends vision and dream with the portrayal of harsh reality. It is this last element that gives the poem its profoundly committed character:

> We live in a land which unsettles the heart
> For even when we are happy we remain ill at ease,
> Even when we have heard the reasons, we feel wronged
> Although we've understanding, we do not understand . . .
> The heart is restless, tossed from side to side.
> As if it would burst out, roots and all.

The poem ends with the evocation of the 'land of the heart's desire' which belongs not to the present, but to the future.

Another long poem, this one by M. E. Nyoka, 'Where, Where is it?' (1962), seems to echo the repression that followed on Sharpeville. The Christian inspiration here combines with the memory of the ancestors to culminate in a passionate questioning of the significance of the suffering endured by the black people and the apparent indifference of the Almighty. At the same time, the poet laments the loss of black pride and the passivity of the warrior who no longer defends himself, even when his enemy's steel penetrates his body. The principal responsibility for the misfortune is however attributed to the (white) Christians, evoked rather than named:

> This lot have come along with their intelligence and
>   their technique.
> They have long since forgotten their holy beginnings.
> They look down on those who have nothing.
> They have forgotten their beginnings.

The poem ends with an appeal to the Lord which is not without a certain ambiguity:

---

* *lobola*: originally, a gift of cattle to seal a marriage.

> Speak to me with understanding
> That I may seek my inheritance.
> I mean
> Turn me towards my home, Holy Trinity,
> Save me, O Lord.

But it is the title poem, 'The Making of a Servant', the work of J. J. R. Jolobe (1902–76), which gives the collection its full significance. Jolobe completed his secondary education in 1926 and published his first poems ten years later. Several are inspired by Christianity. The son of a pastor and himself a minister – he became the African moderator of the Presbyterian Church – Jolobe remained deeply influenced by Christianity, although this did not prevent him from speaking out when he judged it necessary. Given the poem's qualities of firmness and simplicity, it is not difficult to understand why its translators wished to ensure it had a wide circulation at a time when Black Consciousness was beginning to develop.

'The Making of a Servant' is very classical in form: western influence makes itself felt by the use of regular stanzas, and the poem is based on an extended metaphor in which the 'hero', a chained ox, is clearly a representation of the black South African. A series of observations, in the form of aphorisms, serve as brief commentaries by the author, who each time draws the moral of what he is describing. The first stanza is very significant in this respect:

> I can no longer ask how it feels
> To be choked by a yoke-rope
> Because I have seen it for myself in the chained ox.
> The blindness has left my eyes. I have become aware,
> *I have seen the making of a servant*
> *In the young yoke-ox.*[4]

Each of the following stanzas unfolds with its own pithy observation representing a part of the total argument, with the leitmotiv 'I have seen the making' returning each time as the increasingly insistent refrain of the poem. The main argument is the gradual enslaving of the black people, which is hidden behind good reasons ('A good piece of rationalization can camouflage evil'): the yoke, henceforth, becomes the sign of degradation of him who does not have the possibility of choosing his own destiny ('Being trained in one's interest is for the privileged') and leads to conflict between brothers ('The suffering under the yoke makes for bad blood').

If the author left it at that, he would merely be cataloguing the misfortunes that beset the black people, albeit in the guise of a very appropriate metaphor. The second part of the poem, however, represents as it were the other side of a work whose internal dialectic aims to lead to a liberation: the 'advice' takes on a dynamic character:

> To be driven is death. Life is doing things for yourself.
> . . .
> The savour of working is a share in the harvest.

The series of teachings culminates in the last stanza:

> I saw him hungry with toil and sweat,
> Eyes all tears, spirit crushed,
> No longer able to resist. He was tame.
> Hope lies in action aimed at freedom.

It is easy to understand the value of such a poem, the prophetic character of which emerges fully when we note that it dates from 1936. To these 'political' qualities must be added essentially literary qualities: the tautness of the form, the strict framework and the powerful leitmotiv all help to emphasize the argument, which progresses unfalteringly towards a practical conclusion. Moreover, the poet finds in his ancestral heritage the concept of the maxim, which attracts the reader's concurrence and the last of which has the effect of a slogan. Finally, the appropriateness of the similes and the constant drawing of parallels cannot fail to stimulate reflection on the part of the poem's readers, who are presented with a faithful mirror of their lot, while at the same time indicating to them the means of fighting back.

Ten years after the publication of 'The Making of a Servant', Jolobe himself translated several of his poems from Xhosa into English; one of these, written after the First World War, asked that the African soldiers who had served in Europe should be accorded the rights to which they were entitled. The Africans, however, were far from obtaining satisfaction; this point was to be made in his turn by another Xhosa writer, the son of an Anglican pastor, A. C. Jordan (1906–68).

After obtaining his MA from the University of South Africa, Jordan taught African languages first at Fort Hare, then at the University of Cape Town. He left South Africa after the proclamation of the Republic and went to teach in America, where he died in 1968.

Deeply committed during his university career, Jordan – whose writing is forbidden publication in South Africa even posthumously – has left a varied work and did a great deal to make Xhosa culture known. Like Jolobe, he translated some of his poems into English; the most significant of these seems to be 'You tell me to sit quiet', which is closer to protest poetry than Jolobe's. This lament, so tightly controlled and unfolding with such dignity and nobility of language, stresses, again by means of similes drawn from the animal world, the principal grievances the blacks can foster against the whites. Christianity as it is applied in South Africa constitutes, once more and not for the last time, one of the poet's main targets. Less rousing than 'The Making of a Servant', 'You tell me to sit quiet', at least by implication, prophesies in its stanza-like sections the unleashing of the anger to come:

> You tell me to sit quiet when robbed of my manhood,
> With nowhere to live and nought to call my own,
> Now coming, now going, wandering and wanting,
> No life in my home save the drone of the beetle!
> Go tell the worker bees,
> True guards of the hive,
> Not to sting the rash hunter
> Who grabs at their combs.
>
> You tell me to sit quiet when robbed of my children,
> All offered as spoils to the rich of the land,
> To be hungered of body, retarded of mind,

And drained of all spirit of freedom and worth!
Go tell the mother hen
Who sits on her brood
Not to peck at the mongrel
That sniffs at her young.[5]

The Zulu poets

Having come into contact with the whites later than the Xhosa, having also been subject to the influence of the missions and their schools later, the Zulu, who offered armed resistance for the last time in 1906 (the rebellion by Bambatha), can pride themselves too on having had poets who set the tone for protest and black intellectual resistance in South Africa. Two names stand out among the forerunners: Vilakazi and Dhlomo.

Benedict W. Vilakazi (1906–47), first a student at Witwatersrand University, became a lecturer there and was therefore the first African to teach outside Fort Hare. This Zulu, born in Groutville, Natal, but who lived for a long time in the Transvaal, was influenced by the spectacle of the mines which he could see around Johannesburg. Although he never became involved in politics, his writings show that his own privileged position did not make him lose sight of the much more wretched situation of the majority of his black compatriots. He is particularly well known for his work as a critic and a poet. He experimented with the western forms he had discovered, trying to make them serve the sources of his own poetic inspiration and revitalize especially the form of the *isibongo*. Two of his poems illustrate his occasional role as a committed poet: 'Ezin komponi' ('On the Gold Mines') and 'Because'.[6]

Conceived in the form of a long apostrophe addressed to the mine machines, 'On the Gold Mines' has three protagonists: the poet, who identifies with the African miners and speaks in their name; the machines, always present through their noise and movement; and, lastly, the white man, who remains in the background but commands both the miners and the machines. While the poet sometimes admonishes the machines, he also addresses them in a fraternal manner, for he and they both have the same master.

The latter appears only gradually: the first part of the poem focuses the attention of the reader on the arrival of the machines in Goli (Johannesburg) and the subsequent arrival of the African worker:

> Then a steam train hauled you overland,
> Puffing it slid you here at last to Goli.
> What a wail you raised, and there came in view
> All the rock-rabbits bobbing up the line.

This very evocative way of depicting the sudden appearance of the Africans and the activity of a busy multitude by drawing on images from the animal world, which abound in the folklore and the animal lore of Africa, to the extent of their being given a preponderant role in many Creation stories, is to be found again in the fifth stanza, which takes on the character of a tale:

> There's a story told about the mine machines
> That when they shrieked a small black mouse
> Peeped out stunned and in a daze;
> It was trapped and turned into a mole,
> Burrowed in the earth, and so was seen the gleam of gold.

What follows (stanzas 8–11) describes the dispossession of his ancestral land suffered by the African, the loss of his social and political status, his transformation, effectively, into an object. Here, too, we find once more Vilakazi's liking for metaphor, and the way in which the eighth stanza is concluded is reminiscent of the riddles, used as an educational device, which abound in African oral literature:

> We yielded and came up from our thatched huts
> And were herded together like yoke-oxen;
> We left our dark corn and curds and milk
> To be fed instead an alien mess of porridge.
> Our family pride is gone, we are children,
> The world is clearly turned heels over head.
> Wakened up at dawn, stood in a row!
> Where have you known of a man once buried
> Who sees with both eyes and stands alive?

The eleventh stanza, passing from description of the general to description of the individual, portrays the lot of the migrants with a peasant realism, and endows them with strength and character:

> Such towers were not here to scale
> That time I first went underground,
> Still I recall the raw deal that I got.
> I thought, I'll pack my goods and get home,
> But there – ruins and bare fields struck me.
> I scratched my head, went into a hut
> And asked: Where is my wife, her parents?
> They said: The whiteman called them up to work.
> Then I was dumb, my mouth sewn up in silence.

Each of the following stanzas contains a specific criticism of the white overlord: it is the African miner who enables him to become rich (stanza 12) while he himself is treated without pity (stanza 13), and the skyscrapers rise where once the land of his forefathers lay, land which he is not allowed to buy back (stanza 15). What is left for the African whose fatherland has been stolen from him? '. . . I and this whole line of ours/ Who are black are left with nothing of nothing' (stanza 17).

But, although the whole poem seems to lead to an inevitable climax, Vilakazi, after interrogating God and the spirits without response, asks sleep and Death to allow him to forget and to return to the ancestral soil. The account of the African's misfortunes, which are so effectively evoked, and the cry of impatience ('God above be witness, and you spirits gone,/ Can you bring no end to evils such as these?') become blurred, dissolve and end with a turning in on the self, with resignation or a feeling of helplessness.

Are we to see in this anticlimax the fear of going too far or a reflection of the absence of real militancy on Vilakazi's part? Although there can be no doubt that the inter-war period was one of the darkest for the black South African community, it is no less certain that 'On the Gold Mines' is related to the poetry of protest, but still in a minor key.

'Because', shorter than 'On the Gold Mines' (40 lines as compared to 169), has a ring strangely reminiscent of Langston Hughes's 'Minstrel Man' (*The Dream Keeper and Other Poems*, 1932). Vilakazi depicts almost in the same terms a very similar situation, and skilfully plays on the leitmotiv 'Just because . . .', which is repeated with little change in each of the four stanzas:

> Just because of the laugh on my lips
> And my eyes lowered in respect,
> Pants rolled up above the knees
> And my dark hair all dun-coloured
> And thick with the roadside dust,
> My hands swinging a pick,
> And the back stripped out of my shirt –
> You think I'm like a stone
> And don't know what it is to die.
>
> Because at the fall of dark
> When I've unloosened the chains
> Of my long day's labour
> And I fall in with my brothers
> Stamping the ground in a tribal dance,
> And we sing songs of old times
> That stir up our fighting blood
> Driving away all our cares –
> For that you think I am a beast
> That breeds its kind and dies.

H. I. E. Dhlomo (1905–56), a contemporary of Vilakazi, less well known than he as a poet but nevertheless a versatile writer, expressed himself more explicitly in 1936 in his essay 'Drama and the African':

How often one hears people say the African is happy and care-free because he smiles – ignorant of the fact that behind those smiles and calm expression lie a rebellious soul, a restless mind, a bleeding heart, stupendous ambitions, the highest aspirations, grim determination, a clear grasp of facts and the situation, grim resolve, a will to live.[7]

While it is worth noting Dhlomo's resolute tone and the confidence he feels in the black man's capabilities, there is another important point: Dhlomo is the first African to have written an essay, a play and a full-length poem *in English*.[8]

The poem, one thousand lines in length, entitled *The Valley of a Thousand Hills* (1941), was published in Natal, where Dhlomo lived most of his life. A mixture of several styles and poetic tones, it describes the impassioned questioning of a man exposed not only to the ordinary vicissitudes of life but especially singled out by fate by the fact that he is oppressed.

In the form of an allegory, the poet describes the influence exercised on him by Europe and invokes his mother, whom he contrasts with the foreign stepmother. Around him, in this valley which is reputed to be the most beautiful in the whole of South Africa, everything urges him to seek a personal, spiritual solution and to take refuge there in order to find peace at last.

But voices from the Past ring out and offer him the idyllic picture of a perfect society; in contrast, the Present seems even darker:

> This beauty's not my own! my home is not
> My home! I am an outcast in my land!
> They call me happy while I lie and rot
> Beneath a foreign yoke in my dear strand!
> Midst these sweet hills and dales, under these stars,
> To live and to be free, my fathers fought.
> Must I still fight and bear anew the scars?
> Must freedom e'er with blood, not sweat, be bought?[9]

This question is not purely rhetorical: some sixty or so years after Citashe had called on his compatriots to educate themselves and to entrust their pen and their eloquence with the task of fighting for their rights, Dhlomo poses the problem clearly: the African has not received satisfaction in anything; on the contrary, his lot has greatly worsened since the passing of discriminatory legislation by the Pact government. Dhlomo's response is fundamentally different from the one suggested by Vilakazi in 'On the Gold Mines':

> You ask me whence these yearning words and wild;
> You laugh and chide and think you know me well;
> I am your patient slave, your harmless child,
> You say . . . so tyrants dreamt as ev'n they fell!
> My country's not my own – so will I fight!
> My mind is made: I will yet strike for Right.[10]

Here are thoughts that clearly foreshadow the poetry of the seventies; the fact that they are expressed in a language and an imagery that recall the English Romantic poets makes no difference.

Dhlomo, the forerunner, died in 1956, aged 50, when the black writers of the present generation had begun writing: tribal, and therefore linguistic, distinctions no longer had any meaning in spite of the efforts of the South African government to maintain them. It was as Africans, and mainly in English, that the Zulu, Xhosa and Sotho writers now began to express themselves.[11]

Writing in the vernacular languages did not, however, cease: the new racial laws on education increased its production while resulting in a fairly general decline in its quality.[12] There was one notable exception: Mazizi Kunene.

Kunene was born in Durban in 1930 and left South Africa in 1959, on the eve of Sharpeville. For a number of years he lived in London, where he held an important post with the African National Congress in exile.[13] He continued writing in Zulu: he became known to the English-speaking public through his *Zulu Poems*, translated in collaboration with Gillian Frost (Deutsch, London, 1970).

This was in no sense an urban poetry like that which was to be written in the townships from the middle of the sixties: it did not reflect the African's confrontation with the white city and its restrictions; it contained no descriptions of the black ghettos or of humiliating contact with the whites. Several of the poems have a pastoral setting; they are concerned with nature, love and friendship, with the cycle of the seasons and the generations. Yet Kunene is not at all indifferent to what is going on in the world, especially in his own country, or to the clash of cultures. How could he be when for long he travelled the world to bear witness against apartheid and concerned himself with the problems of the Third World?

But, by temperament and because, like Brutus and Pieterse as we shall see, he has other platforms from which to express his political views, his poetry has no trace of the language of protest. He avoids the purely anecdotal and the abstract and seeks within his own culture the images, symbols and metaphors which through their concreteness attain the universal. A quite definite elevation of thought runs through his poems and gives them their life, a combination of dignity and lyricism – a lyricism which is at times contained but which at others expresses itself with force and passion. Indeed, his criticism can be sharp:

> Europe, your foundations
> Are laid on a rough stone.
> Your heart is like cobwebs
> That are dry in the desert . . .
>
> Once I believed the tales.
> Once I believed you had breasts
> Over-flowing with milk . . .
>
> I know the hardness of your visions:
> You closed the doors
> And chose the bridegroom of steel.[14]

While the cry of the poet wounded by the ills that weigh his people down breaks out in 'The Screams':

I offer you screams of a thousand mad men . . .
I offer you voices of a thousand vultures . . .
I offer you the cloth that is torn in the middle
Left in the field
By those who departed before the children were weaned from the breast . . .
I offer you those who sleep alone
With their hands folding the dream . . .
I offer them to you to shout them to the world![15]

In fact, the range of Kunene's poetic talent is extremely wide. There is in 'The Screams' a sense of structure and rhythm which recurs especially in 'Thoughts on June 26'[16] and in 'Europe', the poem quoted above. There is an epic dimension as well, not only as regards the form – at the end of his collection Kunene gives an extract from his 'Anthem of the Decades'[17] – but also in his cosmic vision of people and things. We can see this in 'Place of Dreams', which develops a San proverb:

> There is a place
> Where the dream is dreaming us,
> We who are the shepherds of the stars.
> It stands towering as tall as the mountains
> Spreading its fire over the sun
> Until when we take one great stride
> We speed with the eagle on our journey.
> It is the eagle that plays its wings on our paths,
> Wakening another blind dream.
> Together with other generations hereafter
> They shall dream us like us.
> When they wake on their journeys they will say:
> Someone, somewhere, is dreaming us, in the ruins.[18]

Committed Kunene certainly is, but in the best sense of the word. Beyond the 'situation' itself, it is in the values of his own culture, through recourse in the first instance to his own language, that his commitment and his resistance are expressed. Evidence of this is to be found in the lengthy introduction to *Zulu Poems*, which is a fascinating guide to his own civilization and an invitation to attempt a deeper understanding of his poetry. In spite of the geographical separation, the poet has remained in complete communion with his people. It is with the firm conviction that those who follow him will take up the torch that he writes 'To the Killer':

> If your species multiply
> And all men derive from your image,
> We shall open our doors
> Watching them sharpening their swords with the morning star
> And spreading their blades covered with blood.
> They shall obstruct our passage in our travels
> And cut our heads because we were of alien clan,
> Believing that our blood is desirable.
> But the growing of the powerful buds
> Will not let them triumph;
> They will haunt them with talons of weeds
> Piercing them in their dreams.[19]

And it is as the citizen of a world that he wants to see more just, more upright and worthy, as the defender of the great human values, that he writes:

> When I have fulfilled my desires
> Let me take these grain baskets,
> And fill them up with other men's desires,
> So that whoever crosses the desert
> May never starve.[20]

Through his attachment to his mother tongue and to his African values, Kunene foreshadows the tendencies that will emerge fully into the open with Black Consciousness. He is not concerned with a love for the past or a return to a parochial view of culture harmful to the political battle of the present but with the urge to regain his dignity and force the white man to acknowledge the African, the 'Other', he has so long ignored and humiliated.[21]

In fact, vernacular poetry survives among the people, too. It is the people who are the anonymous and 'plural' author of the songs of resistance and scorn that are provoked by events or inspired by life with all its struggles. Mtshali has included one of these in his poem 'A Roadgang Cry' which ends with a cry of anger that rises from the very depths of oppression:

> It starts
> as a murmur
> from one mouth to another
> in a rhythm of ribaldry
> that rises to a crescendo
> 'Abelungu ngo dam
> Bazibiza ngo Jim —
> Whites are damned
> They call us Jim'[22]

Mtshali was, in fact, the first African after Dhlomo to resume the use of English as a poetic medium, but before him there were three Coloured poets: Dennis Brutus, Cosmo Pieterse and Arthur Nortje.

Notes

1. The written literature of the Xhosa was at that time only about sixty years old, which only serves to emphasize Citashe's remarkable success, prepared, it is true, by centuries of oral literature.
2. Quoted by Professor Albert Gérard in *Four African Literatures: Xhosa, Sotho, Zulu, Amharic* (University of California Press, Berkeley, 1971), p. 41.
3. Ravan, Johannesburg, 1971. The book has since been reprinted several times.
4. Italicized in the text.
5. In *Poems from Black Africa*, ed. Langston Hughes (Indiana University Press, 1963), pp. 111–13.
6. Vilakazi's poems have been collected in *Zulu Horizons* (Howard Timmins, Cape Town, 1962). The lines quoted here are taken from *The Penguin Book of South African Verse* (ed. Cope and Krige, Penguin, London, 1968), pp. 300–5. Professor Gérard quotes another version (op. cit., p. 253).
7. Quoted by Professor Gérard, op. cit., p. 228. Dhlomo's essay was published in *South African Outlook*, LXVI (1936), pp. 232–5.
8. The play is entitled *The Girl Who Killed to Save* (Lovedale Press, Lovedale, Cape, 1936); the poem, *The Valley of a Thousand Hills* (Knox, Durban, 1941).
9. *The Valley of a Thousand Hills*, ibid., pp. 37–8.
10. ibid.
11. There is a literature in the Sotho and Tswana languages, but the special circumstances of these peoples, who retained their independence (their countries are today called Lesotho and Botswana), makes it essentially a literature that glorifies their heroes.
12. See Gérard, op. cit., pp. 91–2.
13. Mazizi Kunene is at present teaching at the University of California, Los Angeles.
14. *Zulu Poems* (Deutsch, London, 1970), p. 76.
15. ibid., p. 52.
16. ibid., p. 4.

17. Kunene's major epic poem, *Emperor Shaka the Great*, was published in 1979 (Heinemann, London). It was followed by *Anthem of the Decades* (Heinemann, London, 1981) and *The Ancestors & the Sacred Mountain* (Heinemann, London, 1982).
18. *Zulu Poems*, op. cit., p. 36.
19. ibid., p. 48.
20. ibid., p. 53.
21. In this context, it should be noted that Kunene wrote the introduction to the English translation of Aimé Césaire's *Cahier d'un retour au pays natal* (Penguin, London, 1969).
22. *Sounds of a Cowhide Drum* (Oxford University Press, London, 1972), p. 13.

Chapter 9
The First Generation of Committed Black Poets

▼▼▼▼▼▼▼▼▼▼▼▼▼▼▼▼▼▼▼▼▼▼▼▼▼▼▼▼▼▼▼▼▼▼

Of the three poets studied here, the first, Brutus, is known especially for his parapolitical activities; the second, Pieterse, as the compiler of anthologies of plays by black writers; while Nortje is relatively little known abroad. Yet all three are authentic and talented poets writing in English and their work is closely bound up with the problem of apartheid.

Being Coloured, they were partially protected from some of the indignities and humiliations to which their black compatriots were subjected, especially the obligation to carry a pass, and they could have remained satisfied with their social situation, which was better than the average.

But they were proud, aware, too, that their position as teachers made them the accomplices of a system which sought to impose an inferior education on the black people, itself a prelude to their condemnation to an inferior status and to a situation which was getting worse year by year.

Brutus and Pieterse, much older than Nortje, fought apartheid at first from within the teaching profession, before becoming more directly committed politically. We shall read about the ups and downs of their lives and how they came to leave their country, Pieterse in 1964, Brutus in 1965. Their work reflects the struggle they have pursued in order to rise above the pettiness of a regime that is ready to do anything to get rid of people of stature as soon as they show any independence of spirit, active opposition and a desire to fight back.

Nortje was only 18 at the time of Sharpeville, and he had to stand by powerless as so many of his friends, who included especially Brutus and Pieterse, were silenced and imprisoned. He, too, went into exile in 1965, driven to despair by apartheid.

Three friends, three different kinds of commitment, three ways, too, of reacting to exile.

Dennis Brutus

Dennis Brutus belongs to the South African Coloured community. He was born in Salisbury (Zimbabwe, then Rhodesia) in 1924, but spent the next forty-two years in South Africa, which he had to leave to go into exile.

Brutus has described in 'Childhood Reminiscences'[1] the environment of his early years: a township in the suburbs close to Port Elizabeth inhabited by Coloureds with modest incomes. As a child, he was prevented for some time from going to school as the result of an accident, and spent much of his time alone, on a piece of wasteland on the edge of the township and the white residential area: 'On the stretch of land below the township, where the bus ran, was an open patch of waste ground. It was full of holes and mounds and littered with builders' rubble and refuse. Beyond this was a high fence and a row of trees'[2]

The poet's imagination later seized on the symbolic value of this place and made it the prefiguration of the destiny reserved by the world for the black man:

> It was a sherded world I entered
> of broken bottles, rusty tins and split roof-tiles
> bits of seashell, black sharp shards
> – the bladed cases of long-dried beetles.
> The littered earth was spiked with menace,
> with jagged edges waiting the naked feet;
> holes, trenches, ditches were scattered traps
> in waste plots where the broken earth was playground.
> This was the world through which I learnt the world
> and this is the image of my vision of the world.[3]

Brutus's parents were schoolteachers, but to augment the income of the family, which included three other children, his father kept their books for the Indian and Portuguese shopkeepers of Port Elizabeth, while his mother gave private lessons or took in washing. They were both great lovers of poetry, but it was his mother who exercised the strongest influence on the child by her choice of poems to recite or relate: the poems of Tennyson, Wordsworth's 'Lucy Gray' and 'The Prelude' and, 'last but not least', the tales of chivalry. The family was also very religious, and Dennis was for a long time a choirboy in his parish.

The primary school Brutus attended irregularly was run by Irish nuns; it was mixed in the South African sense of the word at the time, that is, it was open to children of all races, a factor which had a decisive influence on him: 'You knew so early that there were no real differences, that all differences were superficial and secondary.'[4] Otherwise, the long, solitary days Brutus spent away from school stimulated his inclination to daydream, fed by the stories his mother told him and the reading she encouraged. Soon, the child was reading everything he could lay hands on, provided from various sources, for along with the books his elder brother brought home from school (one of the few to possess a library), there were the books given to his mother by the white families for which she worked.

When he was nearly fifteen, Brutus, who had been kept back by his irregular attendance, entered the junior high school. He very quickly made up for the time lost; he was rapidly promoted, won a first bursary to enable him to continue his studies, and then received one from the City Council which meant he could go on to Fort Hare. He spent four years there, specializing in English literature and psychology; he was a brilliant student in both subjects. His varied reading ranged from St Thomas Aquinas to Marx. He also made a close study of apologetics and theology, taking part in a number of debates organized among Christians and the members of other faiths or atheists.

His parents found themselves in financial difficulties, so Brutus went to teach in a small village in the Karoo. When he completed his studies in 1947, he joined the social services, at the request of the Bureau of Coloured Affairs itself, which had noted the progress of this outstanding student. This experience as a social worker, coming after the experience gained as a teacher, initiated what was to be for him an important period in his life: it gave him access, in fact, to the shanty towns of Port Elizabeth.

He very soon realized that the majority of the coloured and African population live in appallingly unhealthy and promiscuous conditions. He was also able to see the extent to which the black is hounded by his impossible circumstances: not only does the law keep him in inferior and underpaid jobs, but the social services, too, through their lack of resources, are incapable of correcting the basic inequalities. It became clear to Brutus that the evil lay in the system itself.

His experience as a teacher confirmed this realization: with the passing of the new laws on the education of black people, the teacher was obliged to operate syllabuses geared specifically to the kinds of employment the government was prepared to make available to the working population.

In spite of the good reasons he could easily have found for engaging in active opposition, Brutus was not ready to become involved in politics, in the strict sense of the term: he belonged to the Catholic 'camp' and was, by definition, therefore, fiercely opposed to the Communists, many of whom at that time belonged to the left-wing organizations.

As he was in charge of sport at the school where he taught, Brutus once more came up against apartheid: the recent legislation had not spared this important area of South African life. The communities were now forbidden to meet one another in the sports stadiums, any more than they could in the schools; black people were not allowed to train alongside whites, or to compete with them. Moreover, their facilities were old and few in number; only whites were chosen to represent South Africa in international competitions.

While he was thus gaining experience as a future opponent of apartheid through the medium of sport, Brutus had the opportunity to become involved in a more concrete fashion by joining the editorial committee of a teachers' periodical, *Education News*. He contributed – in English, for he refused to write in the language of his oppressors – a monthly column which commented on current South African affairs. He also won the sympathy of the editor-in-chief of a Port Elizabeth newspaper and wrote a number of 'letters to the editor' which enabled him to make known his feelings about what was happening in the country.

Brutus's writings drew a warning from his Principal, who also criticized him for his other activities. Brutus had just, in fact, taken the important step of founding SASA (South African Sports Association), in October 1958. His aim was to draw the attention of the international sporting associations, in particular the IOC (International Olympic Committee), to the fact that the Union of South Africa was infringing the Olympic charter, which stipulates that 'no discrimination . . . is allowed against any country or person on grounds of race, religion or politics'; it also states quite clearly that the national Olympic committees must be 'autonomous and must resist all pressures of any kind whatsoever, whether of a political, religious or economic nature'. In setting up SASA, Brutus wanted to bring into being in South Africa a multiracial sporting organization which could achieve international recognition and, at a later stage, replace the existing organization which practised racial discrimination.

Alan Paton, who became Patron of the new association, emphasized that it was not at all intended that black sportsmen should dominate but to ensure that they would be recognized abroad and could represent their country alongside white sportsmen, if their performance justified it. In the speech he made in January 1959 at the opening session of SASA, Paton stressed that racial barriers are incompatible with the sporting spirit: they divide men instead of uniting them, and establish between them artificial hierarchies and a total lack of sportsmanship. Sport, properly understood, teaches men to know and to respect one another, to admire each other's prowess and to compete honestly.

This, then, was the way Brutus chose to involve himself in the day-to-day struggle against apartheid: it did not require him to surrender his religious convictions, but it was, obviously, non-political in appearance only. The government was not deceived: Brutus was put under surveillance by the Special Branch.

It was the year 1960 that saw Brutus's total commitment: not only did he feel that this was justified by the internal situation of the country but he had also reached the stage when he believed he could take his stand on the left without contradicting his religious loyalties.[5] His commitment, moreover, was now to express itself for the first time in poetry.

He began writing poetry in 1947–8: following a love affair, Brutus wrote a hundred or so poems, mostly sonnets, 'in the manner of Wordsworth and Shakespeare', he was to say later.[6] At university, however, he had specialized in Webster, not so much from preference as from a desire not to do what the other students were doing. His enthusiasm for Browning, whose influence on his first poems he acknowledges, also dates from his university days. Later, he discovered Eliot, Yeats and Hopkins and then, three years after starting teaching, he read Donne, who was to have a great influence on him. He wrote a number of poems which were lost during his travels in the years that followed. Only a few survived; they are contained in his first collection, *Sirens, Knuckles and Boots*.[7] The best-known of these poems is 'Nightsong City', frequently reprinted in subsequent anthologies.

This poem, in which the beloved and the homeland are intimately mingled and confused, was written in December 1960, for a young white woman with whom Brutus was at the time having an affair:

> Sleep well, my love, sleep well:
> the harbour lights glaze over restless docks,
> police cars cockroach through the tunnel streets;
>
> from the shanties creaking iron-sheets
> violence like a bug-infested rag is tossed
> and fear is immanent as sound in the wind-swung bell;
>
> the long day's anger pants from sand and rocks;
> but for this breathing night at least,
> my land, my love, sleep well.[8]

Brutus has explained the circumstances surrounding the composition of this poem, and his explanation enables one to grasp, in all its complexity, the genesis of the committed poem: Brutus speaks, in fact, of the 'electric moment of fusion', of the occasion when he managed, 'as if by magic', to speak at the same time of his homeland and his love:

> But writing for her – I think this is how it happened – I found I couldn't write a Christmas card that said what I wanted to say, so I wrote a little letter instead, which had been taking shape in my mind for some time and which, I think, was

influenced by Auden's poem, 'Lay your sleeping head, my love, human on my faithless arm' . . .
    So, then, I could be talking to her and, at the same time, about the country . . . At the moment I started, I didn't yet know what was going to happen. It was in the process of writing it that I discovered one could do the simultaneous statement, which I've ever since done.[9]

This woman, to whom he was united by links all the stronger for going against religious and racial taboos, was his companion in the underground resistance which was becoming established throughout the country. Thus, the two of them were at the heart of the struggle in this crucial moment of South Africa's history: the tragic events of Sharpeville had taken place in March 1960, the state of emergency had been proclaimed, the African organizations declared illegal and dissolved, and a number of political leaders, both white and black, taken into custody or placed under house arrest. The police patrolled the townships, which were seething with anger, and there was great tension throughout the country. It needed an intimate experience of danger and a total participation in the life of his compatriots, along with an unusually acute lyrical sense, for Brutus to be able, one Christmas Eve, to write:

> but for this breathing night at least,
> my land, my love, sleep well.

The 'as if by magic' suddenly becomes clear; if there is magic, it lies in the poet's capacity to find, at the right moment, the words needed to sing about the woman he loves and his country, without separating them, for they are the objects of a single love; Brutus will say later which should have first place.

But it was not because of his activities in the resistance that Brutus found himself again in the Nationalists' prisons – as a result of which his poetry was to take a new direction – but for the part he had played in SASA and the organization which succeeded it in 1962, SAN–ROC (South African Non-Racial Open Committee for Olympic Sports). Brutus had achieved a first success in 1961: the exclusion from an international competition of a South African team which had been selected on the basis of colour, not merit. After Sharpeville, taking advantage of the state of emergency, the police had confiscated the records kept at the offices of the organization run by Brutus. In 1961, he was forbidden to teach or to publish; at the same time, he was banned from taking part in any meeting of more than two people and from belonging to sporting organizations. No longer able to teach, Brutus decided to return to university and left for Johannesburg: there he found employment as Secretary to the Principal of a private school. He worked in the morning, attended his Law classes in the afternoon, then returned home where he was required to stay between 6 p.m. and 6 a.m.

House arrest was the penalty Brutus had to pay for secretly resuming his activities as secretary of SAN–ROC: he was arrested in May 1963, then released pending trial. It was at this point that the most dramatic event of his life occurred: in August of the same year, Brutus decided to go to Baden-Baden, the seat of the International Olympic Committee, in order to hand over irrefutable evidence of sports discrimination in South Africa and thereby to secure the latter's exclusion from the 1964 Games. When he crossed into Mozambique – legally, for he had a Rhodesian passport – he was arrested by the Portuguese secret police and handed over to the South African authorities. He was taken to Johannesburg where, convinced that the police would seek to eliminate him as it had done in the case of other embarrassing witnesses, he escaped while he was being taken from the central police station to prison. He received a bullet wound to the stomach during the chase and appeared in court after it had healed, to be condemned in January 1964 to eighteen months' hard labour.

It is on Robben Island, off Cape Town, that those who have been convicted undergo their sentence. Here the prisoners are cut off from all contact with the outside world: those with the heaviest sentences could then receive neither letters nor visits. Brutus found himself in the most closely guarded section, in the company of two of the principal leaders of the African resistance movement, Nelson Mandela and Robert Sobukwe. Every day, the prisoners were taken to the quarry where, under a blazing sun, they had to extract stones and reduce the large blocks to pebbles; when the work did not progress fast enough the guards beat them.[10]

In the beginning, it was impossible to write. Later, on the pretext of continuing his studies by correspondence, Brutus obtained a little paper and a pencil; in the end, it was on toilet paper that he wrote the drafts of a few poems.

Brutus was released in June 1965 at the end of his sentence. He was immediately subjected to a series of five-year banning orders: he was banned from leaving his house, attending meetings, teaching, going to the University, publishing and even from 'preparing for publication'. All he could now do was leave, which he did, not with a passport, but with a simple exit permit.

Brutus left South Africa at the end of July 1965. On the 31st, he arrived in London: he was free, but not from his memories:

> I walk in the English quicksilver dusk
> and spread my hands to the soft spring rain
> and see the streetlights gild the flowering trees
> and the late light breaking through the patches of broken cloud
> and I think of the island's desolate dusks
> and the swish of the island's haunting rain
> and the desperate frenzy straining our prisoned breasts
> and the men who are still there crouching now
> in the grey cells, on the grey floors, stubborn and bowed.[11]

Free to travel, free also to speak, Brutus threw himself energetically into action. His collaborators in SAN–ROC based the organization in London and made him its president. It had to be everywhere in the world where international sports meetings were being held, so Brutus had to do a great deal of travelling. At the same time, he was taken on by Canon Collins, the director of the International Defence and Aid Fund, which helped the families of South African political prisoners, often completely destitute as a result of being deprived of their breadwinner. Here, too, Brutus made an enormous contribution.

So began a long series of travels which took Brutus as representative of SAN–ROC or Defence and Aid to the four corners of the world. And to publicize what was going on in South African prisons, Canon Collins and Dennis Brutus published a White Paper: *South African Prisons and the Red Cross Investigation*.[12]

When he left prison, Brutus set himself the task of fighting to reveal the truth, so that South Africa might eventually become a country based on justice and democracy. If the poems he has published since hardly reflect this, it is because he has too high an ideal of poetry to allow it to be used for propaganda. A world still haunts him and he must write about it: he loves his country, but he lives in exile; he is free but his friends languish in prison. Wherever he is, in planes, during stopovers, in the short breaks between missions, he scribbles lines of poetry, but the really important part of his life is not there.

It is not by chance that so many elements of recent South African history reflect, almost literally, the period of the Nazi occupation of France and the Resistance: in both cases, one finds an oppressed people, the same aspirations towards freedom, constant tension, the crucial choice that is made by those who refuse to bow down, the risk involved in the very act of writing, let alone non-escapist poetry.

In South Africa, however, the problem is more complex, since the occupier has been there for three centuries. How, then, does one treat the work of art born of resistance in a different cultural and political climate? The example of Brutus is there to give us an idea: Brutus possesses all the qualities of the great committed poets, who thrill intensely to the rhythm of their country, espouse its causes and make its anger and its suffering their own.

The theme of the troubadour occupies a central position in his work: on it he focuses his devotion to his oppressed country. Brutus sees himself, in effect, as the knight who defends a cause, but it is not an abstract cause: his country became his 'lady' at the time of his affair with his companion in the resistance – a coincidence, as far as the events were concerned, but a lasting source of poetic inspiration:

> for you, you know, can claim no loyalty –
> my land takes precedence of all my loves.[13]

And it is in sexual terms that Brutus will henceforth express his love for his country. If the theme of the troubadour is linked to the theme of love, it is also linked to the theme of the prison: the poet must be able to suffer for his lady and the trials that he undergoes are intended to prove to her all the love the poet–knight feels for her. But, equally, it cannot be separated from wandering, from journeys, and those that Brutus undertakes in the service of his cause, in South Africa first of all then abroad, can only reinforce the analogy he sees between his own life and that of the troubadours. To this must be added, finally, the fact that after 1966 exile (separation from the beloved) reinforces the poet's expression of his yearning for his country, as do also his periodic bitter-sweet reunions with the Mediterranean countries which remind him, by their climate, their vegetation and their life-style, of his native Cape Province:

> A troubadour, I traverse all my land
> exploring all her wide-flung parts with zest
> probing in motion sweeter far than rest
> her secret thickets with an amorous hand:
>
> And I have laughed, disdaining those who banned
> inquiry and movement, delighting in the test
> of will when doomed by Saracened arrest,
> choosing, like unarmed thumb, simply to stand.
>
> Thus, quixoting till a cast-off of my land
> I sing and fare, person to loved-one pressed
> braced for this pressure and the captor's hand

> that snaps off service like a weathered strand:
> – no mistress-favour has adorned my breast
> only the shadow of an arrow-brand.[14]

'Banned' (line 5) refers to the different restrictions that the Nationalist government can place on the movements of its opponents, in particular to the one which forbade Brutus to leave his home. 'Doomed by Saracened arrest' is heavy with political and cultural connotations: Saracen, in its first sense, is the Saracen, the Infidel to whom the Troubadour is opposed in the name of his Faith; but the same term also designates in South Africa the armoured cars that patrol the African townships to impose order and sometimes, as at Sharpeville, terror. The allusion to the 'unarmed thumb' can only be understood if one knows that during the period of passive resistance by the Africans the thumb raised above a clenched fist was the rallying sign and an indication of refusal to collaborate. But, at the same time, the ineffectiveness of passive resistance as a form of combat ('simply to stand') prepares for the introduction of the verb 'quixoting': the struggle is unequal, the weapons of either side totally disproportionate, and the poet's ironic reference to himself tells us that the pursuer will have no difficulty in separating the knight from his lady. And, here, the lady is the motherland and, if it is the first time that the parallel is drawn between the beloved and the poet's country (in the feminine), it is not the last. Hence the allusion in the last two lines: it is not the coloured ribbon of his lady that adorns the poet–captive's breast but the arrow-shaped mark that all South African detainees wear so that they can be identified.

Some ten years after writing this poem, Brutus explained the exact meaning he attributes to the word 'troubadour':

> He [the troubadour], was first of all a soldier, he was a knight, he went to battle; secondly, he made up music, poetry – he fought and he sang. His third element was that he tended to have a reputation as a lover. And these are three elements which merge in my own poetry. It's singing poetry, it's poetry really which sings people to battle, in its own way, and it is about a permanent love-affair, a relationship between me and my country which is often described in male–female terms.[15]

Brutus owes this conception of the troubadour much more to his childhood reading than to dictionary definitions: the latter – the *Encyclopaedia Britannica* to which Brutus could have had access is no exception – only mention the three great sources of the troubadours' inspiration: war, religion, woman. On the other hand, the tales of chivalry that his mother told him helped to blend in Brutus's mind the figures of the knight and the troubadour.[16] This blending was certainly reinforced by the fact that many troubadours were also nobles ('knights'), and therefore involved in the wars of the period. We only need to mention Bertrand de Born, 'the fierce baron roaring in his armour',[17] and his poetry to see this. But in his reference to the sexual aspects of his love, Brutus is much nearer to the first generation of troubadours than to the second, who were influenced by the clergy and gave to their poetry a religious and courtly flavour.[18] We saw in the first stanza of 'A Troubadour' the unequivocal evocation of the lover and his land/lady: '. . . exploring all her wide-flung parts with zest', and the two lines that follow. This same characteristic is found in several other poems.[19]

There is no doubt, therefore, that Brutus, like many other 'troubadour – knights' of times gone by, fights and sings at the same time. It is, on the other hand, less certain that he writes a poetry which urges men to fight ('which sings people to battle'), even with the proviso that Brutus immediately adds ('in its own way').

In fact, Brutus has written few 'militant' poems, or to be more precise, if he has written any, he has published very few of them. This is not surprising in a man who loves fine poetry and who has declared that it is immoral for the artist to introduce propaganda into his work: militant poems are often declamatory, or else they want to convince at all costs. But this is not Brutus's aim, and he has sometimes been reproached for it. Thus, during a public reading of his poetry (in Chelsea in August 1971), when he was criticized by a member of the audience for rarely writing 'political' poems, Brutus retorted that it was true he had no intention of saying in so many words 'apartheid is detestable', but: 'This is apartheid as we live it; it is for you to draw the inescapable conclusions.'

The poem of this period which comes closest to a direct call to action, 'At a Funeral', was written to the memory of a young African woman who died soon after qualifying as a doctor, too rare an occurrence not to be celebrated and its heroine mourned. Nevertheless, although the purity of the intention and the nobility of the idea cannot be doubted, and although the poem also contains political and social allusions, their multiplicity within the restricted framework of a sonnet does it more harm than good. Abstract vocabulary abounds, the homage is inflated into rhetoric, and bombast has replaced the simplicity the subject demands.[20] This is not the case with 'Somehow we survive':

> Somehow we survive
> and tenderness, frustrated, does not wither.
>
> Investigating searchlights rake
> our naked unprotected contours;
>
> over our heads the monolithic decalogue
> of fascist prohibition glowers
> and teeters for a catastrophic fall;
>
> boots club on the peeling door.
>
> But somehow we survive
> severance, deprivation, loss.[21]

Here, the essential idea, which is a simple one but not without nobility given the context, is strengthened by the repetition ('somehow we survive, somehow tenderness survives') and gives the whole the form of a sonata *con variazione*. The veiled way in which the message of hope is addressed to the beloved enables it to be read as if it were addressed to the nation as a whole. The concrete elements prevail over the more abstract references of the third stanza, and the images and metaphors dominate, adding to the threatening atmosphere against which the determination of the protest poet asserts almost with serenity his certainty of better days to come.

In other poems of *Sirens*, the poet uses the weapon of irony: here, we return to poems full of cultural references, as if the writer wanted to show by the ease with which he moves in an environment which, in theory at least, does not 'belong' to him, by the subtlety of his allusions and by his command of the whites' language, that he is their equal, their superior even, for there are some winks, including the title 'Off the Campus', in the direction of the initiated:

> Tree-bowered in this quaint romantic way
> we look down on the slopes of sunlit turf
> and hear the clean-limbed Nordics at their play.
>
> We cower in our green-black primitive retreat
> their shouts pursuing us like intermittent surf
> peacock-raucous, or wracking as tom-tom's beat;
>
> So we withdraw from present, place and man
> – to green-clad Robin with an iron beak
> or Shakespeare lane-leaf-hidden from a swollen Anne.
>
> So here I crouch and nock my venomed arrows
> to pierce deaf eardrums waxed by fear
> or spy, a Strandloper, these obscene albinos
> and from the corner of my eye
> catch glimpses of a glinting spear.[22]

An American critic, Paul Theroux, has accused Brutus of showing racism in reverse by calling the whites 'obscene albinos'.[23] This misinterpretation is easy to make if one loses sight of the fact that the whole poem is written in an ironical vein and involves a subtle criticism of racial stereotyping. It must be said right away that Brutus wrote this poem in Johannesburg when he was a student at the University of the Witwatersrand: although he was permitted to attend classes alongside the white students, he was not allowed to join them on the sports field. It was from a shelter overlooking the campus, but outside it, that Brutus watched the games of his fellow students.

The irony is perceptible from the outset: 'clean-limbed Nordics' stresses the absurdity and the ridiculousness of South African racial vocabulary which seeks to define whites as 'Europeans'. There is also irony in the choice of 'cower' and 'primitive': these words refer once more to white stereotyping in their application to the poet himself who, hidden in his leafy nest, prepares his poison arrows, that is, the cultural weapons that the 'Nordics' have given him. In the last section, Brutus, abandoning the past and the culture inherited from the Colonizer, identifies himself with the first tribes, the Strandlopers, who saw those strangers, more naked in their whiteness than nature itself, coming along the beach resembling their own albinos, themselves objects of suspicion and taboo. Finally, the last two lines link the past to the present: those Hottentots had in fact had spears as weapons, but in 1961 the spear was the symbol of the resistance organization, and it is with this glance towards a 'militant' future that the poem ends.

A final example will show concretely how Brutus saw his role as protest poet during the sixties. This is the four poems Brutus published almost anonymously in February 1963 in *Fighting Talk*,[24] under the general title of 'Tourist Guide', accompanied by the dedication: 'For those confined to the magisterial district of X':

> Sturdy British businessmen
> made this town (and 'Coolies'!).
> Light-festoons along the beach

> dribble away the nutriment
> of glaucous hunger-swollen urchins;
>
> proud men display perverse inverted pride
> as carrier-beasts for lording colonialness;
> the stairs are occupied by ancient odours
> of curry, hospitality and insecurity,
> and the image of incited rampage
> is cherished like a rusted hunting-knife
> amid the bustle of rapacity,
> uncertain liberals and pink gins.

The poem sets out to re-establish several truths. Historical truth, first of all: the English traders did not 'create' Durban *on their own*, they were helped in this by the Indian labourers (known as 'coolies' by the whites) brought into the country after 1860. Moreover, the anti-Indian riots in Durban were, in the view of South African democrats, incited by the Afrikaner Nationalists in order to divide the non-whites, hence the reference to 'incited rampage' and the sentence that follows, which alludes to the frequent use of this argument by those who wanted to bring about this division. The poem also seeks to re-establish a certain social truth: this port built on the edge of a magnificent bay presents a pleasant façade but the show of bright lights must not allow people to forget the malnutrition of a large part of the population; it is not only the whites who come in for criticism, but those who collaborate with them as well ('carrier-beasts for lording colonialness').

Similarly, the three other poems present a more complete, more true-to-life picture of what South Africa is really like; taken together these poems belong to the best poetry of demystification which, without demagogy, without stridency, both asserts the unity of the resistance movement and sees the rebellion that will one day spring from the very existence of the townships created by Verwoerd. Take, for instance, the last lines of 'Johannesburg':

> ... and metal in the clank of teeming shacks
> tocsins the surgeon's cleansing cleaver.

'The surgeon' is an indirect reference to Dr Verwoerd, thus nicknamed because of his autocratic and ruthless policy of separation – hence 'cleaver'.

When Brutus left South Africa and began his travels about the world, Africa, only recently freed politically from colonial tutelage, was beginning to take stock of what remained of its own culture. Following the example of the writers of the independent black states, Brutus was to try and define his own Africanness. The only thing of which he was certain at this stage was that, in acting and writing in the way he had done so far, he had joined the handful of men whose commitment had expressed itself in concrete terms, men like the Tunisian Memmi and the Nigerian Wole Soyinka.

At the same time, his writing was transformed as a result of his experience of prison: the latter had tried him both physically and spiritually and had entailed a re-examination of what he had been and of what he had written. In the face of evil, injustice and continual harassment, in the face of his isolation (few of the letters from friends and family reached him, and he was allowed one short visit every three months), all he had to preserve him from insanity or suicide were his religion and his poetry.

The thirty-odd so-called prison poems (which were written, in fact, during his second period of house arrest, as the dates indicate) provide only a glimpse of the horror of prison life: it is not in *Letters to Martha* that we must seek a unique account of life on Robben Island, but in the articles and reviews Brutus has written in prose.[25] The poems, in fact, reveal the man Brutus rather than the prisoner: a man conscious of the weaknesses inherent in human nature and, in the circumstances, surprisingly understanding towards his enemies, rather than a militant who has given himself unreservedly to a cause.

Thus, to the man whose evidence in court had sent Brutus's brother to Robben Island, the poet wrote 'A Letter to Basil', in which he had this to say in particular:

> To understand the unmanning powers of fear
> and its corrosive action
> makes it easier to forgive.
> And there is even room for pity.
> For how will you endure
> the occasional accusatory voice
> in your interior ear,
> and how will you, being decent, not sorrow?[26]

To mark the anniversary of the defeat of the Zulu King, Dingaan, 'Blood River Day', which is always enthusiastically celebrated by the Afrikaners, Brutus wrote a group of three poems which are far from being one-sided. He indeed emphasizes the rowdy militarism and the bloodthirsty tribalism of the Nationalists ('guilt/ drives them to the lair/of primitiveness/and ferocity'), but he also asks the question:

> – who has not joyed in the arbitrary exercise of power
> or grasped for himself what might have been another's
> and who has not used superior force in the moment when he could,
> (and who of us has not been tempted to these things?)[27]

The second poem in the group develops the militarism theme in terms that make it difficult to be sure whether Brutus, writing in the first person plural, is speaking for the Nationalists or for all South Africans.[28]

His poetry itself has been stripped of inessentials: an extreme simplicity often resulting in the prosaic has replaced the baroque and affected style characteristic of the poems of *Sirens*. And if *Letters to Martha* still contains poems that sing, they are those written much earlier – Brutus was only to restore their chronology in *A Simple Lust*.

Poems from Algiers[29] is a slim volume comprising nine poems of varying length and a commentary running into several pages: the poems were written in Algeria during the first Pan-African Cultural Festival, the commentary a few months later (September 1970). In a very significant way, the collection brings together Brutus's personal reflections, expressed with great frankness, and his self-questioning concerning his 'representativeness' and hence his sense of belonging. But representative of what? And his belonging to what world?[30] In this Mediterranean climate which is so close to that of the Cape, the thoughts he evokes mingle and become confused: does he belong to a clearly defined African or South African world? Or is he, in his fundamental solitariness, the unattached poet who is, by that fact, universal? Hence the poem that opens the collection, 'And I am Driftwood', a meditation on his destiny as an exile which opens out onto the mystery of man as a whole, and not only of the man Brutus:

> (Though we know how clouds gather and have weighed the moon,
> Though we have erected and heaved ourselves
> in some vast orgasmic thrust
> to be unmundane and to trample the moon –
> still the blind tides lunge and eddy,
> still we writhe on some undiscovered spit,
> coil in some whirlpool of undefinable tide).[31]

In the commentary which follows the poems but which is directly related to 'And I am Driftwood', Brutus tries to answer his questions. With the openmindedness which is typical of him, he refuses to allow himself to be enclosed in any particular definition of Africanness: Africa is big enough and varied enough to hold what he represents, that which makes him different as well – only to the extent, however, that he can really 'belong' anywhere. In this brief pause in the troubadour's wanderings – here, the stress is placed on wandering, and affirmation momentarily replaces the questioning – we must note Brutus's conclusions:

> I settle for being the non-totemistic 'new' African artist Ibrahim Salahi spoke about this month, who will simply take his place in the whole of world culture while always bearing certain distinctive features as a result of his origins and experience. And it may be that in some respects our experience is more humane – i.e. is more considerate of human feeling, because we have, up to now, in some measure, escaped the dehumanizing processes or events which have made a mark, or are marking, other societies.[32]

Thoughts Abroad, published in the same year but under a pseudonym to enable it to be sold in South Africa, opens with a very fine poem which, seven years after *Sirens*, establishes the link between past and present:

> When last I ranged and revelled all your length
> I vowed to savour your most beauteous curves
> with such devout and lingering delight
> that they would etch themselves into my brain
> to comfort me throughout the prisoned night.
>
> But waking early in the frosty dawn
> and finding you dishevelled and unkempt
> my heart arose as though you showed your best
> – and then I wryly knew myself to be
> the slave of an habituated love.[33]

Indeed, it is in this collection that the song of exile comes across most powerfully, beneath the overcast skies of London or the bright skies of India with, at each stage and perhaps because of his freedom of movement, the memory of the men who are still in prison. Thus it is that Brutus writes of a visit to Hamlet's castle:

> O might I be so crouched, so poised, so hewed
> to claw some image of my fellows' woe
> hacking the hardness of the ice-clad rock,
> armed with such passion, dedication, voice
> that every cobblestone would rear in wrath
> and batter down a prison's wall
> and wrench them from the island where they rot.[34]

The collection also reveals Brutus's wider commitment to the problems of his fellow men, whatever the colour of their skin. The work of destroying deceptive appearances which so far he had restricted to South Africa he now carries out wherever he feels it necessary to dispel ambiguity. So, on a visit to Bristol, the former centre of the slave trade, of the 'triangular' trade which to a large extent made it possible for Britain to accumulate the capital necessary for its technological development,[35] Brutus addressed the following poem to the Quaker owners of Cadbury's:

> Frys still sell chocolate
> still glean the cocoabean
> and the bean still coalesces to a swollen gleam –
> sweatdrops globed on salt black flesh,
> lambent like blooddrops fresh and red.
>
> A factory sprawls in acres of verdant park
> and the city squats as it anciently did
> on its excremental guilt and dominance –
> and a ragged refuse dump of spilled, screwed,
>   dried, twisted, torn and unforgiven
>   black lives.[36]

In Belfast, when he went to the University to organize a demonstration against a visit of the Springboks, he also attacked economic exploitation, for which racism, in his view, is often only a pretext. In Dubrovnik, he expressed his surprise at the contrast between the ideals of a socialist country and the luxury of its hotels.

Thoughts Abroad is therefore a demonstration of Brutus's growing awareness of the problems of his time and, once again, of his love for his country: but it is also a continuation of his self-interrogation – across the centuries he holds out his hand to that other exile, the French Renaissance poet Joachim du Bellay ('in fruitless search of depths:/only in myself, occasionally, am I familiar'.[37]

Since *A Simple Lust*, which essentially brings together the poems contained in *Sirens*, *Letters to Martha*, *Poems from Algiers* and *Thoughts Abroad*, Brutus has published two slim volumes. *China Poems* consists of a few *haiku* written during a stay in the People's Republic of China in August–September 1973 but published in 1975 (African and Afro-American Studies and Research Centre, University of Texas, Austin). Brutus employs this form, which is not new to him, with varying success; we could quote this particularly fine *hakai*:

> The tree in the Emperor's Garden
> will not accept
> the discipline of marble. (p. 9)

Strains (Troubadour Press, Austin, Texas, 1975) contains older poems going back to 1962, 1966, 1967 and 1968, and about fifteen more recent poems.

Stubborn Hope also contains a few older poems, some more recent ones, and a selection from *China Poems* and *Strains*.

Brutus stayed twice in the USA in 1969–70 as a Visiting Professor, and has now settled there at Northwestern University (Evanston, Illinois), where he teaches. He has not, however, stopped his travels about the world, in furtherance of his efforts to have South Africa excluded from international sporting competitions.

He continues his work for SAN–ROC, in fact, with his London friends; the enormous undertaking begun in South Africa with SASA has borne unhoped-for fruit, for South Africa, unable to prove that it has ceased practising apartheid in sport, has been excluded from the Olympic Games. At the Montreal Games, Brutus succeeded in getting most of the African countries to withdraw in protest against the presence of the New Zealand athletes, who were accused of having competed with South African sportsmen after the events in Soweto. A sour victory, however, to judge by the attacks on Brutus by the press, radio and television of certain countries more concerned with entertainment than moral principles! But a victory, all the same, for the campaign for the abolition of all discrimination (at the level of sport, of course) is growing among white South Africans aggrieved by the isolation from the rest of the world in which the policies of their country have placed them. Brutus and his friends are ever vigilant, to ensure that, in this area as well as in others (for instance, the so-called independence of the Transkei), the South African government does not pull the wool over the eyes of international opinion.

In summarizing our view of this writer who is inseparable from the life of his country and of his century and whose future development is difficult to predict (for Brutus is sixty), it may be best to stress those characteristics which show his originality.

As a man who has protested and as a poet, Brutus clearly deserves to be called a committed writer. With him, the marriage of poetry and commitment is possible and complete only because he is involved in two types of quite separate activity: political and parapolitical activities and poetry. The former enable him to serve in his capacity as a citizen, they are the outlet for his need to act and to speak out. As a result, it has been possible for him to keep his poetry relatively free of propaganda, since he has had the opportunity to make his ideals known in another way. It is no secret that Brutus dreams of being able to devote himself entirely to poetry: the fact that he has postponed the realization of this dream clearly shows that he gives his social and political responsibility priority.

It would, however, be to misunderstand him and the significance of his present struggle against the Nationalist government especially to view his commitment as a limited one.

In fact, in spite of his conscientious pursuit of his political activities and his unswerving devotion to his country, Brutus, as we have seen, seeks universality. One of his contributions to the discussions during the 1967 Stockholm conference, on the subject of commitment, would provide conclusive proof of this if many events in his life and many of his poems were not already there to do so:

> This problem lies at the heart of this conference and at the heart of the writer as a person, that he must commit himself. Not to *African* personality; I believe it is to human personality that he must commit himself. And so, whether we are

Finns or Swedes or Norwegians or whether we come from any part of Africa, we are all committed, at least to one value, the assertion of human value, of human dignity, and that is why we have a special function when we see human dignity betrayed.[38]

In Brutus's own case, it is surely the overflow from his everyday activities that gives his poetry its unique character as the expression of personal confidences, broadened in the first instance to take in the drama which is playing itself out in South Africa, and thereafter the planet as a whole. In his themes and in his concern for human dignity, Brutus is clearly a writer of the second half of the twentieth century, except only that his language is generally not violent: he speaks in tones of moderation, often sadly, where others feel the need to cry out.

As for his influence on the young black generation of his country, it is likely, in the short term at least, to be less important than Mtshali's or Matthews's, if only because, for the time being, his work is still banned in South Africa.[39] As he himself has said, he belongs to the team out front, the one that is making the most effort, in company with his friends Mphahlele and Pieterse; but he has also said that 'the best is yet to come'.

Cosmo Pieterse

There are two well-blended tendencies in Cosmo Pieterse which must not be arbitrarily distinguished from one another, for they are the whole man: the love of words and the love of men. They combine so closely that it is impossible to say which is the stronger; they fill each of his daily activities and they find their expression at all levels of his professional and political life and in his poetry.

In his own country, Cosmo Pieterse was a teacher of English language and literature, as well as a man of the theatre, until his activities as an opponent of apartheid brought down upon his head a number of banning orders. He then continued in exile a career as teacher and lecturer and worked closely with the African service of the BBC, while at the same time writing essays, introductions to the anthologies he has published, and poetry.[40] This illustrates the importance for him as a broadcaster and man of the theatre, and as a teacher who is also a poet, of the world of sound, the world of everyday words, with their semi-magical force, which cannot, however, stop 'saying' because they are the most privileged means of contact between men. The world of the words he uses, although it is sometimes difficult to enter, prefigures, in fact, the world of tomorrow, more intelligent and more open because then culture will no longer be the preserve of a small category of human beings, more just too and freed from all political fetters because words are free and Cosmo Pieterse, Cape Coloured and South African, is not: few writers in exile convey as he does the impression of never having left their country, of continuing to write and to fight as if from the inside.

Anyone who has not heard Pieterse reading or speaking poetry has not experienced the obvious enjoyment, the combination of intelligence and intoxication with which he communicates a language he seems to be discovering for the first time. Although he speaks Afrikaans fluently, and has written a number of poems in that language, it is English he prefers now, an English that he seems to gather from its beginnings, an English that is very close to its original meanings and its many roots. When he discusses poems or recites his own verse, one thinks of the craftsman at his anvil or his workbench, hammering and carving with a conviction that does not exclude a very lively sense of humour the words and sentences he then directs at his fellow men and women with a mixture of strength and tenderness.

In fact, Cosmo Pieterse could be defined in terms of two of the characters in his first book, *Present Lives, Future Becoming*, if it were not that they are two whereas he combines the characteristics of both of them. Nkosi, the first of these characters, appears in the barely fictional part of the book, which deals with the everyday realities of a South African mine. Nkosi is a little like a character from a novel by Emile Zola, to whom Pieterse explicitly refers, but not at all like the Souvarine of *Germinal*, who is the very opposite of the ideas promoted by Pieterse: Souvarine dreams of carrying out on his own an act that is little short of insane, whereas Nkosi is imbued with the idea that only unity in the struggle *and* the education of the masses will enable the latter to free themselves one day from oppression. That is why, along with his work as a militant and a stirrer of consciences, Nkosi continues to educate himself, reading while his comrades are still asleep, so as to be able, one day, to enlighten them, with their help.

The other character from the same book is Bra (Brother) Joe, who appears in the story 'She Been A Cherry Soph'town My Boy' and who is described on several occasions as being 'the man of words, the spinner of a tale, the tongue that sings, the tongue of fire, the fire in my blood, the blood of a poem, the poetry of Sophiatown'.[41]

Cosmo Pieterse no more lived in Sophiatown than he was a faceworker in a mine; yet there is a great deal of Nkosi and Bra Joe in him, a great deal of love for men and for words.

Pieterse's career had been all planned in 1948 when the Afrikaner Nationalists came to power: after going to university, he would become a teacher. In the year that followed, he continued his studies and finally obtained his degree in education, as well as an MA in English.

Pieterse has said that he owes nearly all his education to the influence of his mother, and of two aunts who took him in when his mother left Windhoek, where she had given birth to him in 1930, to go to Cape Town to work as a qualified nurse. It was in the Karoo where they lived, some fifty miles from Cape Town, that Pieterse was to spend ten years of great importance for his education, which he completed at his mother's insistence.

Cosmo came from a Cape Coloured family settled in Namibia (South West Africa), whose origins were mixed in the extreme: at family gatherings, the range of colours went from nearly white to very black. On his mother's side, he was of Sotho–Irish descent, and on his father's side of Xhosa and Hottentot descent. The schools he attended were either mixed (where there were more Coloured than African pupils) or mainly African. His first encounter with the colour problem in South Africa occurred when he was about twelve, at a mission school run by whites but where white nuns in shoes and barefooted black nuns worked side by side. Two influences marked his childhood: Africa and religion. Close contact with the African community made it easy for him to gain access, through an aunt born in Namibia, to ancestral traditions which had survived chiefly in the form of stories relating to everyday life or to African history, with its legends and heroes. As for the religious influence, Pieterse relates how one of his aunts was a member of the Dutch Reformed Church, and since he had been confirmed in the Anglican Church, it sometimes happened that he went to church five or six times on a

Sunday, taking part in the services of both churches.[42] A passage in his childhood recollections published in *Present Lives, Future Becoming* is very revealing (even though it is the adult who records them) about the imaginative proclivities of the child and his taste for music, which was to find its best outlet in the only medium available to him – language:

> And then at 11 o'clock it would be Matins and the organ rolling out peals of thunderous thrills and you shaking and moaning with all that music, making your own noises in your head to echo now the answer then the sounds that made you find depths within you that you would never have been able to recognize or realize if it were not for the church bells chiming, the organ moaning, the homing pigeons and the wild turtle-doves cooing and gurgling amongst the green berries and the jagged outlines of lead, singing together in the windows to make those oblongs of glass into pictures and stories and truths and dimensions and world without end. And you would be kneeling.[43]

His taste for words was to develop when he began teaching. His university studies had led him to the discovery of the writers who were to inspire him: Keats, Hopkins, Dylan Thomas, and Joyce, who was to remain his favourite author. He had, however, begun writing poetry when he was twelve, after the thrill of reading *Macbeth*, whose imagery, more than its language, had impressed him. Later, he was to use his own poems to stimulate the critical awareness of his pupils and develop their creative abilities. It seemed to him that a command of language provided a greater chance of communicating quickly and effectively with one's fellow men. In 1969, he declared on this subject:

> And I love words just to be in a sense toys that one plays with, because it seems to me basically, really, that this is one level at which words do what they should do most effectively. The sheer love of the element we have, of the medium where the medium in a sense is as important as the message because it seems to be the corollary of this idea: that if we learn to enjoy the medium, then the message itself can be much more clear.

But language was also a crucial weapon in his political work, which began in 1952, the year he started teaching, during the Defiance Campaign. The teaching profession was at the time the spearhead of the Coloured opposition to apartheid, and Pieterse was active in the Teachers' League of South Africa. He later became a member of the Non-European Unity Movement (NEUM). It was because of his activities that he was eventually banned from teaching and publishing and had to leave South Africa in 1964: he was 34.

Twenty or so poems read on the radio, others published in various journals (one of these 800 lines long, has all the appearance of an oratorio), the collection already mentioned, comprising prose and poetry, and 150 unpublished poems which the author has not yet weeded out – this is the relatively modest total that the critic has at his disposition to give an idea of a many-faceted poet whose chief quality seems so far to have been above all his ability to *live* with his contemporaries and whose commitment expresses itself in an original and very personal manner. One of the keys for an understanding of Cosmo Pieterse is to be found in his great modesty, which has made him for a long time prefer to publish the writings of his fellow poets instead of his own, and in his professionalism, which required him to *hand over* to the public only those poems he considered ready for publication. This means that the poems which have so far been published have survived the critical examination to which he has submitted them and that unpublished material must be used with great care.

Pieterse's essential characteristic is that his heroes are never alone, however isolated they may be, and that in his poetry the 'I' is never a sign of narcissism or egocentricity. The case of Looksmart, the African National Congress militant whom Pieterse made the hero of his 'Ballad of the Cells', is there to show this.

This long poem is in fact an excellent guide to an understanding of a coherent body of writing at the chronological centre of which (1962) it stands. Looksmart Solwandle Ngudle was born and bred in the Transkei, which he left in order to become a militant in Cape Town. Arrested in terms of the so-called '90 days' law, which allowed the detention without trial for three months of any suspect believed to be in a position to provide the police with information, Looksmart was taken to Pretoria. His interrogators tried to force a confession from him through torture; in vain. When he was eventually murdered, they disguised it as suicide; so Looksmart, who no longer even had the strength to eat, was found hanged in his cell.

The poem takes the form of an oratorio in which several voices are heard, in turn or simultaneously: the narrator's voice, Looksmart's, his torturers' and that of the choir, which represents South Africa – a liberated South Africa. At the same time, it is the narrative of a sort of 'Passion', with Looksmart's torturers trying to make him deny his cause, to betray his colleagues, and above all to lose faith: his friends have deserted him or they have confessed, they say, or they have gone into exile and are composing useless motions while he is suffering in his cell. Besides, in the country itself, the situation is scarcely any better for the opponents of the regime: aren't the communities fundamentally hostile to one another? Only the government 'is doing something'.

As these voices try to sway him, Looksmart expresses his confidence: it is a waste of time quoting the Durban riots or the profiteers who exploit their brothers in oppression – this is merely an attempt to divide which is to the advantage of the white community only. 'Natal gave all birth', cries Looksmart. Then, when he is told that the government is going to give the Africans more land and more rights (in the Bantustans), Looksmart replies with sarcasm and, breaking into a political song of the late 1940s, he attacks the government's allies, men like Kaiser (Caesar) Matanzima, an obscure headman appointed by the government and now, thanks to it, Prime Minister of the Transkei and an African quisling.

Finally, in response to the accusation levelled against those who have gone into exile, to the allusion to the so-called inaction of his black brothers, Looksmart, absolutely certain that the whole country suffers with him and supports him, proclaims, in a paraphrase that adds to Donne's 'No man is an island',

> No man is islanded if hope
> oceans his lone peninsula.[44]

Throughout his passion, Looksmart is sustained by the fleeting vision of his childhood village, his country's landscapes, which stand between his physical suffering and himself. A whirlwind of names assails his spirit, although it is no indiscriminate blending of those that brought shame and those that brought pride to the nation.

The African national anthem, 'Nkosi Sikelelei' Afrika', rings out from time to time, sung by children, symbols of the seeds that are beginning to shoot. At no time does any dichotomy between Man and Nature to which he belongs show itself. The irresistible power that runs through the latter is the same that fills the men of this country with the certainty that the future belongs to them. It is this power that sustains Looksmart during the interrogation sessions and the torture, that enables him to resist the temptation to despair – the 'demonic' enterprise of the police who encircle him, rising to his consciousness in a kind of delirium where the various voices meet, but where, in the end, the 'good voices', those that speak of loyalty and love, triumph, So, this song-poem which begins and ends with the word 'alone' only does so in order to assert that on the contrary Looksmart is not alone, that he is surrounded by the solidarity of a whole people and that his example will serve to inspire those who follow him:

> Alone;
> His ghost haunts me,
> Nor will it leave you alone
> Till his restless corpse
> Tall spirit
> Is grown
> Beyond dark taunts in
> Fenced cities, bitter dorps*
> To its own bright station
> Within our possible time
> That we will inherit
> The ageless all-we
> Whose reasoned elation
> Is rhymed, timeless, sublime.[45]

'Within our possible time' – another key to an understanding of Cosmo Pieterse is, in fact, Time: here lie the certainty and the comfort of the militant and the exile active in the fight, here will be found the realization of his hopes, the promise of the new world. Pieterse's poems often refer to Time and to change: germination, shoots, flowers, fruit and, above all, the berry, the perfect shape, containing both the finite and the promise of future creation. 'The Silver Echo', written in 1962 in memory of the two aunts who brought him up, is a hymn of life and a song of hope which draws its images from the vineyards around Cape Town where he spent the happy period of his childhood. Playing on the word 'must' from the start of the poem, Pieterse links the idea of responsibility with that of the inevitable process of fermentation which releases the essence of things:

> We are, and being, must:
> Must breathes
> Itself and liquefaction
> And in its death
> Bequeathes
> Generation to generation to generation

---

* *dorp* (Afrikaans): small village.

> To regenerate
> And inherit
> Its spirit
> And dust.[46]

Time is insufficient on its own; there must also be the continuous effort of men to gather the harvests of the future. This idea of individual and collective responsibility frequently recurs under Pieterse's pen: the planting of the seeds is merely a promise, only the will and the anger of the oppressed can give them the necessary strength to germinate and to break the obstacles between them and the nourishment they need. The obstacles themselves are not to be found outside oneself: the hereditary enemy has only been able to establish himself in the country because of the disunity that divides and betrays.

'Within our possible time', therefore, also stresses the sense of urgency that Pieterse evokes in his short one-act play, *Doctor in the House*, as well. The character of the old woman, Ma Latu, stands in gentle opposition – for the relationship between the couple is placed under the sign of love – to that of her husband, as if Pieterse wanted to contrast action and procrastination. In reply to Pa Tema, who has just said, 'We must wait', Ma Latu says, 'We must wait. The day does not wait, Tema, and disease does not wait. Day sets the table of weaknesses and disease dines away with his jaws of pain and then death comes along and clears the remains away and there are only left the bare, bleak bones.[47]

This couple's example is not gratuitous; for Pieterse, the unity of the nation is reflected in the unity of the Couple. In order to understand why he constantly returns to this theme, it is necessary to realize the importance, for the birth of a new society, of the liberation of women in societies in which the notion of 'machismo' is particularly strong. In South Africa, the importance of this is reinforced by the fact that the status of the black woman involves a double inferiority. The racial laws and customs make her a person who is virtually deprived of rights; in addition, as is frequently the case in oppressed societies, the male tries more or less consciously to assert elsewhere the 'power' of which he is deprived, in the only place where he can exercise it with impunity and even with the complicity of the dominant culture – in his family, by in his turn oppressing his wife and denying her equal status with him. But the black South African woman, like her North American sister, is often the family's most stable material and emotional support. She distinguished herself, too, very early on in the political battle: partly out of patriotism, but also because she knew that her own liberation was inseparable from that of her companion. The fact of her oppression, her vulnerability before the law, as well as her natural pugnacity, have made her a formidable fighter, and many women have been arrested, tried and sent to prison since the beginning of the protest movement in the 1950s. It is therefore not surprising that Pieterse should have made Nkosi's companion, Mary, the fighting woman, who in spite of their separation conducts her own fight at the same time as she urges Nkosi on and gives him her support. She is indeed, the poet tells us, 'the voice of the forgotten half of the Nation'.

The woman is therefore an essential part of the longed-for renaissance, of the end of the night that the common struggle of Mary and Nkosi promises, metaphorically, in the symbol of the sleeping miners, to the South Africa of tomorrow. She is there, present, not the complement, but the other 'half' without whom the man cannot live, cannot accomplish anything lasting, cannot fulfil himself. By the resistance she offers to life's burdens, by her capacity to receive the regenerative seed, to bear and to give birth, by her physical constitution, which binds her closely to the cycle of Nature, the woman is intimately linked to Time: like it, she 'bears' and sustains.

> For being forbearing
> My darling and wearing
> The mood of the morning
> I love you I love you
>
> For singing past sighing
> And flying past winging
>
> And caring past crying
> For daring and dying
>
> And seeing and hearing
> For being for bearing
>
> I love you I love you.[48]

The daily struggle can only be carried on by people who are equal: the accord achieved by bodies alone is not enough; there must also be the accord born of true dialogue. Here, too, we find once more the cardinal importance of language.

Pieterse probably owes his sense of his roots to his childhood spent in the Karoo, to his familiarity with a truly African environment, and to his late contact with the city. His attachment to the land of his birth is expressed in the first instance through the products of its soil. 'Fruits', placed at the centre of the long poem in fourteen sections entitled 'Exile's Re-initiation', is ample evidence of the poet's closeness to his environment. It is also a striking illustration of the muscular pleasure to be found in *speaking* the poem before writing it. One is reminded of André Spire's prophetic book, *Plaisir poétique et plaisir musculaire*, written a few decades ago and contemporary with the earliest research into the production of sounds. One of Spire's arguments was that our whole phonological system, tongue and teeth included, share in an act of creation which involves tasting both as a sensual and as an intellectual pleasure. 'Fruits' must be read and listened to in this way, and so, too, many of Pieterse's other poems:

> Listen Listen Listen guards
> Listen to the gourds, the sentinel
> Calabashes singing the golden wholesome simplicity
> curved for filling the flesh
> fleshed for feeding the mouth
> mouthed for reaping the water
> water for ripening repeated in the kiss of the
> sun of the golden and open-eyed air
> Listen to the round gourds drinking their water.[49]

In fact, the whole of 'Exile's Re-initiation' (dedicated to the African sculptor Dumile) is his gift to the land of South Africa. In it, the exiled Cosmo Pieterse celebrates his wedding to his land in a debauchery of sounds and resounding colours, but it is a controlled debauchery and a rational intoxication. These sentences that unwind endlessly, without full stops, without apparent pauses, the continuous thread that binds his central ideas for them to be read, are in fact the visible sign of his concept of life and of his political vision, expressed in poetic terms. Indeed, we have here – and in this sense the term 'wedding' is not too strong – a mystical union with the land, with its hills, rivers and fruits, a renewed communion, by means of a veritable immersion, through language, in the names of places, in the nuptial water of words that evoke the beloved land, embrace it lovingly, make it rise up again, not with the pain and poignancy of exile, but beautiful as on the first day for the lover who has never really left it. In this way, the poet takes it with him, celebrates it, daily breaks the bread of its presence and daily, also, tastes its wine which is intoxicating only because it is the wine of freedom.

The opening strikes the reader immediately: because of its ellipses, which set up a coming-and-going between the present and a future that seems to have been lived already, full of meaning on the political level through the insertion of the words 'we shall return'; because of the way words echo one another, and the deliberate playing on words, producing associations that also have a political significance (for instance, the allusion to the Orange 'Free' State). But it is also, because of its sound effects, a poem to be spoken aloud, to be declaimed, to be sung almost, so that its intensity and its majesty can fully emerge:

```
We are shouting    Goodbye
                   Goodbye good land
                   Good Hope good hope
We'll be singing   Welcome when you sing Welcome
                   We'll come
                   home dancing over grey wastes
                          grey clouds and grey seas
                          grey days all of
January February March April
March until all may March right through
            the river of the land
in a climate of rich rivers    KEI and Keiskamma
                   FISH RIVER
                   BLOEDRIVIER
                   AMANZINTOTI
across a grey river into the new orange ripe and free state
of re-birth where all our lands
            cape
But now the land is called granite and locked rock
                        the closed mouth
                        opens crying
                        and in first humble
            breath.[50]
```

The structure of 'Exile' reveals what is truly a dialectic of hope amounting to a final rejection of exile. The general movement is circular, the end being already implied in the beginning, but it also goes from the periphery to the centre, from the seed to the pulp, from the dawn to the middle of the day, from the spring to the autumn. A subtle anthropomorphism blurs the lines and the shapes and simultaneously develops the various processes of maturation: of thought, of fruits.

Cosmo Pieterse plays on the different meanings of the same word so as to bring out the interpenetration of human and natural rites. The constant recourse to animal and plant symbolism means that the poem only gives up its secret and its richness on the level of the images after several readings. The traditional is set side by side with the esoteric and the lyrical without ever jarring, the link being provided by its incantatory character, very appropriate to this celebration so full of sounds, songs and the charm of music. A celebration is always something of a rediscovery, the repossession of a looted or badly managed patrimony. With love and action to guide them, the men who had left and who return at this hour of truth which is midday can cry:

> We shall conjugate every known
> human noun
>
> We shall decline the verb
> 'yield' of our land
> And disturb the universe
> Of song to rehearse
> The new nuptials' high hymn and the
> amen of anther and hymen[51]

Pieterse's commitment is, then, expressed in an original and a very personal manner. He directs what he has to say above all to the men and women of his country: although he does so without any concern for colour or the differences between the communities, it is nevertheless those who are fighting against apartheid that he is addressing, those who struggle, not those who hold the reins of power. There are no personal complaints, no laments: he prefers to speak as a militant to other militants, and he does so in a manly way, but always linking men and women; without ever losing sight of his objectives but, what may seem paradoxical, without for all that using only everyday language. Committed writer as he is, there is in Pieterse too great a love for language, which brings men together, for him not to force it to give up its resources, and more besides. He does not hesitate to experiment in the name of freedom and having in mind those who, once they are freed, will have access to culture and will be able to sharpen their teeth on his poetry. The latter is remarkably free of the dross that committed, even revolutionary, poets often cannot avoid. Pieterse, like Brutus, was lucky to have had in South Africa enough platforms on which to give vent to his political slogans: he was able to put them aside in order to speak another language, but not necessarily to say anything very different, in passing from politics to poetry. Of all the present committed poets, he has the best talent for choral symphonies. It is on these large canvases that those artists who have at heart the progress of mankind best express themselves.

Arthur Nortje

No presentation of Arthur Nortje[52] could separate the poet from the man of colour. A solitary person, this he might well have been with or without the racial laws of his country, but separation was the hallmark of his childhood and adolescence. Friendship and love are two remedies for solitude under any skies, but not here. Love is forbidden if the woman who is loved is white and repression has removed all your friends – they are in prison or have gone abroad. There would still be the countryside, the incomparable beauties of nature, if only the mind were free of its obsession: liberty. Only poetry remains, carrying with it melancholy, but also irony – two chords which are found everywhere in Nortje's work, the poison and its antidote being often present in the same poem.

Then came the day when Nortje in his turn took the road of exile. Legally, as a student, but it was exile all the same: in order to find happiness, he would have to find a way to blot out the past, to forget everything the emigrant takes with him in his luggage, everything he has left behind. This man exiled from himself, this outsider in his own country, uproots himself. Action might have saved him, but Nortje was not a militant. There only remains, then, the bitter taste of conditional freedom, that of the man without a country.

For the passport issued by the oppressor is in no sense the key to some kind of citizenship; it is hardly even a door half-opened onto an elsewhere scarcely more satisfactory than the here denied him. There remain the devices men use to try and deceive their loneliness, shorten their nights, and overcome their incurable malaise: alcohol, drugs, barbiturates – or the quest for the endless repetition of the contacts of the flesh. There also remains death, in which Nortje had served his apprenticeship in his own country, the death that prowled the streets every day in the shape of unexplained disappearance and executions for the crime of resistance. If you must live in solitude, then you might as well choose your own. On 8 December 1970, Arthur Nortje, poet, Coloured, South African, 'took' his own life.

Nortje's poems read like a story: the story of the 1960s, his own story. A story in the form of poems, of fragments of a diary, of letters. Poems in the form of a malaise, of 'ill-being'.

Few can resist the temptation to attribute the suicide of an individual – however talented he may be – to his instability or to his fundamental failure to adjust to the society in which he lived: as if the norm of the majority was necessarily just, or even the only just norm. The nonconformist who prefers to quit the world at the time of his own choosing will always be regarded as a failure: 'He lived on the periphery of life, and now he hasn't even managed to die properly!'

The Afrikaners have reasoned and spoken this way about their poetess, Ingrid Jonker: 'She had marital problems after having had problems with her parents . . . She was morbidly obsessed with death . . .' The inevitable incomprehension that comes between the rebel and the establishment. The latter saw nothing reprehensible in the way they treated the black majority, restricting them to menial jobs and keeping them in a state of subjection by means of terror. She, on the contrary, saw only decay and death around her: the decay of a society which trampled underfoot the Christian principles it claimed to observe, the death of the essential human values, the death of the spirit, with its parallel, the death of innocent people.

Other Afrikaners apart from herself have lived on the edge of their society and have been excluded from it without being driven to suicide. An examination of their situation shows that they have been involved in religious or political action of some kind – such as Beyers Naudé and Theo Kotze of the Christian Institute, or Bram Fischer, a member of the South African Communist Party, who held out for forty years against the opprobrium of his own community.

If militancy provides support because of the active solidarity of every moment, it does so also because it substitutes hope for a situation that seems to offer no way out, the prospect of a more just order in place of the existing order (seen as a 'counter-order'), because it is the intimation of a Utopia which can be achieved *in our own time* and whose inevitable realization will be brought about, precisely, by personal *and* collective action.

Nortje, like Ingrid Jonker, was one of those solitary horsemen or knights – the literature of the western calls them 'loners' – who are sustained neither by political action nor religion.

Certainly, he was not rejected by his own community, but cut off from it by exile after having been cut off by the repressive laws from some of its members, those most likely to attract him. Nortje might have said, like Nerval's hero: 'Je suis le . . . Veuf, l'Inconsolé, le Prince d'Aquitaine à la Tour abolie': El Desdichado, the king without kingdom or companionship except that offered by chance encounters, because his real friends, exiles like himself, are scattered to the four corners of the world.

Not without a certain literary reputation, however, which Nortje sought in Canada after having won it without trying in England. But what if a reputation were merely compensation, and for the lesser talents at that? In that case, one day, without much comprehension on the part of those who remain, you go to the edge of the sea and wait for the tide to come in: this was how Ingrid Jonker died. Or else, like Nortje, you swallow more tablets than you need to get you through the night. Is it weariness or the logic of a situation taken to its conclusion?

In his brief life (Nortje died when he was 28), the four acts which led up to that 8 December 1970 were perhaps merely a long prologue. Act I: the years lived in South Africa and his rapid maturing between 1960 and 1965. Act II: the decision to take on the world, but also the wrench of the Great Separation: London, Oxford, university success, the round of invitations and receptions, but also the heartbreak of exile. Act III: departure for the Great North, two years (1968–9) of which we know only that they were marked by work as a teacher, a deep disappointment in love and a mere four poems from a man who was always writing. Act IV: a period of feverish travels – London, Canada, back to London, Oxford, as if he was too lost and bewildered to know where he would be best off or least likely to run away from himself. Then sudden death.

But what if there had been no Act V? If, in spite of this theatrical gesture, which in our society constitutes a deliberate departure from the scene to which men sometimes cling desperately, there was only, in fact, the intention to cause a break in the 'nonsense' of life, a desire for coherence which would make of his own death the first and last act of his life? The hero dies on the first page of the second volume: everything has gone wrong in the world of literature, but what a beginning to his own dazzling if ephemeral life!

Although Nortje belongs to the same age-group as Mtshali and Serote – he is two years younger than the former and two years older than the latter – a world separates them. His preoccupations, his themes, his style and his 'accent' are all different. It is a question of personality, certainly, but also of circumstances: Nortje, a Coloured, encountered fewer social and racial handicaps than his two contemporaries, brought up in the Transvaal; he started school earlier than they did and was able to go to university. His outstanding academic ability won him a scholarship awarded by Jesus College, Oxford. He thus made his acquaintance with the wider world well before they did, and, especially, he began writing sooner than they did. His age, his rapid maturity, his precocious sensitivity also made him fully contemporary with the events which occurred during the first half of the sixties, that is, the period that runs from Sharpeville to the hanging of John Harris.

Nortje, who was only eighteen at the time of Sharpeville and not a political militant, escaped the repression that followed. So, while Brutus was breaking stones on Robben Island, and Hugh Lewin and David Evans were beginning their long prison sentence at Pretoria Central Prison, Nortje – free in his person but not from the climate of oppression – was writing prolifically. It is the traces of that period that one finds in his 'South African' poetry, the poetry he wrote between 1960 and 1965, the date of his departure for Oxford. This departure occurred at the start of the brief period of recovery by the black community, which was to culminate in 1969 with the birth of Black Consciousness. Nortje on the one hand, and Mtshali and Serote on the other, belong therefore to two periods, to two different styles of expression.

One must not, however, look in Nortje's work for the *details* of the historical events of his country nor, after his departure, for those of a universal history with which he might seem to live in symbiosis. Occasional verse in the strict sense of the word was not for him, or very seldom: a poem on Lumumba's death, another on the shootings in Langa, while elsewhere he 'celebrates' in his own way the twenty-first anniversary of the dropping of the first atomic bomb on Hiroshima or reflects on the semi-fratricidal war after Nasser's death between the Jews and the Arabs. For him, external events were not important except in so far as they might have implications for the individual, for the general climate and for the state of mind it causes in the long term. As a black man, in his own country Nortje was in the direct line of fire; rare are the poems written by him during the period 1961–5 which are not indelibly marked by: 'I suffered under Verwoerd!'

The essential character of a period stands out most clearly, when one first looks at it, if the human imagination has managed to express its impact through symbols. Nothing more clearly indicates the violence various countries have used against their own citizens than these signs: barbed wire, the garrotte, the mental hospital. To these, in the case of South Africa, we can add: the gag. For Nortje, the mortal sin of which white South Africa had made itself guilty was to have completely severed the natural and spontaneous means of communication that people have with one another. In this respect, no one better than he has evoked the emotional and cultural desert into the middle of which the individual has been cast, violated in his character as a social being because forced into silence and separation. Like visible signs on the pages of the poems written between 1963 and 1965, these chilling words are constantly repeated: 'lonely', 'alien', 'alone', 'silent', and these lines:

> silence keeps me home, I'm lonely[53]
>
> I am alone here, now, here living
> with shoals of fragments[54]
>
> Separation seems all[55]
>
> Only that inward poignance craves
> nearness and meaning, totally lonely[56]
>
> The long silence speaks
> of deaths and removals.
> Restrictions, losses
> have strangled utterance[57]

The First Generation of Committed Black Poets

And these premonitory lines, a terrible indictment of the deterioration whose seeds have been sown and tended here:

> The loveless essence
> remains the empty
> nights and years, husks of the exile.[58]

A short poem, 'Synopsis' (1963), provides a better understanding of the general climate and the way in which Nortje interpreted it:

> High white masses
> of cloud delude me.
> Wind floats, mingles
> blue glimpses between.
>
> Occasional rain
> sings by green willows:
> I watch the slant of
> glittering springs.
>
> Is the heart's country
> all this loneliness?
> Sundrops deliver
> docile rainbows.
>
> We've spoken. You
> ignored the syllables.
> Between the sentences
> amass the silences
>
> Where have the men gone
> who fought colour
> theories, cracked spectrums —
> back to the prisms?[59]

The apparent detachment, achieved mainly through the omission of the article (a frequent device in Nortje's poetry) and through the use of short sentences, cannot obscure the profound and chilling despair contained in the poem. But this detachment itself hides a fragility which becomes increasingly evident. The despair is present in lines 10 and 11, but also more subtly in the penultimate stanza with its double meaning, to which one must draw the attention of the unwary reader so that he can grasp its full significance: it is an allusion to the dialogue of the deaf between Colonized and Colonizer (the 'We' and the 'You'); it is also an allusion to the pitiless repression that followed the various protests and demonstrations. Thus 'sentences' refers both to the sentences spoken and the prison sentences; 'silences' to the pauses between the poet's claims and the silence that followed the arrest of the leaders. One can begin to grasp more fully the reality of the expression 'to create a vacuum' in South Africa.

The deliberate breaking down of communication: this is the major theme of most of the poems written by Nortje in South Africa. Speech refused and denied: it has become dangerous for the protester to speak out; dangerous, too, for those who dare to love on the other side of the racial barrier. Knowing that the police are watching and the fear of being denounced give rise to a kind of self-censorship on the part of individuals: people do not speak any more, or only in whispers (Nortje was to write later, recalling this period before his exile: 'no longer need I shout freedom in the house'[60]).

If you add the various laws which, by systematizing geographical segregation and increasingly reducing opportunities for meaningful contact, also organize this silence, you do indeed have the image of a gag being tightly tied. By pulling off the gag you take back the right to speak, you offer resistance – of a kind.

It is obviously his own experience that Nortje is communicating above all, but his poems are also an expression of the general malaise. He introduces the external world by a very personal application, in poetry, of perspective. His hero, most frequently himself, is always situated in his own environment, in a precise place and moment in time. The poet, working as some film directors do, constantly uses the depth of field, panning in now on the environment, now on the individual thinking and feeling within it, and he does so in a continual movement back and forth from him to the world outside him, and vice versa, as we have already noted in the case of 'Synopsis'. In this way, there results a significant expansion of the spatial framework and often, too, thanks to the use of flashbacks, of the temporal framework.

This approach is far from being gratuitous or simply a stylistic device. It is found in producers with more or less conscious social or historical intentions. This is the case with someone like Visconti or, better still, Jean Renoir. By never separating the hero from his context, by constantly returning to it during the action or the dramatization of the hero's thoughts, the artist never loses sight of the environment in which he functions. As a result, the hero comes across not as an isolated individual but as an integral part of a whole within which he lives and struggles.

Even if in Nortje's case it is more accurate to speak of a sociological than a social dimension, the comparison with Renoir is valid, especially as Nortje has a strong poetic feeling for, and an acute perception of, the colours and sounds which contribute greatly to the integration of the hero with his environment. The role played by Nature, with its noises and smells, adds a truly cosmic dimension which helps to create the impression of space that strikes the reader so forcibly.

This results in an intense awareness of the particular situation which, in spite of its being anchored in a specific place and time, is more universal than particular. The accuracy of the metaphors and images has a profound impact on the reader, encourages empathy and allies aesthetic feeling with a purely intellectual satisfaction. This is how we must read 'Soliloquy: South Africa', a love poem, a poem about solitude, about the ever-present violence, but above all a poem about speech, its impossibility and yet its necessity, it risks and its agony. In this poem of 36 lines, there are no fewer than 22 references to speech, not counting the title, of course, which stresses the only possibility available – soliloquy:

> It seems me speaking all the lonely time,
> whether of weather or death in winter,
> or, as you expected and your eyes asked, love,
> even to the gate where goodbye could flame it.
> The last words that issue from the road
> are next day regretted because meant so much.

> All one attempts is talk in the absence
> of others who spoke and vanished
> without so much as an echo.
> I have seen men with haunting voices
> turned into ghosts by a piece of white paper
> as if their eloquence had been black magic.[61]

'Spell Cold and Ironic', written during the same period, links the renewal of nature and all that it promises with the impossibility of real change in South Africa. This cold spell in the heart of spring (September in South Africa is equivalent to March in the northern hemisphere) is also winter in the heart that has looked forward to change. Repression is really to blame, but it is also, Nortje tells us in the third stanza, because of the lack of courage on the part of the oppressed. In spite of its sombre outlook, however, the poem is not at all sentimental. In 1963, Nortje's joy in writing and his intense lyricism once again defused his despair and, instead of giving in to the tragedy inherent in the situation, the poet found the strength to be ironical:

> Streamers of colour in September's opulence;
> water splashed laughs through my fingers, glistened,
> danced my face in the element's brilliance.
> Hatched eggs, flocks of new birds opened
> freedom's country, offered the millions
> blood's fresh chance to change and mingle.
>
> But cold snap shuts one in at zero . . .
>
> Ironcast sky: against the day I'll carry
> something subversive, ash in satchel,
> showing I've studied death's business, am very
> prepared to report in heaven or hell
> (barring of course a security leak)
> that grey day gagged it – spring could not speak.[62]

Who is not aware of the effectiveness and power of speech shared? And what must Nortje's experience of solitude have been in 1963 already, for him to cry out: 'Something speaks on when something listens',[63] before adding that a fly or a moth can act as interlocutors for the prisoner of silence. For breaking the silence and breaking solitude are synonymous. The Oxford scholarship was going to help him to escape the gag, but there is only the thickness of a passport between total exile and the exile of speech.

Death is often spoken of as the 'last journey'. Whether it was for Nortje the first or the last journey, there is no escaping the fact that he was a great traveller: not only in space measurable in miles or kilometres, but also because he so frequently penetrated the 'inner world'.

One could, in fact, describe Nortje as the typical traveller. First, because with each departure he senses the possibility of a real change, and not only a change of décor, and also because he expresses so remarkably well the ambivalent feelings of the man setting out: the sadness of the separation, the joy of the discovery to come; now standing on the prow of the ship, wanting to make it go faster by the force of his own desire, now leaning over the stern, murmuring to himself the words he can no longer say to the woman he loves.

A typical traveller, yes, but with a particular characteristic that makes him a traveller of the kind found more in the twentieth than in earlier centuries: the political exile.

The ordinary traveller is only really happy because deep down he knows he will be able to return. He *knows* that one day he will return to harbour, his eyes, his mind, his heart enlarged by the familiar, as well as the unfamiliar experiences he has had during his travels. It is quite different for the emigrant and, even more so for the political *émigré*, who does not know if he will be able to return or, indeed, who senses already that he will not be able to return in the near future, the world being what it is. And his increasing awareness of power politics as he travels about strengthens that conviction.

Consequently, the ordinary traveller, even if he stays away for several years, has roots in so far as his country still belongs to him. He knows this, and there is nothing to tell him otherwise. On the other hand, *everything* reminds the political *émigré* that his country is closed to him: it has not changed, it does not change! While the *émigré* gets to know the great world and experiences freedom, his country recedes increasingly from him. Was it not suspect, in South Africa, to want to fraternize freely on either side of the racial boundaries? And now that he is abroad, he fraternizes with men and women of every kind!

So, as the gap of time widens and the distance grows, the separation becomes greater, and sharper, too, the pain of knowing that the doors of return are shut, or barely ajar, but then at such cost. For the country was his childhood, his past, the link with himself and his family and friends maintained by 'osmosis', if not by deeply significant contact. Exile exacerbates the suffering; the country acquires a reality which is magnified by memory and nostalgia. Is this not a landscape which one could call 'enchanted' without fear of hyperbole? That most beautiful place in the world, the Cape, with its sunshine and its sea, with its winds that bring the beneficial rain, with its Mediterranean climate and its mountains so close by?

And yet this same country is simultaneously experienced as hostile – an ambivalence of feelings that was to follow Nortje throughout his exile: he is tossed about between the pull of this beautiful land, the land of his birth and of his adolescence, and the rejection of this implacable country that 'organizes suffering'. Unable to separate the permanent from the transitory, the country itself from the regime which makes it a sombre place for the spirit (Nortje calls it 'the grim place'), unable, therefore, to find a commitment which will strip the myth of its unreality, it is impossible for him to reconcile himself with South Africa; impossible, also, not to love it. The country that bore and shaped him, and where his own mother still lives, is experienced as a rigid straitjacket, the very negation of the mother's womb because it rejects growth and change: it prefers harshness to love, tyranny to motherhood.

A frightening psychological and emotional responsibility – and one that causes irreparable damage, since apartheid society makes it impossible to share in those everyday contacts with others, with their risks and dangers, that are a part of the maturing process. It throws Nortje in on himself, it drives him to seek imaginary or artificial compensations which will enable his inner self to restore itself to wholeness, at least temporarily, and to seek everything, consolation and harmony, from another who is nothing but a myth because never really encountered.

Thus, after dividing, atrophying and falsifying human relations in the country itself, after suppressing the free expression of thoughts and feelings and making what is considered normal in modern democracies appear illicit and reprehensible—especially the freedom to choose from among one's fellow citizens those with whom one could have the richest relationships—the policy of apartheid finally plays its role as the supreme uprooter. So it fosters Nortje's unease after having created it and radically undermines his chances of finding a place for himself in the outside world. A stranger in his own land, Nortje was to remain one in the world outside South Africa, discovering its true face behind the prestige with which dreams and imagination had decked it.

It is difficult to give a precise date for when Nortje began to write. He won the Mbari prize for poetry when he was only nineteen. These 'juvenilia' published in *Black Orpheus*, the literary review edited from Ibadan by Ulli Beier and Janheinz Jahn, reveal a Nortje who is still writing confused and affected poetry, still caught up in imitating his great model, Gerard Manley Hopkins. But it is already possible to discern the sharp gaze that the young poet brings to bear on reality and already there is the first, tentative outline of his overall view of the world, with its distinctive pendulum movement.

Nortje's friends and teachers have remarked on his passion for reading and inquiry, his tireless vitality, which, whatever the circumstances—the opportunities for going out or staying up late into the night were frequent in London and later in Oxford—made him write his daily poem or take his daily exercise. For he was convinced, like Eliot and Valéry, that only regular work pays and that the gods only grant you the first line.

He matured rapidly as a poet. In less than two years, the clumsy writer had transformed himself into a highly individual poet. The range of his themes, limited during his South African period to the portrayal of his inner life, the political climate and his amatory experiences, broadened out: impressions of London, which bowled him over (he called it 'the City of the heart'), winter in Oxford, the Beatles, but also, all too soon, descriptions of hangovers from drinking bouts and LSD trips.

When he arrived in Oxford, he began keeping a journal. In it, he noted down the important events of his daily life, critical appreciations of the authors he read, his ideas on writing. And he wrote letters, too, with, one suspects, as much concern for craftsmanship as when he was writing poetry: 'Superb letters make people happy. One's art absorbed there, not so?' he wrote in his journal in February 1966, adding: 'I spend hours carefully chiselling, paring, elaborating, balancing words so they give pleasure. For I love the Beautiful'.[64]

It was this passion, this joy in writing which inspired the remark we find in a letter of June 1966. It concerns the way he always signed his poems with his initials, K. A. N. (for Kenneth Arthur Nortje): 'About KAN, glad you like it. Actually I've always signed my work like that; it was suggested to me by a high school teacher to whom I owe such a helluva lot . . . The English equivalent is the affirmative *can*, as in *can do*'.[65] This is the calm self-assurance of someone who knows his potential, whose devotion to poetry is total and whose ideas on the nature and scope of poetry are already clear. 'Speaking Out' (1966) shows him watching with a critical eye a group of people taking part in a meeting with cultural pretensions, and refusing to play along with the fashions that must be followed in order to please. What he wants is not purely intellectual refinement but the wholeness of a life which, like flint, is shot through with fire ('The world stinks/If one can only find some adjectives').[66]

For this reason, this is already committed writing and, given the joy he gains from the act of writing, it is writing as pleasure, but as depression takes a hold, it also becomes writing as therapy. In fact, the poem fulfils several functions for Nortje. A mirror, at one and the same time an act of narcissism and the desire to know himself, with the wish to pass over to the other side, to go in search of the reality which evades him and frightens him. Writing as speleology, as archaeology of the Self: the poem as narrative of the Voyage to the Centre of Oneself, the poem as exorcism, to expel the demons that assail the divided poet, the poem as confession in which Nortje tells everything without hiding the most unflattering details, into which he pours pell-mell the sublime, the noble and the sordid because these are all elements of human nature, *are* human nature: 'Give me the whole experience to savour . . . !'

The turning-point in Nortje's life occurs in 1966–7: the profound disappointment in love he experienced then was one of a series of circumstances which undermined his self-confidence, without harming his poetic output, which became its echo, its tormented reflection. For 'the whole experience' also meant despair. Between the beginning of 1966, when Nortje, who had recently arrived in England, wrote: 'If I stand and wonder/nothing where I am/can make the soul not bleed',[67] and September 1970, three months before his death, when he noted: 'I too walk on the thin edge, a figure in Kafka',[68] there is no break, only the discovery that the state of exile and the condition of modern man simply duplicate the experience of isolation he had known in South Africa, but *on a much larger scale*. Nortje suffered from an existential anguish which perhaps had its roots in his very early childhood, but which was fostered and developed by apartheid, and which goes far beyond any specific geographical setting – or the episode of his disappointment in love, as painful as it was. The external signs of sociability were there and yet he felt himself an outsider. Already in 1964 he wrote: 'There are no people I can closely know',[69] and the history of his relations with women illustrates the precariousness of his efforts to conquer loneliness.[70]

But his anguish is also anchored in the kind of life which is characteristic of the modern western world: standardized, compartmentalized, hardly socialized in spite of appearances, and conditioned by impersonal and commercialized relationships.[71] Nortje sometimes rejected this world, sometimes went along with it, but, unable to change it and reluctant to change himself, was always angry with himself for continuing to live a lie, for not putting an end to his lack of consistency. Until the day he decided to recover his liberty by the one act over which he still had freedom of choice: his death.

What we find in the poetry Nortje wrote before leaving South Africa is an enthusiasm for the theme of departure and lyrical descriptions of the elsewhere from which one expects everything, because where one is is so dark. He was given his opportunity to escape, and he thought that that was freedom; he needed a little time to realize that 'there are destinies as well as destinations'.[72]

Then followed the harshness of disillusionment, the disappointment at discovering that the world he dreamed about in the country of his oppression was not as friendly as he had imagined: violence exists on a universal scale, the thirst for possessions is as general as the relentless struggle in the modern jungle. Nortje soon saw that he belonged to the fringes of this new society: 'There are those who hope like me, not to arrive.'[73] Like those others who lived on the fringes of society, the beatniks, the hippies and the flower people, Nortje attacked the race after money, in which men act towards one another not even like wolves but like rats. As was the case with them, his political philosophy was vague: not in any sense a Marxist, he criticized the power of money, the financiers whom he held responsible for all the world's evils, but also the lack of human fraternity. Like them, too, in order to forget the grey world around him (the adjective 'grim' which he used in his own country is replaced by the word 'grey'), in order to escape even briefly from his alienation, he turned to drink and drugs:

> The milk that cannot permeate the blue
> steel existence, quietly in the glass
> syringe affords me some drab ecstasy . . .
>
> What other indicators, evidence,
> of love and identity do we need?
> They are importing the exotic narcotic,
> sugar from Cuba, Indian hemp and seed
>
> of poppy, and the grey world should be grateful.
> They make you remember ruined peoples
> and make you forget that your teeth are rotting.
> There are things that will wreck us, things that will help us.[74]

'Things that will wreck us, things that will help us' – among the latter, we can list writing and, for a while at least, love; among the former, which weigh more heavily in the balance, the growing difficulty of living with his contradictions, and a very exacting conception of the self which made him write one day when he felt himself particularly unworthy: 'the soul/ glimmers feebly in its bed of pork';[75] but especially the feeling of being abandoned, of being uprooted, the anonymity of the exile, which is summed up in the words: despair and solitude.[76] Several times he returns to the leitmotiv which in his work poses the character of a bitter diagnostic:

> lack of belonging was the root of hurt.[77]
>
> for often it's been found
> that the heart is not a void
> but barren ground
> where roots have struggled and died.[78]
>
> Peach aura of faces without recognition,
> voices that blossom and die bring need of death.
> The rat-toothed sea eats rock, and who escapes
> a lover's quarrel will never rest his roots.[79]

Cut off now from his country, Nortje turns back towards it with nostalgia. As the product of a very special kind of world, he never ceased to miss the climate of the Cape, which brought its inhabitants in colourful crowds into the streets – its sun, its seascapes and, right up to his last day,[80] its vitality and its rhythm. This would, in fact, exert such a pull on him that he found it difficult to throw off its charm, and he had to make a special effort to persuade himself that it went hand in hand with repression.

The phenomenon is worth dwelling on, for it constitutes a major component of Nortje's sense of unease abroad and was a cause of the discontent he felt with himself. For he who stripped South Africa of its mask – of the official image intended for the tourists and the investors – to reveal the falseness of a partial vision which only showed the beauties of the landscape and the climate, found himself talking about it as if it were a paradise, but a paradise from which he had been excluded.

But that was the truth of the situation, its unbearable violence, the one-too-many acts of persecution from which he never recovered: he had been excluded, he whose family and 'racial' roots went deep into the country's memory. Excluded because of his mixed descent, because of his colour. Excluded from what was legally his, from what rightfully belonged to him. The first exile, Adam, had at least 'sinned'. In his case, there was no sin, only a stigma, the colour of his skin – in other words, the absurd. The absurd repeated thousands of times, at every moment of your daily life; the absurd perpetuated by the system of education of which Nortje knew he would make himself the accomplice if he went back to his country to teach; the absurd which burned into his mind as he recalled it over and over again throughout his long journey of exile.

It was a constant inner struggle which left a bitter taste in his mouth, as he went from constant regret to the rejection of a past from which he perhaps only ever escaped at all in the poem 'Questions and Answers', referred to below. Rejection only comes as an afterthought, after reflection, which is proof that his memories were deeply rooted in him and overwhelmed him. 'In Exile' expresses very well the emotional damage caused by these imponderables – the colour of the sky, a change in the direction of the wind which, like Proust's madeleine cake, suddenly bring back an atmosphere and plunge the individual into a past which the reason ends by rejecting, leaving a feeling of emptiness:

> Open skies flare wide enough
> to make me vaguely anxious.
> Nimbus wisps
> trace patterns of the past.
>
> Wind sweeps between the towers
> through tunnels, old and new.
> My heart is
> hollowed with the boots passing through.
>
> Garments gather and play about
> my limbs: they tremble to a return
> gust. Leaves and transient
> streetscape conjure up that southern
>
> blue sky and wind-beautiful
> day, creating paradise.
> Otherwise,
> the soul decays in exile.[81]

Because the past has remained desirable in spite of everything ('Bitter though it be, it is life somehow'),[82] because Nortje no longer belongs to the place he comes from, any more than he belongs to where he is now, the exiled poet 'lives' in an extremely unhappy situation which he accurately describes as a limbo and which feeds his bouts of depression. But at the same time as it overwhelms and torments him, his feeling of exclusion leads him to seek spiritual roots for himself, roots of which the exiled poet could never be deprived. Thus Nortje reaffirms in many poems his sense of belonging to South Africa as his ancestral home, from the only perspective available to him: history. This is how, by returning to his mixed origins and presenting himself as the heir of the Xhosa and Zulu chiefs who resisted the oppressor, he establishes his belonging. Thus, he gives himself comfort, while at the same time holding himself up to the eyes of the world as a true citizen who must give witness by his presence: 'You are required as an explanation.'[83]

Nortje then goes on to compare himself to the other exiles, to try and define his position in relation to those who are engaged in activities to further the restoration of the lost country. During his period in South Africa, he had felt guilty for not joining the resistance. 'Poem', written in 1963, emphasized the fact that he stood on the sidelines while others paid for their involvement by going to prison.[84] 'Autopsy', written some years later, shows him to be still reserved and embarrassed towards those who had preceded him and had sung of their country and the need to fight.[85] It is only now that he sees that he can contribute something through his writing.

> Some will storm the castle,
> some define the happening.[86]

'Questions and Answers', one of Nortje's last poems, goes further in terms of verbal commitment: it is, in fact, his only overtly militant poem, the only one that gives way to passionate declamation. But the only one, too, to be fundamentally despairing. For this poem, with 'I Who Wear',[87] which is clearly an earlier version, is full of that rage known to those who live in exile, or to those who are condemned to belong for ever to the symbolic opposition which the oppressive regime keeps alive in order to lend itself an appearance of democracy. This rage leads Nortje to imagine the end of the order he hates and whose end he cannot see except in the wish-fulfilment of the poem. This does not in any way minimize the poem's qualities: it is still essentially a lyric poem, but it is the despair which so powerfully creates the atmosphere of violence so unusual in Nortje's work.[88] The poem has frequently been used for propaganda purposes at anti-apartheid meetings: its inner dynamism derives as much from the revolt that is openly expressed as from the oratorical style which lashes and tears those responsible (sometimes naming them) for the infamy that has been perpetrated over the centuries. It is a call to battle, a frequently repeated assertion that the day will come when speech, or even cries, will no longer suffice, when only action will bring about change. What committed poet would not identify with the poem's conclusion, which is universal in spite of the specific references to South Africa:

> Who but to save me but myself?
> I bred words in hosts, in vain, I'll have to
> bleed: bleed for the broken mountains, lost
> Umshlanga, Hangklip, Winterberg,
> the starving rivers wait for me to plunge through
> to the forefront,
> the mud has hardened on my boots.
> Ancestors will have their graves uprooted,
> uncouth will be the interrogations and bloody the reprisals.[89]

The cry of vengeance expressed here as in the rest of the poems comes perhaps partly from the feelings of revenge which were current among the South African exiles who were more and more finding their way to London, where Nortje had returned from Canada in September 1970. There is no doubt that this poem gives voice to the frustration of a collective conscience: the 'I' which Nortje uses here is often a plural 'I'. But the personal factors must not be forgotten: Nortje seems to be firing his last shots as an exile, as someone on the sidelines of the world, but also as a Coloured – in other words, once again, as an outsider. Direct and indirect references to Nortje's double origin are not lacking in his work; in Canada, a few months previously, he had described himself as being in an awkward position, halfway between the whites and the blacks of his country and experiencing his mixed descent as an additional factor of exclusion in his isolation. The ending of 'Questions and Answers', in linking this theme with the theme of exile, clearly stresses, yet again, the difficulty in finding roots encountered by a child of the South African ghettos:

> White trash
> coursing through my blood
> for all the unalienable seasons,
> and I have an incurable
> malaise that makes me walk restlessly
> through the sewers of these distant cities.[90]

The attainment of self-knowledge is the denial of Death. A moment of courage restores lost unity and the innocence that preceded one's birth. Reconciliation with oneself is achieved by abandoning self-deception, which can only continue at the cost of one's integrity; for one can deceive others, but not oneself. Putting an 'end' to one's life is, in this sense, to give it a meaning once more, to be honest towards what one has been and, if one was unable to beat the odds, to show that one has regained one's purity. K. A. N. – 'Can, as in can do': this initialling of his own life reflects the initialling of his poetry, and the exile sets out on his first real voyage to 'the land of the heart's desire'.

Nortje's work itself turns its back both on the partisans of militant poetry and on those of pure poetry. For, if the author of *Dead Roots* was never able to commit himself in the sense understood by the political parties and organizations, he showed just as much hostility towards an art that isolates the individual from his social context and just as much contempt for intellectual activity which is incapable of opening out onto life as a whole. The fact that only a sixth of his work 'directly' concerns apartheid is not proof of a lack of interest. The route he followed, it is true, was above all that of poetry. But he was born a black South African, in other words on the side of the oppressed. He was above all a victim. Extremely self-centred though he was, he spoke nevertheless in the name of all the victims of apartheid, of those who were born and who have lived under the sign of separation. In spite of 'Questions and Answers', he was only a pre-revolutionary, in the manner of Maxim Gorky's heroes, conscious of the evils that assail society but unable as yet to join forces in a collective resistance and a collective struggle. Hypersensitive and gifted as he was, he revealed to the world the damage caused by the hidden evil, by the cancer called apartheid. But it would be mistaken to see in him only the Coloured victim of a society determined to deprive him of his humanity: his anguish as a human being is that of many people in our twentieth century, and the journey from Port Elizabeth to the room in Jesus College, Oxford, is merely one expression of an experience that many others have undergone. It is essentially through his work that he is linked with the suffering side of humanity as a whole and that he escapes his solitude.[91]

Notes

1. In *The Writer in Modern Africa, African–Scandinavian Writers' Conference*, Stockholm, 1967, ed. Per Wästberg (Scandinavian Institute of African Studies, Uppsala, 1968).
2. ibid., p. 95.
3. In *Stubborn Hope* (Heinemann, London, 1978).
4. Interview with Professor Lindfors, London, August 1970.
5. Brutus's evolution is described in *Resistance Against Tyranny*, ed. E. Heimler (Routledge & Kegan Paul, London, 1966).
6. Interview with Lindfors, op. cit.
7. Mbari Publications, Ibadan, 1963.
8. *A Simple Lust* (Heinemann, London, 1973), p. 18 (future references will be made to this edition).
9. Interview with Lindfors, op. cit.
10. His disciple, A. Nortje, wrote later (in *Dead Roots*, Heinemann, London, 1973, p. 53):

    > 36,000 feet above the Atlantic
    > I heard an account of how they had shot
    > a running man in the stomach. But what isn't told
    > is how a warder kicked the stitches open
    > on a little-known island prison which used to be
    > a guano rock in a sea of diamond blue.

11. *A Simple Lust*, op. cit., p. 102.
12. International Defence and Aid Fund, London, 1967.
13. *A Simple Lust*, op. cit., p. 24.
14. ibid., p. 2.
15. During a reading of his poems in Chelsea in August 1971.
16. Cf. what Brutus wrote in 'Childhood Reminiscences', op. cit., p. 98.
17. In André Berry, *Florilège des Troubadours* (Didot, Paris, 1930), p. 115.
18. Cf. R. Briffault: 'There is in no work by any troubadour of the twelfth century any ambiguity as regards the sensual character of the emotions of the love relationship that constitute its theme.' In *Les Troubadours et le sentiment romanesque* (Les Editions du Chêne, Paris, 1945), p. 105.
19. *A Simple Lust*, op. cit., pp. 16, 31, 36, 37, 42, among others.
20. ibid., p. 17 (the poem is accompanied by the following note: 'Velencia Majombozi, who died shortly after qualifying as a doctor').
21. ibid., p. 4.
22. ibid., p. 12.
23. 'A Study of Six African Poets', in *Introduction to African Literature*, ed. U. Beier (Longman, London, 1967).
24. It is tempting to regard these poems as unpublished: they are not included in any of Dennis Brutus's collections. In fact, he had forgotten their existence, for they had appeared in 1963 during his period of house arrest, above the initials B. K. (the name of his woman companion during the Resistance).
25. Especially in *Christian Action*, Winter 1967, and *South African Prisons*, op. cit.
26. *A Simple Lust*, op. cit., p. 74.
27. ibid., p. 79.
28. ibid., p. 78.
29. Originally published by the African and Afro-American Research Institute (University of Texas, Austin, 1970).
30. Here is what Brutus wrote on this subject in his commentary on the poems (not included in *A Simple Lust*): 'I was naturally delighted to be invited, but en route became

increasingly filled with misgivings about my right to be called an "African voice"; how far were my ideas and opinions and art peculiarly African?'
31. *A Simple Lust*, op. cit., pp. 141–3.
32. *Poems from Algiers*, op. cit., pp. 26–7.
33. *A Simple Lust*, op. cit., p. 42.
34. ibid., p. 127.
35. See on this subject what Ronald Segal says in *The Race War* (Pelican Books, London, rev. edn, 1966), p. 46.
36. *A Simple Lust*, op. cit., p. 116.
37. ibid., p. 121. The whole poem should be read, however, with its pessimistic view of Africa, which is not tempered in any way by any reference to the alienating effect of the cultures evoked.
38. *The Writer in Modern Africa*, op. cit., p. 34.
39. The editors, Butler and Mann, of *A New Book of South African Verse in English* (Oxford University Press, Cape Town, 1979) stress in their preface that, in spite of repeated requests, they were refused permission to include poems by D. Brutus (p. 16).
40. Poetry: *Present Lives, Future Becoming* (Hickey Press, London, 1974).
   Prose: *Protest and Conflict in African Literature*, co-editor and contributor (Heinemann, London, 1969).
   Books which Pieterse has edited, on his own or in collaboration:
   Ten One-Act Plays (Heinemann, London, 1968).
   Seven South African Poets (Heinemann, London, 1971).
   Five African Plays (Heinemann, London, 1972).
   Short African Plays, editor and author (Heinemann, London, 1972).
   Nine African Plays for Radio (Heinemann, London, 1973).
41. *Present Lives, Future Becoming*, op. cit., p. 72 (abbreviated henceforth to *Present Lives*).
42. It was, however, the Catholic Church that he preferred until he lost his faith, when he was about 14 or 15 years old.
43. *Present Lives*, p. 14.
44. In *Short African Plays*, op. cit., p. 134.
45. ibid., p. 131.
46. Unpublished.
47. *Present Lives*, p. 41.
48. Unpublished.
49. *Present Lives*, p. 66.
50. ibid., p. 1.
51. ibid., p. 78.
52. Poems published in *Black Orpheus* (Ibadan), *Modern Poetry from Africa* (ed. Beier and Moore, Penguin, rev. edn, London, 1968), *African Arts/Arts d'Afrique* and *Seven South African Poets* (ed. C. Pieterse, Heinemann, London, 1974).
   Two posthumous collections: *Lonely against the Light* (Rhodes University, Grahamstown, 1973); *Dead Roots* (Heinemann, London, 1973).
53. *Dead Roots*, op. cit., p. 9.
54. ibid.
55. ibid., p. 18.
56. ibid.
57. ibid., p. 24.
58. ibid.
59. ibid., p. 4.
60. 'Up Late', in *Modern Poetry from Africa*, op. cit., p. 217.
61. *Dead Roots*, op. cit., p. 5.
62. ibid., p. 8.
63. ibid., p. 5.
64. In *Lonely against the Light*, op. cit., p. 5.
65. ibid.
66. ibid., p. 36.

67. *Dead Roots*, op. cit., p. 36.
68. *Lonely against the Light*, op. cit., p. 60.
69. *Dead Roots*, op. cit., p. 15.
70. It would be inappropriate to deal with this subject here. There is no doubt, however, that Nortje's love life is an image of his relations with others: the need to communicate at a deeper than superficial level but also hesitation at committing himself beyond a certain limit – that of his independence. Who is holding back from whom? Is he holding back from others, or others from him? Unless the exchange can be made on his own terms . . .
71. See on this subject: R. Jaccard, *L'Exil intérieur: Schizoïdie et Société* (PUF, Paris, 1975).
72. *Dead Roots*, op. cit., p. 88.
73. ibid., p. 73.
74. ibid., p. 73.
75. ibid., p. 66.
76. The two themes are constantly linked; 'Waiting' (*Dead Roots*, op. cit., p. 90) is particularly representative of this characteristic, and also specifically mentions the word 'limbo', referred to below.
77. *Dead Roots*, op. cit., p. 62.
78. ibid., p. 20.
79. ibid., p. 39.
80. ibid., p. 146.
81. *Lonely against the Light*, op. cit., p. 35.
82. *Dead Roots*, op. cit., p. 105.
83. ibid., p. 93.
84. In *Seven South African Poets*, op. cit., p. 103.
85. *Dead Roots*, op. cit., p. 52.
86. ibid., p. 118.
87. *Lonely against the Light*, op. cit., p. 60.
88. Nortje's own sense of violence, for his poems are full of the violence of the present regime.
89. *Dead Roots*, op. cit., p. 141.
90. ibid.
91. Hedy Davis, in 'Arthur Nortje: The Wayward Ego', *The Bloody Horse* (no. 3, January–February 1981), throws some light on the mystery that still surrounds the fascinating personality of Arthur Nortje; at the same time this new magazine announces the publication of unpublished work of Nortje by the Bateleur Press, Johannesburg.

Chapter 10
The Black Man Holds Up His Head

▼▼▼▼▼▼▼▼▼▼▼▼▼▼▼▼▼▼▼▼▼▼▼▼▼▼▼▼▼▼

The situation of the colonized South African is not far removed from that of the slave. Like him, he possesses none of the fundamental liberties: he is not free to move about as he pleases, to choose a profession and his place of work, to live where he wants, including with his own family. When we add that his access to education is regulated and, more often, denied him altogether, we realize that for him to speak out is a major step on his part. This is what the followers of Black Consciousness have recently done. This first step, by which the colonized South African, after having considered the nature and extent of his oppression and the weight of his chains, finally lifts up his head and prepares to confront the colonizer, is central to the poems of Mtshali, Serote, Mattera and their contemporaries. It is through their works that we can see how attitudes have changed: the black man speaks first, and only then resorts to arms. To take what is his due.

O. M. Mtshali[*]

Isolation is one of the principal characteristics of South African society, affecting all its constituent communities, albeit in differing degrees, and writing and *publishing* are the privileged means of breaking it. In South Africa, writing is not only an act of personal liberation, it is a response to the vital need to communicate with the members of a society from which one is separated by innumerable barriers. If Mtshali, who was born in 1940 in the province of Natal and is the author of *Sounds of a Cowhide Drum*,[1] wrote and published in Zulu, his mother tongue, he would only reach the few million Zulus who live in South Africa.

If we also accept that South African society is a gagged society in which freedom of speech, especially among black writers, is very restricted, we must draw the inference that any writer who wants to communicate more than mere banalities will either have to avoid certain subjects or disguise his ideas in order to get over the obstacle of the censor: 'There are many tricks for pulling the wool over the eyes of a suspicious State', Brecht once wrote in praise of antiphrasis.[2] As we shall see, the range of techniques Mtshali uses to express himself is very wide indeed. But, of course, the 'How to say it?' is inseparable from the 'What to say?' And, first of all, why does Mtshali write?

---

[*] A shortened version of this chapter appeared in *Commonwealth, Essays and Studies*, vol. II. 1976 (ed.: R. Mane).

A question of identity

On examination, one of the motives behind Mtshali's poetry seems to be the desire to acquire a face and a voice, both of which are denied him by the white man. To the colonizer, in fact, the colonized person has no face: it is smooth and transparent. He does not even have a name, or rather it is the name the colonizer has given him once and for all so as to make his own life easier.[3] In Lionel Rogosin's film *Come Back, Africa!*, the white housewife asked the Zulu peasant who had come to Johannesburg in search of work (in 1959):

'What is your name?'
'Zachariah.'
'All right. I'll call you Jack.'

As far as the whites of South Africa (the English-speaking ones, at any rate) are concerned the African is invariably Jack, John or Jim.[4]

This simplification of names is closely linked with the psychological blindness of the colonizer: it is equivalent to denying the existence of the Other. The Afrikaner writer Laurens van der Post records having encountered this phenomenon among many, often well-intentioned, whites,[5] and André Ungar argues that without this blindness, more often than not deliberate, it would be impossible to keep one's sanity in South Africa, impossible even to stay in the country. He writes: 'If a white man *begins to see*, his revolt has in fact begun. For a white man born in South Africa, such an acquisition of full sight is an aching and terrifying experience.'[6]

Indeed, if the Other exists, then his suffering and his poverty begin to exist too, as well as the injustice with which he is treated. By denying the existence of the colonized person, the colonizer casts him into limbo; he can then enjoy his privileges without qualms.

Mtshali frequently refers to the way the colonized person, in this case the black, becomes aware of the white man's blindness. It is, however, in the moving opening to 'The Master of the House' that Mtshali best expresses the suffering of the man without a name or a face. He does it with restraint, without emphasis, with the dignity and the simplicity of the slave who is unknown to his master and who at last leaves the shadow and dares to speak:

> Master, I am a stranger to you
> but will you hear my confession?
>
> I am a faceless man
> who lives in the backyard
> of your house.[7]

What speaking means

The search for an identity, the recovery of dignity by speech and writing, can be realized in a minor key, but they imply for all that the same fundamental need: to open the white man's eyes. To this end, he must be shown how the black man lives, he must realize the absurdity and inhumanity of his laws, the inequalities they have created in society, the misery and tragedy they cause the Africans. Mtshali's poems can therefore be read as documents. They do not, however, have the dryness of the sociological study: the reader will find no statistics in them, no abstract terminology, except, once only, for the word 'ideology', but rather scenes taken from the everyday reality of the blacks and marked with the seal of truth and realism.

Thus 'The Master of the House' not only tells of the anonymity into which the blindness of the whites has cast the black man – in it, Mtshali also talks about the inferior status of the black population ('in the backyard/of your house'), their inequality ('As the rich man's to Lazarus/ the crumbs are swept to my lap'); the impossibility for the blacks employed as servants of leading a normal family life ('I am the nocturnal animal/that steals through the fenced lair/to meet my mate/and flees at the break of dawn/before the hunter and the hounds/run me to ground'). There is nothing here that does not correspond to reality, and yet everything is transformed by the poet's vision: the narrator, who appears in the poem in the first person, passes imperceptibly from the condition of the slave to that of the hunted animal: the process of depersonalization is complete. The metaphor that describes it ('I am the nocturnal animal'), very eighteenth-century with its vocabulary characteristic of the hunt ('fenced lair', 'run to ground'), is exact down to the smallest detail ('The hunter and the hounds'): in South Africa, the police who have the job of raiding or checking servants' quarters at night are accompanied by wolf hounds.

Yet Mtshali is very discreet indeed. The title, which plays on the word 'house', can be read as 'The Master of the House' or 'The white man who rules' (the narrator's 'I' would, in the first place, designate the individual, in the second, the black people). And, however suggestive the poem may be, it still stays within the strict bounds of the law: no incitement to revolt can be found in it, and if it contains a call to reflection – it would be more accurate to say, an appeal to the heart and the mind – it is directed at an educated public, as the cultural references prove. Is it therefore ineffective? On the contrary, it seems.

The book of poverty and fear

Mtshali's poems are intended in the first instance for the fringe of the English-speaking white population that reads poetry. But, although this public may well be educated, it is no less ignorant of the real conditions of the African with whom it rubs shoulders without seeing.

So, when Mtshali demands the right to speak, when he reveals to the whites the 'hidden face' of South African society, he is undertaking a political act of which only the black prose writers of the late fifties and early sixties who are now banned in South Africa were capable. Although he never presents the communities in a position of conflict, although he always adopts a restrained albeit firm tone, although he plays at being naïve the better to attack, he nonetheless fulfils his role as the revealer of the truth, in other words, as a man of protest.

Rather than restrict himself to the more usual portraits, Mtshali prefers to sketch characteristic little scenes which enable him to reveal some fundamental features of the African's situation. Thus, he constantly switches from the swarming crowds of the township, where the African lives at night and at weekends, to the white city, where he works during the day: from the one to the other and vice versa, in the constant back-and-forth movement of the pendulum that is the underlying pulse beat of the urban life of South African blacks.

The dominant impressions conveyed by the township are all confirmed by the sociological surveys: hunger, poverty, fear, for the majority; a relative prosperity and violence for the rest. For in this world of the underprivileged, an inverted order has established itself in which for those who live on the fringes, the tsotsis reign supreme.

It is a world in which one attends classes at the University of Life where the classrooms are the shebeens, the hospitals and the prison cell; a world in which, on the same day, one can consult the witchdoctor and the priest; a world from which one escapes briefly through drink, drugs or jazz, unless one seeks refuge in one of the messianic sects which promise a future, inverted life in which the white will knock in vain on a perpetually closed door.

The themes of poverty and hunger are chiefly introduced through children. It is possible to see in this a desire to move the reader more effectively, to stir in him feelings of compassion, or even to show the future adult in the suffering child. The reality is simple: the great majority of Africans live below the poverty line and black children are the first victims of malnutrition.

There is nothing surprising, therefore, in Mtshali's taking a black child as the model for his allegory of hunger, 'The Face of Hunger':

> I counted ribs on his concertina chest:
> bones protruding as if chiselled
> by a sculptor's hand of famine.
>
> He looked with glazed pupils
> seeing only a bun on some sky-high shelf.
>
> The skin was pale and taut
> like a glove on a doctor's hand.
>
> His tongue darted in and out
> like a chameleon's
> snatching a confetti of flies.
>
> O! child,
> your stomach is a den of lions
> roaring day and night.

In 'A Brazier in the Street', the reader's attention is focused on four urchins huddled together around a brazier: they try to forget their hunger by smoking cigarette ends and telling stories. The cry of one of them betrays their obsessions and the principal theme of their conversation: 'I once ate a loaf of bread with nothing . . .'. A woman comes out of a nearby house and fetches the brazier to prepare her meal, for night is falling.

Here, as in the previous poem, the evocative quality derives as much from the acute observation of details as it does from the use of new and forceful metaphors, drawn mostly from the animal world ('The wintry air nipped their navels/as a calf would suck the nipple'). The ending of the poem is particularly interesting: a comparison with a mad dog enables the poet to introduce the metaphor of devouring night, giving the scene a cosmic dimension:

> And quicker than a rabid dog
> leaps to swallow its tail,
> the starless night gaped
> and gulped down the foursome.

In 'An Abandoned Bundle', it is no longer through the symbolic linking of the harshness of nature and poverty that Mtshali seeks to create a feeling of the tragedy of the African's condition. In this poem, the whole city seems to secrete misfortune. The huge collection of individuals known as White City Jabavu* only allows its chosen victims to leave if they pay cruelly for the privilege. Between the girl caught in the trap of maternity who has abandoned the body of her newborn child on the public tip and the dogs that scramble to devour the corpse, the reader cannot help wondering for a moment who is really guilty.

The reply is in the poem: for Mtshali, it is the city, that running sore, and therefore men. Only 'intelligent' readers will make the next connection and realize that the ones who bear the responsibility are those who make South Africa's laws and create the rubbish tips that are its cities. It is not by chance that Mtshali returns to this theme in another poem entitled, in fact, 'White City Jabavu'.

In this poem, he plays on the bitter irony of the word 'white', with the cultural connotations, for South Africans as well as Americans, of 'white is right'. The poet does not really need to ask himself what is satisfactory about this city where the misdeeds of the tsotsis are the cause of so much sorrow.

'The Day we buried our Bully' paints the portrait of a tsotsi who is a shameless robber and rapist, while 'Nightfall in Soweto' evokes the fear of the inhabitants as night falls. Mtshali exclaims:

> Nightfall! Nightfall!
> You are my mortal enemy.
> But why were you ever created?
> Why can't it be daytime?
> Daytime forever more?

The African's night

This wish, in its metaphorical as well as its literal sense, is very indicative of what obsesses the Africans. The daytime that will last 'forever more' is the exact opposite of an omnipresent night – and not just the real night – with which the Africans of the great South African cities are familiar:

> I go to work
> for five days a week
> with a thousand black bodies
> encased in eleven coaches
> that hurtle through stations
> into the red ribbon of dawn
> crowning the city skyscrapers[8]

The alienating life of the African, which begins thus before dawn with the journey he must make to get himself to work – a constant reminder, even if it remains at an unconscious level, of the attraction–repulsion phenomenon which is the basis of black–white relations in South Africa – continues in this white city where he is subject to prohibitions, to official discrimination and to contempt.

---

* D. D. T. Jabavu: a Xhosa leader, journalist and politician of moderate views (1859–1921).

The Black Man Holds Up His Head

Deprived of a face and a name, restricted to the status of an underpaid servant, he leads there a life in parenthesis, a life that reduces him to a nothing: the night of the soul, the nightmare night, for at almost every step he is required to show the document that literally entitles him to live and which he may not forget or lose, his pass. The night is in this sense a reflection of the condition of the black South African.

One must not conclude from this that *Sounds of a Cowhide Drum* is nothing but a long string of complaints. Besides his irony, Mtshali possesses a sense of humour which some South African whites – who are not afraid of stereotypes – describe as 'unfailing good humour' (*sic*). And it is true that life in the townships can also be gay and exuberant.[9] But Mtshali only needs to incorporate one or two particularly moving scenes into his ironical portraits and descriptions of situations to strike the dominant note and give us the key to the Africans' condition.

In 'Always a Suspect', we are given a close-up of the double curse under which the African lives: the biological one, which clings to him like the colour of his skin, and the social one, which makes him suspect as soon as he puts on clothes other than those of the employee or the labourer:

> I get up in the morning
> and dress up like a gentleman –
> A white shirt, a tie, and a suit.
>
> I walk into the street
> to be met by a man
> who tells me 'to produce'.
>
> I show him
> the document of my existence
> to be scrutinized and given the nod . . .
>
> I trudge the city pavements
> side by side with 'madam'
> who shifts her handbag
> from my side to the other
> and looks at me with eyes that say
> 'Ha! Ha! I know who you are;
> beneath those fine clothes
> ticks the heart of a thief'.[10]

The same fatalism is expressed by the hero of 'This Kid is no Goat': this poem is about a young African whose anger has led him to the conclusion that, try as he might, he cannot be both black and honest ('black and straight') in a world that has been 'twisted' by the whites ('in this crooked white world'). He explains:

> If I tell the truth
> I'm detestable.
> If I tell lies
> I'm abominable.
> If I tell nothing
> I'm unpredictable.
> If I smile to please
> I'm nothing but an obsequious Sambo.

Mtshali can do his best to show his detachment from the characters he portrays, but he still creates the Kafkaesque atmosphere which conditions relations between Colonizer and Colonized: the former denies the equality of the latter and can acknowledge him only as an inferior, and therefore as dumb. There is no possibility of dialogue, and there can be no real dialogue between someone who calls his servant John or Jim and someone who is treated as an invisible man or the clothes horse on which one hangs one's clothes. In all the poems in the collection which deal with whites and blacks, we only hear the voices of the whites giving peremptory orders; the only dialogue is between inhabitants of a township.

Since the roles have been allocated once and for all, the relations between white and black are predetermined in an absolute sense. This is emphasized by 'Two Chimney-sweepers', which is almost a fable in its brevity and in the conciseness of its conclusion:

> I saw
> two chimney-sweeps
> scraping the soot
> inside a stack.
>
> They came out
> and wiped
> their faces
> and one said to the other:
> 'I'm white and
> I'll always stay so.
> You're black
> You'll remain so!'

So the African oscillates continually between his township, with its poverty and violence, and the white city, which is open to him only in a false kind of way: what solution can there be, then, when the white asserts that nothing can change, ever?

Mtshali, according the poet a hypersensitive awareness of reality, has every reason to exclaim, at the end of a poem which expresses his disillusionment:

> Black is the hole of the poet,
> a mole burrowing from no entrance to no exit.[11]

The Christians' responsibility

In this metaphysical night which has become his own, Mtshali reflects on the origins of the Evil which he sees everywhere around him and which is also within him. How can the African avoid feeling hatred for the person who keeps him in his state of oppression? How can the Master tolerate the sight of his faithful servant reduced to the status of a Beast? The answer lies in the presence or absence of love or charity. Although Mtshali never mentions this last word, which is nevertheless present by implication in many a poem, he frequently returns to the absence of love and its tragic consequences.

In 'Walls' he lists the famous walls that keep people apart but, he says, in the form of a metaphor, the one wall that cannot be scaled is the one that encircles hearts and in whose moats stagnates the water of fear. In 'A Voice from the Dead', Mtshali returns to this theme in a dramatic dialogue between the author and his mother, who speaks to him from beyond the grave:

> Yes, Heaven is in your heart.
>
> God is no picture
> with a snow-white beard.
>
> WHAT!
>
> Yes, God is
> that crippled beggar
> sprawling at the street-corner.
>
> There is no hell burning
> with sulphur and brimstone.
>
> WHAT!
>
> Yes, Hell is
> the hate flickering
> in your eye.

This Johannine conception of the love of God, symbolized here by the sentence 'God is that crippled beggar', is expressed more explicitly still in 'Just a Passer-by', in which Mtshali condemns hypocrisy with an even greater sense of commitment and through a pointed, almost caricatured, use of symbol. For the first time, moreover, the words 'neighbours' and 'brothers' are closely linked: as in the case of Paton, they refer to those who live under the same 'roof', that is to say, in the same country:

> I saw them clobber him with *kieries**,
> I heard him scream with pain
> like a victim of slaughter;
> I smelt fresh blood gush
> from his nostrils
> and flow on the street.
>
> I walked into the church,
> and knelt in the pew,
> 'Lord! I love you,
> I also love my neighbour. Amen' . . .
>
> Back home I strutted
> past a crowd of onlookers.
> Then she came in –
> my woman neighbour:
> 'Have you heard? They've killed your brother.'
> 'Oh! No! I heard nothing. I've been to church.'

Although Mtshali avoids attacking any particular community, there is one subject, however, where he does not beat about the bush: Christianity. If his criticism of Christianity is unequivocal, it is because it postulates the law that man should love his neighbour but, in South Africa at least, this remains at the level of a principle.

---

* *kierie*: club.

In a poem already mentioned, 'This Kid is no Goat', Mtshali evokes an 'angry young African' who has left his mission school thinking that his rosary would be like an amulet to protect him from discrimination. Disillusioned, he stops going to church, where the priest's sermon seems to him to be like

> a withered leaf
> falling from a decaying pulpit tree
> to be swept away
> by violent gusts of doubt and scepticism.

He does not care if his wife and children continue attending church. As far as he is concerned, he is not so stupid (hence the title of the poem): he wants his heaven here and now, this heaven is to be found in the fine white suburbs.

In 'An Old Man in Church', Mtshali shows how the Church is the accomplice of the power that exploits the African proletarian masses. During the week, the old man – he does not specify that he is an African[12] – is a machine that works flat out but, says Mtshali, his productivity would be affected if he did not recharge his batteries every Sunday in church. We witness the old man's fervent prayers, the scorn that greets his modest contribution during the collection; then the poem ends with the preacher's voice: 'Blessed are the meek, for they shall inherit the earth.'

This last claim, which is contradicted everywhere in the poem, is taken up again by Mtshali in 'The Washerwoman's Prayer', which he dedicates to his mother-in-law: in this poem, the poet argues with bitter irony that the Church helps to perpetuate the existing situation by teaching resignation. Behind the image of the washerwoman who has worked hard all her life without complaining to accomplish the degrading tasks set her by her master, it is difficult not to discern the symbolic representation of the black people kept in bondage for so long, at least in part through religion. The concluding stanzas of the poem express quite unambiguously the fact that the washerwoman's patience is at an end and that Christ's arguments seem specious to her:

> One day she fell and fainted
> with weariness.
> Her mouth a foaming spout
> gushing a gibberish.
>
> 'Good Lord! Dear Lord!
> 'Why am I so tormented?
> How long have I lamented?
> Tell me Lord, tell me O Lord.'
>
> 'My child! Dear child,' she heard,
> 'Suffer for those who live in gilded sin,
> Toil for those who swim in a bowl of pink gin.'
>
> 'Thank you Lord! Thank you Lord!
> Never again will I ask
> Why must I carry this task.'

An astonishing frankness which is 'acceptable' because of its good dose of innocent humour. In fact, Mtshali has considerable skill in hiding the barbs he aims at the whites from the heart of poems which give the impression of dealing generally with the theme of Evil. But the alert reader can pick out the tiny details that prevent any real ambiguity, as for example in the key line of 'The Marble Eye':

> The marble eye
> is an ornament
> coldly carved by a craftsman
> to fill an empty socket
> as a corpse fills a coffin.
>
> It sheds no tear,
> it warms to no love,
> it glowers with no anger,
> it burns with no hate.
>
> Blind it is to all colours.
>
> Around it there is no evil
> to be whisked away
> with the tail of a horse
> like a pestering fly.
>
> Oh! the marble eye –
> if only my eyes
> were made of marble!

In fact, Mtshali can be said to be, *fundamentally*, more subversive than he seems: we find in his work a series of messages addressed to his fellow Africans.

The mask and its transparency

At the heart of the poems directed especially at the black community, Mtshali returns constantly, and in several places fairly explicitly, to the same crucial idea: the chief enemy of the oppressed is not the white man but the black man himself – because of his passivity and his lack of courage and aggressiveness. He allows himself, in fact, to be exploited, to be reduced to the state of an animal, to accept the imposition of the fatality of colour distinction in which white is the symbol of domination and monopoly, and all without the slightest protest. All he does is turn to prayer, drink or drugs, which are of little effect against the weapons of the white man. In this way, he wastes his vitality and sweeps aside the heritage of his ancestors. In other words, Mtshali invites the Africans to radically change their thinking.

This is something that would have difficulty in getting past the censor if the message were clearly stated: even in a country where the potential audience for poetry is minimal, there are limits the regime would not allow to be exceeded. Mtshali was well aware of this, so out of necessity, as well as from personal preference, it seems, he veiled his thoughts and used 'the language of the slaves' – a network of allusions, references and hints which are clear only to those who share his culture.

There has already been the example of the Negro spirituals of the nineteenth century, whose religious references could be interpreted in a political sense without losing any of their other connotations, and the work songs of the black American convicts in the twentieth century. In *Sounds*, we also have – but in reverse – the example of the 'freedom train'. During the period of slavery, this expression referred to the Gospel 'train' which would take the repentant sinner to heaven; it also referred to the underground network – the underground railroad – that enabled a number of black slaves to escape to the North and to freedom. In one of the poems of *Sounds*, Mtshali describes a group of convicts who get into the train in which he is travelling early one morning. They are sub-humans stripped of all human dignity whom he compares to cattle being led to the slaughterhouse. The last stanza ends with one of the prisoners appealing to the sun: 'Oh! Dear Sun!/ Won't you warm my heart/with hope?' The poet's reply falls like the blade of the guillotine: 'The train went on its way to nowhere'. This train is, in fact, the train of resignation, of futile recourse to outside help; it cannot lead to freedom.

This warning is by no means an isolated one: it is contained in the 'microstructure' of poems like 'A Washerwoman's Prayer', 'Snowfall on Mount Frere' and 'Men in Chains', which are themselves integral parts of the 'macro-structure' of the collection as a whole.

'Snowfall on Mount Frere' offers an approach which is both more secret and more allusive. The poem is presented as the description of a snow-covered landscape in the Transkei; the snow is everywhere, weighing everything down, the animal and the trees call in vain for the winter sun to come to their rescue, but it remains absent or distant. The people huddle in their cold huts, saying nothing: they submit.

This summary does not bring out the extent to which nature is personified, along with the animals and the elements, nor the amusing quality of some of the comparisons. These characteristics would not, however, be enough in themselves to justify the inclusion of this poem, the only 'landscape poem' in the collection, if it were not for the fact that it is placed between 'A Washerwoman's Prayer' and 'Men in Chains' and is therefore an essential element in an overall argument.

> Trees sagged
> and grunted
> under the black-breaking
> flour-bags of snow.
> Breathless
> they cursed and waited
> for sunrays
> to lift their burden . . .
>
> Birds huddled helplessly
> against the whiplashing wind;
> and raised their frozen feeble voices
> in protest to the skulking sun.
>
> No tribesmen
> ventured out.
> They were marooned
> in their heartless huts
> by the vast white sea.
> They cringed like drowning gorillas
> chained in cold steel cages.

For the personification of nature is balanced by the 'animalization' of man: protest and defiance come from the animals and the trees, while the image of degradation and powerlessness is provided by the tribesmen.

But the personification itself, which is really a rather trite device, has here a special function: it is given an air of simplicity so as to put the reader off his guard. In fact, when we look at it closely,[13] we realize that the snow is associated with the weight that bends the backs (back-breaking=black-breaking), with the burden, and if we notice that, just as the snow is everywhere, at the end the author evokes 'The vast white sea', there can be no missing the comparison: the poem is quite clearly a veiled reference to white oppression.

Mtshali describes this omnipresent whiteness as 'papery'. This word can be understood in various ways, but there are at least two significant connotations that exist side by side:[14] legalism, the laws on which it all hangs, but also their lack of consistency, their fragility. (Pieterse speaks elsewhere of 'bullets of white paper', and Delius constructs the conclusion of *The Last Division* on the wall of paper that will separate the Neths/Nationalists from the rest of Hell).[15]

Thus, the message becomes richer as the explanation – one could almost say the decoding – of the poem progresses. Mtshali tells the Africans: 'Look at yourselves! You have been reduced to the level of animals and you let it happen!' But also: 'Is the power of the whites so great that you cannot breach it?' (fourth stanza).

However, the Africans of 'Snowfall' are inhabitants of the Transkei (Mount Frere is in the Transkei and Mtshali uses the term 'tribesmen'), a Bantustan devoid of real power where the South African government keeps the Africans in a state of semi-servitude ('chained in cold steel cages'). The chains are therefore not only those of oppression, but also the new chains of 'separate development' hidden behind the always unfulfilled promises of the whites. The pie in the sky[16] here becomes a Kit-Kat biscuit covered in chocolate. One might even think that the allusions to the sun are so many references to the whites, both government and liberals. 'Aproned sunshine', 'slice it' are culinary references which might well suggest the whites' 'cookery' constantly denounced by the followers of Black Consciousness.

The message has therefore become richer still[17] and one does not seem far from the kind of work that introduces real characters under fictitious names. If there is still any doubt about this, read 'If you should know me', placed at the very heart of *Sounds* like the apple it evokes:

> Once concealed
> like the Devil
> in the body
> of a serpent –
> as an apple of sin
> in the hand
> of a temptress –
> I am the biter.
>
> For all
> I bare my heart
> to see the flint
> to be ignited
> into a flame
> shaped like three tongues
> that tell me –
> look, listen and learn
> what surrounds me.

In fact, in order to bring the truth home to the whites, as well as to the Africans, of South Africa, Mtshali employs a wide range of techniques, especially the fable, the dramatic dialogue, the spiritual and antiphrasis, much vaunted by Brecht.

We also find the language of the slaves in 'Song of Sunrise'. This poem begins in the form of an allegory with the description of the morning's St George-like triumph in its combat with the night, but it continues at a more ordinary level which, without ceasing to be poetic, destroys the initial emphasis and serves as a veritable eye-opener, which is a frequent technique with Mtshali:[18]

> The sword of daybreak
> snips the shroud
> of the night from the sky,
> and the morning
> peeps through the blankets
> like a baby rising
> from its cot
> to listen to the
> peal of the bell.

What does the bell say?

> Arise! Arise!
> All Workers!
> To work! To work!
> You must go!

The sound parallel made between the first and the third lines introduces a development which strengthens the injunction and is therefore likely to become fixed in the memory. The last stanza, on the other hand, after a short transition which indicates the general activities of the Africans on their way to work, is in a completely different register:

> I shuffle in the queue
> with feet that patter
> on the station platform
> and stumble into the coach
> that squeezes me like a lemon
> of all the juice of my life.

Thus the debunking of the opening allegory, which discreetly set the tone (a contrast between the tired cliché and the more prosaic reality), parallels the demythification of work and its alienating effect, since the journey itself from the township to his place of work empties the African of everything he possesses in the way of creative vitality. The last two lines place in their right context the injunctions contained in the second stanza, of which there now only remains the barely ambiguous refrain, like an implied coda:

> Arise! Arise!
> All Workers!

The Black Man Holds Up His Head

The fact that this poem could be applied to the working masses of all industrialized countries in no way minimizes its specific relevance to South Africa, where it is the Africans who constitute the basic proletariat.

Mtshali therefore implicitly invites his reader to read and reread his collection carefully. If there is 'a message instead of a lizard underneath every stone',[19] then *Sounds of a Cowhide Drum* can be read as a coherent whole in which the poems do not simply have an obvious documentary value, but also a political significance. They develop an argument which can be briefly summarized as follows:

> We are not liked, we are treated like animals, less than animals even, for they are allowed to do certain things.

> The white man says it will always be this way; his religion promises us heaven, but it does not help at all to improve our lot on this Earth.

> Our misfortunes are great, our children suffer from starvation, many of our women are prostitutes.

> We are like sheep, our courage is dissipated in drunken quarrels, our blind violence brings us into conflict with one another; but we are only in chains because we resign ourselves to our situation.

> We must recover our manhood and our courage, we must return to our roots, Africa.[20]

A dynamic architecture, then, which leads in stages to the idea of a necessary and vital liberation.

This 'thesis' is borne out by the three poems placed at the end of the collection: 'My Shadow, Courage', 'Dirge for my passing Years' and 'Sounds of a Cowhide Drum'.

The first two are accounts of dreams, or nightmares rather, which suggest an obsession with castration and the theme of the loss of courage linked with the theme of the growing effeminacy of the individual. These themes, which we shall find more fully developed and stressed in Serote, are here intended, on a personal level which is never far from the experience of the community itself, to emphasize one last time the African's powerlessness to regain his lost manhood.

Although one needs to be careful in applying Jungian patterns literally to a society which has its own meanings and symbols – and the study of which has only just begun – one cannot, however, help noticing the large role played by the Night and Shadow in this dream reconquest of a Self which is clearly unsatisfactory as it is:

> I looked at myself.
> There I was. Shadowless there I was.
> Empty, like a hulk
> waiting for a demolition squad.

A strong desire for death seems to have overcome the individual: regression and a return to the infantile become apparent as the poet descends into the tomb in quest of his childhood and his mother, found intact but *unusable*, in spite of the man/child's wish that she should still be alive:

> In the grave I meet my mother
> black as ebony
> smooth as ivory

> sweet as syrup on a cake.
> Her body lies embalmed
> in a handkerchief of my tears.

The father's heritage, however, is symbolic but derisory: all that he has passed on to his son are his genital organs, and they only serve as a tasty dish, a spice to heighten the flavour of the insipidity of everyday life:

> My father is not there.
> He had left me, a child,
> with his penis to eat for a boerewors*
> and his testicles to slice as onion and tomato
> to gravy my dry and stale mieliepap†.

It is at this point that we reach the last poem in the collection, the one which gives it its title. The drum that can already be heard in the north of Africa ('I hear it far in the northern skies') announces the various struggles for liberation. It calls upon the neophyte to take part in the 'cultural' struggle: the poet openly expresses here something he has not so far said explicitly:

> Boom! Boom! Boom!
> I am the drum on your dormant soul,
> cut from the black hide of a sacrificial cow.
>
> I am the spirit of your ancestors,
> habitant in hallowed huts,
> eager to protect,
> forever vigilant.
>
> Let me tell you of your precious heritage,
> of your glorious past trampled by the conqueror,
> destroyed by the zeal of a missionary.
>
> I lay bare facts for scrutiny
> by your searching mind,
> all declarations and dogmas . . .
>
> Boom! Boom! Boom!
> That is the sound of a cowhide drum –
> the Voice of Mother Africa.

This same example of the fighting ancestors, 'above the heads' of the fathers who have failed, will recur in Serote. Here already Mtshali joins the battlefield of Black Consciousness which, among its other objectives, is anxious to hasten the African community's attainment of self-awareness, to shake it from its passivity and restore its sense of pride in its colour.

---

* *boerewors*: a kind of sausage.
† *mieliepap*: maize porridge.

The importance of Mtshali

Steve Biko, the black leader murdered in prison in September 1977, wrote in 1972: 'We have felt and observed in the past, the existence of a great vacuum in our literary and newspaper world. So many things are said so often to us, about us and for us *but very seldom by us*.'[21]

This is what is interesting about Mtshali, for he painted the portrait of the colonized African as he was raising his head to confront his situation. Along with the other black poets, Mtshali helps to fix this moment for posterity, to give it the appearance it will henceforth always have.

But he also accomplishes, just as unwittingly perhaps, another task: that of ennobling a literature hitherto despised by the purists of the English language in South Africa and contemptuously referred to as 'township art'. It is true that there are popular features in this literature and that the English it uses is not the 'King's English'. It mixes classical and popular styles, African and Afrikaans vocabulary, and it borrows its slang, adapted to Soweto, from North America. But it has an extraordinary vitality and the mixing is to be found again at the level of its imagery and symbols: images taken from the pastoral civilization from which Mtshali comes, like many detribalized Africans, comparisons that are drawn with a daring which indicates the absence of cultural complexes, and symbols which betray the influence of the Bible and Christian education.

This particular acculturation is to be found also in the obsessions and emotional impulses that underlie this poetry. A psychoanalytical reading shows how much Mtshali is a product of a society on which the white has unilaterally made his impression, a society towards which the African is drawn while at the same time wanting to reject it. So, the frequency with which food is evoked in *Sounds* does not only represent a major obsession among many badly paid Africans; linked in the collection with its opposites, vomiting and frequent defecation, it expresses the wish to get rid of that which is no longer bearable, by violence if necessary and here symbolically. We shall find this again in the poetry of Serote, especially in his famous 'What's in this Black "Shit"?'[22]

It is in comparison with the 'bad mother' represented by contemporary South Africa that Africa itself, called 'Mother Africa' in this last poem, is symbolic of the 'good mother'. Attraction and rejection are the visible equivalents of the pendulum movement which affects all the communities living in South Africa, and Mtshali has been very good at putting this across.

Mtshali's success – 16,000 copies of *Sounds* were sold in a year, and the book is now published in England where it has already twice been reprinted – has inspired a large number of young African poets. Whether or not he has hastened the growth of awareness among a majority of Africans is less certain; it is too early yet to know. Besides, to the difficulty poetry generally encounters in working on people's minds must be added the obstacles placed in the way of education and culture among the black people, which of themselves restrict the size of the reading public. It is also likely that it meets with a certain hostility on the part of the followers of Black Consciousness because it uses white channels of publication and marketing.

As for Mtshali's white public, which has ensured the literary success of *Sounds*, it is found principally among the liberal fringe. Applauded after a reading of his poems, Mtshali confided to a BBC interviewer: 'It's quite sickening to hear somebody say "Oh I enjoy your poetry"; in other words, he or she is saying they're enjoying my suffering.'

Mtshali left South Africa in 1974 for the United States. Before his departure, he told his white readers: 'I am not going to publish any more poems. When I read you my poems you appreciate them, but you will not acknowledge me as a person when we meet in the street.'[23]

Mtshali is now back in South Africa with a doctorate obtained in the United States. His second collection of poems, published by Shuter and Shooter (Pietermaritzburg, 1981) has been banned.

Wally Serote

Serote was born in 1944 in Sophiatown, but he has lived most of his life in Soweto and Alexandra; it is the latter township that he constantly evokes in his poetry. After his secondary schooling was interrupted at fourth-form level, Serote spent nine months in detention under the Terrorism Act, until he was released without charges being preferred against him. He left South Africa in 1974, spent some time in the United States where he obtained a degree in fine arts from Columbia University, then went back to southern Africa: he now lives in Botswana.

The three collections of poetry[24] he has published are far from forming a monolithic entity. The first, *Yakhal'inkomo*, comprises poems written for the most part between 1967 and 1971, the period during which Black Consciousness developed. Violence plays a large part in these poems but the overriding feeling is that the black has reached the bottom of the pit and is now on his way up again; confidence and optimism dominate.

The two other collections, *Tsetlo* and *No Baby Must Weep*, are books in which the author gives vent rather to passionate questioning and doubt. In *Tsetlo*, the tone is bitter and violent and the typography itself, with the splitting up of poems and words, reflects the poet's confusion as his hopes for a rapid liberation seem temporarily frustrated. *No Baby Must Weep*, a single poem running to sixty-four pages, is a meditation in which the different stages of a return and a rebirth are linked together until finally the poet emerges from a baptism of fire, undaunted and confident.

Taken together, the three volumes express well the ups and downs and the deep currents of feeling that have been experienced by the black South African over the last ten years, and more particularly the tension between death and growth, slavery and liberation, the spirit of submission and desire for revolt.

A descent into hell

The objective situation of oppression which is that of the South African African justified the anguished portrayal of an existence that seemed too often doomed to futility. Contrary to Mtshali, who *also* describes the truculent vitality of the black townships, Serote is like a fist clenched on violence and resentment; one senses in him the constant desire to shake people into awareness.

In order to achieve this, Serote, like Mtshali, turns to the daily life of the people; as he reviews the activities that stand out most, he can point out its constants and highlight very precisely where the blame lies. It is very much as a teacher, then, that Serote works, for the colonized individual is so used to his deficiencies that he believes them to be part of him and he can no longer tell, from among the innumerable difficulties he encounters in his attempts to survive, which of his evils are avoidable.

The large place Serote gives to tsotsis[25] and to prostitution must not be misunderstood for, while he calls upon the tsotsis directly to stop spilling the blood of their brethren,[26] he knows perfectly well that the tsotsi phenomenon is the product of apartheid, and therefore the fault of the whites, and can only come to an end with the demise of apartheid. Behind his particularly realistic descriptions of scenes of violence, with the cries of its victims calling in vain for help, with the grief of mothers and sisters, Serote shows better than anyone else how the energies of the Africans are being turned aside from their real target, the struggle against the whites.

The prostitutes play an equally harmful role: they undermine the Africans' energy, not only because they dispense the alcohol which on pay-day sets the men fighting with one another, but also because they sell false love which does not lead to maternity and therefore to life. Serote's outlook becomes more radical with his second volume: his description of the prostitutes is no longer simply picturesque but becomes a violent denunciation of women seen as empty, sterile shells devouring the life-force of the men ('the dark and the beer-house where the whores are made/eat people').[27]

But is procreation really so desirable in a society where hope is impossible? By his stand on the subject of prostitution, Serote would seem to be replying in the affirmative. In fact, he is giving expression in his work to one of the tensions and contradictions which are in no sense attributes of his people: on the one hand, the bitter recognition that such an existence is not worth the living ('If my mother's milk was wise enough/as wise as the corn of the field/I would not be here'), and on the other hand an almost animal – certainly not logical or rational – wish to procreate ('. . . but I keep on, I want corn/for I can make milk in some woman/ somebody to suck').[28] 'Murderer, his Mother and Life', which brings together symbolically a tsotsi and a prostitute, shows that evil, by attacking the children, saps the vital forces of a nation and seriously undermines the future. It is this realization that leads Serote to exclaim bitterly:

> Black-experience
> let no man touch my shoulder;
> life is dead,
> is a shadow sprawled over bleeding ruins . . .[29]

The expression of this bitterness is, in fact, part of a dialectic which uses the technique of shocking people into awareness as one of the means of change. For, while Serote reflects, both in *Yakhal'inkomo* and *Tsetlo*, on the end of a life based on futility and doubt, each time the questioning goes deeper and expresses a tension towards another kind of life to which the present bondage communicates a kind of urgency to seek:

> What are we living for?
> For nothing it seems.
> I do not know wealth, nor poverty,
> I know a want,
> A ravaging hunger like of a rage.[30]
>
> I miss what I do not know
> for what I know I wish not to have known.[31]

The examination of his own existential situation thus leads Serote to talk less of the specifically physical suffering of the black people than of their moral poverty, which destroys in man all vestige of resistance or sends him off in the wrong direction. For him, the real hell is resignation to one's fate, the spirit of submission, the lack of courage and the will to fight, in a word the lack of virility, both on the part of his fellow Africans and himself. Through him, the whole South African black community speaks and voices the difficulties it encounters in trying to free itself.

Indeed, this community bears the heavy inheritance of the past generations who bent their backs in the belief that their docility and imitation of the white man would win them his favour and improve their lot by gaining them access to his 'civilization'. Serote shows the people of his own generation as being at a crossroads: their responsibility towards the generations to come is immense and they cannot escape it. This is his greatest quality, as is the fact that he expresses it so well.

In 'Anonymous Throbs+A Dream', the throbs in question, nine in number, are snapshots to which Serote assigns the function of illustrating certain major aspects of the Africans' condition, their poverty and their submission, but also the insensitivity and the cruelty of the whites. What strikes the reader here is the vitality of the images and their crudity. The third stanza (Throb III) treats the theme of submission by developing, in the full sense of the word, the image of the docile white man's dog by which the American and South African blacks designate the zealous servants of the whites:[32]

> I did this world great wrong
> with my kindness of a dog
> my heart like a dog's tongue
> licking too many hands, boots and bums
> even after they kicked my arse
> voetsek, voetsek*
> shit. I still wagged my tail
> I ran away still looking back
> with eyes saying please.[33]

This spirit of submission is also summed up by Serote in a way which appeals vividly to the popular imagination when he evokes the lack of virility in the men or, more metaphorically, the complete absence of men:

Look now this black woman looks at me
with eyes sticking out as big as her arse
shouting at me to look between my thighs . . .

inside the whole world
where mothers call their children, children crying and swearing
I don't know where the men are
dogs roam near the doors staring straight into the eyes of women and children
dogs here do eat shit

---

* *voetsek*: Go away!

their tails wag above dustbin brims
or their backs slide across the donga
I do not know where all the men have gone[34]

Elsewhere, it is the passivity of his brothers that Serote castigates, telling them that there is no time to be lost and that sacrifices will be needed to attain the freedom they desire. Dreams and nightmares follow one another; their images reveal the obsessions of a man who seems suddenly to have realized that the people are struggling, way behind the advance of Black Consciousness, and that he himself is in a no-man's-land between this world, which he rejects, and a world whose shape he cannot yet clearly distinguish. Some lines resemble the neat phrases which the militants pump out at political meetings to shake people into a state of awareness: 'Everybody's back is facing the future'.[35] At other times, Serote's poetry bursts with cries of anguish and pain that express his rage before such poverty and resignation:

> I'm justified to do anything
> including banging God's door
> that's what I mean.[36]
>
> My heart bleeds through my eyes
> for indeed my eyes are a bloody memory.[37]
>
> nobody looks any more
> or hears
> or even sleeps
> everything is fucked up
> children cry all night and all day
> while their mothers and fathers can't even make love
> these dead things
> which sleep through a nightmare
> snoring
> sleeping with open eyes
> ears shut to everything except the alarm clock
> ears always ready to listen to lies[38]

However, Serote's poetry is also often able to enclose within a classical and highly restrained structure the lesson he wants to put across to his brothers. The following poem, which stresses a person's responsibility at a time when major decisions likely to change the face of a country are being taken, has a universal application which goes well beyond the context for which it was written. It is the mark of great poetry for a poem to be able to remain in people's memories long after the specific historical occasion which produced it has died away:

> Everyone of us
> throbs footsteps inside the chest of the earth
> for we belong there.
>
> the earth is always tight-lipped
> but only talks to itself
> perturbed by its throbs.

> Each of us will answer
> when the worms dig in and out us for the truth,
> below the earth.[39]

The watcher for the dawn

The other side of Serote's work is the prophecy of the advent of the new man he longs to see and to whom he lends his voice. In spite of the disappointments recorded in *Tsetlo*, there is enough to justify the hope of a change, the responsibility for which lies in the hands of the younger generation, the children and the young men and women of the seventies. They will not be afraid to address the white man on equal terms, they will not fear to hate the authors of their centuries-old suffering. They will regain the courage of their ancestors and hear from across the seas the message of liberation addressed to them by their brothers who have gone into exile in Europe and the United States. There would be nothing new here that was not already spoken of by Mtshali, except that Serote says directly, in his own voice, and *clearly*, what Mtshali hinted at or expressed by means of a fable. Serote – and this is the chief characteristic of Black Consciousness – dares to look the white man in the eye and, especially, to speak to him plainly.

He is, however, less anxious to speak to the white man or to reveal to him the 'hidden face' of South African society than to speak to his fellow Africans, not in the language of the political militant, like Stokely Carmichael, for instance, but by trying to bring about the cultural and psychological transformation that must necessarily precede political action proper. If we add that his work also shows his rejection of the white liberals, the prophecy of a retributive violence and a stress on what is and is not to be done, we can say that Serote is the voice of the Black Consciousness movement, minus its didacticism but with the lyrical power of the poet.

It is not, therefore, by chance that the poem that opens *Yakhal'inkomo* defines the peripheral zone in which black and white met until then without really talking to one another, merely rubbing shoulders, because they were both victims of fear – the fear of the white man trapped by his inhumanity and his lack of love, the fear of the black man who has placed the white man on a pedestal he does not deserve. Beneath an apparently respectful exterior – Serote uses the word 'baas' several times – the poem prefigures and announces their future encounters, when the black man will be truly present ('It's just that I appeared'), having at last come out of the shadows, abandoned his anonymity and, in short, left behind him his non-existence:

> Do not fear Baas.
> It's just that I appeared
> And our faces met
> In this black night that's like me.
> Do not fear –
> We will always meet
> When you do not expect me.
>
> I will appear,
> In the night that's black like me.
> Do not fear –
> I will blame my mind

> When I fear you
> In the night that's black like me.
> Do not fear Baas,
> My heart is as vast as the sea
>
> And your mind as the earth.
> It's awright Baas,
> Do not fear.[40]

This places the emphasis squarely on the sharing of responsibilities, a theme Serote was to return to later. However, if we seek a poem to serve as a banner for Black Consciousness, a poem which bears the mark of the new relationship between the young generation of Africans and the whites, we must turn to 'What's in this Black "Shit"?' This poem is an expression of self-assertion and courage, in the metaphorical form suggested by the title: Serote implicitly returns to the dialogue idea only to leap immediately from servile or forced submission to the orders of the white man to categorical refusal. In both cases, there is denial of the other man's words, but in the second the roles are reversed, the only way, say the followers of Black Consciousness, for the African to regain his dignity and make an impression on the white man.

Apart from this, still in the same poem, the scatological vocabulary and the naturalistic descriptions are not merely details intended to create a vivid effect: they are there to show from what century-old depths come this disgust, for the white man and for oneself, and the desire for revolt that has never been articulated; they prepare for the conclusion which is all the more resounding and forceful for having been withheld for so long. Disrespect is part of the newly acquired courage and the verbal violence prefigures violence of another sort which shows that the era of the Kumalos is well and truly over:

> It is not the steaming little rot
> In the toilet bucket,
> It is the upheaval of the bowels
> Bleeding and coming out through the mouth
> And swallowed back,
> Rolling in the mouth,
> Feeling its taste and wondering what's next like it . . .
>
> I'm learning to pronounce this 'Shit' well,
> Since the other day,
> At the pass office,
> When I went to get employment,
> The officer there endorsed* me to Middleburg,
> So I said, hard and with all my might, 'Shit'
> I felt a little better;
> But what's good, is, I said it in his face,
> A thing my father wouldn't dare do.
> That's what's in this black 'Shit'.[41]

---

*endorse: to post, send.

The last poem of the series, 'Ofay-Watcher'*, with its stanzas of unequal length, its blend of aphorisms and poems and its calls to the reader to reflect, is particularly effective as an illustration in miniature of the relations between whites and blacks in South Africa. We witness the unfolding, step by step, of a train of thought which is organized in the form of associations of ideas, hence the importance of the verbal echoes, which help the transition from one step in the reasoning to the next. The argument is put together by the repetition of fragments which are progressively assembled around a common core ('from there'):

> I come from there,
> The children there have no toys, they play with mud . . .
> I come from down there,
> the parents there are children of other men and women,
> there the old just sit and wait for death
> like people wait for a train.
> I come from down there below,
> my friends are tender people who look old . . .
> they are meek like sheep following the other blindly.
> They and I come from down there below,
> down there below the bottom.[42]

Serote's detached tone, used even to talk of everyday dramas, stresses the tragic quality of this life; the hints and the allusions contribute to the effect by their concision:

> My younger brother is quiet, like a tree holding its leaves,
> Not to shake,
> But the wind is blowing.[43]
>
> My younger sister is a seed
> Or has a seed.[44]

The poem's ending asserts the need for change and stresses the idea of a shared responsibility:

> White people are white people,
> They are burning the world
> Black people are black people,
> They are the fuel.
> White people are white people,
> They must learn to listen.
> Black people are black people,
> They must learn to talk.[45]

Elsewhere, Serote gives a metaphorical picture of the change he sees taking place around him between the preceding generations and his own, or he shows, within his own time, what separates the past from the present. Thus, he contrasts the seated position, which signifies stagnation and passivity, with walking, the sign of

---

* Ofay: white (Americanism).

rebirth and will. In this new *Pilgrim's Progress*, Serote takes his symbols and his movement from the journey, and his tone and his use of repetition from the Negro spirituals. So, 'Hell, Well, Heaven' contrasts the present and the past with the leitmotiv 'I do not know where I have been/But Brother,/I know I'm coming', which marks the various stages of a veritable Stations of the Cross and which finally leaves the reader with the conviction: no, it's not Hell any more, it's Heaven:

> I do know where I have been,
> But Brother,
> I know I'm coming . . .
> Hell! where I was I cried silently
> Yet I sat there until now . . .
> I come like a tide of water now,
> But Oh! there's sand beneath me! . . .
> I do not know where I have been
> To have despair so deep and deep and deep
> But Brother,
> I know I'm coming.
> I do not know where I have been
> But Brother,
> Was that Thoko's voice?
> Hell, well, Heavens![46]

Another symbol of this hope which may not be fully realized until the next generation is that of sowing seeds. The two collections, especially the second, are full of children to whom the poet talks, or young animals, especially cats, symbols of resistance, contrasted with dogs and their bad reputation and with rats, which represent misfortune. 'The Seed and the Saints', like other poems, draws on this symbolism, while at the same time showing the reader what influences Serote and the followers of Black Consciousness have undergone:

> I'm the seed of this earth
> ready with my roots to spread deep into reality
> I've been a looked after
> black seed; by black saints and prophets
> by Sobukwe Mandela Sisulu
> Fanon Malcolm X George Jackson.[47]

The first volume, especially, is full of poems evoking the joy of a soul discovering its new strength, feeling that it is 'growing wings'. There is nothing gratuitous about the images chosen from the world of nature: images of growing trees and plants, of ripened fruit ready to fall, as, for example, in 'The Growing',[48] which again uses a language of allusion. Or else it is images of rivers in flood, or the image of the turning of the tide, suggesting the poet's faith at the end of the sixties:

> We are caught up in a turning tide,
> The river flows, the river ebbs,
> The bubbles form and burst
> And foam oozes out our scalps,
> The turn is long, turn is wide,

Hands and mind retract, craving to touch,
There at the wide and long turning . . .
The turning tide, we are caught up there
Where the waves break before they ripen,
Many will break there,
Many will not become waves, they will peep and perish,
There at the turning tide . . .
One day we'll wake up,
And on the rocky cheeks of the bank there'll be huge droplets flowing
And the reeds of the river will be dry like skeleton bones;
And the river shall be heard,
Flowing, flowing on, and on
The route will be long and straight,
The bubbles will burst, like eyes looking back,
But the river shall flow like the song of birds.[49]

Such is the power of this collection that the reader comes away from it as if invigorated. This is not so much protest poetry, with its accusations and its endless appeals to the whites, as the song of the watcher who sees the dawn coming and proclaims the fact out loud. From the centre of the shadow that is still spread all around him, the poet asserts with lyrical serenity that the day will break. The titles themselves seem to belong to a music programme: 'Waking up. The Sun. The Body' or 'Movement. Moulding. Moment':

> The sun has slept,
> There are no more shadows following anything,
> The fright is gone under cover
>
> Of darkness.
>
> The night throbs,
> Through the silence of the footsteps of the shadow
> The truth hides, only seen by the stars
>
> Of darkness.
>
> Something is breathing,
> There is a silent life in the light walking to the horizon.
> The moon follows the sun
>
> Of dawn.[50]

'But seasons come to pass'

The poems and extracts quoted above are all evidence of Serote's true quality as a poet: the power of his images and symbols, the vigour of his ideas and his language, his profound lyricism are present in all of his poetry, together or by turns. Is the awareness of his art enough, however, to encourage a writer to continue writing when nothing in the political structure of his country changes, because its masters, those who have the arms, the money and the backing of so many foreign countries, do not themselves change? What use is literature?

To speak to others so as to make them think—and we know that in this respect the poet has greater freedom than the prose-writer; to speak to himself so as to clarify his own ideas; to speak quite simply so as to 'pour out his heart', to exorcize some of his nightmares; to speak, finally, so that the world will know. From the South African prison Serote's voice is heard, along with a few others. It tells of the tragic lot of a people left to the folly and the arbitrariness of their rulers:

> When i take my pen,
> my soul bursts to deface the paper . . .
> my crimson heart oozes into the ink,
> dilutes it
> spreads the gem of my life
> makes the word i utter a gasp to the world.[51]

Would what he has to say be as valuable if his poetry were not devoid of Manichaeism, if his questioning and his doubts did not add consistency to his and his contemporaries' experience? Would he be such a great poet if, presenting it as he does, the magnitude of the problems that still need to be resolved by the Africans on their way to freedom did not reveal the fragility of their hopes and, as a corollary of this, the responsibility of the 'free' world? For the power of literature does not depend on the writer alone: words are seeds which can only germinate in the consciences of others, after surviving the winter of despair and being warmed by the spring of anger. If the seed does not die . . .

That is why Serote's work is worth listening to and reflecting upon: the account he gives of his daily fight reduces our own fears to more modest dimensions. His own struggle with the angel, which is constantly having to be begun all over again and at the end of which he finally wins back his human dignity, is also our struggle in a way, not to serve as a catharsis but to be pursued in spite of the distance, in spite of the obstacles to which a world based on the overlapping of interests endlessly adds.

Of course, what he has to say is inseparable from that of Matthews and Mtshali. His greatness, if we compare him with the former, lies in the way he presents an insight into the black man's experience which is much richer, much more complex, much more subtle; his work is not that of a propagandist, even if the cause justifies this approach a thousand times over, but that of a man who has felt very deeply the greatest doubts and hopes, all those tensions, in fact, without which even violent writing remains desperately flat.

Serote's work is also profoundly original in relation to Mtshali's, rich as the latter is. It is, certainly, less colourful than Mtshali's, and Mtshali's naïve, yet corrosive, humour is almost completely missing from Serote. But Serote's poetry gains as a result in concentration; it is kept alive by a constant fire within, and it burns with the intensity of an emotion which is never superficial.

A last poem can be cited in this discussion about the power of literature; it is the poem entitled 'For Don M [Mattera] – Banned'. The message of hope Serote addressed to him – one will note the play on words ('it's a dry *white* season'), is also the one he spoke to himself when his patience ran out. For time in the long run is against the oppressor, and the certainty of the dawn is contained in the eternal cycle of nature and the seasons:

> It is a dry white season
> dark leaves don't last, their brief lives dry out
> and with a broken heart they dive down gently headed for the earth,

not even bleeding.
   it is a dry white season brother,
   only the trees know the pain as they stand erect
   dry like steel, their branches dry like wire,
   indeed, it is a dry white season
   but seasons come to pass.[52]

Don Mattera*

Besides Serote, several writers have dedicated their work to Don Mattera as a mark of esteem and admiration for his indomitable spirit, as a sign of encouragement for one who has been silenced by decree, as a token of friendship for a man who has never failed them or the people of Azania.[53] But Don Mattera is more than an authentic militant for the black cause, he is also one of the most significant poets of the present generation.

The Mattera family put down roots in South Africa in 1904 when Francesco Mattera, then 26 years old and a sailor from Naples, jumped ship while in Cape Town and married a Griqua woman. He went to work in the Kimberley mines, made some money there, and eventually founded one of the first bus companies for Africans in Johannesburg. He settled in nearby Sophiatown where the family, through interracial union or marriage, became as cosmopolitan as the city itself which then numbered some 200,000 inhabitants. Don Mattera, Francesco's grandson, was born there in 1935.

Left at first in the care of his paternal grandparents, he was later sent to a Catholic school in Durban which accommodated orphans and children from broken homes. There he was brought up the hard way, his rebellious spirit grew; there he learnt the English language and 'English' manners; there, too, he became an expert boxer.

When he went back to Sophiatown in 1950, the Mattera 'clan' was no longer holding itself together, the Nationalist party had come to power, and Johannesburg was one of the worst places for tsotsism and crime. Mattera joined one of the youthful gangs whose leadership he assumed very quickly. He had several brushes with the police and even served a brief spell in jail. Yet he somehow managed to finish school, and passed his Matriculation in 1957.

By then, he was having second thoughts about making his way in life through the power of the fist or the knife: a son had been born to him, and there were more useful things to be done by a youth whose political awareness was growing.

It was in Sophiatown, too, that Mattera came to know the quite popular figure of Father Trevor Huddleston, and a few white radicals such as Joe Slovo and Dennis Goldberg, the latter later condemned to a life sentence as one of the accused at the Rivonia Trial (1964).

Don Mattera belonged for a while to the Youth League of the African National Congress then joined the more radical Pan-Africanist Congress, but both organizations were banned after Sharpeville, and it was only at a later stage that he entered the Coloured Labour Party, which was the only body where he could still be politically active.

---

*This essay was first published in *Kunapipi*, University of Aarhus, Denmark (vol. 2, no. 1, 1980), although in a highly condensed form. The English text is by the author.

But he was yearning to struggle again side by side with his darker brothers, an opportunity which presented itself in 1971 when the Black People's Convention was founded. Don Mattera took a large share in the conscientization then taking place under the auspices of the Black Consciousness organizations. However, his activities were brought to an abrupt end in 1973 when a five-year banning order was issued against him forbidding him, among other things, to address meetings, to be in groups of more than two persons, to leave his place of residence, to publish and/or prepare for (personal) publication.[54] This order was renewed in 1978 for a further period of five years. Like Karel Kosik, the Czech philosopher and dissident, Don Mattera could very well say: 'My existence has taken two forms: I am and I am not; I am dead and yet at the same time I live . . .'[55] In 1979 he addressed an 'Open Letter' to all white South Africans, depicting in detail what the life of a banned person is like; he complains notably that he has been transformed into a 'near vegetable': 'I am so demeaned', he adds, 'that I can no longer truly fulfil myself as a poet and a person.'[56]

Don Mattera belongs to the group of 'Coloureds' who, at a very early stage, considered themselves as 'blacks' because they knew that their fate was inseparable from that of the African and the Indians. The political and social events that have taken place since 1948, the oppression, repression, expulsions to which all the 'non-whites' have been subjected indiscriminately have proved them right. In Mattera's case, the fact that his beloved mother was a Tswana, as well as several incidents in his early life, not only convinced him of the basic need for solidarity and unity: it instilled in him the pride of being an African – or as near to it as possible;[57] this appears throughout his poetry and prose.[58]

His autobiography, *Gone with the Twilight*, will, when it has been published, rank among the most fitting tributes paid to the Sophiatown that was. Like his two predecessors, Bloke Modisane (*Blame Me On History*, 1963) and Can Themba (*The Will To Die*, 1972), Don Mattera, some ten years younger than they were, evokes magnificently the multiracial community which lived in Sophiatown before this very togetherness was forbidden by law. Don Mattera relates his childhood and youth, the moments of happiness and those of sorrow, the partings and the reunions – the former more frequent than the latter. He describes his family and friends and the motley crowd of the teeming, bustling township, the exploited and the exploiters, the priests of various denominations, the gangs and the police . . . They all come alive in a wealth of picturesque details, like chunks and slices of a rich, pithy life with its mixture of little joys and dramas, its humour and tenderness, and the overall humanity that transcended the barriers of language and colour. The descriptions themselves seem to come straight from his youth, passionate, idealistic, vibrant with indignation or pathos. More lyrical passages occur when he relates the actual destruction of the houses where they had lived, and tells of the feelings of dispossession and uprootedness that were theirs. Here is a moving, though precise, testimony on the disappearance of a community and the passing of an era.

His poems will appeal, first of all, to those who seek in the literature of the oppressed the direct reflection and expression of a people's mentality. His poetic output[59] straddles the period from Sharpeville and its aftermath of defeat and doubt to the post-Soweto days with their spirit of challenge and defiance. Since most of them are dated, they provide so many landmarks in the evolution taking place within the black community during those vital twenty years, and they document the progress of Black Consciousness.

Mattera's early poems are what one might call protest poetry 'of the first kind' because they 'simply' enumerate the evils. They concentrate mainly on the depersonalization of the black man, subjected as he is to exploitation and oppression. Here, black men queue up for their passes, mere objects still who 'stare fixedly/at the powerful rubberstamp . . ./ in the white man's hand' ('Rubber Stamp'). Or they are seen waiting for their pay, 'head bowed in seeming gratitude/ mouth spitting out the usual/thank you, my baas' ('Payday'). There, a beggar murmurs the same 'thank you, my baas' to one of his black brothers whose hand his poor eyesight has failed to recognize. But there is already the deep-felt conviction that this situation will not last for ever. 'Payday', mentioned earlier, ends with the clear warning:

> So, thank you, my baas,
> but it will not always be like this.

From the end of the sixties, and for at least the next few years, two themes recur more or less frequently. The first one is linked both with the life of misery and deprivation Mattera has just described and with the consequences the obdurate refusal of the whites to change must automatically entail. Thus the plight of the black man is but a prefiguration of the plight of the whole country, a country for which Mattera feels immense love. This he expresses in warm terms: like Dennis Brutus, Mattera addresses South Africa as a lover would address the loved one:

> Sea and sand
> my love my land
>   God bless Africa
>   but more the South of Africa
>   ('God Bless Africa', 1969)

> I weep for you my country
> that you should some day
> bear testimony
> to that final folly
> when men turn against each other

> When those who killed
> for seeming love
> must die for lack of it
> and the trodden rise to dethrone

> I weep for you South Africa
> and dread the long nightfall
> we so hastily beckon
> I weep for you my love.
>   ('Lament for My Country', 1972)

> And so,
>   my country
>   my deepest love
>   you that drank my tears
>   cannot mend my grief.
>   ('The Heart', 1973)

The second theme is couched in far more bitter terms, for Mattera takes the white man to task for his lack of true religion and for his inhumanity. These are no Christians, he says, who make such cruel laws and limit their religious practice to church-going and an occasional breast-beating. One recognizes here a theme familiar to all committed poets, both black and white. But in Mattera's poems, the various stages through which the oppressed have gone, from puzzlement to outward rejection, appear clearly: the tone changes because the attitudes themselves have changed.

The white man is thus at first referred to indirectly as 'They' and the poems merely state the bare facts, in a concise way that lends them strength and credibility. 'Limitation' (1970) shows the white man's generosity for what it really is:

> Because I believed they loved me
> because I believed they cared
> I asked them for my freedom
>
> Then, they took back the wheatfield
> and took back the well
> and tightened the chains
> and told me I asked too much.

Not even twelve months later, the tone has become sharper, and the white man is addressed with a vindictive 'You':

> To say that you love
> and offer it
> to a dream
>
> To say you love that dream
> and offer it
> to man
>
> To say that you love man
> and yet offer him
> to God as Cain did his brother
>
> To say rather no such love
> nor dream nor offering
> and what of no God?

Still one more year and the white man is pushed into the background: since he won't listen, since he won't change, there remains for the poet/ conscientizer to turn towards his brothers. Like his colleagues of the Black Consciousness movement, Don Mattera has realized that the black man is truly 'on his own', that his passivity and lack of combativity are playing a role in the perpetuation of apartheid. As he makes it quite clear in 'Of Reason and Discovery' (1973):

> I have discovered, yes,
> the fault not in the God
> nor the pain, but the sufferer
> who makes virtue of his anguish

> and waits meekly on the God
> for deliverance
> though white scavengers rip flesh
> from his battered black bones.

If the time for reasoning and praying is over, then the black man must 'stand up for his rights': indeed, 'the slogan repeated by the oppressed [is] DON'T MOURN, MOBILIZE'.[60] Hence, the direct appeal to the black man to 'look him [the white man] in the eye' as in 'No Time, Black Man':[61]

> Let him hear it
> if he turns his face and sneers
> spit and tell him shit
> it's all or nothing
> he's got all
> and you have nothing.

From then on, the interjection: 'we've had enough' will recur over and over again with mounting force, at first a cry of anguish and then a declaration of war. In 'No More':

> Hell, God, someone must pay
> for all this mad wicked destruction
> strong against the weak
> armed against the unarmed.

Or in 'Of Life, Of Death':

> Even as we live
>   let us remember the dying
>   as we clench our fists
>   against the robbery of life
>   cursing our subjugation . . .
>
> As for me,
> I have reached the cross
> if there is love, then it will be shared
> with them that are moved by it
> if hatred is to be, then
> it will be learned
> for what it teaches and not
> what it would make of me.

Thus the protest poetry of the early stages has gradually evolved into a defiant, militant one. Yet, even then, the liberation of minds is more difficult to achieve than it might appear at first: hatred cannot be 'learned' that easily, and probably far less so for Mattera's own generation: there are numerous signs in Mattera's poetry and prose, as indeed in many of his contemporaries', of the reluctance, unwillingness or even inability to resort to the same violence as that of the rulers. Thus, in 'A Sure Reminder':

> This hatred was not in me
> but in the guns of the overlords
> mine was a song singing to be free
> theirs the thunder of repression.

The poet is even more explicit in 'And Yet':

> I have known deep silences
> when thoughts like angry waves
> beat against the shores
> of my mind
> revealing the scars
> of brutal memories
> of trampled dignity
> and the murder
> of my manhood
>   and yet
>   I cannot hate
>   try as I want to
>   I cannot hate, WHY?[62]

One finds here a situation unlike those described by Fanon in *The Wretched of the Earth*: for various reasons,[63] the South African world is not as Manichaean as one might imagine. Mattera himself, in his 'Open Letter', finds it difficult to address the whites as a 'nation' because of the 'many valiant white men and women [who] have raised their voices, offered their lives and the lives of their families in the cause of freedom for all people.' He also says he cannot forget 'those white men and women who have stood up to be counted, and are dead and suffering as a result of their consciences'. Thus there is no wish, except perhaps from a tiny minority of blacks, to want to 'expel the colonizer from the panorama' (Fanon). The society envisaged by Mattera is *probably*[64] of a socialist type, but it is definitely a non-racial one, and his most ardent wish is that this should be achieved without bloodshed. Mattera's basic humanism and intense generosity of heart shine out in 'God Bless Africa', but one should also note that the word 'love' is the one that recurs most frequently throughout his work:

> God bless the children
> of South Africa,
> the Black and the White children
> but more the Black children
> who lost the sea and the sand
> that they may not lose love
> for the White children who took the land.

However, Mattera is torn by a situation which sees the rulers safe in their seat of power and using the latter with the utmost ruthlessness. His own absence of aggressiveness and that of his black brothers is at the same time noted and regretted: for if the whites will not change, the blacks themselves change too slowly (interpret: are too submissive still, not daring enough). Anger and impatience grow as the years go by: they sometimes embrace both oppressed and oppressors:

> This land,
> this damned stupid submissive sonofabitch
> of a land, needs to be rumbled out
> of its indifferent fear
> by a volcano of anger
> and tell the world
> > NO MORE
> > HELL GOD
> > WE HAVE HAD ENOUGH.
>
> ('No More')

Mattera must have thus seen with a mixture of pride and horror the uprisings of 1976–7: the children had 'found the answers', dared to stand up – and paid dearly for their courage.

If the political import of the poems mentioned so far points to a growing didacticism on the part of Mattera, the blame for this is not the writer's. For Don Mattera is no politician suddenly turned to literature, nor a prose-writer converted to verse: there is in him a genuine urge to write poetry, and to write of other things than those pressed on him by 'the situation'. The number of lyrics is important: some end up with the poet's main preoccupation, others develop fully and reveal sensitivity, sense of structure and unquestionable talent of expression.

The lyricism is there from the very beginning: in the first version of 'Sophiatown' (1960), not printed in *Azanian Love Song*, Mattera describes graphically the atmosphere prevailing in the bulldozed township; but he links it quite appropriately with the Sharpeville and Langa massacres and ends up on a very personal note:

> The guns are quiet now
> > bullets lie hibernating
> > in their common vaults
> > the blood has been washed
> > from dusty pavements where
> > thumb-in-air congress folk
> > called Africa back
> Even the wind is chained
> > to the unforgotten horror
> > of Herod's march
> > on the innocent Black child . . .
>
> Sophia, Sophia, Sophiatown
> > we walk and lie beaten in the dust
> > drained of defiant fire
> > and lean against the
> > we-won't-move-sign
> > laughing at the passing show of defeat
>
> > But, in the long dark night
> > when police flashlights
> > and barking alsatians
> > have ceased their manhunt

> we crouch sexually and crawl
> into each other
> to count our scars
> and weep and wait and call
> the God in whose name
> we are destroyed.

The poems that follow in the late sixties and early seventies are mostly classical in form: they develop one idea through the use of extended metaphors, each stanza carrying its own weight of the argument through to the last line which serves as a 'parting shot'. Such is the case of 'Offering', 'Limitations', and 'Not There', the latter an echo of Rev. Msimangu's sombre words[65] that the whites may turn to loving when it is too late, when the black man is 'not there' . . .

The texts written in the next few years, although more often than not addressed to the black community, are not all meant to 'teach a lesson': besides poems common to all committed poets about the difficulty of writing songs and not dirges in a police state, there are others where Mattera's lyrical qualities appear uninhibited. 'An Old Woman Speaks' denotes a fine sense of observation while recapturing the girlish fervour of one who lived 'before machines gave birth/to concrete cities':

> Time's pins have pierced my limbs
> rivers of wrinkle
> bend and twist
> on my aged face
> my eyes have lost their sparkle
> the doek* is tattered and worn
>   I am old now
> It was not always so
> once Time and I were partners
> we chased the Rising Sun
> through fields of sunflowers and corn
> there was fire in my eyes then
> yellow and orange like my skin . . .

Two poems hint at the theme of negritude: 'Departure', the longer one, with its evocation of the Nile, 'jungle fruit' and freedom, as opposed to 'this city/seething in unrest and injustice'; and 'Freedom, the Bird', in a strikingly powerful, though concise, allegory:

> And it was in a dream
>   that the earth trembled
>   and released a Bird,
>   gargantuan and Black
> I was the Bird,
> It was in me.

---

* *doek* (Afrikaans): head scarf.

There are more personal poems where Mattera's tone is elegiac or passionate, as the occasion demands, and some bitterness understandably creeps into the later poems. 'At least' shows the poet at his best: he has dropped for one day 'the heavy cloak/of bitter resolve/to welcome the infiltration/of warmth and love and beauty'. With heightened lyricism, Mattera 'simply' begs to function again *fully* as an ordinary man and as a poet:

> For these brief
> somewhat fleeting hours
> while the crisp laughter
> of the wind fills me deeply
> O my land
> at least for this untroubled day
> let me unclench my being
> to stroke the yellow flowers.[66]

If Don Mattera, then, is no professional like many other black writers of the last decade, he has vital things to say and he often says them well. Some of his poems antedate those of his fellow poets while others echo them. If there is in his poetry less humour than in Mtshali and fewer bold, graphic images than in Serote, he is more of a 'teacher' than they are – at least more directly so, until his banning – and in this he is closer to James Matthews. His influence and example remain, though.

Notes

1. *Sounds of a Cowhide Drum*, with a preface by Nadine Gordimer. First edition: Renoster Books, Johannesburg, 1971. Revised edition: Oxford University Press, London, 1972 (the edition to which reference – abbreviated to *Sounds* – is made in this text).
2. In 'Cinq difficultés pour écrire la vérité', *Europe*, January–February 1957.
3. It is interesting to note the same phenomenon in connection with that other 'colonized' person, the domestic servant; see M. Lamouille and L. Weibel, *Pipes de terre et pipes de porcelaine* (Ed. Zoé, Paris, 1978).
4. See *Sounds*, pp. 13, 46.
5. In *The Heart of the Hunter* (Penguin, London, 1965), p. 123.
6. In *Resistance against Tyranny* (Routledge & Kegan Paul, London, 1966), p. 37.
7. *Sounds*, p. 55. Hereafter, the pages will be given only for those poems whose title is not indicated.
8. ibid. p. 50.
9. On this point see, among others, Nkosi, *Home and Exile* (Longman, London, 1965), and Modisane, *Blame Me on History* (Thames & Hudson, London, 1963).
10. The dust-cover of the English edition aptly remarks: 'The loaded image of that "handbag", the irony of those "fine clothes", the choice of the inhuman verb "ticks"? (timepiece or timebomb?) are the marks of a poet of rare quality.'
11. *Sounds*, p. 27.
12. But identification is easy in a country where class barriers correspond with racial classification.
13. If we note the cluster of signs: weight=(op)pression=snow=white.
14. The tendency is common among many committed (especially black) poets.
15. Pieterse's poem is 'Song', in *Poets to the People* ed. Feinberg, (Heinemann, London, 1980), p. 158.
16. See below, p. 210.

17. One should also examine the possible significance of the animals and colours for the cultural milieu at which the poem is directed.
18. See especially *Sounds*, p. 27.
19. The image is André Breton's, in 'Epervier Incassable', *Clair de Terre* (Gallimard, Paris, 1923).
20. The poems have none of the didacticism of this summary.
21. In *Black Viewpoint* (Spro-Cas, Durban, 1972), p. 7.
22. See below, p. 191.
23. For other statements by Mtshali, see *Issue*, A Quarterly Journal of Africanist Opinion, vol. VI, no. 1, Spring 1976, ed. B. Lindfors.
24. *Yakhal'inkomo* (Renoster Books, Johannesburg, 1972). *Tsetlo* (Ad. Donker, Johannesburg, 1974). *No Baby Must Weep* (Ad. Donker, Johannesburg, 1975). Since this chapter was written, another book of Serote's has been published: *Behold Mama, Flowers* (Ad. Donker, Johannesburg, 1978). Serote's first novel *To Every Birth Its Blood* was published in 1981 by Ravan Press, Johannesburg.
25. It is worth recalling here that the violence of the tsotsis is directed above all against the African community. Criminals and victims, in spite of themselves, play a predetermined role for which political oppression and poverty are chiefly responsible. See on this subject S. Thion, *Le Pouvoir Pâle* (Ed. du Seuil, Paris 1969).
26. In *Yakhal'inkomo*, op. cit., p. 19.
27. In 'A Glance', *Tsetlo*. op. cit., p. 39.
28. ibid., p. 42.
29. ibid., p. 46.
30. *Yakhal'inkomo*, op. cit., p. 10.
31. *Tsetlo*, op. cit., p. 26.
32. Also called 'Uncle Tom', from the name of the old slave in *Uncle Tom's Cabin* by Harriet Beecher-Stowe, and 'Kumalo', from the name of the black pastor in Paton's *Cry, the Beloved Country* (see above).
33. *Tsetlo*, op. cit., p. 53.
34. ibid., pp. 50, 54.
35. ibid., p. 13.
36. ibid., p. 52.
37. ibid., p. 21.
38. *No Baby Must Weep*, op. cit., p. 27.
39. *Tsetlo*, op. cit., p. 25.
40. *Yakhal'inkomo*, op. cit., p. 1.
41. ibid., pp. 8–9.
42. ibid., p. 48.
43. ibid., p. 49.
44. ibid.
45. ibid., pp. 50–1.
46. ibid., pp. 16–17.
47. *Tsetlo*, op. cit., p. 34.
48. *Yakhal'inkomo*, op. cit., p. 13.
49. ibid., p. 44.
50. ibid., p. 26.
51. *Tsetlo*, op. cit., p. 9.
52. ibid., p. 58.
53. André Brink's book, *A Dry White Season*, has popularized Serote's poem but not the man for whom the poem was written. Among other testimonies written for Don Mattera, see Len Morgan's 'The Fugitive' and Christopher van Wyk's 'They would've banned your eyes, Don', in *Staffrider* (May–June 1978), as well as the glowing tribute inscribed on the opening page of *Forced Landing* (Ravan Press, Johannesburg, 1980) by editor Mothobi Mutloatse. Mattera was eventually unbanned in May 1982.
54. Reverend Theo Kotze, a director of the Christian Institute of Southern Africa, himself a banned person who escaped to Great Britain, declared in a speech delivered at the Royal

Institute of International Affairs, Chatham House, London, on 7 November 1978: 'Under the Internal Security Act, the Minister of Justice is enabled to ban a person if he is satisfied that he/she engaged in activities which endangered the maintenance of public order . . . Of course, the so-called evidence for this is always secret and probably by paid informers. I know of no instance where reasons for the banning of a person were either publicly given or proved.' Let us add that no banned person has ever been brought to court and stood trial – except in the case when he/she had allegedly broken his/her banning order.

For further evidence on bannings, see *The Silenced* (South African Institute of Race Relations, 1979).

55. This is a letter addressed to Jean-Paul Sartre in 1975.
56. See *Index on Censorship* (vol. 9, no. 1, February 1980) and *Focus on Political Repression in Southern Africa*, International Defence and Aid Fund, London, (no. 25, November/December 1979). After being a social worker in the early sixties, Mattera had turned to journalism: he was still on the staff of *The Star*, one of the leading English-speaking newspapers in Johannesburg, though only as a sub-editor because of his banning, but he resigned in 1983 to protest against the sacking of MWASA (Media Workers Association of South Africa) of which he was Vice-President.
57. See the very significant episode in *Gone With The Twilight* where Don Mattera, having been beaten by an African policeman despite what he thought were his privileges as a 'Coloured' (i.e. not having to produce a pass), goes and complains to his mother:

'"Now you know a bit . . . It's bad when your skin is black. Now, I'm happier that I gave you to your father's people, otherwise you would have suffered," she told me without pity.

'I argued that the policeman was an African and yet he beat me without regard for my age. She replied that he stopped being an African when he wore a police badge. He became something totally different. A tool. A robot. Something else but not an African. Being an African was something great, transcending and valuable, with an open heart, she said. I loved her for giving me something better than pity. She helped me to understand and believe that being an African was beautiful and I wanted more than anything else to become one.'
58. I am indebted to *Index on Censorship* (London) for providing great help during Mattera's banning in letting me have free access to Mattera's manuscripts.
59. His poems were published in 1983 (see *Azanian Love Song*, op. cit.).
60. Cecil Abrahams in *World Literature Written in English*, vol. 18, no. 1, April 1979.
61. See above, p. 39.
62. This theme is taken up again almost verbatim several years later in Mattera's 'Open Letter'. But Mattera adds: 'My children watch me closely: laughing when I laugh, crying when I am sad, asking me, forever asking me why is it that I endure so much pain and humiliation. Or why the setting sun no longer moves me. Or why I have rejected Christianity [Mattera has been converted to Islam]. They will find the answers.'
63. Some of them being the length of contact between Colonizer and Colonized over more than three centuries in the case of the 'Coloureds', the influence of Christianity, the fact that quite a number of whites – Liberals, Communists, Radicals – have sided with the blacks and paid for it, the emergence of a black lower middle-class . . .
64. I have not had any access to Mattera's theoretical texts and can only deduce the 'idea' of socialism from some of the poems, although class and race are nearly always identified as one.
65. In Paton's *Cry, The Beloved Country*.
66. I have kept the first version of the poem. Mattera's second version appears in *Azanian Love Song*, op. cit., p. 20. For a recent interview of Don Mattera, see *Index on Censorship*, London, vol. 12, no. 3, June 1983.

Chapter 11
The Black Man at the Crossroads

▼▼▼▼▼▼▼▼▼▼▼▼▼▼▼▼▼▼▼▼▼▼▼▼▼▼▼▼▼▼▼▼▼▼▼

James Matthews

James Matthews's poetry appeals directly to the heart and the mind, perhaps because it talks simply, in linear fashion, of simple and obvious things. 'Simply' does not mean, though, that it is lacking feeling: Matthews has nothing of the person to whom the sad inheritance of three centuries of servitude and an increasingly severe oppression have given the psychology of defeat, nothing either of the poet who would content himself with bewailing a life dominated by injustice and discrimination. The tone of his poetry is one of passion and violent protest, but with a violence very inferior to that of the regime he is attacking.

And yet *Cry Rage!*[1] (1972) is far from being the Manichaean kind of work in which the whites are simplistically categorized as the oppressors and the blacks as the victims. Certainly, the withholding of rights and the hard-heartedness are unequivocally condemned, but Matthews takes as his targets only those really responsible: among the whites, those who make the decisions and who tolerate the injustices, that is to say, the rulers of the country, their officials and those who are indifferent to the way things are; among the blacks, those who betray their brothers and are unmistakably the allies of the regime. With regard to all of these, Matthews spares neither his criticism nor, during the course of the volume and increasingly as it approaches its conclusion, the promise of well-deserved punishment, with the result that the government, worried by this new radicalism, was led to ban the book.[2] It is also this directly political aspect of his work which distinguishes Matthews from the other committed poets of his country.

Matthews who, in terms of his age (he was born in 1929), is the contemporary of Cosmo Pieterse and Dennis Brutus and who, in terms of his work – until the end of the sixties, at least – was essentially a short-story writer, turned to poetry at a moment when it seemed more effective than prose as the vehicle of protest. His poetic style is awkward, and Matthews himself rejects the title of poet (although he still takes part in literary meetings and poetry readings), but he uses his poetry as the tool of a political vision which is, in large measure, that of Black Consciousness. More than Serote and Mtshali, whose poetic temperament drew them to only certain aspects of the oppression to which the black man is subjected, Matthews gives us what is effectively a catalogue of the evils currently due to apartheid. In doing so, he does not resort as they do to allusions and veiled comment accessible only to the most educated of his fellow blacks, but goes straight to the point. This is where he is original, and this, too, is what gives him his importance. There is in him a desire to convince which reveals him as a true teacher in the field of protest.

Cry Rage! is manifestly intended for two kinds of reader, by definition very different from each other: to his white readers, Matthews shouts his disgust and warns of the approaching 'day of anger', while he tries to open the eyes of his black readers to their subjection and to instil in them courage and pride. What links these two kinds of reader in the course of daily life is the official terminology behind which the ruler (white) tries to hide from the ruled (black) the 'harsh facts of reality'.

Persuasion is in fact an important element in the preservation of power by a totalitarian regime thrown up by a minority. As it cannot rest for ever on an equilibrium created by terror, besides the permanent show of force and authority it also needs the support provided by the kind of propaganda perfected by specialists in psychological warfare. Hence the apparatus of arguments and official pronouncements, the bludgeoning of opinion in the press, on the radio, and now on television, all intended to put across the official point of view, not only as unrepressive but as liberal and progressive. By using the slogans and catchwords of the Nationalists to show up their emptiness and/or their hypocrisy, Matthews demonstrates what all this talk really means and so the mask slips. He is no longer merely concerned to show the effect of unjust laws but, by going back to their origins, to show what they are like at the moment of their conception: an ideology in the service of exploitation or, at its best, a caricature of the 'Christian democracy' which white South Africa claims to be.

Matthews's protest didacticism makes ample use of the simple, indeed simplistic, arguments of official propaganda. He incorporates them into the fabric of a logical argument, gives them flesh and blood by means of similes and metaphors taken from the language of everyday life or the Bible, and assures them a 'memorable' quality by the skilful use of repetition and leitmotiv. In this way he tries to *show*, to *demonstrate* the situation by means of logical argument and to *move* his readers by the association of the concrete/imaginary with real life.[3] The themes are linked together in small groups and taken up from one poem to the next, developed and enriched in a continuity created by the way they constantly echo one another. Matthews organizes them under a few major headings: loss of land and fundamental rights, humiliation, white hypocrisy, the lack of brotherliness and communication among men, the universal violence of the whites, the blind violence of the black delinquents. Matthews develops all these in a vast canvas which gradually expands until it culminates in the final theme: in order to resolve a situation blocked by the whites' refusal to change, violence is necessary and is bound to come sooner rather than later because it is inherent in the growing resentment and discontent. Matthews clearly reflects the frame of mind of a large sector of the black population, a frame of mind that led to the explosion of anger that occurred in the summer and autumn of 1976.

The short stories Matthews wrote before *Cry Rage!* had none of the didactic purpose of his poetry, and there is nothing in their technique to make one expect a move in this direction: they are 'slices of life' that unfold in the Coloured environment in which Matthews grew up; they are not lacking in humour, but it is a sense of frustration that predominates.

'The Park' is the most poetic of these stories. It is the story of a little boy who returns at night to the 'public' garden which he is not allowed to enter because of his colour; he has a last go on a swing before the arrival of the attendant, who is also Coloured and who invokes the regulations. The most political is 'Azikwelwa' ('We

Will Not Ride'), an account of a bus boycott by African workers. Matthews tells how a bus company decides arbitrarily to increase the fares and the Africans from the townships decide to walk to the city rather than pay them. The story has more than a purely personal significance; while it tells how a Coloured man joins what he had at first considered to be exclusively an Africans' fight, it also shows that a common endeavour carried out with determination can make the whites give in.[4] This story is taken up again in one of the poems of *Cry Rage!*: a comparison between them shows that Matthews has a clear idea of the differing possibilities of prose and poetry. Where the former seeks to inform, the latter aims at making a rapid and effective impact on the reader. The short story conveys in detail the inner feelings of the hero, which hold it together, while at the same time bringing out its significance; the poem, on the other hand, stresses mainly the power of the people taking part in the boycott, and its rhythm and imagery give it a vigour which communicates itself to the reader. When Matthews writes, for instance:

> unlike castrated bulls
> herded in their pens
> they showed their might
> with a stampede of walkers
> the people of gelvandale . . .[5]

he is doing more than describe a real event; he is interpreting it in terms of resistance to oppression and gives it its value as an example. The reference to cattle and the stress on the castration of the bulls (which suggest strength and virility) is both an historical reminder and a call to honour, while 'might' indicates the potential force of the Africans – who only rarely resort to it. These characteristics all recur in *Cry Rage!*

A first example is provided by an examination of the group of poems that deal with the lack of civil rights for black people. The official policy is to explain this absence of representation by the argument that the Africans can vote in the Bantustans and the Coloureds can make their opinions known through the Coloured Representative Council. Matthews points out that this Council is simply intended to echo official policy and was manipulated by the government until 1974, while the Bantustans are above all places of concentrated poverty with derisory powers. The so-called policy of dialogue is merely a sham, he says, based on nothing and leading nowhere.

Thus poem 3 develops in linear fashion, framed by the word 'dialogue', which serves as introduction and conclusion. Matthews sets out to denounce the lie with the help of simile, metaphor or catachresis (marked a, b or c respectively in the following extract):

> Dialogue
> the bribe offered by the oppressor
> glitters like fool's gold [a]
> dazzling the eyes of the oppressed [b]
> as they sit around the council table
> listening to empty discourse promising empty promises
> beguiled by meaningless talk
> they do not realize ointment-smeared words [c]
> will not heal their open wounds [b]

> the oppressor sits secured with spoils
> with no desire to share equality
> leaving the oppressed seeking warmth
> at the cold fire of [b]
> Dialogue.

The next poem continues with this theme of futile promises, in the shape of an extended metaphor. The juxtaposition of related terms: 'pie in the sky' and their masters' meal which the blacks witness from outside ('through the window') shows up the dishonesty of a policy that goes no further than pious intentions: equality is for the whites only, the English-speakers as well as Afrikaners. Metaphor (marked 1 in the following extract) leads naturally to (2) and (3); (4) as a result takes on additional connotations: the rumbling of the belly suggests the idea of suppressed revolt while 'hunger' subtly evokes 'anger':

> We have been offered
> pie in the sky [1]
> but never smelled it
> neither will it appease
> our hunger for rights [2]
> that are rightfully ours
> we watch through the window
> as they sit feasting
> at a table loaded with equality [3]
> and grow frantic at its flavour
> how long can we contain the rumble [4]
> of hunger in our belly.

Poems 6, 7 and 8 work in exactly the same way. In them, Matthews attacks the policy of resettlement through which the South African government eliminates people from the 'white' towns and the 'black spots'* that it deems to have become superfluous: women and old men with few resources, sick people and recalcitrants. Nadine Gordimer had attacked this inhuman procedure at the beginning of 1971 in an article of unusual verbal violence:[6] at the time, nearly a million people had already been uprooted and deported to uninhabited areas. Cosmas Desmond, a Franciscan missionary working at Dimbaza, had also publicized in *The Discarded People* the facts about these human dumping grounds.[7] Matthews himself has no intention, in the few poems he devotes to these people, of rivalling this documentation. On the contrary, he wants to sensitize his readers by portraying the situation realistically, and to stir their imagination and their feelings by the deliberate use of allegory, which enables him to bring the abstract to life, and also, as before, by means of simile and metaphor. Thus, in poem 8:

> The people of Limehill† and Dimbaza
> like those of Sada and Ilinge
> are harvesting crops of crosses
> the only fruit the land will bear . . .

---

* 'black spots': places, districts or towns which are arbitrarily redistributed, generally to whites.
† Limehill, Dimbaza, Sada, Ilinge: some of the many places where people are dumped.

> Cinderella resettlement areas, government gifts,
> are graveyards they stumble through
> as hunger roosts on their shoulder
> waiting for them to fill the earth
>
> Villages of old faces and wasted frames
> of children thin as reeds
> dark shadows staining the soil
> of women who lay with aching loins
> their beds empty of men
> with the lion of the kraal
> an ox in the city

At the same time, Matthews stresses the whites' responsibility for the situation and develops rather effectively the theme that charity should begin at home, if it begins at all. This idea is the focus of poem 6, which is the one most likely to bring home to the whites how illogical they are in helping people at the other end of the world while they leave their own poor to suffer and, what is worse, themselves organize their poverty. The poet sets out here to demystify the conveniently distant and the forgotten here-and-now: in this sense, one can say that poetry surpasses even the most prolix prose and that a short poem has a stronger impact and a much greater economy of means than a long treatise:

> they speak so sorrowfully about the
> children dying of hunger in Biafra
> but sleep unconcerned about the rib-thin
> children of Dimbaza
> they spend their rands to ease the plight
> of the suffering in Bangladesh
> but not the thought of a cent to send
> to relieve the agony of Ilinge
> they raised their voices in horror at
> the killing of eleven jews at Munich
> but not a murmur of the thousands
> of killings of my people all over the land
> black people are driven to death by white law
> yet, they will say that they never knew.

While Matthews's systematic exposition of his ideas on the level of the understanding is on the one hand prevented from being monotonous by the density and variety of his imagery, his use of repetition strengthens rather than weakens it on the other. In fact, repetition is used not only to link one poem with another in an almost uninterrupted chain, but also within the poems themselves, the better to persuade or move the reader.

This highlights in fact the popular character of Matthews's poetry: he has rediscovered, more by intuition than by intention, the techniques to which ordinary people everywhere have always turned in order to express their suffering, their hopes and their anger. The following poem could have been written in any underdeveloped country, yet it definitely originates from South Africa, where so many African babies die before they are four years old:

> through the window of the bus I saw
> five mourners walking to the grave
>
> they carried their grief wrapped in linen
> five mourners walking to the grave
>
> through the busy street they passed
> five mourners walking to the grave
>
> the infant dead, a parcel for disposal
> five mourners walking to the grave
>
> what they said I could not hear
> five mourners walking to the grave
>
> I looked at them and shared their pain
> five mourners walking to the grave
>
> the bus moved on and they were gone
> those five mourners walking to the grave.[8]

So, when we read – or, rather, hear – Matthews we have the impression that sometimes it is a ballad, at others a protest song that we are listening to. Yet there is frequently a more specific echo of the Negro spiritual, from which Matthews clearly borrows the structure, vocabulary and symbolism of his poems; only the situations are different.

Poem 13 develops in this way the theme of dispossession, and the punishment that awaits those who are guilty of it:

> They have driven us hard, Lord,
> stripped us of our land
> lashed us with their laws
> but the walls of Jericho will fall . . .
>
> terrifying like thunder will be
> the trumpet roar of our rage
> that will rend prison cages asunder
> as the walls of Jericho fall.

Poem 63 returns, in more or less the same terms, to the theme of slavery and the awakening of the slaves, but the imagery and its associations are again those of the Bible:

> Lord, how long Lord, how long
> must we watch the rapine of our minds
> reducing us to citizens of no class
> who have no say in their destiny
> and must suffer every injustice imposed
> upon us by the white pharaoh
>
> Lord, how long Lord, how long
> must we contain ourselves and turn the other cheek
> and endure the harshness they display

> to turn us into eunuchs and not men
> who dare to take a stand
> and wreak vengeance for what they had done
> Lord, how long Lord, how long?

However, Matthews can also put aside these traditional models and adopt a form based on repetition, which is constantly varied, but always simple: simplicity is crucial, because the themes are often stark, but it is a simplicity which has an immediate impact on the reader's emotions through the discreet repetition of the key elements.

Thus, in poem 36, which deals with arbitrary arrest and detention, each stanza is developed around the words 'I know fear', 'I know terror', where only the complement changes each time, reverberating like a muffled death knell until the last stanza, in which the poet evokes the deaths caused by the Special Branch, who have thereby acquired an unfortunate celebrity:

> I know fear.
> Fear is the knock
> at the fourth hour after midnight
> when the house is hushed in sleep.
>
> I know terror.
> Terror is the feeling
> that turns your body limp
> as they drag you from your bed.
>
> I know death.
> Death is your fate
> and it will come in the shape
> of a slip on a stair or flight through air.

A detailed enumeration would be tedious. Suffice to add that, as a result of this technique of repetition, the themes became firmly fixed in the memory and lead progressively and dynamically to the final explosion. And, indeed, the most violent and the angriest poems come at the end of the collection; anger marks the rising tone and the poet's cries crack like a whip:

> the word of the white man
> has the value of dirt. (poem 5)
>
> white man
> who needs your double-faced morality? (poem 14)
>
> white south Africa
> you are mutilating my soul. (poem 40)
>
> white man
> why not take my heart? (poem 55)
>
> white man my wrath will find you. (poem 62)
>
> white man
> get lost and go screw yourself. (poem 64)

When we finally come to the title poem, its impact is all the greater for this:

> Freedom's child
> you have been denied too long
> fill your lungs and cry rage
> step forward and take your rightful place
> you're not going to grow up
> knocking at the back door
> for you there will be no travelling
> third class enforced by law
> with segregated schooling and sitting on the floor
> the rivers of our land, mountain tops
> and the shore
> it's yours, you will not be denied anymore
> Cry rage, freedom's child.[9]

As one reads these poems, with their impassioned pleas and their directness of tone, in which accusation precedes not protest but the explosion of a vengeful anger and the promise of retribution, it is easy to see why the whites, on reading the volume, felt as if they had been slapped in the face. They were accustomed to the black man's submissiveness; they had come to think that he would never stand up and defy them with such vehemence, that he would never contest their authority so frankly and openly, with the result that *Cry Rage!* seemed to be the expression of a South African version of Black Power.[10]

And yet! . . . there is in Matthews a debate, of which he is himself perhaps not entirely conscious, between his fundamental humanism and the radicalism which a growing number of young blacks regard as essential for the liberation of the black man in South Africa. His poem on the rainbow of colours,[11] the one in which he attacks the Immorality Act in the name of the right of people of different colours to love one another,[12] runs counter to the slogans that proclaim the beauty of the black man and the superiority of the black woman over the white woman.[13]

Similarly, Matthews wavers between condemnation of the whites in racial, therefore global, terms, and the distinction between true and 'false' white liberals.[14]

Apart from displaying a certain illogicality in his attitudes, these contradictions – which are, in fact, very few – show yet again in concrete terms the difficulties confronting most black people, especially those of Matthews's generation, who try to adopt a thoroughly radical stance and to respond with violence to the violence of the present regime. Matthews is a good example of the paradox which, some believe, will determine the change in human and political relations that will eventually occur in South Africa: the white man does not know how to love and the black man cannot manage to hate.[15]

One could say of James Matthews's poetry that, because it borrows so much from the political and journalistic language of its period, it belongs to its time and is full of the weaknesses that an ability to distance himself from his work would have enabled him to avoid. Its virtue, however, is precisely that it *is* deeply rooted in its time and that it reflects the process of history which it helps to shape. Judged by the yardstick of poetic quality alone, his poems are certainly of a quite different order to those of Serote, Mtshali and Sepamla: Matthews does not have the inner fire of the first, nor, in spite of his varied use of metaphor, the richness of the last two; moreover, it cannot be denied that some of his poems have a prosaic ring. It may, however, be fairer to say that they are *different*. Michel Borwicz once said that you cannot judge the poetry of condemned or deported men according to the criteria for 'judging' traditional poetry.[16] There is, in effect, in James Matthews's poetry a need to convey a message of such urgency that it outweighs all aesthetic considerations.

In any case, poetry has its own life, which is to some extent determined by historical conditions. To lay down criteria of literary worth in an oppressed society would be to reduce poetry to a simple exercise, which is something totally incompatible with the revolutionary poetry with which Matthews's has much in common, a poetry that rejects the cultural models of the dominant class in order to use the language of the people and so to speak directly to them.[17] For revolutionary poets, 'awkwardness', 'affectation' and 'naïvety' have no meaning. And yet, no more in their case than in Matthews's can the poem be reduced to the one cry, the simple injunction: 'Forward! Awake! *Rebel*!' Man's indignation sometimes produces songs that stir his emotions or sustain him in his struggle against oppression. And there can be little point in those who write being as modest as Matthews and rejecting the title of poets if what they write *is* poetry even when they deny it is:

> To label my utterings poetry
> and myself a poet
> would be as self-deluding
> as the planners of parallel development
> I record the anguish of the persecuted
> whose words are whimpers of woe
> wrung from them by bestial laws.
> They stand one chained band
> silently asking one of the other
> will it never be the fire next time?[18]

Matthews was arrested, along with many other black intellectuals, after the riots in the South African winter of 1976. He was held without trial for four months and released on 22 December without being charged. While in prison, he wrote fifty or so poems collected under the title *Pass me a Meatball, Jones*.[19] In this volume, Matthews is less declamatory, more inclined to introspection, more lyrical, too. This is prison writing in the broadest sense of the term, in spite of some references to the situation of the black South African deprived of citizenship and rights:

> Thoughts hurry into the mist
> to spread the news that
> I never was from the start.[20]

Sipho Sepamla

Sipho Sepamla is a writer whose poetry makes the reader see and think: he has a gift for the precise, incisive stroke and he knows how to find the words best suited to the description of his aspirations and those of his fellow blacks. As a satirical poet, he has a solid sense of irony and humour. As a lyric poet, he can be both fiery and tender, and he can rise above the demands of the 'situation' to express the most universal human emotions.

Sepamla's activities are many and various. In his early forties, he is a man of the theatre, a critic and a poet.[21] He also edits two literary reviews, *New Classic* and *Sketsh*.[22] In the former he publishes both poets and short-story writers, white and black; in the second, in appearance and content more popular, he provides his readers with a review of the main theatrical events as well as extensive extracts from new plays. His editorials are essentially inspired by the daily life of the South African black, and it would be true to say that after the departure of Mtshali and Serote, along with Matthews, he became one of the principal driving forces in his community.

A master of irony

His first collection of poems, *Hurry Up to It!*, is characterized by a movement from submission to self-awareness, and from self-awareness to the declaration that it is time things *really* changed. The themes intersect in a series of generally short poems – parables or sketches – the last paragraph of which contains a moral or a caustic conclusion. Humour, irony and a sharp sense of imagery provide their vitality.

The first poem in the collection, 'To Whom It May Concern', appears to be on the lines of a letter of introduction, but it is in fact advice to 'the bearer', to enable him to travel from one place to another on condition that he is careful to observe the required instructions. The use of repetition (in which opposites destroy one another) and of asides (which reading aloud makes even more effective) stress the reification of the African:

> He [the Bantu] may roam *freely* within a *prescribed area*
> *Free only* from the anxiety of conscription . . .
> And [he] *acquires a niche* in the said area
> As a *temporary* sojourner
> To which he must betake himself
> *At all times*
> When his services are *dispensed with for the day*.

The official terminology is *denounced* as it is spoken by the slave with a knowing air, by being revealed for what it is: a mixture of trickery and pseudo-scientific reasoning. The poem's conclusion then plays the trump-card of irony:

> Please note
> The remains of R/N 417181
> Will be laid to rest in peace
> On a plot
> Set aside for Methodist Xhosas
> A measure also adopted
> At the express request of the Bantu
> In anticipation of any faction fight
> Before the Day of Judgement.

In the early forties, W. H. Auden had written with a fine irony about the *homo industrialis* of the twentieth century, reduced to his registration number and his needs entirely provided for him by the State, including the function of thinking. While criticizing various aspects of contemporary society, Auden nevertheless made it clear – no doubt so as to goad him into action – that this man was sufficiently content with his lot never to have rebelled against it. The poem itself was called 'To JS/07/M/378 This Marble Monument is Erected by the State'.[23] Sepamla's poem is certainly a more corrosive attack on white society, which can easily be seen behind the way the South African African is treated, and its long-term effect is rather like the slow burning of the fuse leading to the mine or to the time-bomb.

'The Will' has the same impact and the same relevance, and the play on words becomes evident from the second line: it is not in any way, as the title might lead one to suppose, a will drawn up by a free man, but instructions *dictated* to someone who has been expelled and in whom one has no difficulty in recognizing the black man subject, in all its rigour and to the point of absurdity, to the so-called Group Areas Act. A comparison with Matthews's poems dealing with the same theme immediately reveals the originality of 'The Will'.[24] In this poem there is no story-line, no pity, no invective, only the enumeration of objects that the man who has been expelled must leave behind him. The increasing seriousness of the poem derives from the nature of the objects mentioned, from the sense of total dispossession, which is made even more cruel by the mockery of the word 'share' applied to the Bible: an example filled with terrible irony which lashes the pseudo-Christianity of South Africans and which is further stressed, in spite of the apparent modesty of the tone, by the final image of the 'black and white' cat which only God will be able to 'divide' between the legatees:

> The house, by right,
> you will have to vacate
> surrender the permit
> and keep your peace
>
> The burglar-proofing and the gate
> will go to my elder son
> so will the bicycle
> and a pair of bracelets . . .
>
> The peachtree uproot
> it might grow in the homelands
> so might it be with your stem
>
> The Bible
> you will have to share
> for you will always want its Light
>
> The cat spotted black and white
> you will have to divide
> for that you'll need God's guidance.[25]

This note of seriousness does not run through the whole collection: *Hurry Up to It!* is a profoundly optimistic book and it could not be otherwise, for it retraces the beginnings of the black man's liberation and shows how, from being a forced labourer, manipulated and impotent, he has stirred himself into action and, raising his head, has become aware of his possibilities.

The advent of the new black man is announced

And so, a third of the way through the volume, 'Remake the World' explodes from the page, high and clear. This is one of the most perceptive poems yet written on the cultural depersonalization and the psychological subjection of the colonized man by the colonizer *and* on the liberating effect of the former's new self-awareness. A sister poem to Serote's 'Black Bells' and Stanley Motjuwadi's 'White Lies',[26] 'Remake the World' declares:

> I want to remake the world
> For everything about me is white
> The lush green grass is white
> The pitch-black night is white
> The dream I scream is white
> God! where can the end lie
> If not in me.

A whole group of poems dwells on this theme of the African's transformation with evident happiness and joy. So, 'My Name Is' returns to the quest for black identity, or rather its reconquest – a theme Mtshali had dealt with in 1971[27] – but in order to assert very forcefully:

> Let them know the name
> It's been gone too long
> Your vacant face unknown
> Its number
> munched easily by a computer
>
> Thixo*! We want to rejoice
> Celebrating the birth of a new age
> For gone is Kleinbooi†
> No more Sixpence†
> John is neither here nor there
> Mary lives no more for tea only!

'Mother of Men' tells of the new Africa the poet sees riding on the horizon; in contrast, 'Portrait of Another Brother' presents a relic of the conventional Africa in the person of a black man ashamed of himself and his brothers. Finally, 'Go Slow' rejects the so-called gradualist policy behind which the whites have always hidden their refusal to make real changes and introduces the third phase of the evolution of attitudes in the South African black community.

Indeed, the last poems of the collection, with their constant reference to the time factor, emphasize the urgency of the situation. Thus, in 'A Pause', Sepamla insists that the situation has lasted long enough and that it is time to bring it to an end ('We want to bid the whole thing goodbye'), while in 'Talk, Talk, Talk', the poet attacks the Africans' endless attempts to reason out their condition, their hesitation, their fear of speaking out and saying they have had enough of this dog's life.

---

* Thixo: an African word meaning 'Lord!'.
† Kleinbooi, Sixpence: pejorative nicknames given by whites to black people.

The Black Man at the Crossroads 219

'Hurry Up to It!', which ends the collection, also embodies a course of action in its title. Yet one could miss its implications if one paid attention only to its apparently restricted subject: a father begging his son to marry before it is too late. In fact, the poem returns one last time to the theme of the black man subservient to the laws of the country but, although oppression is being denounced at the level of the family, it is equally clear that the father's advice to his son has a wider application:

> And son
> You must hurry
> Hurry up for your sake and mine
> For age moves ahead of wishes.

The same approach has already been evident in 'Hats Off in My House'. Beneath the simple anecdote (which tells how, during a family drinking session, a father finds the courage to order a representative of the law to take off his hat in his house) lies the injunction 'Be master in your own house!', a slogan of considerable significance at the political level.

Sepamla's volume is therefore a good illustration of the evolution that has taken place in the African community during these last few years. 'To Whom It May Concern', with which it begins, dates from 1971-2, 'Hurry Up To It!', from 1974-5. To this internal evidence, one could add a comparison between another of Sepamla's poems, 'Darkness', and the opening poem of Serote's *Yakhal'inkomo*, which was written when Black Consciousness was just beginning. In 'Darkness', the African has unquestionably changed, he speaks to the white man as an equal, he has got the measure of him. His confidence is evident from the first line: 'Yes, sir, I have arrived . . .', and the word 'sir' is itself significant, for not once does the word 'baas' appear in Sepamla's volume, not even in mockery.

> yes sir i have arrived
> walk the night if you dare
> there i reign over death
> 'swonder you legislate the night
> i walk erect in the night
> you crouch in retreat
> crowding each nook in fear
> of the stench of my blackness
> agitated by a darkness.

Optimistic, then, in the way it underlines the uncheckable movement towards the liberation of the black South African, this collection also reveals its optimism through the author's talent. Snapshots of everyday life and images taken directly from the real African world are scattered throughout the volume. Often heightened by a touch of humour, they strengthen the concrete character of the poetry, as when they simply create a picture, in 'Pimville Station', for instance, or when, as in 'Go Slow' for example, they capture so vividly the character of South African paternalism.

> We are born into a blinkered existence
> Our trial effort made stillborn
> by an aged fabrication:

> everyone is for us
> even breast-beating in the process
> eyes raised
> never allowing for our thoughts
> not even our solemn thanks
> always told:
> Go slow, the last cow leaves the kraal also.

Here, the cattle metaphor is only touched upon in passing so as to prepare for the African proverb at the end, elsewhere, it runs through the whole poem and thus gains in forcefulness. 'Jam Tin' is therefore an African variation on the theme of the Voltairian orange: the African, too, is rejected when he is no longer useful. The theme could lend itself to bitterness or recrimination; but there is none of this here, for the black poet is master of the situation.

'The Applicant' illustrates very concretely, and in a very picturesque way, the inevitable emergence of Black Consciousness: Sepamla also develops, metaphorically, the theme of a blood transfusion, truer on a poetic more than a biological level. With great humour, he plays on the terms 'yellow fever' and 'red pox' to refer to the foreigners the government thinks responsible for the recent evolution of the African in South Africa. The poet says that when black corpuscles have replaced the white corpuscles in his blood – a transparent allusion to the deculturation of the African – he will cease to be invisible.

Finally, Sepamla is the first of the African poets to use language itself as a source of humour.[28] To do this, he takes as his starting-point the township slang or the imperfect English spoken by the African masses, who have only benefited from two or three years' schooling. Hence the linguistic play in 'The Bookshop', in which the language is 'massacred' with just enough fantasy to turn the mockery against the white man.

If we recall, in fact, the poem in which Mtshali dealt bitterly with the way his colour fatally determined the African's social position,[29] we can appreciate more fully the contrasting lightness of tone used by Sepamla to describe the experience of a young man chased by a shopkeeper who suspects him of stealing books from his display.

'Reclaimed' in this way, slang becomes a weapon, and it is the so-called thief who dominates the situation, to the extent, even, of exploiting the irony of the double meaning in 'taken all sorts of things':

> Suddenly I hear: 'Excuse me please?'
> Strangers leaves me dumb
> I sees this one grab my newspapers
> 'Can I see what you have there?'
> 'Sure! I never had anything to hide!'
> Not a moment later: 'Excuse me but
> One lady inside said you had taken all sorts of things.'
> 'Not the first time!' I answers
> And I proceeds.

Irony, humour: this is how destiny is dominated and lucidity sharpened. Bitter-sweet words, because they convey the nature of the experience; magic, liberating words, because at the same time they transcend it. Humour, irony: the ability to distance and detach oneself, the intelligence turned against force, the characteristic of people who have suffered a great deal – the Irish, the Jews, the blacks.

The lyric poet

When a man manages to raise his meditation above the everyday life that nourishes it but at the same time threatens to drive it off course, when he finds symbols to express it which are the more apposite for being the simplest, then all he needs to reach the higher level of lyricism is the fire that has been kept alive by his joys and his sufferings. Sepamla attains this lyricism in several poems, whether they be poems of circumstance, like the reminder of Sharpeville,[30] or deal with everyday elements that the poet has been able to read and interpret.

In 'The Sea-gull', Sepamla devotes five or six short stanzas to the description of a gull engaged in winning its food from the sea which threatens all the time to engulf it. The air and the water attack one another in a dialectic of agility and power, intelligent waiting and blind force. It is only in the last stanza, however, that Sepamla gives the poem its full impact:

> In that instant
> I felt the agony
> of being
> I saw the whirl on
> a wing
> I saw myself
> hover
> at all times.

Here the poet depicts the destiny of the living creature in confrontation with the elements in a continual battle for life, while in the background only, thanks to the context of the volume as a whole, the more particular destiny of the African in South Africa stands out in profile. Sepamla leaves it to the reader of the year 2000 to decide whether it is a metaphysical poem or a committed poem in the most universal and timeless sense of the term.

Similarly, 'Adriaanspoort' is shot through with a fresh and youthful lyricism: the poet can look about him, bathe in the spectacle that surrounds him and draw out the higher meaning of what is otherwise a prosaic event – a picnic:

> Down there below
> where I can see no spoor
> of man or
> animal
> there is a winding
> of what used to be
> there is a swaying
> of lanky tufts of grass
> there is a meandering
> of leafy protea trees
> there is an ageing
> of variegated pelindaba rocks
> and there is a thought

of dead spirits
once clashing by day
only to retreat at sunset
leaving these parts wild at night
yet serene under the moon.

The stanza has a musical quality which reinforces the gentleness of the description, to which the many *-ing* endings certainly contribute. In addition, the poem is surrounded by a halo of mystery which the African tradition enables us to interpret as the subtle and permanent presence of the ancestors, which is confirmed by what follows:

> There is a spirit moving where we are
> we turn faces to avoid it
> hardly being successful
> for we are part of the being of things.

Thus, the past and the present mingle, but not at all in the desacralized and often psychological manner to which the West is accustomed. The poem ends with an invocation to the rain, which must fall: it is perhaps possible to detect a discreet reference to the future when Sepamla notes:

> There are clouds gathering above our heads
> we say it will not rain
> hardly being correct
> for the earth needs to be swept at times
>
> it rains . . . pula! . . . it rains . . . pula!

A similar simplicity, although essentially of a very different kind, runs though 'The Loneliness Beyond'. This poem should be compared with Mtshali's on the black inhabitants of the suburbs.[31] The author of *Sounds* observed the workers at their departure, Sepamla observes them on their return. Mtshali stressed the lot peculiar to the black workers and emphasized their alienation; Sepamla goes much further in developing the theme of the individual's isolation in a modern industrial civilization. A certain number of documentary details situate the description: reference to the demands made by the masters ('spirit maimed by commands . . . the grouse of mouths/that never rest/from grinding complaints . . .'), to the many accidents that happen to the trains the Africans use ('like sheep herded into a kraal/ they crowd numbered coaches/hopeful of a safe landing'). But more general is the nakedness of the faces as a result of exhaustion, powerfully conveyed by the description. And the poet's immense sensitivity breaks out in the lyrical conclusion:

> I've watched the multitude rub shoulders
> and I've wondered what they do
> with the loneliness beyond;
>
> I've seen throngs of people
> disappear into little holes of resting
> and I've pondered what might be happening
> with the loneliness beyond.

On the other extreme, 'The River' transports the reader into the heart of the country. In spite of its apparent simplicity, the poem is in fact a very conscious construction: a subtle network of repetition and alliteration creates a weightless web and composes an intimate music with the help of the trochaic and iambic rhythms of its succession of very short lines. The poem moves fluidly towards the last stanza, which ends in a whispered exchange of confidences: is it pure chance that the final word of the poem, itself the penultimate in the volume, should be 'hope'?

> At the ears of the river
> hugging the tortured course
> are squeals of a donkey
> and the pealing churchbell
> angry with the mean sun
> to quench man's parched voice
> for neither here nor there
> are voices heard crystal-clear
>
> The clouds that gather
> they go and they come
> they come and they go
> leaving the river without water
>
> Intimate whispers
> the river in between
> sources of a murmuring
> they tell of hope.

For completeness, one should mention one last feature of Sepamla's lyricism, closely associated in this case with humour and producing poems which blend emotion and laughter. The example is the love poem entitled 'Dear Lovely' which here again uses the English of the black proletariat:

> My heart cough little bit
> Minute I touch touch for you
> This here and that there
> Oh my mostest beautifullest
>
> How I was being born
> And you was born or coming front or back
> Just the devil can know
> Oh my number one thing

It can be seen that Sepamla's deep sense of commitment in no way interferes with his qualities as a poet. But this commitment, as unambiguous as it may be, extends well beyond the frontiers of his own community. For here is a man who is convinced that the South Africa of tomorrow will be built with the help of all its inhabitants. His poems constantly place the emphasis, not only on the common biological identity shared by all the people of his country, but also on the common destiny that binds all South Africans. These are the ideas that emerge in 'Da Same, Da Same' and 'The Blues Is You in Me'.

In the first, written in 'murdered' English,[32] after asserting that all men have a heart that beats in the same way and that it is cruel to inflict on others the suffering one would not want to endure oneself, Sepamla cries:

> when da nail of say da t'orn tree
> scratch little bit little bit of da skin
> I doesn't care of say black
> I doesn't care of say white
> I doesn't care of say India
> I doesn't care of say clearlink*
> I mean for sure da skin
> only one t'ing come for sure
> an'da one t'ing for sure is red blood
> dats for sure da same, da same for avarybudy

'The Blues Is You in Me' begins like a real 'blues' and for a moment gives the impression that the singer, or the speaker, is addressing his beloved, who does not return his love – a theme that is dear to 'blues' literature:

> When my heart pulsates a rhythm
> off-beat with God's own scintillating pace
> and I can trace only those thoughts
> that mar the goodness of living with you
> then I know I've got the blues for howling[33]

This impression does not last: as the throbbing refrain on the theme suggested in the title recurs, the poet develops the series of everyday factors that have contributed to his disquiet. It then emerges that the 'You' to whom he is speaking is white South Africa:

> the Blues is the shadow of a cop
> dancing the Immorality Act jitterbug
> the blues is the Group Areas Act and all its jive
> the blues is the Bantu Education Act and its improvisations
>
> the blues is you in me
> I never knew the blues until I met you

In spite of the vocabulary borrowed from America (cop, jitterbug, jive), the reader has no doubts at all about where he is, and if the last line quoted above indicates the whites' responsibility for the situation, the last stanza, on the other hand, establishes the common destiny of all South Africans:

> I want to holler the how-long blues
> because we are the blues people all
> the whiteman bemoaning his burden
> the blackman offloading the yoke

---

*clearlink: used here for 'Coloured' (Afrikaans *'kleurling'*).

Here, there is no wide-eyed humanism, nor any tendency to see things in too schematic a way; of course, it is the white man who makes the laws, but by letting himself be manipulated, the African allows them to be imposed upon him. 'Offloading the yoke' is the aim of Black Consciousness; it is also the underlying theme of Sepamla's first collection. The title, *Hurry Up To It!*, retrospectively gains its full force: the sooner the African is freed ('the how-long blues') the better.

As we can see, the general structure of *Hurry Up To It!* is very reminiscent of that of *Sounds*: as in Mtshali's volume, the progression towards the main idea is made by alternating satirical or humorous poems with poems of more general interest. As with Mtshali, a great deal is left to the power of suggestion, and Sepamla also speaks in a first person who represents the African in conflict with white civilization.

This, however, is where the comparison ends: Sepamla does not in any way hide behind a mask, and above all the general tone of the volume indicates an optimism which is missing from Mtshali's volume, in spite of his humour. Sepamla, more than Mtshali, and in this more also than Serote and Matthews, is aware of the possibilities the poem offers: its development, its structure, the value of the skilful use of repetition, the technique of extending a metaphor to draw out its maximum effect, the hitherto unexploited potential of the English of the townships and the slang spoken there. Sepamla also seems more conscious of the musicality of words, of the effectiveness of alliteration, of the power of rhythm and breaks in rhythm in bringing out the full value of a poetry which must be read aloud. His use of irony, more powerful and more varied than Mtshali's, shows too that he has learnt from the masters of the technique: his education, which he carried further, has certainly helped him here. He does not have Serote's forcefulness nor the militant vigour so evident in Matthews. But it must also be said that he is not writing at the same stage in the evolution of Black Consciousness. It is not by chance that he is writing *after* the decolonization of Angola and Mozambique: his optimism, his serenity, his lack of aggressiveness and especially of hate are without doubt – in part at least – due to the certainty South African blacks now have that the hour of deliverance is at hand.

On the eve of Soweto, Sepamla and Matthews seemed to be showing the two directions in which the blacks could go: a middle way, resulting from an understanding between themselves and the whites *on an equal footing*, which would ensure a place for the latter while completely eliminating apartheid – a solution which might result in, or from, the creation of a black bourgeoisie; and a more radical stance, which would be aimed at hastening change on all fronts, since the men in power seem to want to delay indefinitely the blacks' achievement of their rights.

In the wake of Soweto, it is difficult to be so categoric, at least as far as the tone is concerned. The poems Sepamla published under the title *The Soweto I Love* certainly do not call for revenge. But, while they reflect the poet's horror at the massacre and the imprisonment of very young children, and at the number of detainees who died in suspicious circumstances, they express above all his pride in seeing the young people rebelling and confronting the police head-on and without weapons. He pays them homage unequivocally, with lyricism and eloquence. Thus, in 'At Sunset', Sepamla cries:

> It was a moving moment
> when youth embraced in unity
> shouting a delirious cry
> Power! Power! Power![34]

While in 'At the Dawn of Another Day' he graphically describes the role played by the young generation and the decisive turning-point that has occurred in South Africa in the relations between whites and blacks:

> At the height of the day
> youth rage spilled all over the place
>   unleashing its own energy
>   confounding the moment
>   exploding the lie
>
> take away
>   your teachings
> take away
>   your promises
> take away
>   your hope
> take away
>   your language
> give
>   me
>   this
>   day
>   myself . . .
> i shall learn myself anew
> i shall read myself from the trees
> i shall glean myself from all others
> i shall wean myself of you . . .[35]

These last remarks seem to date the black renaissance from the events of Soweto, whereas in fact, as we shall see with Pascal Gwala, it antedated them by several years. It nevertheless remains that Sepamla, with *The Soweto I Love*, was playing the role of witness; he also records the signs of the decline of white power ('The Island'), while, in 'The Land', he asserts, in majestic fashion, the growing confidence of the blacks who, however permanent the rejection with which they are faced, know they are the rightful occupiers of this land that belongs to them:

> I have never had to say
> this land is mine
> this land has always been me
> it is named after me
>
> This land defines its textures by me
> its sweat and blood are salted by me
> I've strained muscles yoked
> on the turning wheel of this land
>
> I am this land that is mine
> I have never asked for a portion
> there's never been a need to
> I am the land[36]

Mafika Pascal Gwala

Gwala can be justly regarded as the symbol of the 'new black' dreamed of by Serote and Sepamla, and foreshadowed by Matthews and Mattera. There is, indeed, a determination on his part 'not to be taken for a ride' either by the mirages and traps of the consumer society, in the South African version of the western model, or by the change constantly being promised by the white politicians but always postponed.

He never gives way to self-pity, nor does he ever appeal to the humanity or to the understanding of the white: the black as he appears in his theoretical writings and poetry is in no sense the predestined or consenting victim to be manipulated at will by the men in power. He is a determined fighter, who stands erect and looks the whites in the eyes, as Don Mattera wanted it. Gwala is also a man who constantly relates the virtues of the past to the present fight, with the aim of making the black man someone who is proud to be what he is, and proud therefore of his national (South African) and pan-African heritage.

Finally, more than the other poets of his generation, Gwala is a kind of lay poet–preacher who unremittingly tries to convince his brothers of the bankruptcy of western civilization on both the individual and the collective levels, of the futility of seeking to imitate the dubious values of this civilization, of the need for a real change that can come only from the black man himself, and of the unavoidable struggle that must be engaged to achieve this change. Gwala has at his disposition a wide range of means: his writing is full of irony and humour as well as lyricism, detachment as well as the most ardent passion. Although he can exploit the destructive effect of the veiled allusion, he much prefers direct attack. His tone is most frequently sharp and incisive. Generous in his intentions, he can, when the occasion demands, be cutting without being bitter. He has not only a 'temperament' but also a 'tempo'.

It is not by chance that Mafika Pascal Gwala is the youngest of the poets so far studied, and therefore closest in age and feelings to the young people who revolted in Soweto and in the many other South African townships in 1976 and 1977. Born at Verulam, near Durban (Natal), in 1946, in a region where the Zulus and the Indians make up the bulk of the population, Gwala evokes in a 'letter' dedicated to an Indian friend the life of the two communities before the rigid enforcement of segregation.

> Verulam has undergone unheard of metamorphosis
> With the Group Areas Act having ploughed our lives
> Leaving no other seed except boredom and germinating thoughts
> Remember mixed and united Verulam?
> All that is a dream circling round people's minds
> In rotation of the barrel setting of a pepperbox[37]

Gwala was 8 years old when the Nationalists began to separate the ethnic groups in the educational sphere, 14 at the time of the peaceful demonstrations organized in response to the call from the Pan-Africanist Congress, which were crushed at Sharpeville with the shedding of blood, and 18 at the time of the Rivonia trial which marked the end of organized resistance. In other words, his childhood and adolescence saw the introduction of legislation that marked the institutionalization, and then the radicalization, of apartheid: as with the other young people of his generation, the impact of all this on him was profound.[38]

Gwala passed his Matriculation at Inkamana High, one of the two secondary schools for Africans at Vryheid, and then enrolled at Ngoye University (the University of Zululand). It was during this period that SASO was founded: Gwala abandoned his university studies and devoted himself with his companions in the struggle to the development of Black Consciousness, while earning his living in a variety of jobs.[39]

He contributed to the student organization's *Newsletter* and edited *Black Review 1973* for the Black Community Programmes (BCP). He also took part in the Black Renaissance Convention held at Hammanskraal, Transvaal, in December 1974. This significant event brought together some 300 delegates from all the urban centres and represented a broad spectrum of opinion in the black community in a period characterized by great hopes and profound disappointments.[40]

Gwala made a speech that attracted a great deal of attention, entitled 'Towards the Practical Manifestations of Black Consciousness', in which he expressed with utter frankness his opinion of the regime's collaborators and the 'separatists' (the supporters of separate development, in other words the Bantustan leaders). Gwala did not pull his punches, either, when speaking of the Movement's intellectuals, who tended to cut themselves off from the working masses in the towns and the rural areas. Emotional but well argued, at times harsh, Gwala made his appeal in this speech to the imagination of his brothers in the struggle and insisted that more emphasis should be placed on the practical than the theoretical. He also stressed the importance of taking the socio-economic factors of their oppression (and therefore of their struggle) into account, and warned against pushing Black Consciousness in the direction of the 'cultural'.[41]

By the time of the Black Convention, Gwala had already been writing and publishing for some while: short stories and poems, which appeared in several anthologies published in 1974, as well as an important theoretical essay entitled 'Towards a National Theatre'.[42] It was only in 1977, however, that his first complete volume was published, *Jol'iinkomo*. Since then, Gwala has contributed to the multiracial review *Staffrider*, mainly as a poet, but also as a critic and essayist.[43] Thus, action, creation and theory run parallel in his work, nourishing one another in an individual style and approach.

Africa redeemed

In 1972, Ben Koapa wrote of Pascal Gwala: 'His poetry is directed mainly at the blacks and their situation. It seeks to awaken a sense of pride and dignity in them and make them seek to live like human beings apologizing to no one for their blackness.'[44] This clearly stresses one of his principal characteristics. Gwala, unlike his elders, skipped the stage of recrimination and calling on the whites to acknowledge the damage being caused by apartheid in an attempt to appeal to their humanity, criticizing this approach in his speeches and theoretical writings. Right from the start, he adopted the stance of the black and the fighter.

He is black in the most natural sense. He does not indulge in the ecstatic proclamation of his blackness, in lyrical claims to have (re)conquered his lost identity; he seems to have felt no need to do this.

There are various reasons for this: his age, his fighting temperament, his participation from the start in the student movement, the influence of his reading

The Black Man at the Crossroads

during the sixties,[45] and the polarization sought by the whites themselves. Nevertheless, he continued to develop his Africanness, and he wanted to restore to the black man his pride in being black, without making that 'black pride' an end in itself: it is only a stage in the liberation of the black man: a liberation from the stereotypes created by the white and which have become second nature to the black man, another skin; a liberation which has to be achieved to some extent at least by a return to Africa. While this means the rediscovery of the African values that existed before colonization, Gwala draws a clear line between the possibilities and the limits of this return to sources:

> The stress on black art is the re-instatement of indigenous culture – with its modern complexities and the stripping of its inferiority labels . . . The people must be made to respect their past, their dance, their music, their arts and crafts, their language. They ought to be made aware of the different contexts between the preconquest indigenous culture and the post-conquest indigenous culture. So as to make them more able to put into perspective their tribal culture before the coming of white ways into their lives . . . More, to make them see the common link that binds the two together, rural and urban, into the black culture. Thus, in the process, making them see better – without conscience pangs – why we can't go back to the 'beshu' and 'Umkhonto'.[46]

For the time being, and because of an inevitable return of the pendulum in a society dominated by the prejudices that force one to make comparisons in derogatory terms between 'white' and 'non-white', 'European' and 'non-European', civilized and uncivilized, Gwala stresses the virtues of African society. Thus, in 'The Children of Nonti', he evokes without undue emphasis the traditional virtues of understanding, solidarity, unity, keeping one's word and concern for truth, while at the same time exalting, already, the spirit of resistance:

> There are no sixes and nines be one
> with the children of Nonti. Truth is truth
> and lies are lies amongst the children of Nonti . . .
>
> Sometimes a son rises above the others
> of the children of Nonti. He explains the workings
> and the trappings of white thinking.
> The elders debate;
> And add to their abounding knowledge
> of black experience.
> The son is still one of the black children of Nonti
> For there is oneness in the children of Nonti.
>
> And later, later when the sun
> is like forever down . . .
> The black children of Nonti will rise and speak . . .
>   the children of Nonti will stand
> their grounds in the way that Nonti speared his foes
> to free his black brothers from death and woes;
> They shall fight with the tightened grip
> of a cornered pard. For they shall be knowing that
> Nothing is more vital than standing up

> For the Truths that Nonti lived for.
> Then there shall be freedom in that stand
> by the children of Nonti . . .[47]

Later, in 'Soul Afternoon', Gwala expressed these ideas in much stronger terms, and the conclusion of this poem is striking for its breadth and power:

> Here we rest
>   facing the sea
> As the children of Blackness;
> Bringing together Black Mother Africa
>   onto the shore,
> To find our Blackness
>   which has been mysticated
>   by drear distortions
>   in dull books
> bound in the essence of breaking
> our proud ancestry.
> We count the virtues wherein:
> Blackness spills no foreign blood
>   – no blood for gold
>   – blood for paper money
> Blackness mixes no tequila
>   for foreign investment
>   – no tequila for investors
> Blackness pegs no claim
>   for expropriation of property
>   – no claim for people's property
> Blackness blacktalents . . .[48]

Thus, the negative assertion of otherness ('I situate myself in relation to the white man') is replaced by the positive assertion: the black has his own values. It is to the extent that he believes once more in these that the black person creates his own qualities: 'Blackness blacktalents'.

It is just as important, in the context of the present struggle and of the struggle to come, to remember the example of the heroes who have distinguished themselves in resisting the white man. So, Gwala recalls his Lala ancestors and the courageous Zulu warriors who fought so gallantly at the battle of Isandhlwana.[49] With the same pride he also evokes the fighters of the ANC, people like Nelson Mandela, 'Ma' Ngoyi and the freedom fighters, the authors of the Goch Street and Silverton attacks.[50] In other words, he rejects the tribal barriers that are as harmful to African unity as the ideological barriers that can undermine the common front of the black communities suffering from oppression in different ways.[51]

For Gwala, the attempt to throw down roots in the recent or more distant past of South Africa (one finds many examples of this in his poems) must not be accomplished at the expense of a broader vision of Africa: there is a deliberate intention on his part to break down the insularity of South Africa (created by the whites) in relation to the rest of the African continent.

Thus, while on the one hand he evokes the Namibian heroes Morenga, Witbooi and Maherero in 'Jol'iinkomo', he also refers to Patrice Lumumba's supporter, the

Congolese Pierre Mulele, in 'There is'.[52] Generally, one senses in him the desire to unearth Africa from the sands in which the colonizers had thought they had buried it for ever.

It is in 'Words to a Mother' that Gwala's pan-Africanism is most evident. The fact that in this area, as he himself admits, he is still something of a novice – 'I am still learning to say Mother/Yet I wish to share your dreams;/How much should I know of you/That I should know more of me?' – is of little real importance. While in Mphahlele, Serote, Mtshali and Sepamla there are only passing references to Africa as the mother, there is in Gwala, on the contrary, a very distinct effort at identification with his African roots. The whole of Africa is a space in which a common spirit is expressed:

> While Alexandra chokes
> Your torrents freshen the buds
> of wild flowers born of your nature, Mother
> Across the veld at Dindela,
> In the dusty evenings of Mabopane
> They hail you, Mother:
> Where many a son of yours
> has been deballsed by free world larceny
> that chains you to the yesteryear
> of slave cargoes and piracy.
> Yet you once roamed free with your sons
> to fountains of learning at Rabat
> You sniffed the high walls of Baghdad
> You threatened the Alps of Italy
> You mothered the Lion of Judah . . .[53]

Gwala is not the only poet currently writing in *Staffrider* who refers frequently to the rest of Africa – a task of great pedagogic importance. He also shares with some of them a readiness to revert to their mother tongue, thereby practising what he preached in his 1974 speech. Whereas 'Bonk' Abajahile'[54] introduces Zulu 'in strips', as one might say, 'A Reminder' skilfully blends Zulu and English by playing with great subtlety, in its evocation of the heroes of the resistance and of Black Consciousness, on the meanings of the African names.[55] 'Uphondo' ('the Horn') is written entirely in Zulu.[56] Gwala therefore shows himself to be the worthy successor of Mqhayi, Jolobe and Kunene, especially the last two. The pastoral setting of some of his poems, the cultural and linguistic references they contain, their imagery and even their tone give them an undeniably authentic character.

In a discussion of Gwala's 'defence and illustration' of Africanness and Africa, there is also, finally, the way he makes full use of the many resources of oral literature. More than in any of those who currently write in *Staffrider*, he tries to link teaching and song, rhythm and incantation, poetry and word music. The eighth and last stanza of 'Getting Off the Ride' provides an excellent illustration of this. By way of reply to the question 'What is Black?', Gwala uses a concise formula that he will later go on to explain at length: 'Black is when you get off the ride'. By this he means not simply refusing to be scorned any longer, but also reacting by fighting back with, or in spite of, all the risks that this involves. The poet goes on:

> Sometimes there's a fall
> when a brother gets off the ride,
> and the fall hurts;
> A fall is a hurt to every black brother.
> Then I smell the jungle
> I get the natural smell of the untamed jungle;
> I'm with the mamba
> I become a khunga-khunga man
> I'm with the Black Ghost of the skom jungle
> I get the smell of phuthu in a ghetto kitchen
> The ghetto, a jungle I'm learning to know
> I hear the sounds of African drums beating
> to freedom songs;
> And the sounds of the voice come:
>   Khunga, Khunga!
>   Untshu, Untshu!
>   Funtu, Funtu!
> Shundu, Shundu!
>   Sinki, Sinki!
>   Mojo, Mojo!
> O–m! O–oo—M! O—hhhhhhhhhmmmmmmm!!![57]

    This is a fine example of his inspired mastery of language, helped along by repetition and accretion as well as by sound effects, the whole blending to create a pattern in which meaning and sensibility are inseparable. Apart from the vocabulary borrowed from the culture of the black ghettos, there is the positive connotation given to the word 'mamba' which was already to be found in the militant poetry of the early seventies.[58]

'Black is struggle!'

Enhancing the sense of African identity, and restoring it to those of his fellow Africans who may have lost pride in their culture, are necessary endeavours, but not ends in themselves. When back in 1973 he had argued that Black Consciousness ought not to be either an object of intellectual curiosity or a form of narcissism, or even an outlet for cultural activism, Gwala was already stressing its political character. And when he declared, in his speech to the Black Renaissance Convention, 'Right, now we have come to terms with our Blackness, what about it?', he was stressing the importance of a praxis which his comrade Ben Koapa had summed up in the formula: 'Being Black is not enough, one must be Black and ready together!'[59] Gwala echoes this in 'Gumba, Gumba, Gumba':

> Been watching this jive
> for too long.
> That's struggle . . .
>
> You seen struggle
> If you have heard:
> Heard a man bugger a woman, old as his mother;
> Heard a child giggle at obscene jokes
> Heard a mother weep over a dead son;

> Heard a foreman say 'boy' to a labouring oupa*
> Heard a bellowing, drunken voice in an alley.
> You heard struggle.
> Knowing words don't kill
> But a gun does.
> That's struggle.
> For no more jive.
> Evening's eight
> Ain't never late.
> Black is struggle.[60]

Gwala returned to this theme some years later and developed it in 'Getting Off the Ride' which, like many of his poems, is at once the profession of faith of a militant, a concrete analysis of the situation, a call for the mobilization of effort and an affirmation of determination to resist the oppressor.

Eminently lyrical in spite of its didactic content, 'Getting Off the Ride' is an important part of a many-sided argument entirely geared to the theme of *real* change, with its indispensable corollary, the struggle to attain it. The poem – the longest Gwala has so far published – is constructed around a leitmotiv, acting as a kind of thread linking the stanzas and expressing the feeling of having had enough of being 'taken for a ride'. Never before has this theme, common to the poets of the Black Consciousness generation, been exploited so fully, so skilfully and in such an original manner:

> I get off the bus ride
> after long standing
> listening to black voices
> that obliviate the traffic noises;
> A billboard overwhelms me,
> like an ugly plastic monster with fiercy eyes
> it tell me what canned drink
> will be good enough to quench my thirst;
> I eye-mock the plastic arrogance
> 'Cos I know, shit, I know
> I'm being taken for a ride.[61]

'Billboard' and 'canned drink' are simply metaphors for all the insults that the blacks have to 'swallow': the following stanzas prove just how well founded what he says is. Concrete examples drawn from the life of the ghetto all around him show the consequences of this continual deception. At first, the poet uses the first person singular to identify himself with each and every one of the victims of the system and their acceptance of it, but in the fourth stanza he speaks for himself:

> I'm the lonely poet
> who trudges the township's ghetto passages
> pursuing the light,
> The light that can only come through a totality
> of change:

---

* *oupa*: literally 'grandfather', i.e. old man (Afrikaans).

> Change in minds, change
> Change in social standings, change
> Change in means of living, change,
> > Dreams and hopes that are Black
> > Dreams and hopes where games end
> > Dreams where there's no end to man's
> creation of gas chambers and concentration camps.
> I'm the Africa Kwela instrumentalist whose notes
> profess change.[62]

While the seventh stanza expresses his confidence in the resistance latent within the black man's soul, designated by the phrase 'the Black Ghost', the eighth stanza constitutes the third step in his argument ('I hate this ride') and also prepares the way for Gwala's definition of what it means to be black:

> I ask again, what is Black?
> Black is when you get off the ride.
> Black is point of self-realization
> Black is point of new reason
> Black is point of: NO NATIONAL DECEPTION!
> Black is point of determined stand
> Black is point of TO BE OR NOT TO BE for blacks
> Black is point of RIGHT ON!
> Black is energetic release from the shackles of Kaffir, Bantu, non-white.[63]

So, the poet has clearly defined the objectives, as well as the targets and those with whom the dialogue must be engaged. We must now look in detail at the approach Gwala adopts towards those who must be criticized and to inspire the rest with courage and confidence.

The militant and the poet

Gwala rarely talks about the whites. When he does, he wastes no words, for he has long since seen through them:

> . . . The 'W'?
> I hate it, I said.
> All it means is
> 'M' for man . . . inverted[64]

Gwala is more concerned to attack white values than the white man as a 'person'. The criticism of western civilization, already present in the work of his elders,[65] here takes on a wider scope. It does not dwell on the hypocrisy of the false Christians in power and of the many who support them, for this attitude has been adequately denounced by his contemporaries, from Paton to Horn and Jensma, from Mtshali to Matthews and Sepamla.[66] It extends to the planet as a whole. It finds its evidence in those forms of technical progress that have proved themselves to be disastrous and goes on to list the examples of carnage that have occurred in the world, both since the beginning of colonization and during the twentieth century (in the concentration camps, in Vietnam and in Africa). A destructive civilization whose dubious values are the frantic urge to acquire stimulated by the slogans of a consumer society based on capitalism, the fierce struggle for survival and the rat-race, individualism carried to the extreme and that frequent spiritual poverty that is the daughter or the companion of excessive consumption – a civilization of the artificial and the sham symbolized by plastic and opposed to the 'unadorned beauty' of Africa, a theme which recurs often in Gwala's work. Besides feeling that he is fully justified in having no complexes with regard to the whites – 'I swore, I swore never to say "sir" or "master "/because of skin colour',[67] he bases all his hopes for change on the activity of the 'black magic hands'.[68]

As far as his own country is concerned, his certainty that the defeat of the whites in power is inevitable – and through their own fault – is total. Signs of this are to be found in the numerous references to the sunset in his poems, especially 'Sunset' (his only landscape poem, like Mtshali's 'Snowfall on Mount Frere' and which can be read on a political level).[69] And there are many other poems in which he treats this theme.

In 'Before the Coming', included in *Jol'iinkomo*, and especially in 'Bluessing In', a later poem, Gwala uses Humpty Dumpty of the English nursery rhyme as the perfect representation of the white frozen in his superiority and inability to change – a superiority and a power which are in reality very fragile: a human figure reduced to an enormous head-egg, once he has fallen to the ground and broken into a thousand pieces, Humpty Dumpty cannot get up again.[70]

Although, in the first of the poems mentioned, Gwala contents himself with suggesting a coming-together by playing on cultural associations, he is, on the other hand, absolutely explicit in 'Bluessing In'. In eleven six-line stanzas, each of them marking a significant historical stage, Gwala takes the reader–listener from 1884 to 1994 – and to the decolonization of South Africa:

> Blues, blues
> Azania blues 1994
> We buried Humpty Dumpty
> on a hill at Magaliesberg
> A monument marking his grave reads
> 'He didn't want change'[71]

The same fate awaits the gradualists of all persuasions whom he addresses in 'Paper Curtains':

> And if you cry change
> you shall not shrink
> at the slightest shaking
> of the speed needle
> as it races across the meter of our lives
> to register the pace of the motor
> that drives home freedom. Sacrifice.
>
> For if you shout:
> You're going too far!
> YOU'RE severing peaceful relations!
> If you cry: You're overhasty!
> You're running too fast!
> Then my friend you are a hypocrite

> Then you're a stuntist fraud in a dead
> And mighty fall.
>
> You won't pull your curtains
> if they are made of paper
> (I warn you Don't)
> You won't look at life outside
> You won't keep sunlight in your room
> Paper curtains, my friend, are not flexible enough.[72]

It is therefore up to the blacks themselves (at least, to all those worthy of the name) to hasten the achievement of this change: by the continuous critical analysis of the policies followed by those in power, but also of the black community itself, and therefore by means of an ever greater lucidity and determination to fight.

It is easy then to understand in this context why Gwala does not temper his criticism of those who seek to divide the communities and who support separate development, accusing them of contributing to the myth of the national 'homelands' (cf. his 'Black is point of: NO NATIONAL DECEPTION!' quoted above) or of those blacks, particularly among the nascent middle class, who are or who would be tempted to imitate the whites or to sell their birthright for purely material improvements or a simple resurfacing of the façade of apartheid.[73]

In 'No Mirth for Bantus', and especially in 'Black Status Seekers', Gwala rounds upon them in no uncertain terms:

> To say bullshit! to you all
> with the gusto of Mongane
> is not meated bone for y'all.
> Maybe this jive is not for bluessing;
> But then who's to lament?
> You all know it
>   you
> blacks with so-called class
>   you
> you non-Whites, you.
>
> Black grownup kids
> munching cream crackers
> can't reach
>   the beauty of
> a Black toddler suckchewing
> the black soil;
> You all know it.
>
>   . . .
>
> Your non-white women
>   rouge themselves
> redder than Jesus' blood,
> They make Cutex play mommon games
> on their faked finger nails;
>
>   . . .

The Black Man at the Crossroads

> Non-Whites you've become
> a fuckburden to Blacks.
> Non-whites you're hardboiled eggs;
> Your golden intentions are a threat
> to the nation's health.[74]

Elsewhere, in 'Grey Street', named after the commercial centre set aside for Indians in Durban, Gwala attacks the profiteers, taking care, in several places, to make it clear that he is not attacking the Indian community as a whole.[75]

Gwala is just as hard on his fellow Africans who run away from reality (and their responsibilities) in alcohol, prostitution and blind violence against blacks. However, he places his emphasis – and this is where his originality lies in relation to his elders – on the need for a genuine and immediate commitment.

For him, to struggle means to fight to the end, to have the strength of one's convictions, not to speak of change without engaging in those concrete activities that will bring it about. It is significant, in this respect, how many poems Gwala devotes to the possession (or lack) of the virtue which goes hand in hand with struggle: courage. In a poem dating from the early seventies, the young poet had already written:

> In my journey through the bored streets
> of Durban's Grey Street complex
> I see many an acid-belly face
> of the morning-after;
> Then there's a hangover
> What I wish to see still
> is a hangover from the
> mass rallies of the nineteen sixties.
> The current that should
>   flash, flush, rush
> is the current of change.
> Change. Against the deceiving comfort
> of Castle Beer, Wimpy Bars and Kentucky Chickens.[76]

The allusion to the mass rallies implies the idea of solidarity, a theme that refers back to the beginning of the poem and to the need for courage.

'Beyond Dreams', which was published in 1974 in *Black Voices Shout*, ends with the injunction:

> Brother, trim the crazy thing,
> Beyond dreams lies hope;
> Crazy is the world of living dreams
> And dreams we have to burn into hopes;
> Hopes we have to bend into reality;
> It's where freedom lies.[77]

Over the years, in the various issues of *Staffrider*, we find the same call ('Time of the hero/is when leftovers give blacks constipation/is when ghetto trains/spill out race cards thru the windows/with blacks refusing to bet on their poverty anymore . . .'),[78] the same encouragement ('So it be said/The voice is loud and clear/the sound is Black and near').[79] 'Africa at a Piece', which is subtitled 'On Heroes Day' (the reference is to 21 March 1980, the anniversary of the Sharpeville massacre), seeks to convey the same faith in a present justified by past struggles and those now taking place:

> Our blackman's history
> is not written in classrooms
> on wide smooth boards
> Our history shall be written
> at the factory gates
> at the unemployment offices
> in the scorched queues of dying mouths . . .
>
> Our history shall be written
> on laps in the bush
> or whizz out of a smoking steel mouth
>
> Our history is being written.[80]

In general, the poems Gwala has written since 1978 show an unwavering militancy, whether it be in his reflections on politics, as in 'No More Lullabies'[81] or in his injunctions as to what should be done ('A Poem').[82]

It is in this sense that we can talk of a 'sermon' – one that is not given from the elevation of a pulpit but from within the black ghetto itself. According to Gwala, the artist must serve the community in which he lives, *with* it and not *from above* it. Hence the didacticism of 'The Children of Nonti' and 'Gumba, Gumba, Gumba', already mentioned, but also of other longer or shorter poems: discursively in 'Perspectives',[83] friendly in 'Things'[84] and impatient in 'Circles with Eyes'.[85]

The poems 'Bonk' Abajahile' ('Everyone is in a hurry') and 'Uphondo' constitute a diptych on the only choices still available. The first of these ends with a series of questions ("Talk, should we not talk with deep, open voices?/Wait, should we wait until the cows come home?"), to which the second, written entirely in Zulu, seems to provide the elements of a reply:

> Dlothovu, so would it not be better
> if we blew away our peace dreams
> if we counted the rivers we still have to cross
> and the grasslands we shall have to track across
> in running battles?
> So's when our maidens
> stamp their feet and chant at the outlets of rivers
> would it not be better
> if the young men belted on their guns
> at all the river crossings?
> What more else, when the battlehorn's water
> has spilled
> when the sun is nearing sunset
> darkness be waded through solemnly
> – the darkness of yesterday's mind-aches;
> Our forefathers long ago won fortitude

against this here misery;
Even Chakijane and Bhambatha son of Mancinza
will resonate bravo.[86]

Gwala's militancy, no more than his at times crude language and the frequent use he makes of township slang, does not at all obscure the very real poetic qualities of his work. If there can be any doubts after reading the few examples already quoted, at least the following characteristics should be mentioned, although they do not exhaust a subject that is beyond the scope of this study.

First, a lyricism which can best be qualified by the adjective 'fighting': contributing effectively to it are the use of the imperative, of expletives, the lively and sustained rhythms, the incisive formulas that go straight to the essentials, and the vitality that runs right through the poems. We have here the talent of a born orator and what, at the beginning of this study, I referred to as a 'temperament' and a 'tempo'. In the language of jazz, a form of music close to Gwala's heart, we can talk of a 'hot' style ('Gumba, Gumba, Gumba', for instance), paralleled by a 'cool' style, in which the rhythm is slower, the phrasing more deliberate. This last style corresponds to another aspect of Gwala's temperament: an ability not to take himself too seriously, to dominate the situation, however distressing or dangerous it might be. In 'Kwela-ride' and 'Winter',[87] for example, everything is in half-tints, suggested rather then expressed. The same restraint characterizes the two love poems, 'Promise' and 'We Lie under Tall Gum-trees', which avoid the usual clichés,[88] while 'My House is Bugged', a more recent poem, is striking for its subtle irony and quiet strength that belie what is at stake.[89] Sometimes even, the two styles merge, as in 'An Attempt at Communication':

> Hot it cool, right
> We have the music-blues
> to bury the dead blue
> in us.
> Give yourself a forwardpush
> Africa rhythm –
> Start off and go.
> Then you're jazzhappy.
>
> Cool it hot, yes
> That Mbaqanga
> stirs you too?
> I can do my own
> Rock, Twist, and Jive.
> For I also have
> my muscles to loosen
> and cringe.
> When it befits me.[90]

Perhaps his most distinctive characteristic, however, is the way he works on language to give it power and vitality: obviously, there is in this the strictly utilitarian intention of strengthening his rhetoric. But there is also the very real pleasure Gwala so evidently takes in playing with words, in juggling with them, matching in his own way adjectives, nouns, verbs and adverbs, so as to transform them into word-images and striking metaphors.

Thus, he talks of 'barefoot-toe sensitiveness', of 'intoed curiosity' and 'plying a talk-channel' in that little masterpiece, 'When it's all Double-You', which ends with the following lines:

> We embrace in silence – gesture love-wise.
> I KNOW she has understood[91]

We saw earlier expressions like 'I eyemock the plastic arrogance' and 'blacktoddlers suckchewing the black soil'. Elsewhere, speaking of 'playwhites' and 'non-whites', he uses the terms 'bagged with empty class'[92] and 'eelsleepering the argument'.[93] In fact, a systematic listing of the examples of this endless capacity for linguistic invention, of his puns on words and names, remains to be done. There is no doubt that of all his contemporaries, Gwala, along with Nortje but in a different register, is the black poet who handles the English language with the greatest freedom. Contrary to the fears of some purists, it is less a case, in fact, of his exploiting it than of his serving it, since he contributes so much to its renewal.

It is also important, finally, to draw attention to a more classical aspect of his lyricism, linked to nature, to the elements, to the African fauna, in a word to his own culture. 'Beyond Fences', one of the newest poems in *Jol'iinkomo*,[94] is one example, but there are others:

> The waters of the Inyalazi
> have crocodiled me to Umthunzini
> Where men received the drilled patience
> of a root doctor
> When shall I inhale once more the gardenia fragrance
> of the Umngeni Valley in mid-Spring?
> Let me take the lithe of the tiger
> Let me steal the speed of the cheetah
> Let me track the paths
>   of my hunting forefathers . . .
> Let me cheat the wind
>   with the hiss of the black mamba
> Let me go the way of the elephant –
>   and trumpet the past into the future . . .[95]

It detracts in no way from the achievement of his contemporaries to say of Pascal Gwala that, from several points of view, he is profoundly original compared with them. He is an angry young man, an angry African, an angry poet. An ardent promoter of Black Consciousness (he is currently engaged in assembling a collection of his writings on the Black Consciousness Movement), he is clear in his own mind that it is only a phase in the struggle for the real South African nation where one will no longer think in terms of 'race'.[96] Although he emphasizes the need for unity among the blacks, therefore for the polarization of South African society at this time, he is equally aware of the fact that the day will come when the people of all the South African communities will be able to speak of one another with equal understanding. Already in 1973 he wrote of Athol Fugard that, albeit a non-black himself, it was the existential experience of the blacks that he was describing in *Boesman and Lena*. And in *Jol'iinkomo*, he justly observes that 'ghetto

Blacks dig Wopko Jensma', whose 'South-Africanness' has been discussed elsewhere in this study.[97]

If he is an angry man, his anger is rational and derives from the highest of motives. This is why, returning for a moment to a point made earlier, he has never wasted time in recriminations. This is not only because it is not in his nature; it is also because he can read the signs. He is not waiting for the dawn; he has seen it coming and he calls upon his fellow Africans to hasten its arrival, for it is in their power to do so. Close in this to Serote, he does not, however, share the latter's moments of doubt. He also has the assurance that Sepamla displays in 'The Land'. But whereas Sepamla described in terms of the future (see his 'At the Dawn of Another Day')[98] the black man's break from his dependence on the white, for Gwala, on the contrary, this is already a thing of the past (dating back to the early seventies thanks to Black Consciousness) and it is definitely in terms of the present that he places their hope:

> Rough, wet winds
> Parch my agonized face
> as if salting the wounds of
>   Bullhoek
>   Sharpeville
>   Soweto,
> unbandage strip by strip
> the dressings of Hope;
>   I wade my senses
> through the mist;
>   I am still surviving
> the traumas of my raped soil
> alive and aware;
> truths jump like a cat leaps for fish
> at my mind;
> I plod along
>   into the vortex
> of a clear-borne dawn[99]

Only a very few years separate Brutus, Pieterse and Nortje from the poets of Black Consciousness; yet a whole generation seems to be between them. What a difference in their styles, their choice of themes and even their aims!

For Brutus and Pieterse, exile eliminated a real public; the poet soliloquizes, speaking aloud of his love for his distant homeland, speaking *of* his people but not *to* his people. The elevated nature of his views and his generosity are as much reflections of his personality as they are of his humanist education and his reading of the classics. Without having to break with his background, the wide world is open to him and is, as it were, familiar to him. It seems quite natural to hear Brutus state, as he did at the Stockholm conference in 1967, that he felt himself committed to the defence of the human rather than of the African personality.

The black poets of the second generation also want to defend the human personality, but they see this as being achieved essentially by rebelling against the lot reserved for the blacks of their country. This attitude is filtered through a rethinking of the way the African sees himself; and if Mtshali is preoccupied with morality, it is always the specific example of South Africa to which he refers his readers. There is a close correspondence between the ideals of Black Consciousness, explained earlier, and those expressed by the poets studied in the last chapters. Never before has there been such complete identification between the mentality of a whole generation and the poetry it writes.

The latter derives from living conditions and an education which Brutus and Pieterse did not know. Between the two generations of writers came the two important landmarks of Sharpeville (1960) and the Bantu Education Act (1954–9). Sharpeville was the massacre we know about, but it was also the symbol of the radical turn taken by repression since then – expressing itself blindly in 1976 and on an even greater scale in 1977.

It was after the promulgation of the Bantu Education Act that the compartmentalization of society became stricter still and a ghetto mentality developed: the blacks, who wanted nothing to do with a 'dialogue' with people who claimed to be their superiors, were very sensitive to the inequalities and the humiliation that were and remain their daily lot.

In the wake of all this, what Mtshali, Serote, Mattera, Matthews, Pascal Gwala and Sepamla write seems more utilitarian, more community-oriented than personal, more 'local' than universal, much less concerned with stylistic perfection than with finding the means to express an urgent message; more functional, therefore. What Mtshali said about his reasons for writing ('I write to liberate my people')[100] could be echoed by all the poets, young or not so young, who have followed him.

For another characteristic of the new generation is that they have literally assumed the right to speak without complexes and thereby contribute to the liberation of people's minds. To the poets to whom Royston's anthology drew attention,[101] must now be added Themba Ka-Miya, Nkathazo Kaminyayiza, Basil Somhlahlo, Mandlenkosi Langa, Shabbir Banoobhai, Christine Douts, Essop Patel, Ingoapele Madingoane, Fhazel Johennesse, Christopher van Wyk and many others.[102] Among them, as with the leaders of Black Consciousness, we find the same taste for the concrete, the same stress on the importance of the direct message, expressed either explicitly or symbolically, the same blend of simplicity and forcefulness, the same taste for imagery, daring similes and extended metaphor.[103]

The lyricism of these writers is not limited to the expression of a few truths uttered in everyday language. There are many examples where, like Serote and Sepamla rather than Matthews, the poets manage to express, with accuracy and feeling, the condition of the black man today, that is to say, the extreme oppression to which he is subjected and the will to resist. If they do not shape their thoughts in the traditional mould and if, in this respect, they are very free with the 'Great Tradition', if, unlike the older generation, they show little evidence of formal research, they do not hesitate to turn to those natural and spontaneous aesthetic elements which can serve their purpose – chiefly alliteration and repetition, which they use in combination with a great variety of rhythms that are part of an oral tradition that is still very close.

This poetry, alongside its remarkable capacity for *showing*, also has great power of suggestion. It makes much use of ambiguity, chiefly because it serves its main weapon, irony: the play on words, here and there a wink, an insinuation and other allusions are intended for the black readers whom it wants to make its accomplices. This poetry is certainly, to revert to Nadine Gordimer's expression, at one and the same time a hiding place and a megaphone.[104]

Ultimately, the Black Consciousness poets are closer to forerunners like Vilakazi, Jolobe and Jordan than Brutus, Pieterse and Nortje. There is, on the other hand, no such gap in the continuing use of allusion and irony as weapons in the fight.

Nortje has been left deliberately to one side in making these comparisons. This is because the author of *Dead Roots* and his poetry represent the transition between Brutus and Pieterse on the one hand and the poets of Black Consciousness on the other.

Through his education, he belongs to both: a primary and secondary education in a mission school, followed by higher education at the Coloured University of the Western Cape. He is both very South African in his themes and his illustrations, and very universal. His lyricism is more 'English' than African, but the increasing violence of his tone, even though it can be explained also in terms of personal considerations, heralds the period that follows immediately after him. He is the only poet to have been able, or to have known how, to capture the spirit of the short period between the Resistance and the emergence of Black Consciousness. He is in a way in a no-man's land: this factor contributed in no small measure to his tragic destiny, but also to his originality and the power of his poetry.

Notes

1. *Cry Rage!* (Spro-Cas Publications, Johannesburg, 1972); this also contains some ten poems by Gladys Thomas.
2. It has also banned the anthology of poetry prepared by James Matthews, *Black Voices Shout* (BLAC Publishing House, Athlone, 1974), which contains about twenty poems by Matthews.
3. That is, similes, metaphors and catachreses.
4. James Matthews, *The Park and Other Stories* (BLAC Publishing House, Athlone, 1974). An enlarged edition of the book was printed by Ravan Press, Johannesburg in 1983.
5. *Cry Rage!* op. cit., p. 61.
6. 'Pack, Black Man, and Move', in *Herald Tribune*, 13 January 1971.
7. The film *Last Grave to Dimbaza* has since publicized this aspect of South African policy.
8. *Cry Rage!*, op. cit., p. 26.
9. ibid., p. 68.
10. The force of some of Matthews's expressions is greater for his white South African readers than the poetry of black Americans was to their white compatriots: the politico-racial context had not until now allowed the direct expression of their feelings by South African blacks. Note especially poem 65:

    > rage sharp as a blade
    > to cut and slash
    > and spill blood
    > for only blood can appease
    > the blood spilled
    > over three hundred years . . .
    >
    > you have taught us
    > that you have no reason
    > so reason not with us
    > when our rage will find you

11. Poem 38.
12. Poem 39.

13. Poem 69. See also my analysis of Matthews's short story 'No Exit' in *Genève- Afrique*, vol. XVIII, no. 2, 1980.
14. This theme is treated in poems 30–5 inclusive: they praise the priests and white students who do not hesitate to face the police to protest on behalf of their fellow citizens deprived of rights. Poem 33, however, violently attacks the Jewish liberals, although they constitute a large proportion of white protesters and some of them have been sent to prison (see the indirect witness to them in Brutus, *South African Prisons and the Red Cross Investigation* (International Defence and Aid Fund, London, 1967); Lewin, *Bandiet* (Heinemann, London, 1981).
15. We also find in Matthews reference to a 'community of destiny' which unites the blacks of South Africa and their 'brothers' in the United States and Great Britain. However, Matthews goes further than this racial identification: he also proclaims his solidarity with the voices that rise from the underground in Eastern bloc countries.
16. In *Ecrits des Condamnés à Mort sous l'Occupation Nazie* (Gallimard, Paris, 1973).
17. This assertion needs modifying, for some poems have a more sophisticated vocabulary than others.
18. *Cry Rage!*, op. cit., p. 70.
19. BLAC Publishing House, Athlone, 1977.
20. ibid., p. 8. James Matthews has since published a new collection of poems, *No Time For Dreams* (BLAC Publishing House, Athlone 1981).
21. The play is *Morning, Noon and After*, still unpublished. Poems:
    Hurry Up to It! (Ad. Donker, Johannesburg, 1975).
    The Blues Is You in Me (Ad. Donker, Johannesburg, 1976).
    The Soweto I Love (Rex Collings, 1977).
    Children of the Earth (Ad. Donker, Johannesburg, 1983).
    Sepamla is also the author of an important theoretical essay: 'The Black Writer in South Africa Today: Problems and Dilemmas', in *The New Classic*, no. 3, 1976, and of two novels: *A Ride on the Whirlwind* (Ad. Donker, Johannesburg, 1981 and Heinemann, London, 1984) and *The Root is One* (Rex Collings, London, 1980).
22. These two publications, quarterly in principle but in fact appearing irregularly, have their editorial headquarters in Dube, the most 'middle-class' township in Soweto.
23. W. H. Auden, *Collected Poetry* (Random House, New York, 1945).
24. Cf. Matthews, *Cry Rage!*, op. cit., poems 8, 16, 19, 21. Sepamla has devoted another poem to the same subject: 'The Start of a Removal', in *Hurry Up To It!*, op. cit., p. 40.
25. The word 'stem' (line 8) is probably an allusion to *Die Stem*, the Afrikaners' national anthem. The word, written here with a small 's', and which also means 'voice' in Afrikaans, would refer to an independence on a small scale.
26. See below, pp. 263–4.
27. See above, p. 171.
28. Sam Weller in Dickens's *The Pickwick Papers* expresses himself in this way. In South Africa, Delius (*The Last Division*, Human & Rousseau, Cape Town, 1959, Canto III) and Sydney Clouts, in *One Life* (Purnell, Cape Town, 1966), have used this technique to render coloured speech.
29. See above, p. 175.
30. 'I remember Sharpeville', in *The Blues is You in Me*, op. cit., p. 21.
31. See above, pp. 174 and 182.
32. See above, p. 40.
33. *The Blues Is You in Me*, op. cit., p. 70.
34. *The Soweto I Love*, op. cit., p. 4.
35. ibid., pp. 6–7.
36. ibid., p. 17.
37. *Jol'iinkomo* (Ad. Donker, Johannesburg, 1977) p. 37 (henceforth abbreviated to *Jol*). Note also this declaration made by Gwala: 'I grew up in a mixed environment. I have Coloured and Indian cousins, nephews and nieces, uncles and aunties, some who even pass for whites . . .' (*Staffrider*, vol. 2, no. 3, July/August 1979).
38. A recollection of this period occurs in 'To my Daughter on Her Sixteenth Birthday', *No*

More Lullabies (Ravan Press, Johannesburg, 1982), pp. 57–9 (henceforth abbreviated to *No More*) which contains most of the poems published by Gwala in *Staffrider* since 1978. 'You are the song/of crumpled rolls of tears/The day Mandela was given life sentence/for standing up to be a true blackman . . .'

39. According to the back cover of *Jol*, Gwala has worked as a legal clerk, secondary school teacher, factory worker, personnel assistant and publications researcher.
40. The year 1974 saw the simultaneous decolonization of Angola and Mozambique in the wake of revolution in Portugal, Matanzima's unilateral decision to accept the principle of Transkeian independence (which became effective two years later), and the repression by the South African government of members of SASO and the BPC.
41. See *Black Renaissance: Papers from the Black Renaissance Convention*, ed. Thoathlane (Ravan Press, Johannesburg, 1975). The compiler makes specific mention of Gwala's contribution, 'which perhaps is the most hard-hitting and carries the greatest indictment of the Black People, [which] nevertheless is likely to provoke the greatest soul-searching by Blacks' (p. 9). Gwala was, several years later, to assess critically Black Consciousness in 'Steve Bantu Biko', *Reconstruction*, ed. Mothobi Mutloatse (Ravan Press, Johannesburg, 1981).
42. Poems in *It's Gettin' Late (and Other Poems from Ophir)*, ed. Peter Horn and Walter Saunders (Ravan Press, Johannesburg, 1974); in *Black Voices Shout*, ed. James Matthews (BLAC Athlone, Cape, 1974); in *To Whom It May Concern*, ed. Robert Royston, (Ad. Donker, Johannesburg, 1974). 'Towards a National Theatre' appeared in *South African Outlook* (Rondebosch, Cape), vol. 103, no. 1227, August 1973.
43. Cf. his 'Black Writing Today' (*Staffrider*, vol. 2, no. 3, July/August 1979), written in 1976 but only published three years later; in this essay Gwala prophesied, with remarkable insight, the renewal of the short story and the novel among black writers.
44. *Black Review 1972*, ed. Ben Koapa (BCP, Durban, 1973), p. 209.
45. The black American writers and certainly Frantz Fanon, whose *The Wretched of the Earth* was published in English translation in 1965.
46. 'Towards a National Theatre', *South African Outlook*, August 1973, p. 132.
47. *Jol*, pp. 47–8.
48. ibid., pp. 51–2.
49. The Lala are a branch of the great Zulu nation who won a brilliant victory against a British force at Isandhlwana in 1879. The Zulus, who were finally incorporated into Natal in 1897, rebelled again in 1906 (the Bambatha rebellion).
50. Lilian Ngoyi, a member of the women's league of the ANC, over a long period subject to a banning order, died in 1980. The Goch Street shooting in 1978 resulted in the death sentence being passed on Solomon Mhalangu, a member of the ANC, although he had not in fact used his weapon. Silverton is the Johannesburg suburb which saw the first taking of hostages in a bank by members of the ANC; since then, acts of sabotage have greatly increased.
51. This, even if he uses to designate South Africa the term Azania, adopted by Black Consciousness and increasingly used by the majority of blacks and liberal whites.
52. See *Jol*, p. 70, *No More*, pp. 1–2.
53. *No More*, pp. 13–16. Elsewhere, he evokes the resistance by the Ethiopians ('Winter', *Jol*, p. 25), the Basuto, and the Ashanti ('Getting Off the Ride', *Jol*, p. 65).
54. *No More*, pp. 3–6. His vision of Africa is far from idyllic: the fifth stanza of the same poem evokes the bad sons to whom Africa has given birth. His realism even leads him, after expressing his hopes for the birth of an Azania freed from hate and shared by all, to ask the question which ends the poem:
    Mother
        am I going too far?
        am I pushing too fast?
    Mother
        do you hear me?
55. ibid., p. 63. On the subject of African names and their importance and meaning for the individual concerned and the whole community, see the thesis of the Zulu scholar,

Sibusiso Mandlenkosi Emmanuel Bengu: *African Cultural Identity and International Relations: Analysis of Ghanaian and Nigerian Sources 1958–1974* (Shuter & Shooter, Pietermaritzburg, 1976), pp. 52–6.
56. See below.
57. *Jol*, p. 67.
58. See especially *Black Review 1973*, ed. Pascal Gwala (BCP, Durban, 1974).
59. In *Black Viewpoint*, ed. B. S. Biko, Spro-Cas/BCP, Durban, 1972.
60. *Jol*, pp. 29–31.
61. ibid., p. 60. Although 'Taken for a Ride' by Stanley Motjuwadi has another meaning – that of being thrown into a Black Maria (in South Africa, 'Kwela'), reference and homage are no doubt intended to the precursor of Black Consciousness whose poem 'White Lies' is quite remarkable in this connection (see *To Whom It May Concern*, op. cit., pp. 12–13). It is also worth noting that with Gwala, the word 'jive' is often synonymous with the word 'ride'. This was seen in 'Gumba, Gumba, Gumba', and it appears again in 'The Jive' where it is fully developed: 'we jive through our problems/all that is left/of the black miseries jive . . ./the ja-baas jive scares cowards/with Frankenstein monstereyes and the jive continues/but we blacks got the wizard in us . . .' (*Jol*, p. 45).
62. *Jol*, p. 64.
63. *Jol*, p. 66–7.
64. *Jol*, p. 12. It is obvious that if Gwala plays on the letter 'W', it is not only on a semantic level. Reversing that letter to turn it into an 'M' and adding 'for man . . . inverted' is already to denote the opposite of what is human ('inverted') and the white himself ('The Man' in Afro-American slang). Thereafter, 'W' takes on an additional meaning in the enumeration of questions beginning with this letter ('Who', 'Where', 'What') asked by the white officials at the 'pass office' in robot fashion, another example of the dehumanization of the man (*sic*) in power.
65. Notably in Sepamla's poem 'Civilization aha' in *The Soweto I Love*, op. cit.
66. See above. We find, however, in 'Words to a Mother': 'Mother/they lied to me Jesus/about brotherly love and Salvation/they lied to me/about the biblical piece', *No More*, p. 14.
67. In 'VO NGUYEN GIAP: A Tribute to Vietnam: 5 May 1975', ibid, pp. 82–8.
68. *Jol*, p. 11, 'Black' and 'magic' are both adjectives.
69. See *Jol*, pp. 20–1.
70. This is how it goes:

    Humpty Dumpty sat on a wall
    Humpty Dumpty had a great fall
    All the King's horses and all the King's men
    Couldn't put Humpty together again.

71. *No More*, pp. 32–4.
72. *Jol*, pp. 14–15.
73. See on this subject, Judy Seidman, *Apartheid Uplift* (IDAF, London, 1980).
74. *Jol*, pp. 33–4, 'Mongane' refers to Serote.
75. If one needs convincing, it will be enough to read the lines in which he asserts: 'Only your rich go on Haj to Mecca', or else, 'Grey Street/You're trying to fight against the Mahatma's manly spirit', and in an even clearer way in the lines: 'Grey Street/power fists are clenched in Chatsworth too' (Chatsworth is an Indian district).
76. *No More*, p. 26.
77. *Black Voices Shout*, op. cit., p. 15.
78. *No More*, p. 71.
79. ibid., p. 77.
80. ibid., pp. 44–6.
81. ibid., pp. 91–3.
82. ibid., pp. 18–19.
83. *Jol*, pp. 11–12.

84. ibid., p. 17.
85. *No More*, p. 49.
86. ibid., pp. 73–4.
87. *Jol*, pp. 28 and 25 respectively.
88. For 'Promise', see *It's Gettin' Late*, ed. Horn and Saunders (Ravan Press, Johannesburg, 1974); for 'We Lie under Tall Gum-tree', see *Jol*, p. 53.
89. *No More*, p. 49.
90. *Jol*, p. 62.
91. ibid., pp. 12–13.
92. ibid., p. 24.
93. ibid., p. 34.
94. Of the 33 poems in the collection, 16 had already appeared in other publications – see the acknowledgements at the end of the volume – although it omits 'Night Party', published in the last number of *Ophir* (*Ophir 23*, Spring 1976).
95. *Jol*, pp. 42–3.
96. See especially 'Black Writing Today', where Gwala declares: 'Black Consciousness can be seen to be a transient force, an idealism; but not an ideology. As part of national consciousness, it can only be subjected to the trend that national consciousness takes . . .' (*Staffrider*, op. cit., p. 56).
97. The reference to Fugard can be found in 'Towards a National Theatre' (*South African Outlook*, August 1973). For Jensma, see "Words Are Also Born", *Jol*, p. 55.
98. See above.
99. 'Tap-tapping', one of three of his poems included by Gwala in his study 'Black Writing Today', op. cit.
100. Cf. Mtshali's statement at the symposium on contemporary South African literature at Austin (March 1975): 'This is an obligation I have taken upon myself to carry out, in my own modest way, through my poetry: the liberation of my people.' (In *Issue*, vol. VI, no. 1, Spring 1976, ed. B. Lindfors, p. 28.)
101. See above, p. 38.
102. Their poems can be found mainly in *Ophir* (now defunct), *New Classic* and *Staffrider*, also Madingoane's *Africa My Beginning* (Ravan Press, Johannesburg, 1979), Johennesse's *The Rainmaker* (Ravan Press, Johannesburg, 1979), Banoobhai's *Echoes of My Other Self* (Ravan Press, Johannesburg, 1980), Patel's *They Came at Dawn* (BLAC Publishing House, Athlone, 1980) and Christopher van Wyk's *It is Time to Go Home* (Ad. Donker, Johannesburg, 1979). See also the second edition of *Poets to the People*, ed. Barry Feinberg (Heinemann, London, 1980). Banoobhai and Patel belong to the emerging Indian South African writers, as do Ahmed Essop (see above, p. 40), Achmat Dangor, *Waiting for Leila* (Ravan Press, Johannesburg, 1981), *Bulldozer* (Ravan Press, Johannesburg, 1983) and the playwright Ronnie Govender, *The Lahnee's Pleasure* (Ravan playscripts 5, Johannesburg).
103. We have noted Sepamla's liking for extended metaphor. Similes, mostly very original, often daring, are to be found in great numbers among the new poets, especially in Mtshali. There are more than fifty in *Sounds*.

    As for the practice of making the abstract concrete, we have seen many examples of this in the preceding pages.

    With Serote, the lyrical quality of his poetry often derives from this process of making the abstract concrete, as when he resorts to unexpected personification (cf. *Tsetlo*, op. cit., pp. 16, 56) and it often gains its forcefulness from the blend of alliteration and repetition, coming in ever longer waves. It is the chief characteristic of *No Baby Must Weep*.
104. In *The Black Interpreters* (Spro-Cas/Ravan, Johannesburg, 1973), p. 52.

Conclusion and Evaluation

The time has come to assess the information gathered along the way and to draw conclusions, albeit provisional, as the reader will readily understand: the 'situation' is far from resolved and the poets themselves, whether in exile or not, continue the work that has been begun. The reader will find, therefore, in the pages that follow a broad sketch of the general characteristics of their poetry and an account of the elements which, beyond the various barriers, are common to all these poets from different communities.

Two of these elements are sufficiently important to be the subject of closer examination: these are, on the one hand, the broader perspective that the committed poetry seems to have transmitted to the whole of South African poetry, and, on the other hand, the specific contribution the committed poets have made in the sphere of language.

Finally, there is the question that has frequently been asked in these pages: what poetry can do when confronting authority, in other words the relationship between literature and change, and this leads to a variety of contradictory answers. On the one hand, there are those who accord poetry an elevated role. Baudelaire's remark, 'The only great men are the poets, the priests and the soldiers', implies a certain degree of effective influence, at least on people's consciences. On the opposite side, however, are those who assert that literature has no power, that at most it is able to reflect the spirit of the age – a not insignificant role. The question has been asked in the past in connection with Uncle Tom's Cabin *and the assessment of the real influence of this popular work in preparing minds to accept the emancipation of the slaves. The historians' response was to stress the way different factors* converged, *and this included the literary factor, which they considered in the case of Harriet Beecher-Stowe's work to be crucial.*

As far as South Africa is concerned, the situation, because of its complexity, needs a variety of responses. It should be said at the outset that in a sphere where there are not many objective elements, one subjective factor cannot be ignored: this is the poet's own feeling that literature can, in fact, contribute to change. This feeling supports the writer, enables him to give the best of himself in the never-ending struggle against compulsion and arbitrary power, which threaten the fundamental values of his society. It is more than a sign of hope; it is the belief that in man the instinct for life dominates the instinct for death. Poetry written in the worst possible conditions and in spite of all the material and spiritual obstacles proclaims this from the roof tops.

General Characteristics

In order to win recognition as a person, the colonized African had literally to impose the fact of his presence upon the Colonizer, force him to *see* him and to realize that he had the courage and determination to throw off the yoke of slavery. This is exactly what the black demonstrators did in 1976 when, marching into the heart of the white cities, they declared their determination to the oppressor's face. Serote's poem 'What's in this Black "Shit"?', published in 1969 in the review *Ophir*, heralded the rebellion of the young people of Soweto seven years before the event. We can therefore say with Jean-Paul Sartre that 'the first revolutionary will herald the advent of the black soul; he will be the forerunner who will tear off his negritude to offer it to the world'.[1] Black South African committed poetry has given itself the triple aim of informing, accusing and exhorting, and in its endeavours it has enjoyed the by no means fortuitous support of committed white poetry.

A Poetry that informs

The writings of the black poets list the numerous abuses to which the black population is subjected in all spheres of social, economic, political and psychological life. The result, on a strictly documentary level, is a mine of precise information concerning a way of life created by the requirements of an industrial society based on a caste system built up over a long period of time with encouragement and support from a variety of sources.

The black poetry of the seventies stresses the presence and the reality of a city dweller and a city landscape which were only beginning to become known in the sixties thanks to the autobiographical works of black prose writers. The information they contained on contemporary reality has been confirmed and updated, for apartheid has worsened and affected the totality of the black man's life. It has produced a new image of South Africa and destroys the one created by publicity and propaganda films. For, if skyscrapers and ultra-modern buildings reach up into the skies of southern Africa, it is because the black townships and the white cities are joined by the circulation of a vital blood that feeds the common heart: it is this unbroken link that keeps the whole of South Africa alive.

A comparison of the themes to be found in the poetry of black writers of the first and second generations shows the importance accorded to the portrayal of everyday life, a sign of the hold that this factor has on virtually everyone: minimal in Pieterse, more extensive in Brutus and especially Nortje, it occupies a very large place in the life and work of the poets writing at the moment. Through the depiction of the everyday emerges a clearer portrait of the colonized person whose status as a 'non-person' is equalled only by his new-found determination to assert himself against the white man in terms of what he wants to be: a free man, responsible for his own destiny.

There is no doubt that the black committed poet reveals the 'hidden face' of South African society as represented by the condition of the black peoples. But the role of the white committed writer is no less significant for what it reveals about his own community: through the symbolic topography of the cities and the portrayal of the South African state of mind to be found in Horn and Jensma, the reader discovers the reality behind the mask: behind the real prosperity of a part of the population, and behind the general complacency, one discovers a world typified by guilt and schizophrenia, a world from which one's fellow men – those 'unlike likes' – have been banished.

In addition, this poetry 'records' rather like a video-tape: the picture captures a three-dimensional image of this 'new' reality, while the ironic or accusatory commentary of the poets can be heard on a sound-track over swelling voices talking all the languages of South Africa.

A poetry that accuses

This poetry is not content with simply recording and reproducing: it accuses and stresses the heavy responsibility of the whites vis-à-vis the blacks. It denounces the poverty, the appalling living conditions, and all the discrimination and inequalities, and, looking behind what can be seen on the outside, it reveals the way the blacks are dehumanized by the laws of the country, the deculturization to which they have been subjected over the centuries, the alienation caused by their being called and then immediately rejected by the whites, and their complete exclusion from the sharing-out of their country. The particular emphasis with which all the committed poets condemn formalistic Christianity detached from any social application of its teachings adds, to their moral condemnation, the weight of the religious argument. The whole body of contemporary committed poetry amounts to a great indictment written in letters of fire; its target is this republic, this Christianity, this humanity reserved for the 'happy few'.

The poetry written by the white committed poets confirms that this is indeed the case, as the white characters in *Cry, the Beloved Country* had illustrated. But the long-standing and persistent nature of this acknowledgement coming from the camp of the oppressor himself only goes to prove that the situation has not in any way changed over the years. It must be said, in fact, that it has continued to get worse: scenes of violence, already present in the poetry of the Resistance, are much more frequent in what is being written now, although – theoretically at least – South Africa is at peace. The blind violence encountered in the streets, which was once the work of the tsotsis, has become that of the police, but there is also and above all the deliberate violence of the regime, which has been incorporated into coercive laws and whose most visible manifestations can be found in the numerous incidences of torture and the frequent deaths in suspicious circumstances of people who are detained.

The poetry of the whites also shows the damage caused within the white community itself: it establishes the frightening fact of the degradation the executioner himself undergoes through the suffering he inflicts on his victims. Jensma, Horn and their successors present the many and various aspects of the guilt all the whites must share, although the majority of them seem oblivious of the contagious effect of tyranny and violence and of the inevitable repercussions of the policies hitherto followed.

A poetry that warns and exhorts

South African committed poetry does not limit itself to revealing the facts of the situation and to emphasizing where the responsibility lies: it also aims to warn and to exhort. The first of these tasks is assumed chiefly by the white poets, the second by the blacks; for both of them the aim is to make known the urgent need for change.

Conclusion and Evaluation

The role of writer–prophet has all along been that of the white poet whose eyes have been sufficiently open for him to 'have seen', whose conscience has been stirred to 'want to speak' *before it is too late*. It is a literature that comes from beneath the volcano: there is a clear link running from Paton to Delius to Horn to Jensma, each of them, in his own way, arriving at the same conclusion. A great quantity of evidence and signs has been accumulated: because it is 'getting late' and 'time is running out', the point of no return must soon be reached and tomorrow the sun may rise on a world that has been destroyed. 'It's gettin' late', says one of Jensma's poems, echoing the many warnings issued by one or other of the enlightened members of the two communities, and the same Jensma cries: 'Let's/spell it out: we have no future.'

The black poet's aim is to galvanize his people into a response: so, where his white colleague seeks to frighten, he seeks to shame.

For the blacks, in fact, the overriding priority is to get their fellow blacks to transform their outlook, to get them to liberate themselves psychologically and culturally: they must accept a heavy responsibility if they willingly continue to wear their chains. They insist that a way of life fashioned and imposed by the white man's laws is in no sense an irreversible destiny over which the black man has no control and to which he must therefore meekly submit: on the contrary, he himself holds the keys of his deliverance.

Hence the constant appeals for him to shake off his passivity, for him to regain his lost dignity and pride: by finding his courage again, if one bears in mind the example of ancestral Africa, which has never ceased to struggle against the white invasion; by realizing that the white man's real strength has been exaggerated; and by acquiring a clear understanding of the nature of the consumer society he has imported.

The political implications of these appeals become increasingly explicit as the years pass, developing the elements of a multi-faceted pattern of arguments which revolve in essence around a few crucial ideas: the rejection of paternalism and weariness with being treated like children; the rejection of gradualism; the denunciation of the pitfalls inherent in the consumer society and the risk of being deceived by what is actually a mere facelift; finally, explicit or implicit, the general feeling of having had enough, which was already discernible at an early stage in this poetry but which has only begun to be expressed on a large scale since the ideals of Black Consciousness have taken a hold on the minds of the young.

However, contemporary black poetry does not in any way claim, on behalf of the community from which it comes, an unconditional surrender on the part of the white man: in presenting the white man with his list of demands with a new-found assurance, the black man is still offering the present master of the country the chance to change with a minimum of risk. If one were to try summing up the wishes expressed by contemporary black poetry, it would not be 'All the whites into the sea!' but 'Let the black man have his share!' For what the black community has always suggested to the whites, for years now and with remarkable patience, is a marriage of reason and the terms of a real union between equal partners. It is, however, quite apparent now that the black will want to take his share of power and prosperity from the whites by force, if they persist in their refusal to share. The growing impatience and the radical nature of what is being said are evidence of this, as are the numerous acts of sabotage.

This explains the pessimism increasingly detectable in contemporary white poetry, at least in that poetry which, in the wake of Horn and Jensma, seeks to take account of the situation of the country as it really is and not to be lulled by illusions.[2]

Common themes

Although the black and white committed poets do not, because of their very different life experience, have the same emphases in their presentation of what they see and in their denunciation of abuses, they nevertheless have certain themes in common.

The rejection of the ivory tower

All the poets have rejected the concept of the ivory tower. Perhaps because they are – the blacks at least – constantly 'assailed by History',[3] perhaps simply because, as Brutus says, it is difficult to act in any other way in South Africa: 'In South Africa commitment is not a problem. You don't have to be a hero to be committed. You are involved in a situation so fraught with evil that you are brought into collision with it.'[4]

This approach is just as evident in the white poets who teach or study in the white universities, where poetry is the main form of creative expression. The white students and their teachers would need blinkers not to see the repression that exists both on and off their campuses. Ivory towers have only paper walls and papier-mâché doors as protection against the redoubled outcry. It is therefore easy to understand Peter Horn when he says, on behalf, it seems, of all the new poets:

> I do not walk in the forest
> admiring flowers and trees
> but among policemen
> who check my passport
> and my political background.[5]

The rejection of banalities

The corollary of this attitude is the elevated status the poets accord poetry. We recall the lines in which James Matthews says he does not have the heart to write ballads; these words are echoed by Peter Horn's on St Francis of Assisi, as seen by the poet in South Africa in the 1970s:

> I met him again
> at the street corner
> no longer speaking to the birds
>
> I have no time for that now
> he said
> somebody must worry about these
>
> about these children
> they are hungry
> and they need a home[6]

And Jensma, in a poem dedicated to the black sculptor and painter Dumile, writes of the danger of being a successful artist in a society which wants at all costs to forget its problems and the misery they create:

> one day you got tired
> tired of your soft voice
> tired of being their darling[7]

The poet's role consists therefore in speaking: speaking so as not to connive, through one's silence, with the regime; speaking to awaken dormant consciences; speaking, finally, because this act, synonymous and parallel with the attaining of intellectual lucidity, is an indispensable therapy in a society in which another set of 'values' has been substituted for those of democracy.

But speaking to what purpose? To open people's eyes to the misery, repression and alienation being suffered by the men and women of this country; to fight against the attempt to anaesthetize everyone, against the conditioning of public opinion by government propaganda; to reveal the truth and to show the disorder and sickness hidden behind the unruffled monotony of self-satisfaction. And the same Peter Horn writes:

> My silence is gold
> to those
> who are afraid
> to be exposed.[8]

The rejection of the fabricated image and hypocrisy

All these poets want to enlighten the South African reader and, beyond him, the overseas reader, about the true state of affairs in South Africa; some of them refer explicitly to their work of demystification, others are content to turn the full glare of the lights onto the darkest corners of the South African 'domestic' scene. On the one hand to show up the falseness of appearances, and the most visible of these, the ones that 'sell' the best: the attractiveness of the climate and the landscape:

> Nothing outwardly grieves
> so luxuriant are the trees.
> Leaf-rich boughs ride past with Spring's ease.
>
> Yes, there is beauty: you make
> the understandable mistake.
> But the sun doesn't shine for the sun's sake.[9]

On the other hand, to reveal a less rosy reality: not the reality of the tiny minority of privileged inhabitants, but that of the majority. In this wish to give a true account of life in South Africa, manner and style differ; the objective is nevertheless always the same: to present a global picture of the country so as to provide a clearer impression of the impoverishment of a life lived under so many handicaps. A world of deprivation emerges, a world in which people who are missing or dead are at the centre of the picture.

And so develop the themes of the screen that deceives, of the façade that gives birth to illusion, the theme of a world of make-believe erected into a government system, which leads to the conclusion that South Africa does not even begin to live up to the reassuring image put forward by official propaganda.

This moral role assumed by the new poets is strengthend by their attacks on the hypocrisy of a society whose claim to be Christian is not confirmed by its actions. There is complete unanimity on this point – from Delius, with his evocation of the 'furtive Calvinists cheating the Bible', to Jensma, Mtshali and Sepamla. They all point to this one absolute evil: the absence of love for one's neighbour, or rather that selective conception of love for others which excludes black people: 'In this country which claims to be Christian, you can be a Christian ten thousand times over; but if you are not white, you are treated like a dog.'[10]

It is an absence of love which one would expect to lead to hatred on the part of the oppressed, but this is a feeling which few of the latter have so far managed to find within themselves.

The rejection of the status quo

All these poets are opposed to the perpetuation of South Africa as it exists at the moment; they all reject a society which is compartmentalized and unequal. However, they do not content themselves with criticizing the type of society that exists; they talk of the world they would like to see – in most cases, a multiracial society.

In the new 'Waste Land' represented by the South Africa of the 1970s, the paradise preached by the white poet is togetherness. This togetherness, the opposite of the hell of separation, occurs in the 'visions' of Paton in *Cry, the Beloved Country* (the scene in the church), of Delius in *Black South Easter*, and Horn in 'Voices from the Gallows Tree'.

Although some black poets express the same 'ecumenical' view (it is the case with Sepamla and even Matthews, who dedicates *Cry Rage!* to *all* South African children), Paradise is, for the moment at least, more in the shape of a South Africa freed from fear and the complexes of the blacks than one freed from the whites, towards whom, however, there is a growing hostility.

The idea that this new world, this New Jerusalem, can be achieved only through violence is being expressed by many of the new poets: the Evil that has been established and maintained by violence can only be made to give way through an upheaval of apocalyptic proportions, when chains will be broken and walls will fall: there is reference to Jericho in Matthews, to the thunder in Mtshali, to fire in Serote and Matthews, to hurricanes in Horn and Brutus, to the South Easter in Delius. But it is interesting to note that the change is not visualized in terms of a political ideology: the chief targets are racism and totalitarianism, with only occasional references to capitalism.

All these poets take on the roles of prophet and stirrer of consciences mentioned earlier and in so doing resort to the techniques of the prophet and the preacher. It is, indeed, the fable and the parable that one encounters more frequently than the elegy, together with, in a general sense, whatever can whip people into action (exhortation, for instance), stir the imagination and ensure the ready accessibility of ideas and situations (dramatic dialogues, poems that project into a dark future), apart from direct appeals to God, in the Negro spiritual tradition, and the 'time-bomb' effect of epigram and antiphrasis.

There is another characteristic that accompanies this new prophetic spirit: all the poets, including those of the first generation, make numerous religious references – the mark of a society strongly impregnated with Christian culture, the mark also of the mission education many of its members have received. It is, indeed, an eschatalogical literature, but also necessarily a literature that looks forward to the advent of a better world.

This does not prevent it from being, in terms of its aims and methods, a political literature – far from it. Whatever the regime hides or keeps quiet about this poetry speaks of and reveals. Concerned with freedom and rebirth, it implies the need for change in the political structures which alone can produce fundamental change in the country. To this end, it speaks to all the people of the country, citizens and helots. What it can or cannot hope to achieve in the face of apartheid is discussed later: before we do this, we need to note another of its characteristics.

A widening of the perspective

There is another theme common to South African committed poets – the theme of the heroes and martyrs who have emerged throughout the long struggle against apartheid: major figures of the Resistance, guerrilla fighters who have died unknown on the very frontiers of their country, martyrs of the South African prisons whose murder has been covered up by the authorities as suicide, poet-resisters, many of whom have been imprisoned or have taken their own lives. The poems that evoke them are not so much hagiographies as acts of homage on behalf of the community of which the poet has made himself the spokesman, or a final affectionate farewell to a comrade killed in the same fight. Although they sometimes contain biographical details, they are more usually an occasion to return to general principles likely to provide food for thought: the witness of a life entirely devoted to resisting oppression – Bram Fischer celebrated by Lewin, Evans and Jensma; the courage and determination of the guerrilla fighter or the humble hero – Basil February, sung by Pieterse, and Japhta Majola, sung by Hugh Lewin; the tragic fate of detainees who have died under torture – Imam Haron, evoked by Matthews and Paton, Ahmed Timol by Shabbir Banoobhai and A. N. C. Kumalo, Saloojee, again by Kumalo, and Looksmart by Pieterse; and the figure of a leader like Luthuli, celebrated by poets as diverse as Jennifer Davids, Paton and Dennis Brutus, and finally that of Steve Biko, to whom several of the new poets refer.[11]

The tragic fate of the four writers discussed earlier (Ingrid Jonker, Nat Nakasa, Can Themba and Arthur Nortje) leads David Evans to wonder about society's responsibility towards those whose exile – internal or external – it has earlier caused or intensified:

> Jonker, Nakasa, Themba, Nortje,
> did you spurn life or did life spurn you?
> The poets of our time are born in a mess of blood
> and those who don't die in a mess of blood
> may drown or jump or, the horror ingested,
> choke after the last lonely supper in a mess of spew.[12]

The names of these writers, who represent the white, black and Coloured communities, recur frequently in the work of their fellow poets.

We saw how William Plomer linked Nakasa and Ingrid Jonker symbolically in *Taste to Remember*.[13] Jensma places Can Themba's name at the head of his volume *Sing for Our Execution*. And Cosmo Pieterse deplores Ingrid Jonker's death; she herself had so movingly voiced her indignation at the murder of the black child in Langa.[14]

Nortje, in his turn, was to receive posthumous homage from Brutus and Evans. The latter, who had already written a long poem to the memory of Nat Nakasa in 1964–5, dedicated one of his finest poems to him and read it at his funeral in Oxford. How better to do homage to a poet of such talent than to incorporate in the lines composed in his memory the sounds and words of the motherland once so loved and so feared, and to play with them, as Nortje himself used to do, so as to enrich our perception of the world? These words and sounds are borrowed from all the languages spoken in South Africa, to achieve an effect as significant as Jensma's multilingualism noted earlier.[15]

> When a poet dies
> certain scents which ride in the wind
> colours which lustre across the veld
> sounds which dassie* along the krantzes*
> lapse and are lost
> not because they aren't there to find
> but because we needed him to find them.
>
> When a poet dies
> who was fashioned and fired by the anguished land
> then the git*, the drums, the penny whistle
> the gogog harp* and comb mondfluitjie*
> on which our country's urban tunes are played
> the blackwhite klavier* of the Korsten ghetto
> the voice which sings of District Six, Soweto, Langa, Cato Manor
> are stilled
> until his hard rebirth
>
> > Die skollie boy digter is dood
> > die kuns is lank en die lewe is kort.†[16]

This list is far from complete, but the living are not forgotten, those who have been condemned to silence, like Don Mattera to whom Serote dedicates his poem of encouragement, 'But Seasons come to pass,'[17] and those who huddle on the cement floors of Robben Island gaol (Brutus, in several poems, and Delius in 'The Island').

The recent names in this long interracial martyrology are Onkgopotse Tiro, Mohapi and the children who died at Soweto, who exemplify the new spirit of resistance. Tiro, celebrated by both Serote and Breytenbach, had delivered a very courageous speech at the University of the North, which resulted in his being put under house arrest and having to abandon his studies. Breytenbach's poem recalls the circumstances of his death:

---

* *dassie*: rock rabbit; *krantzes*: mountain faces, cliffs; *git*: guitar; *gogog harp*: a rudimentary harp made from a petrol can and a bow the cord of which is plucked; *comb mondfluitjie*: comb used as a mouth organ; *klavier*: piano.
† 'The poet–hooligan is dead, art is long and life is short.'

and still before he could be banned to the place of the living dead
he left his native country
for a village with the name Gaberones in a country
with the name Botswana in the desert
with little flames of a struggle for freedom everywhere
which made his words ignite
and the boss had to show that a nigger
has to know his place, otherwise . . .
and the boss has sent a book to Tiro
and Tiro lies in his own blood
and Tiro lies in his own blood
and Tiro is the inner flame inside the red flame.[18]

Breytenbach's poem is entitled, in Afrikaans, 'Boeke is bomme: vir my dooie broer, Tiro' ('Books are bombs: for my dead brother, Tiro'). This word 'brother' illuminates and gives their full sense to these references, these posthumous gestures of homage and affectionate greetings to the detainees, the guerrilla fighters and the innocent victims of apartheid.

Indeed, in a country whose laws have tried to erect watertight barriers between people, these rebels re-establish the fraternity that has been denied and flouted and reaffirm their common destiny. The committed poets, in their turn, proclaim the binding force of interracial friendships in the face of the divisions, the forced colour distinctions and the social exclusion practised by their society.

By recalling the tragic events that have affected the whole of the South African community – Sharpeville, Langa, Cato Manor, Carletonville, Soweto – and which have inspired still more poems, they stand in opposition to the edited official history, which omits any reference to blatant compulsion and the refusal to live as one community. They are writing the history of the South Africa of tomorrow, a *common* history for the nation that must be born, a nation that will acknowledge the heroes of all communities considered as South Africans in the full sense of the term and no longer classified separately as whites, blacks, Coloureds or Indians.

It may still be too soon to talk of a national literature, but it is now possible at least to refer to its birth. It is also now a possibility that the widening of perspectives, of which there is other evidence as well, has rung the death knell of separate, partisan literatures which deal only with the linguistic communities from which they spring.

While the poetry of the sixties for the most part kept its distance from the contingent, the poetry of today, as the foregoing pages show, is deeply rooted in the present and only uses the past to ensure the more effective presentation of the themes of the here-and-now.

The white poetry of the early seventies becomes aware of the presence of a fellow inhabitant, the black man, whose existence (or, rather, non-existence) creates a problem. The new white poetry discovers itself through its perception of the Other: it looks at the black man, and his suffering and humiliation turn it back towards itself. It listens to the black man, and his cry of protest forces it to doubt itself and undermines its confidence (or over-confidence). A play of mirrors is set up which is illustrated in the following poem by the poet-psychiatrist Bernard Levinson:

> I remember once
> you were in the backyard
> wearing my pajamas –
> for one bizarre moment
> I thought you were me –
> and it was I
> standing in the darkness
> coming out of the servants room
> hearing a noise –
> and walking to the window.
> It was I
> who looked in
> at the white face –
>
> 'Is everything alright Baas?'
> 'Yes', I said,
> 'Everything is alright now . . .'[19]

The broadening of its themes to include not only the preoccupations of the oppressed and despised majority, but to treat, at last, also the basic problems of modern South African society, has enabled the poetry that is being written at the moment to attain a certain maturity: it has become adult to the extent that it now dares to speak openly and frankly about its innermost secrets.

For the first time, the South African in the fullest sense, and not only the white South African, becomes the central figure in the poet's canvas: not the conqueror nor the explorer, not the founder of empires, not the colonist fighting *bloodthirsty savages*, but the contemporary South African. This sense of the here-and-now is already discernible and is the dominant feature of the new poetry being written in English; it is no exaggeration to say that to a large extent it owes this to the influence of the committed poetry.

Such a claim deserves a fuller examination, which is beyond the scope of this book. There is, however, a useful short-cut provided by anthologies, which are as revealing of their times as they are of their authors.

The most recent of these, edited by André Brink under the title *A World of their Own: Southern African Poets of the Seventies* (1976),[20] provides irrefutable proof of this widening of perspectives: in the very wide choice of authors,[21] in the themes it treats and the aspirations it reveals and, finally, by its tone and style – but also, and even more explicitly, in Brink's own introduction, of which the following two points are worth noting:

> After a very long and often hesitant development – a hesitation concerning, among other things, a choice between Europe and Africa – this new explosion of the Seventies . . . implies nothing less than a definitive emancipation from the last vestiges of literary colonialism.

> In the Blues or Jazz or Rock rhythms of Mtshali, Sepamla, Serote and Jensma one often finds . . . an effort to define the self in terms of the shocking landscapes of personal experience – above all, the experience of this land. For that, after all, is what it really concerns: exploring and evaluating the experience of living in Africa, of being Black or White in this South Africa. This is the common denominator in poems otherwise poles apart, like those of Serote and Christopher Hope.[22]

Reflections on language

Any consideration of the language in which the black poets write reveals differences which, at first sight, seem fundamental.

The poets of the first generation express themselves in a very studied English. Whereas Brutus, in his admiration for Donne and Hopkins, plays with quotations and implicit references to assert his mastery of a language and a culture which are denied him, Pieterse, full of the joy of discovering in English a tool that enables him to play with words, and therefore with meanings, finds the language itself a personal freedom which no one can take away from him – language which is a launching pad for high flight, words with which to test his delving into life, words which say without exhausting what they say, words that open into the infinite – like the 'must' which has already been quoted and which, obviously enough,[23] means 'ought', but much more, too, through its association with wine-making.

It is different especially with Serote, Sepamla and Gwala – not only, however, because unlike their elders they did not go to university, not only therefore because of *what they lack*. Times, too, have changed. Brutus and Pieterse lived at a time when a multiracial society was possible; culturally, at least, there was evidence for thinking this. For the younger generation, this possibility has vanished: the generation that received its education in the sixties did so in institutions that were strictly separated. But what has changed most of all are the attitudes.

It is no longer a question of consciously or unconsciously identifying with the white, of raising oneself to his level or simply asserting one's equality, of winning his respect by conforming to his own criteria or by showing that one can do just as well as he – which is, in effect, a way of asserting oneself and claiming one's right to a place. Now it is a question, on the contrary, of claiming one's right to one's *own existence*. And these poets do not have a common language in which to speak to one another. They can write only in English, which has an ambiguous status in South Africa: it is the language of a minority in the country (but a minority that still retains a certain economic power), a language which is preferable to that of the country's political masters, Afrikaans, but a language which is suspect because it is the bearer of a dominant culture. This is where the black writer feels trapped, and yet it is impossible for him to write in any other way: because it is impossible for him not to write, not to make himself heard by as many people as he can, in South Africa as well as abroad, but also for obvious political reasons, for the South African government follows a policy of enforced tribalization, and therefore of linguistic fragmentation.

English has, therefore, for these young poets the same attraction and repulsion as the white civilization that goes with it: its ambiguities can be readily exploited; but in allowing himself to be moulded by it, the poet is dominated by it and he assimilates, even without realizing it, elements which are foreign, indeed profoundly repugnant, to him.

A poem by Serote admirably illustrates the relations of the colonized African with the language imported by the colonizer: 'Black Bells'. It takes as its subject a man's desperate efforts to throw off the coat the colonizing society has dressed him in but which, like Nessus' tunic, cannot be removed. The rejection of this coat, of this culture which generations of a common social, religious and political life, have accumulated, is a noble goal when one considers that the reward is the recovery of one's identity and self-respect. But then the colonized African comes up against a last, and by no means trivial, obstacle: he cannot rid himself of the colonizers' language, or rather, for lack of a language to replace it, he can only fall into the unintelligible. It is a cruel dilemma which Serote expresses at the end of his first volume in a particularly eloquent way:

> I wonder who trapped me,
> for I am trapped,
>   Twice,
>
> Like
> A word can mean two things,
> Who, and Whitey
> Trapped me.
> I read.
> Words,
>   WORDS.
> Trying to get out
> No. No. No. By Whitey.
> I know I'm trapped.
> Helpless
> Hopeless
> You've trapped me whitey! Meem wanna ge aot Fuc
> Pschwee e ep booboodubooboodu blllll
> Black books,
>   Fresh blood words shitrrr Haai,
>   Amen.[24]

The deliberate use of slang at the end, with its expletive ('Fuck!') but also its phonetic rendering ('me i want to get out') by which the poet seeks to escape into another language consisting of barely articulated words and cries, eloquently proclaims the intense and deeply felt drive for release. This ejection of blood and matter, this effort which is rather like defecation or childbirth ('flesh') show how difficult it is to write 'black books' with 'white' words. The final 'Amen' ends the poems *and the volume*, linking scatology and eschatology, while the cry from the depths ('Haai') expresses both suffering and release.

There remains, in fact, the solution of partially reappropriating the language, of following through to the end the logic of one's peripheral linguistic status – that is, of writing in the language spoken by the people. This English, which the purists regard as debased but which is no longer the tool of the dominant minority (which holds majority political power) but of the real majority (although not effectively one, and for that reason a minority because it is dominated, deprived of rights and a voice), this English has a better chance of being representative of the new culture, of this detribalized and acculturated African proletariat, partially cut off from its roots.

This could explain the linguistic line adopted by Serote in his second collection of poems. He does not use the extended development of ideas characteristic of the form in *Yakhal'inkomo*; the poet now seems to limit his role to the transcription of spoken English and the creation and/or the propagation of a spoken language, which is *subversive* because it is the language of those who oppose the South African regime. Serote could 'conform'; he has shown that he is capable of writing 'like everyone else'. He does not do so, proving that syntax, a means of enslavement, can, when it is rejected or denied, express revolt.[25]

Conclusion and Evaluation 263

It is by unashamedly asserting the value of this language spoken in the townships and having it printed that Serote takes the first step in liberating himself from the colonizer. Since the latter judges education by the criterion of the correct use of grammar and vocabulary, Serote will increasingly use the everyday forms employed by the mass of people who have not benefited from an education, the property of the country's masters, and will in this way be closer to the people:

> I have went inside me
> made love with the gaping wounds
> and the lost gut
> lost in the terrible battle with fear[26]
>
> I fear to see the stars at night
> why because the brothers charge my life
> the brothers are bloody restless
> why because they are wounded bulls[27]

Among the whites, the same thing is being tried at the same time by Horn and Jensma. In Horn's case, this experiment remains tentative: apart from a few very colloquial or slang terms, the undisguised crudity of a few expletives and occasional liberties taken with the syntax, Horn's English remains relatively controlled, as one might expect from a university teacher—especially if he is compared with Jensma.

The imperative, which is much used by Jensma, shapes a language transformed into cries and vociferation into the stuttering of machine-guns, a verbal machine-gun that seeks to destroy myths, hypocrisy and language itself, as if a new way/world ought to emerge from this regenerative act of destruction.

For regeneration, rebirth is perhaps implied in his inclusion of the minor/major languages, hence the use of African vocabulary, or major/ minor languages, hence the use of Afrikaans vocabulary. An attempt to rearrange the territorial boundaries of poetry through language:[28] Jensma's poetry can be seen as looking forward to a national semantic unity as well as a national political unity.

Jensma's case shows clearly, in fact, that this rearranging of the boundaries of poetry involves the whole domain of language. This is what happens in Serote and Mtshali, but also in most of the Black Consciousness poets, especially Pascal Gwala. These writers help, in fact, to enrich the language with what the French philosopher, Paul Ricoeur, has called 'living metaphors'.[29]

Thus 'brainwashed', although it came into existence quite recently, has already lost its force: 'brainwhitewashed', coined by Stanley Motjuwadi, is on the other hand a 'living metaphor': it restores the element of surprise while at the same time bringing out the coloration of the colonial culture; it shows more than it states that the ideology of the white man sees everything in terms of force, that his propaganda, which he is determined must succeed at any cost, has become, as it were, the manic propagation of a single reality in which everything is represented in the image of the white man:

> I know pure white,
> a white heart,
> white, peace, ultimate virtue.
> Angels are white

>   angels are good.
>   Me I'm black,
>   black as sin stuffed in a snuff-tin.
>   Lord, I've been brainwhitewashed.[30]

These composite words, these portmanteau words that do not exist (not yet, at least) but which, once created out of necessity, have such a clear meaning that one is surprised they have not always existed, are all living metaphors. 'I am no big blackman/I am a blackmanchild', writes Serote. And thanks to him we can see the paradox of contemporary black psychology: on the one hand, maturity and a lack of aggressiveness, on the other – and simultaneously – the promise inherent in the word 'child':

>   I am a blackmanchild,
>   I am he who has defeated defeat
>   I am a surprise which surprises me.[31]

Other living metaphors are the 'concertina chest' mentioned in Mtshali's 'The Face of Hunger' and, one of many examples to be found in Gwala's poems, 'whitelonely suburbs', full of double meaning, especially alongside 'Whites only'.[32]

Mencken had already observed this daring, this absence of complexes in relation to English in the United States. Is it, then, the sign of an emerging civilization? Yes, provided we immediately add that in South Africa this characteristic is to be found especially in communities directly concerned with production and until recently still in contact with a rural environment. Yet we notice this characteristic also in the more highly educated Brutus and Nortje.[33] Perhaps we ought to go back to Pieterse's 'rediscovery' of the English language, with his excitement at the discovery of an extremely varied and musical world of sounds, a world of words to be played with. Christopher Hope summarized very well the contribution being made by the black poets on the level of language when he wrote in his report of a poetry conference in Cape Town in 1974:

> The poetry that we heard in Cape Town had just one common feature: it was, all of it, written in English, in South Africa. And, as such, it reflected in microcosm the rich possibilities of the language. Whether you speak it as pidgin, or BBC, or Gammat, or American, or African, the language offers a potential for raw expression together with a vocabulary which enables the most delicate precision. It is no closed system, no artificial construction; indeed it thrives upon abuse and assault. It looks to those who undermine it and subvert it for new energy and new forms. It is emphatically not in need of protection.[34]

What can poetry do against apartheid?

One has to be frank: South African committed poetry has no more effect on the life or death of the South African government than pinpricks on a hippopotamus's hide.

The government feels itself to be strong: it has so far had the massive support of the white electorate to convince itself of this. Otherwise, it has relied on the

Conclusion and Evaluation

international situation, which has been in its favour, on the support it knows it has had from the major nations with which it trades, on the weakness and divisions of its opponents and on its military strength.

The poet is tolerated for so long as he influences only an extremely small part of the population. The arguments he adopts to try and bring an end to what he sees as a general anaesthesia of society cannot outweigh the two-faced bogeyman used by the Nationalists since they set out to win power and then to retain it: the Communist threat and the black peril. The situation in South Africa is such that the survival instinct of a *minority* population, which knows it can last only by force and intransigence, is stronger than anything else.

In any case, why should the government make more enemies by censoring the poet? By letting him speak, it guarantees itself a reputation for fair play on the pseudo-liberal fringe. Better still, in allowing the poet, increasingly violent in his invective and increasingly bitter in his criticism, to indulge his rage to the extent of questioning the very foundations of South African society and its existing structures, the government provides itself, at little cost, with additional proof that it would be very dangerous to relax its vigilance and liberalize its policies.

The poet therefore finds himself in a double trap: because his poetry can reach only a very tiny minority which can or wants to read him, and because the louder he cries the more he conforms to the stereotype of the agitator – in contemporary South African society, not to have the same ideas as everyone else is to be beyond the pale. What effect, then, can poetry have against the overwhelming power of the regime? Does it have any influence at all, and if it does, what influence?

It is undeniable that writing plays a crucial role in man's constant pursuit of self-knowledge: it is the unavoidable route from concept to reality, from the unformulated to the concrete and even, for some, from ignorance to sudden discovery. The work of art reveals the poet's own truth as he writes. It has the same relation towards him as it has towards History; in the same way as it captures the latter and gives it a recognizable appearance while at the same time going beyond it, so also is it the irrefutable evidence of a *moment* in the life of the individual, but a moment which is also transcended. If poetry had only one power left, it would be this one, which is to enable the writer to understand better, to understand *himself* better, to have a clearer grasp of his thoughts and, at the same time, to apprehend the world and to enable others to apprehend it better as well.

The power of creative writing, in this sense alone, goes much further in South African society. There the danger of losing sight of democratic values is not inconsiderable; indeed, a counter-ideology aimed at dispelling people's fears and easing their conscience has been launched and each day steamrollers society.

Here the *subversive* ideas are those that in other countries the masses have had so much difficulty in getting kings and tyrants to acknowledge and which the people still have considerable difficulty in getting totalitarian governments to respect: equality of opportunity and the fundamental freedoms without which every country must slide into injustice and arbitrary rule. It is easy to understand Peter Horn when he says:

> I speak words that I have forgotten:
> Freedom. Justice. Love. This is
> Not enough. But it is a beginning: I gather words
> And drag nets through the past and the present.
> I speak wishing to be

>   Rid of these confusions
>   I speak. That in itself is good . . .
>   And I remember words: Equality. Brotherhood.[35]

Comfort in his solitude, a man's recourse against falling into discouragement or madness. In the concentration camps, men wrote on their mess-tins with a stone or the handle of a spoon; and the poet–publisher, Pierre Seghers, writing about the poets who sent him their manuscripts from the prison camps, says:

> Turned in on themselves, brooding on their patience, with only the practice of the high creative language to safeguard their humanity, inactive or utterly exhausted, deprived of human contact or the exchange of talk, they resort to poetry. This is the true gift, the one man offers to prayer as he does to love. Thanks to poetry, which they win back or recreate, they reconstruct their world and reconstruct themselves.[36]

Does poetry then only have an inner function, for the benefit of the writer alone? We need to look at this more closely.

Poetry cannot, it is quite true, have any *direct* influence on events. But it can do a great deal to help a people to discover its own spirit. Poetry is a dazzling short-cut which, by its brevity and its power of condensation, goes straight to the heart of a problem. It is the plummet dropped into the depth of the collective unconscious, and from the movement of everyday life, where incidents and accidents, mud and clear water mingle, it extracts the essential and highlights the deeper meaning of it all.

Obviously, poetry does not speak *logically*, it does not *demonstrate*, it would not be poetry if it did. It needs the poet's talent, under the pressure of circumstances, to renew its vitality; it must reopen old wounds, stir people's energy, make itself convincing through its symbols as well as through its lyrical qualities. Know yourself! say the Black Consciousness poets to the black community. Throw off your chains! You can do Everything! Wake up!

But what if the public are blind or deaf? What if they block their ears so as not to hear what they know must disturb them? Or what if they are nearly all illiterate?

This is effectively where the book comes to a halt, where it can do nothing more, where its role is finished. But it has issued its warnings, others must take up the challenge; and even if they have not read the poets, men will take up the challenge when their anger boils over. Then the poet is free to close his manuscript, to put down his pen and take up the gun or any other weapon of liberation. Soyinka in Nigeria, Brutus in South Africa, after René Char in France; the citizen takes over from the poet, supposing there had ever been a separation between the two.

For, if white committed poetry, representing liberal thought, *has failed* to awaken the conscience of the whites, and has therefore failed in its role as a force for change, it leaves black committed poetry with the chance to contribute in *the preparation* of this change by the wakening of black self-awareness. It has already heralded, and perhaps prepared, years beforehand, the awakening represented by the upheavals of 1976–7.

So, if the white will not share power, the black will have to wrench it from him. This is the significance of the failure of committed poetry (white or black) *aimed at the whites*; it perhaps explains the success of black committed poetry *aimed at the blacks*. The day will come when the people will be ready for action, stirred by what

Conclusion and Evaluation

has been the collective consciousness of their time. One can therefore understand these words of Yves Buin, which I set down at the end of this study to show quite clearly the limits of the power of poetry and literature after having indicated its greatness.

> Literature must be seen as success because it culminates in the book, as failure because it can do nothing for and against reality and because men must get away from books.[37]

Notes

1. 'Orphée Noir', in L. S. Senghor, *Anthologie de la nouvelle poésie nègre et malgache* (Presses Universitaires de France, Paris, 1948), p. xv.
2. This note is particularly evident in *Cape Drives* (London Magazine Editions, 1974) by Christopher Hope, one of the most talented of the young generation of white poets.
3. Cf. Charles Dobzynski: 'The ivory tower is unknown to those who are assailed by history' (in 'Introduction à la poésie yiddish', *Miroir d'un Peuple*, Gallimard, Paris, 1971).
4. Cyclostyled report of an international conference on the role of the writer, Uppsala, 1968.
5. *Walking through our Sleep* (Ravan Press, Johannesburg, 1974), p. 23.
6. ibid., p. 3.
7. 'Portrait of the Artist' in *Sing for our Execution* (Ravan Press, Johannesburg, 1973), p. 72.
8. *Walking through our Sleep*, op. cit., p. 45.
9. Nortje, *Dead Roots* (Heinemann, London, 1973), p. 25.
10. Statement by Zephania Kameeta, director of the Paulinum Theological College in Namibia. Quoted in *Pro Veritate*, vol. 14, no. 8, December 1975, p. 7.
11. Pieterse's poem is at the beginning of *Apartheid: A Collection of Writing on South African Racism by South Africans*, ed. Alex La Guma (Lawrence & Wishart, London, 1972).
    Banoobhai's poem is in *Ophir*, 21, July 1975.
    The poems by A. N. C. Kumalo (a pseudonym) are in *Poets to the People*, ed. Barry Feinberg (Allen & Unwin, London, 1974, Heinemann, London, 1980), pp. 35, 38. Jennifer David's poem is in P. Rodda, 'Poetry under Apartheid, a selection of South African Poetry', *Transatlantic Review*, February, 1976, pp. 53–4.
12. *Poets to the People*, op. cit., p. 17.
13. See above, p. 23.
14. See above, p. 26.
15. See above, p. 104.
16. *Poets to the People*, op. cit., p. 16. The poet quoted in the last two lines is Baudelaire.
17. See above, p. 195.
18. Translated from the Afrikaans by R. Leigh-Loohuizen. Tiro was killed by a parcel bomb in 1974.
19. *From Breakfast to Madness* (Ravan Press, Johannesburg, 1974), p. 37.
20. Ad. Donker, Johannesburg, 1976.
21. In spite of certain omissions, some of which (Brutus, Matthews) the editor explains as being due to banning orders, others (Peter Horn) are less explicable.
22. op. cit., pp. 9, 11. It should be noted that the way Brink describes the authors' use of rhythm is far from accounting for its variety and richness.
23. Reference to Pieterse's poem quoted above, p. 149.
24. *Yakhal'inkomo* (Renoster Books, Johannesburg, 1972), p. 52.

25. This point, with examples from other cultures, is developed by L. Calvet in *Linguistique et Colonialisme* (Payot, Paris, 1974).
26. *Tsetlo*, (Ad. Donker, Johannesburg, 1974), p. 19.
27. ibid., p. 54.
28. This point is developed in connection with Kafka's use of German in *Kafka: pour une littérature mineure*, by Deleuze and Guatari (Editions de Minuit, Paris, 1975).
29. P. Ricoeur, *La métaphore vive* (Editions du Seuil, Paris, 1975).
30. 'White lies' in *To Whom It May Concern* (ed. Royston, Ad. Donker, Johannesburg, 1973), p. 18. A good example, in fact, of the functional use of fairly erudite techniques; is this not in fact an example of what G. N. Leech calls polyptoton, but used with a comic effect in mind? (See *A Linguistic Guide to English Poetry*, Longman, London, 1969, p. 82.)

    'Black is *sin stuffed* in a *snuff-tin*' is a play on words and sounds – on the difficulty – which is already present in the pronunciation of the line – of getting sin into a snuff-box – in other words of limiting the black man, of trying to force him to fit into categories. Motjuwadi belongs to Mphahlele's generation, which may explain his professionalism.
31. *Tsetlo*, op. cit., p. 20.
32. *Jol'iinkomo*, op. cit., p. 30.
33. One example, perhaps the most striking and successful one, taken from 'The sun on this rubble after rain' will do for Brutus. This is the line used to indicate the resolution of Brutus and his friends and fellow resisters: 'Sharpevilled to spearpoints for revenging', 'Sharpevilled', from Sharpeville, is infinitely more eloquent than 'sharpened'. There could be a great many more examples from Nortje, for he was influenced by Dylan Thomas. But they are far from being limited to the 'situation' and they are to be found especially in the part of his work written after his departure from South Africa. Here he describes the oppressive atmosphere of his country:

    > with butter milk sky covering space
    > and beauty of the countries south
    > gestapoed into disbelief
    > we who have tarzaned, o my brothers,
    > will find the air aciduous
    > the muse expired.

    ('Leftovers', in *Dead Roots*, op. cit., p. 111)
34. 'The Elephants are Taking Driving Lessons', in *Bolt*, no. 10, May 1974, p. 49. I have mentioned earlier a marked return to the vernacular. Any issue of *Staffrider* will provide ample evidence of this, but also many of the plays written in the last few years reveal the abundant recourse to one or several of the African languages.
35. *Walking through our Sleep*, op. cit., p. 50.
36. *Poètes Prisonniers* (Introduction, Seghers, Lyons, 1943).
37. *Que peut la littérature?*, ed. Y. Buin (Collection 10/18, Paris, 1965).

Appendix
Panoramic view of the main committed poets

The 1950s

1948: Nationalist victory and the institution of apartheid

Growth of Nationalist representation in Parliament
Passing of laws enforcing segregation:
  Mixed Marriages Act (1949)
  Population Registration Act (1950)
  Group Areas Act (1950)
  Bantu Authorities Act (1951)
  Bantu Education Acts (1953–1959)
  Promotion (sic) of Bantu Self-Government Act (initiating the Bantustan policy) (1959)
Growth of opposition outside Parliament. United campaigns: Congress of the People, The Freedom Charter (1955)

Key
P: long period of imprisonment
→: in exile

PATON (b. 1903)
DELIUS (b. 1916) →

The 1960s

1960: Sharpeville

The Nationalist advance continues with the support of votes from the English-speaking community.
Repressive laws:
  General Law Amendment Acts ('Sabotage' Act) (1962 and 1963)
  Publications and Entertainments Act (1963) (introducing censorship)
  Criminal Procedure Amendment Act (detention without trial for renewable periods of 180 days) (1965)
  'Terrorism' Act (1967)
Defeat of the opposition outside Parliament and of the armed resistance: The Rivonia trial (1964)

BRUTUS (b. 1924) P then →
PIETERSE (b. 1930) →
NORTJE (1942–70) →
EVANS (b. 1935) P then →
LEWIN (b. 1939) P then →

Poets writing in other languages
Zulu: **KUNENE** (b. 1932) →
Afrikaans: **SMALL** (b. 1936),
INGRID JONKER (1933–65),
BREYTENBACH (b. 1939) P then →

The 1970s

1968: Beginnings of Black Consciousness

Record Nationalist representation in Parliament (131 seats out of 170)
New security legislation
Police raids and several deaths in detention
Urban blacks allocated to Bantustans (1973)
Major strikes in Durban (1973)
Development of Black Consciousness: Black Renaissance Convention (1974)
Decolonization of Angola and Mozambique (1974)
1976 and 1977 uprisings
Steve Biko dies in detention (September 1977)
Banning of BCM organizations (October 1977)
Growth of ANC sabotage acts

MTSHALI* (b. 1940)
SEROTE (b. 1944) →
MATTERA (b. 1935)
MATTHEWS (b. 1929)
JENSMA† (b. 1939)
HORN (b. 1934)
SMALL‡
SEPAMLA (b. 1932)
GWALA§ (b. 1946)

1976: Soweto

*****MTSHALI** also writes in Zulu
†**JENSMA** also writes in Afrikaans
‡**SMALL**, now writes in English
§**GWALA** also writes in Zulu

Bibliography

▼▼▼▼▼▼▼▼▼▼▼▼▼▼▼▼▼▼▼▼▼▼▼▼▼▼▼▼▼▼▼▼▼

The poets: poetic works and principal work in prose

Breytenbach, Breyten, *And Death White as Words*, ed. A. J. Coetzee, Rex Collings, London, and David Philip, Cape Town, 1978. (Bilingual selection.)
In Africa Even the Flies are Happy. Selected Poems 1964–1977, trans. Denis Hirson, John Calder, London, 1978.
Skryt, Meulenhoff Nederland bv, Amsterdam, 1972.
A Season in Paradise, Jonathan Cape, London, 1980

Brutus, D., *Sirens, Knuckles and Boots*, Mbari Publications, Ibadan, 1963.
Letters to Martha and Other Poems from a South African Prison, Heinemann, London, 1968.
Poems from Algiers, University of Texas, Austin, 1970.
Thoughts Abroad, Troubadour Press, Austin, Texas, 1970 (under the pseudonym of John Bruin).
Denver Poems (mimeograph), Denver, 1971.
A Simple Lust, Collected Poems of South African Jail and Exile including Letters to Martha, Heinemann, London, 1973.
Strains, Troubadour Press, Austin, Texas, 1975.
China Poems, The University of Texas, Austin, 1975.
Stubborn Hope, Heinemann, London, 1978.
Prose: *South African Prisons and the Red Cross Investigation*, International Defence and Aid Fund, London, 1967.

Delius, A., *An Unknown Border*, Balkema, Cape Town and Amsterdam, 1954.
The Last Division, Human & Rousseau, Cape Town, 1959.
A Corner of the World, Human & Rousseau, 1962.
Black South Easter (a *New Coin* supplement), Rhodes University, n.d. (1965).
Prose: *Border*, David Philip, Cape Town, 1976.

Evans, D., see *Poets to the People*, ed. Feinberg, rev. edn.
Theatre: *The Choice* (radio play), 1965; *Beneath Olympus*, 1978.

Gwala, Mafika Pascal, *Jol'iinkomo*, Ad. Donker, Johannesburg, 1977.
No More Lullabies, Ravan Press, Johannesburg, 1982.

Horn, Peter, *Walking through our Sleep*, Ravan Press, Johannesburg, 1974.
Silence in Jail, Scribe Press, Claremont, Cape Town, 1979.

Jensma, W., *Sing for our Execution*, Ravan Press, Johannesburg, 1973.
Where White is the Colour, Where Black is the Number, Ravan Press, Johannesburg, 1974.
I Must Show You My Clippings, Ravan Press, Johannesburg, 1977.

Jonker, Ingrid, *Selected Poems*, trans. Jack Cope and William Plomer, Jonathan Cape, London, 1968. (Original in Afrikaans.)

Kgositsile, Keorapetse, *Spirits Unchained*, Broadside Press, Detroit, 1969.
For Melba, Third World Press, Chicago, 1970.
My Name is Afrika, Anchor Books, New York, 1971.

Kunene, Mazisi, *Zulu Poems*, Deutsch, London, 1970. (Original in Zulu.)
Emperor Shaka the Great, Heinemann, London, 1979. (Translated from the Zulu by the author.)
Anthem of the Decades, A Zulu Epic, Heinemann, London, 1981.
The Ancestors & the Sacred Mountain, Heinemann, London, 1982.

Lewin, H., see *Poets to the People*, ed. Feinberg.
Prose: *Bandiet. Seven Years in a South African Prison*, Barrie & Jenkins, London, 1974; Penguin, London, 1976, Heinemann, London, 1982.

Mattera, D., *Azanian Love Song*, Skotaville Pubs., Johannesburg, 1983.

Matthews, J. (ed.), *Cry Rage!*, Spro-Cas Publications, Johannesburg, 1972 (in collaboration with G. Thomas).
Pass me a Meatball, Jones, feelings gathered while held in detention in Victor Verster Maximum Security Prison, Paarl Sept.–Dec. 1976, BLAC Publishing House, Athlone (Cape), 1977.
Black Voices Shout, Troubadour Press, Austin, 1976 (Reissue of the original edition published in South Africa in 1974 and immediately banned.)
Images. Photographs by George Hallett, text by James Matthews, BLAC Publishing House, Athlone (Cape), 1979.
No Time for Dreams, BLAC Publishing House, Athlone (Cape), 1981.
Prose: *The Park and Other Stories*, BLAC Publishing House, Athlone (Cape), 1974. Enlarged edition, Ravan, Johannesburg, 1983.

Mtshali, O. M., *Sounds of a Cowhide Drum*, Foreword by Nadine Gordimer, Renoster Books, Johannesburg, 1971; rev. edn, Oxford University Press, London, 1972.
Fireflames, Shuter and Shooter, Pietermaritzburg, 1981.

Nortje, A., *Dead Roots*, Heinemann, London, 1973.
Lonely Against the Light, Rhodes University, Grahamstown, 1973.

Paton, A., Poetry and prose: *Knocking on the Door*, David Philip, Cape Town, Rex Collings, London, 1975.
The only volume that collects most of Paton's poems. The volume also contains lectures, essays and stories no longer traceable or still unpublished in 1975.
Prose: *Cry, the Beloved Country*, Jonathan Cape, 1948, Penguin, London, 1958.
Too Late the Phalarope, Jonathan Cape, London, 1955.
Debbie Go Home, Jonathan Cape, London, 1961.
Hofmeyr, Oxford University Press, Cape Town, 1964. Abridged ed., Oxford University Press, Cape Town, 1971.
An excellent biography which is particularly helpful for the period 1925–48.
The Long View, ed. E. Callan, Praeger, London, 1968.
A very enlightening introduction by Callan on South African liberalism. The articles included in the volume appeared in *Contact* during the period when Paton was at the head of the Liberal Party.
Kontakion for You Departed, Jonathan Cape, London, 1969.
Written after the death of his wife, Dorrie, *Kontakion* contains a number of autobiographical elements.
Case History of a Pinky, South African Institute of Race Relations, Johannesburg, n.d. (1972).
Apartheid and the Archbishop, David Philip, Cape Town, 1973.
Towards the Mountain, David Philip, Cape Town, 1980.
(An autobiography to 1948.)
Ah, But Your Land is Beautiful, Jonathan Cape, London, 1981.

Pieterse, C., Poetry and Prose: *Present Lives, Future Becoming*, Hickey Press, London, 1974.
Echo and Choruses: 'Ballad of the Cells' and selected shorter poems, Ohio University Center for International Studies, 1974.
See also: *Poets to the People*, ed. Feinberg, and *Short African Plays*, below.
Prose (contributor and co-editor): *Protest and Conflict in African Literature*, Heinemann, London, 1969.
Prose (ed.): *Ten One-Act Plays*, Heinemann, London, 1968.
Seven South African Poets, Heinemann, London, 1971.
Five African Plays, Heinemann, London, 1972.
Short African Plays, Heinemann, London, 1972.
Speak Easy Speak Free (with A. S. K. Mbeki), International Publishers, New York, 1977.
Nine African Plays for Radio, co-ed., Heinemann, London, 1973.
African Writers Talking, Heinemann, London, 1972. (in collaboration with D. Duerden).

Pringle, T., *African Sketches*, Moxon, London, 1834.
Prose: *Narrative of a Residence in South Africa*, Moxon, London, 1835. Exceptionally interesting for an understanding of Pringle and English colonization of the 'frontier', and for an account of the state of race relations in southern Africa around 1820. This work, which is very well written, makes delightful reading.

Sepamla, S., *Hurry Up to It!*, Ad. Donker, Johannesburg, 1975.
The Blues is You in Me, Ad. Donker, Johannesburg, 1976.
The Soweto I Love, Rex Collings, London, 1977.
Children of the Earth, Ad. Donker, Johannesburg, 1983.
Prose: *The Root is One*, Rex Collings, London, 1980.
A Ride on the Whirlwind, Ad. Donker, Johannesburg, 1976 and Heinemann, London, 1984.

Serote, M. W., *Yakhal'inkomo*, Renoster Books, Johannesburg, 1972.
Tsetlo, Ad. Donker, Johannesburg, 1974.
No Baby Must Weep, Ad. Donker, Johannesburg, 1975.
Behold Mama, Flowers, Ad. Donker, Johannesburg, 1978.

Small, Adam, *Kitaar My Kruis*, Hollandsch Afrikaansche Uitgevers Maatschappij, Cape Town, rev. edn, 1973.
Black Bronze Beautiful, Ad. Donker, Johannesburg, 1975.

Anthologies

The chronological order followed here shows the relative order of appearance of the poets whose names are bracketed.

Butler, Guy (ed.), *A Book of South African Verse*, Oxford University Press, Cape Town, 1959.
(Delius, Paton.)

Gordimer, Nadine and Abrahams, Lionel (eds), *South African Writing Today*, Penguin, London, 1967.
(Brutus, Delius.)

Kesteloot, Lilyan, in French trans.: *Anthologie Négro-africaine*, Marabout Université, Verviers, 1967.
(Brutus.)

Cope, Jack and Krige, Uys (eds), *The Penguin Book of South African Verse*, Penguin, London, 1968.
(Delius, Paton, Page Yako, Vilakazi, Small.)

Beier, Ulli and Moore, Gerald (eds), *Modern Poetry from Africa*, Penguin, London, rev. edn, 1968.
(Brutus, Nortje.)

Kavanagh, Robert and Qangule, Z. S. (eds), *The Making of a Servant and Other Poems*, Ravan Press, 1971.
(Jolobe, Mqhayi, Nyoka, Page Yako.)

Royston, Robert (ed.), *To Whom it May Concern*, Ad. Donker, Johannesburg, 1973.
(Mtshali, Sepamla, Serote et al.)
English edition entitled: *Black Poets in South Africa*, Heinemann, London, 1974.

Pieterse, Cosmo (ed.), *Seven South African Poets*, Heinemann, London, 1974.
(Brutus, Nortje.)

Horn, Peter and Saunders, Walter (eds), *It's Gettin' Late, and other poems from Ophir*, Ravan Press, Johannesburg, 1974.
(Gwala, Horn, Jensma, Mtshali, Serote.)

Feinberg, Barry (ed.), *Poets to the People. South African Freedom Poems*, Allen & Unwin, London, 1974; new enlarged edition: Heinemann, London, 1980.
(Brutus, Lewin, Mtshali, Nortje, Pieterse, Serote.)

Alvarez-Péreyre, Jacques, *Poètes engagés sud-africains*, Maison de la Culture, Grenoble, 1975.
(Horn, Jensma, Mtshali, Matthews, Sepamla, Serote.)

Vaillant, Florence, *Poètes Noirs de l'Afrique du Sud*, Présence Africaine, Paris, 1975 (bilingual).
(Jolobe, Matthews, Mtshali, Serote, Sepamla, Small.)

Brink, André (ed.), *A World of Their Own. Southern African Poets of the Seventies*, Ad. Donker, Johannesburg, 1976.
(Jensma, Mtshali, Sepamla, Serote.)

Rodda, Peter, 'Poetry Under Apartheid, A selection of South African Poetry' in *Transatlantic Review*, 53/54, London, February 1976.
(Delius, Matthews, Mtshali, Jensma, Lewin, Horn, Serote, Sepamla.)

Portejoie, Pierre, 'Poètes de la Résistance en Afrique du Sud' (trans. of poems from *Poets to the People*), in *Le Temps Parallèle*, no. 16, March 1978.

Butler, Guy and Mann, Chris (eds) *A New Book of South African Verse in English*, Oxford University Press, Cape Town, 1979.
(Jolobe, H. I. E. Dhlomo, Delius, Kunene, Sepamla, Small, Jensma, Lewin, Mtshali, Nortje, Serote, Gwala.)

Couzens, Tim and Patel, Essop (eds.), *The Return of the Amasi Bird*, Black South African Poetry 1891–1981, Ravan Press, Johannesburg, 1982.

South African reviews or periodicals which publish or have published poetry and/or critical articles

Asterisks indicate those that have ceased (*) or have had to cease (**) publication.

*Africa South**
Blac (Athlone, Cape Province)****
*Bolt**
The Bloody Horse (Johannesburg)

*Classic**
Contrast (Cape Town)
*Donga***
English in Africa (Rhodes University, Grahamstown)
*Fighting Talk***
*Izwi**
*New Age***
New Classic (Benoni, Transvaal)
New Coin (Rhodes University, Grahamstown)
*Ophir**
*Pro Veritate***
*The Purple Renoster**
Reality (Pietermaritzburg, Natal)
Sketsh (Benoni, Transvaal)
South African Outlook (Mowbray, Cape Province)
Staffrider (Ravan Press, Johannesburg)
UNISA English Studies (University of South Africa, Pretoria)
WIP (Work in Progress) (Students' Union, Witwatersrand University, Johannesburg)

General works concerned wholly or in part with the South African poets studied in this book

A Select Bibliography

Beier, Ulli (ed.), *Introduction to African Literature*, Longman, London, 1967.
 A collection of articles appearing over the years in *Black Orpheus*.

Callan, Edward, *Alan Paton*, Twayne Publishers, New York, 1968.

Coetzee, A. J., *Poësie en Politiek*, Ravan Press, Johannesburg, 1976.
 A study in Afrikaans in which Small, Jensma and Breytenbach are frequently mentioned.

Doyle, Jr., John Robert, *Thomas Pringle*, Twayne Publishers, New York, 1972.

Duerden, Dennis and Pieterse, Cosmo, *African Writers Talking*, Heinemann, London, 1972.

February, V. A., *Mind Your Colour: The Coloured Stereotype in South African Literature*, Routledge Kegan Paul, London, 1981.

Gérard, Albert S., *Four African Literatures: Xhosa, Sotho, Zulu, Amharic*, University of California Press, Berkeley, 1971.
 An essential work on the vernacular literatures and the beginnings of writing in English.

Gordimer, Nadine, *The Black Interpreters*, Spro-Cas/Ravan, Johannesburg, 1973.
 A brief but perceptive analysis of several African and South African writers.

Heywood, C., *Aspects of South African Literature*, Heinemann, London, 1976.

Jones, Eldred Durosimi, *African Literature Today*, no. 6, *Poetry in Africa*, Heinemann, London, 1973.

Killam, G. D., *African Writers on African Writing*, Heinemann, London, 1973.
 Contains an excellent essay by Nadine Gordimer, 'The Novel and the Nation in South Africa.

Lindfors, Bernth, (ed.), *Issue*, A Quarterly Journal of Africanist Opinion, Brandeis University, Massachusetts, 1976.

Contains the lectures and main contributions of Brutus, Pieterse, Mtshali, Serote, Mphahlele, Kgositsile, Kunene, to a symposium on South African literature in Austin in 1975.

Lindfors, Bernth, Munro, Ian, Priebe, Richard and Sander, Reinhard, *Palaver: Interviews with Five African Writers in Texas*, University of Texas, Austin, 1972.

Mphahlele, Ezekiel, *Voices in the Whirlwind*, Macmillan, London, 1973.
The African Image (rev. edn), Faber, London, 1974.
The second is a reissue, considerably updated, of the first edition published in 1962.

van Niekerk, *Dominee, Are You Listening to the Drums?* Tafelberg Publishers, Cape Town, 1983.

Nkosi, Lewis, *Home and Exile*, Longman, London, 1965.

Olney, James, *Tell me Africa. An Approach to African Literature*, Princeton University Press, 1973.
An excellent study of autobiography in Africa, with a chapter on South Africa.

Pieterse, Cosmo and Munro, Donald (eds), *Protest and Conflict in African Literature*, Heinemann, London, 1969.

Rive, R., *Selected Writings*, Ad. Donker, Johannesburg, 1977.

Wästberg, Per, *The Writer in Modern Africa*, African–Scandinavian Writers Conference, Almqvist & Wiksell, Stockholm, 1967, Uppsala, 1968.

Wauthier, Claude, *The Literature and Thought of Modern Africa*, 2nd edn, Heinemann, London, 1979.

Wilhelm, Peter and Polley, James, *Poetry South Africa. Selected papers from Poetry 1974*, Ad. Donker, Johannesburg, December 1976.

Zell, Hans M., Bundy, Carol and Coulon, Virginia, *A New Reader's Guide to African Literature*, Heinemann, London, 1983.

Index

▼▼▼▼▼▼▼▼▼▼▼▼▼▼▼▼▼▼▼▼▼▼▼▼▼▼▼▼▼▼▼▼

Abrahams, Cecil 206n
Abrahams, Lionel 22, 24
Abrahams, Peter 5, 6, 8, 15
Achebe, Chinua 19
Adams, Perseus 22
Anderson, Maxwell 63
Aragon, Louis 20
Arendt, Hannah 113n
Auden, W. H. 134, 216
Augustine, St 107

Baldwin, James 22, 49n
Bambatha 245n
Banoobhai, Shabbir 242, 257
Banton, Michael 11n
Barnato, Barney 76
Baudelaire, Charles 250, 267n
Becker, Jillian 43
Beecher-Stowe, Harriet 56, 205n, 250
Beier, Ulli 161
Bengu, Sibiso 246n
Bennet, Arnold 50n
Benson, Mary 21–2
Bérimont, Luc 20
Bernstein, Lionel 17
Berry, André 167n
Bertrand de Born 137
Bezuidenhout 59n
Biko, Steve 185, 245n, 257
Bonhoeffer, Dietrich 102, 113n
Borwicz, Michel 215
Botha, P. W. 49n
Brecht, Bertolt 170
Breton, André 205
Breytenbach, Breyten 18, 26, 29–30, 31n, 37–8, 44–5, 49n, 258, 259
Briffault, Robert 167n
Brink, André 29–30, 37–8, 113n, 205n, 260
Britten, Benjamin 44
Brown, Rap 48

Browning, Robert 133
Bruin, John 50n
Brutus, Dennis 5, 21, 22, 30, 64, 85, 94, 113n, 126, 128, 130–45, 156, 198, 207, 241, 242, 243, 244n, 251, 254, 256, 257, 258, 261, 264, 266, 267n, 268n
Buckton, Margaret 5
Buin, Yves 267
Bunting, Brian 9
Butler, Guy 5, 9, 14–6, 18, 22, 24, 31n, 40, 41, 44, 49n, 68, 78, 96, 168n
Butler, Jeffrey 33n

Callan, Edward 82n
Calvet, Louis-Jean 267n
Campbell, Roy 18, 43, 73
Carmichael, Stokely 190
Césaire, Aimé 48, 129
Chaka 41
Char, René 266
Citashe, I. W. W. 3, 117, 128n
Clayton, Archbishop Geoffrey 61
Cloete, Austin 49n
Clouts, Sydney 22, 43, 44, 244n
Coleridge, Samuel T. 57
Collins, Canon 90, 135
Cope, Jack 21, 22, 27, 33n, 44, 49n

Dangor, Ahmat 247n
Davids, Jennifer 257
Davis, Hedy 169n
Davis, Ossie 78
Darwin, Charles R. 68
De Blank, Archbishop Joost 9
De Nerval, Gérard 155
Deleuze, Gilles 268n
Delius, Anthony 9, 10, 22, 31n, 43, 44, 52, 61, 65, 67–81, 82n, 83n, 181, 244n, 253, 256, 258
Delvaux, Paul 98
Desmond, Cosmas 210
Dhlomo, H. I. E. 5, 124–5, 128
Dhlomo, R. R. R. 116
Dickens, Charles 40, 244n
Dingaan 41, 107, 108, 114n, 141
Diop, David 48
Dobzinski, Charles 267n
Donne, John 5, 261
Douglas, Josephine 81n
Douts, Christine 49n, 242
Doyle, J. R. Jr. 60n
Driver, C. J. 21, 95n
Du Bellay, Joachim 143
Dubow, Neville 20, 32n
Dues, Mike 49n
Dumile 151, 255
Duncan, Patrick 9

Eliot, T. S. 133, 161
Emmanuel, Pierre 20, 114n
Essop, Ahmed 40, 49n
Evans, David 30, 52, 84–6, 90–4, 112, 156, 257, 258

Fairbairn, John 54, 55, 56, 57
Fanon, Franz 193, 201, 245n
February, Basil 257
Feinberg, Barry 267n
First, Ruth 21
Fischer, Bram 18, 38, 86, 88, 92, 94, 110, 154, 257
Ford, Henry II 42
Francis, of Assisi, St 254
Freud, Sigmund 68
Frost, Gillian 125
Fugard, Athol 23–4, 42, 240
Fugard, Sheila 33n

Galileo, Galilei 104

Index

Gandhi, Mahatma Mohandas 8
Gardner, Colin 24–5, 36
Gérard, Albert 128n
Gerhart, Gail M 48n
Goldberg, Dennis 17, 86, 92, 196
Gordimer, Nadine 14, 16, 21–2, 24, 31n, 32n, 39, 49n, 204n, 210, 242
Gorky, Maxime 166
Govender, Ronnie 247n
Guatari, Félix 268n
Gwala, Mafika Pascal 36, 38, 39, 49n, 226, 227–41, 242, 245n, 261, 263, 264

Haron, Imam Abdul 257
Harris, John 18, 22, 62, 86, 88, 155
Heimler, Eugene 167n
Hirson, Baruch 48n
Hofmeyr, Jan Hendrick 62
Hope, Christopher 41, 49n, 260, 264, 267n
Hopkins, Gerard Manley 6, 133, 147, 161, 261
Horn, Peter 36, 52, 63, 65, 67, 80, 87, 96–104, 113n, 234, 245n, 251, 252, 253, 254, 255, 256, 263, 265, 267n
Huddleston, Bishop Trevor 7, 85, 93, 196
Hughes, Langston 124
Hutchinson, Alfred 21
Huxley, Aldous 31n

Jabavu, Noni 5, 11n, 21
Jaccard, Roland 169n
Jackson, George 193
Jacobson, Dan 43, 44
Jahn, Janheinz 161
Jensma, Wopko 36, 52, 64, 67, 80, 87, 93, 96, 104–11, 112, 234, 240, 254, 255, 256, 257, 258, 260, 263
Jeyifous, Abiodun 11n
Johannesse, Fhazel 242, 247n
Jones, LeRoi 49n
Jonker, Ingrid 23, 26–7, 29, 154, 155, 257
Jordan, A. C. 9, 121–2, 243
Joseph, Helen 13n, 21
Jouve, Pierre-Jean 111

Joyce, James 147

Kafka, Franz 162, 176, 268n
Kameeta, Zephania 267n
kaMiya, Themba 242
Kaminyayiza, Nkathazo 242
Kane-Berman, John 48n
Kani, John 42
Kathrada, Ahmed 17
Kavanagh, Robert M. 50n, 118
Keats, John 40, 113n, 147
Kente, Gibson 50n
Kgositsile, Keorapetse 2, 19, 46–8
Kirkwood, Mike 49n
Koapa, Bennie 228, 232
Komai, Felicia 81n
Kosik, Karel 197
Kotze, Theo 154, 205n
Krige, Uys 2, 20, 22, 27, 33n, 113n
Kruger, Paul 80
Kumalo, A. N. C. 257
Kunene, Mazizi 125–8, 231
Kuper, Leo 10, 11n, 12n

La Guma, Alex 21, 267n
Langa, Mandlenkosi 43, 242
Lanham, L. W. 41
Lawrence, D. H. 40
Leech, G. N. 268n
Leigh-Loohuizen 12, 267n
Leroux, Etienne 33n
Lessing, Doris 15, 31n
Levinson, Bernard 259
Lewin, Hugh 30, 52, 84–90, 93–4, 112, 156, 244n, 257
Lewin, Julius 10
Lindfors, Bernth 167n
Livingstone, Douglas 2, 49n
Looksmart, Solwandle 91, 148–50, 257
Louw, P. P. 17
Lumumba, Patrick 48, 156, 230
Luthuli, Chief Albert 10, 22, 85, 257

Macaulay, Zachary 55
Mackay, Ilva 49n
Madingoane, Ingoapele 242
Maherero 230
Maiakovski, Vladimir 19
Maimane, Arthur 9

Majola, Japhta 257
Majombozi, Velencia 56n
Makana 75, 76, 77
Malan, D. F. 62
Malcolm X 193
Mandela, Nelson 8, 17, 41, 48, 135, 193, 230
Mann, Chris 168n
Marquard, Leo 12n
Marx, Karl 68, 101, 131
Matanzima, Kaiser 42, 148, 245n
Matshikiza, Todd 9
Matshoba, Mtutulezi 40, 49n
Mattera, Don 39, 170, 195, 196–204, 227, 242, 258
Matthews, James 20, 21, 38, 39, 41, 49n, 93, 145, 195, 204, 207–15, 216, 217, 225, 227, 234, 242, 244n, 254, 256, 257, 267n
Matthews, Joe 9
Maximin, Daniel 12n
Mbeki, Govan 17
Meiring, Jane 59n
Meiring, Sheila 23
Memmi, Albert 21
Mencken, Henry 264
Mhalangu, Solomon 245n
Mhalaba, Raymond 17
Mhalangeni, Andrew 17
Michaelangelo 87
Miller, Ruth 22
Millin, S. G. 14
Modisane, Bloke 9, 21, 197, 204n
Mofolo, Thomas 116
Mohapi 258
Moore, Gerald 168n
Morenga 230
Morgan, Len 205n
Motjuwadi, Stanley 38, 218, 245n, 263
Motscaledi, Elias 17
Motsitsi, Casey 9, 38
Mphahlele, Esk'ia 2, 4, 5, 6–10, 21, 38, 39, 45–6, 50n, 82n, 145, 231
Mqayisa, Khayalethu 42
Mqhayi, S. E. Q. 118, 231
Mtshali, Oswald 36, 37, 38, 39, 40, 43, 50n 60n, 128, 145, 156, 170–86, 190, 195, 204, 207, 214, 216, 220, 225, 231, 234, 235, 241,

242, 247n, 256, 260, 263, 264
Muggeridge, Malcolm 82n
Mulele, Pierre 231
Mutloatse, Mothobi 40, 49n, 205n
Mzamane, Mbulelo 40, 49n

Nakasa, Nat 9, 13n 23, 92, 257, 258
Nasser, Gamal Abdel 156
Naudé, Dr Beyers 36, 48n, 154
Ndebele, Njabulo S. 38
Ngoyi, Lilian 230, 245n
Nkhulu, Sob. W. 118
Nkosi, Lewis 4, 5, 9, 11n, 12n, 21–2, 23, 30, 33n, 82n, 204n
Nortje, K. A. 22, 92, 93, 128, 130, 153–66, 240, 241, 243, 251, 258, 264, 268n
Ntshona, Winston 42
Nxumalo, Henry 9, 13n
Nyerere, Julius 35
Nyoka, M. E. 119

Oppenheimer, Harry 79, 80, 99
Orwell, George 19, 27

Patel, Essop 242, 247n
Paton, Alan 6, 9, 10, 14–16, 19, 21, 30, 44, 52, 57, 59, 61–7, 68, 74, 80, 81n, 82n, 84, 85, 87, 94, 96, 97, 111, 112, 132, 205n, 206n, 234, 253, 256, 257
Page Yako, S. J. 118
Philip, Dr John 56
Picasso, Pablo 20
Pieterse, Cosmo 5, 22, 82n, 113n, 126, 128, 130, 145–53, 181, 207, 241, 242, 243, 251, 257, 261, 264
Plaatje, Sol 116
Plomer, William 14, 23, 43, 44, 59, 73, 257
Polley, James 49n
Prévert, Jacques 102
Prince of Wales (Edward VIII) 118
Pringle, Thomas 31n, 52, 53–60, 112
Proust, Marcel 164

Qangule, Z. S. 118

Rabie, Jan 33n
Ramopo, Makhudu 33n
Reeves, Rev. Ambrose 9
Renoir, Jean 158
Rhodes, Cecil 68
Ricoeur, Paul 263
Rive, Richard 9, 13n, 21, 49n
Roberts, Sheila 49n
Rodda, Peter 267n
Rogosin, Lionel 171
Royston, Robert 38, 245n
Rubadiri, David 82n

Salahi, Ibrahim 142
Saloojee, Babla 257
Sampson, Anthony 9, 12n
Sartre, Jean-Paul 21, 112, 251
Saunders, Walter 36, 49n, 113n, 245n
Schreiner, Olive 14, 59
Scott, Sir Walter 53, 54
Segal, Philip 11n, 18
Segal, Ronald 9, 30, 168
Seghers, Pierre 19, 266
Seidman, July 246n
Sekukuni 80
Senghor, Leopold S. 267n
Sepamla, Sipho 2, 38, 39, 40, 60n, 214, 215–26, 231, 234, 240, 242, 246n, 256, 260, 261
Serote, Mongane Wally 36, 38, 39, 43, 49n, 156, 184, 185, 186–96, 204, 207, 214, 216, 218, 219, 225, 227, 231, 240, 242, 247n, 251, 256, 258, 260, 261–4
Shakespeare, William 40, 133
Simons, H. J. 9
Sisulu, Walter 17, 193
Slovo, Joe 196
Small, Adam 22, 25, 27–9, 40, 113n
Smith, Pauline 44
Smith, Steven 49n
Smuts, General Jan 4
Sobukwe, Robert 8, 11, 41, 135, 193
Sölle, Dorothee 102

Somerset, Lord Charles 54, 58
Somhlahlo, Basil 242
Soyinka, Wole 266
Spire, André 151
Stein, Sylvester 9
Stone, David 25
Stone, E. V. 10

Takavarasha, Benjamin 49n
Tennyson, Alfred 131
Themba, Can 9, 12n, 197, 257
Theroux, Paul 139
Thion, Serge 205n
Thoathlane, Th 245n
Thomas Aquinas, St 131
Thomas, Dylan 147, 268n
Thomas, Gladys 243
Thoreau, Henry 54
Timol, Ahmed 257
Tiro, Onkgopotse 258, 259
Turner, Richard 36

Ungar, André 9

van der Post, Laurens 43, 171
van Wyk, Christopher 205, 242
Verwoerd, Dr Hendrik 65, 69, 70, 99, 140, 156
Vigne, Randolph 22
Vilakazi, Benedict W. 9, 122–4, 243
Visconti, Luciano 158
Vorster, J. B. 24, 36

Walshe, Peter 48n
Webster, John 133
Webster, Mary M. 114n
Weill, Kurt 63
Welsh, Anne 42n
Wilberforce, William 55, 112
Willhelm, Peter 48n
Witbooi 230
Wordsworth, William 113n, 131, 133
Wright, Richard 49n

Yeats, W. B. 133

Zola, Emile 146